THE STAR AND CRESCENT

Being the Story of the 17th Cavalry from 1858 to 1922

Major F. C. C. Yeats-Brown

The Naval & Military Press Ltd

Published by
The Naval & Military Press Ltd
5 Riverside, Brambleside, Bellbrook
Industrial Estate, Uckfield, East Sussex,
TN22 1QQ England
Tel: +44 (0) 1825 749494
Fax: +44 (0) 1825 765701
www.naval-military-press.com

In reprinting in facsimile from the original, any imperfections are inevitably reproduced and the quality may fall short of modern type and cartographic standards.

KHAN BAHADUR MAULVI QAZI ABDUL HAKIM KHAN.

The Maulvi Sahib joined the regiment as a young man when it was re-raised in 1885 and followed its fortunes until the end. A man of fine presence and simple mind, he succeeded in keeping friends with everyone, while never for a moment losing his hold over the regiment as its Religious Leader. Especially was his power for good evinced over the more "*jungli*" and less sophisticated sowars. During the troublous times of the Khilafat and the Hijrat, it was his sound teaching and unquestioned piety that kept the regiment straight, so that all through the war, and after, there was never a word said against the loyalty of the 17th Cavalry, although no sowar could have remained indifferent to that strange pilgrimage into Afghanistan which so closely affected the land and families of our men. Tall, handsome, full-bearded, as the Holy Prophet was, his life is a shining example of true religion.

Copy Number 65

THE STAR AND CRESCENT

Being the Story of the 17th Cavalry from 1858 to 1922.

Printed for Private Circulation only.

INTRODUCTION.

The History of the 17th Cavalry would never have come into being, but for the enthusiasm and hard work of Major F. C. C. Yeats-Brown who not only originally conceived the idea, but who also compiled the history contained in the following pages from such sources as were found to be available. The appendices to the history were also collected by him from those whom he considered were best qualified to contribute.

As he is scarcely mentioned in the narrative it is felt that some words by another hand are needed to fill this blank. He joined the 17th Cavalry in 1906 at Bannu, and although by natural inclination primarily a man of letters he soon proved to be a soldier also, and in 1913 he succeeded Dodd as Adjutant of the regiment. He was a fine instructor of remounts and recruits, a great supporter of polo and pigsticking and withal a painstaking and efficient "quilldriver" in the regimental office.

After returning safely from France in the early part of the War, he proceeded to Mesopotamia with the Flying Corps and had the misfortune to become a prisoner in the hands of the Turks through an aeroplane accident. In his book "Caught by the Turks" will be found an account of his adventures told in his own pleasing and delightful style.

It is a misfortune both for the 15th Lancers and for such of his old companions in arms who are still serving in India that he has decided to return no more to the East but to try his fortunes in the Great Republic of the West. Major Yeats-Brown has since become Assistant Editor of the "Spectator" (1926).

His departure and his decision not to return have much delayed the publication of the history which he was obliged to leave in a somewhat unfinished state. Its belated appearance is due to this fact. Possibly its literary merits have in some degree suffered from its author never having had an opportunity of seeing the book except in a very rough manuscript form, because, under the circumstances, it became necessary for another hand to carry out the proof-reading and publication. At the time of his departure he had in hand some further material which he had proposed to incorporate in the history which he had already written. Owing to lack of time he handed this over and requested that it should be inserted in the narrative. It was however felt that to do this might involve considerable revision of what had been already written, yet on the other hand it would have been a pity to have omitted the information that these contained. It was finally decided therefore to publish the notes on Robarts and de Kantzow, and the sketches of life in the regiment between 1886—1894, as appendices to the main history and to leave the latter in the form in which it was originally written.

It is hoped that this book which has been compiled with much labour and research will, despite its somewhat disjointed nature, enable generations yet unborn to picture the lives of their fathers in those pleasant days of Indian soldiering which have now apparently passed away to return no more.

Appendix xii, containing the records of the services of the British and Indian officers of the regiment has been compiled with the greatest care, and research from every source available. It is however possible that errors are contained in this Appendix. Any reader noticing any mistake or important omission in this or in any other part of the book is requested to communicate with Lieutenant-Colonel H. S. Stewart, Cavalry Club, 127, Piccadilly, who will make the necessary corrections in the records, and who if the corrections are in any way important will issue an *errata* embodying them to all subscribers.

PREFACE.

In August 1910 a regimental magazine, called "The Star and Crescent," was started in Bareilly by the present writer at the suggestion of Kenneth Barge. A few extracts from the first number will explain the objects of the last number that will ever be published. "We wish to draw, if possible, the bonds still tighter which hold us to the Indian ranks, both high and low; to cement more strongly, if this can be, that feeling of solidarity which now exists in the regiment, and which it would be as unseemly in us to extol as it is desirable to possess. We wish to chronicle, now that they are vivid and vital and veracious, the happenings of our time in Bareilly. To commit to paper some remembrances of those dim but delightful days when we were at Umballa, Ferozepore, Loralai, Pindi and Bannu. To keep some record of our prowess by field and flood. To learn of the lives and interests of our comrades from the Punjab and beyond. To uphold a spirit of brotherhood within the regiment. To keep some record of our dumb staunch friends who live their little span and then go down to oblivion. In places we do not know of, away in the cool green country overseas, the future officers of the regiment are being wheeled here and there in 'prams,' or are hurrying to school, according to their various ages. It is for *these* we write, so that they may know of what happened in Bareilly in the dark ages of 1910, before every *sowar* had learned to spell, before the flying warships and the Baghdad railway. Yes, it is for *these* we write, and for *those* others who were just going to school when we wrote these words and who are with us now and have caught something of the spirit that made us a great regiment. We write for them to forge a link between 'Then and Now.'

Colonel Burton, who recruited and afterwards commanded the regiment, has nobly expressed this idea in his preface to our Digest of Services:—

"The 17th Bengal Cavalry rose to being at a stormy and critical period of the history in India of the British Power. The officers and men who formed its nucleus were accordingly actors in, and spectators of, great events. It is not fitting, therefore, that the red swords of de Kantzow and his brave companions should be washed in *Lethe* and forgotten. And now for a period of fifty years from that time the stream of events in which the regiment was involved, has pursued a less tumultuous course. Yet, however obsure the careers of men, oblivion is bitter: and the desire to live in the memory of posterity has inspired the incomparable energy of the greatest minds. Moreover events of little note may appear important to contemporary actors and their record be of interest to future times, when compared with a changed condition of things. The uneventful record, therefore, of the parades and marches of those who trod in peace the hard and narrow path of duty should still be written down, until such time as the regiment may be called upon to draw the sword in the cause of a rising, or perchance of a declining empire, and by that great incentive may be once again urged onward to renown. And thus the perusal of this digest is recommended to those who, whether they ride over the broad plains of Asia on which the rays of the sun fall in golden showers, or wander in the green fields of England or the vast and gaslit desert of London, are yet approaching the bank of the Stygian stream beyond which their predecessors await them."

"Damna tamen celeres reparant cœlestia lunæ.

Nos ubi decidinus

*   *   *   *

Pulviset umbra sumus."—*Har. Car.* Lib. IV, 7.

London, 1910.   (Sd.) E. B. BURTON.

*   *

Our first officers were actors in, or spectators of great events, and we the last officers, have also seen Kingdoms rise and wane, and the destruction of Empires; so that we write not for the moment, but for a posterity that shall read with curiosity, and perhaps with interest, of the days when we were people of some account. It is for this reason that personalities have not been spared. We want "to rescue from oblivion men and events worthy of a better fate" and keep thereby our memory a living thing. For it is only in the past that a man as a regiment, truly lives : the instant gone makes the instant present : what we planned and what we built make the regiment of to day. It is the past that makes the present. Such as we were, such as we are, this last number of "The Star and Crescent" being the Regimental Records of the last all-Mahomedan Indian Cavalry regiment to survive in the service of the Government of India, sets forth the things we did, and also the things we tried to do : so that when we and our hopes have vanished in the dust and oblivion that covers all this broad land, we being dead may yet speak. All things have an end "Pulviset umbra sumus." Yet shadow and dust though we are our history has a certain historical completeness. We chronicle the days of British supremacy in India, and with the close of our history closes also the pleasant story of life in a silladar cavalry regiment.

Y. B.

TABLE OF CONTENTS.

	PAGE
Introduction	iv
Preface	vi
Table of Contents	viii
List of Illustrations	x
The History of the 17th Cavalry from 1858—1922	1
Envoi	151
Stations of the 17th Cavalry	155
Appendix I.—Notes on Colonel C. J. Robarts and Colonel C. A. de Kantzow	157
,, II.—Sketches of Life in the 17th Cavalry, 1886—1894	162
,, III.—The 17th Cavalry Stud Farm	173
,, IV.—The East African Squadron, 1915—17	183
,, V.—Polo in the 17th Cavalry	199
,, VI.—Some Racing Reminiscences of the 17th Cavalry	211
,, VII.—Pigsticking Recollections of the 17th Cavalry	225
,, VIII.—The Weekly Darbar	254
,, IX.—The rise and fall of the Silladar Cavalry of India with explanation of the System	257
,, X.—Statements of the Regimental Accounts of the 17th Cavalry, showing the financial position of the regiment at the time of its conversion to a non-silladar basis	266
,, XI.—The Regimental List as it stood at the time of amalgamation	273
,, XII.—The Full Lists of the British and Indian officers of the 17th Cavalry	275
,, XIII.—Officers and men of the regiment who have been killed or who have died from wounds or disease contracted on active service	336
,, XIV.—Copies of the Deeds executed regarding the funds and property of the Officers' Mess and of the Polo Club of the 17th Cavalry	338
,, XV.—List of Rewards awarded to Indian members of the 17th Cavalry for good service	348
,, XVI.—Copy of the Deed placing the Private Silladar Fund of the 17th Cavalry in Trust	359

LIST OF ILLUSTRATIONS.

	PAGE.
Khan Bahadur Maulvi Qazi Abdul Hakim Khan	*Frontispiece.*
Colonel C. J. Robarts	6
Colonel C. A. de Kantzow	6
Facsimilies of a letter from Robarts to de Kantzow	10
Sketch of Abdul Ghyas (Robart's son or adopted son)	12
Photograph of a sketch done by Captain H. B. Swiney on the Wall of Fort Mackeson shortly before his death	12
Colonel F. W. Grabham	16
Colonel T. J. Watson	16
Group at Ferozepore	24
Group at Amballa	24
Groups at Rawalpindi 1901 and 1902	28
Group at Rawalpindi 1903	30
Riding Class at Rawalpindi	30
Group at Rawalpindi 1904	32
Men of the regiment	32
Orderly dafadar and mounted orderly	34
The Drill Major	34
Colonel E. H. E. Kauntze	36
Colonel R. W. Sartorious, V.C., C.M.G.	36
Major-General W. A. Lawrence, Colonel of the 17th Cavalry	38
Colonel C. W. Muir, C.B., C.I.E.	38
Brigadier-General F. G. Atkinson, C.B.	40
Major-General Sir Hamilton Bower, K.C.B.	40
Sketches by Warre-Cornish	42
Sketches by Warre-Cornish	44
Sketches by Worre-Cornish	48
Sketches by Warre-Cornish	52
Sketches by Warre-Cornish	56
Captain F. T. Warre-Cornish	68

	PAGE
Major F. C. C. Yeats-Brown	68
The 17th Cavalry Pipers	72
A Camel Sowar	72
Brigadier-General E. B. Burton, C.B.	80
Brigadier-General E. W. Boudier	80
Group at Bannu	86
Group at Bareilly	86
Mounted Combat	88
Men of the regiment	88
Snapshots of the Cavalry Manœuvres	90
Groups at Bareilly	92
Trumpeter Major Shah Wali Khan as a Herald's Trumpeter at the Delhi Durbar	94
The 17th Cavalry escorting Her Majesty Queen Mary at the Delhi Durbar	94
The Recruits at Bareilly	96
C. Squardon at Bareilly	98
Group in Full Dress at Bareilly	100
Jumping at the Bareilly Horse Show	102
Point-to-Point in Bareilly	102
Snapshots at Bareilly	104
Snapshots on the March	106
Group at Jhansi 1917	118
Group at Dera Ismail Khan 1921	118
Groups at Lahore 1918 and 1919	122
Risaldar Rukan Din Khan	126
Group at Lahore 1920	126
Risaldar Kumrodeen Bahadur	130
Risaldar-Major Rustam Ali Khan	130
Risaldar-Major Mahmud Khan	130
Risaldar-Major Izat Khan, Sirdar Bahadur	130
Risaldar-Major Mohamed Akbar Khan	130
Risaldar-Major Saadat Khan	130
Risaldar-Major Mohamed Amin Khan, Bahadur	132
Risaldar-Major (Honorary Captain) Hamzullah Khan, Sirdar Bahadur	132

	PAGE.
Risaldar-Major Malik Dost Mohamed Khan, Bahadur ...	132
Risaldar-Major (Honorary Lieutenant) Zikryia Khan ...	132
Risaldar-Major Rahmat Sher Khan, Bahadur	132
The Trenches in France	138
A group in India	138
Lieutenant-Colonel R. C. Barry Smith	142
Lieutenant-Colonel H. S. Stewart	142
Group taken at Lucknow before amalgamation	144
Group showing uniforms worn by the officers of the 17th Cavalry	144
Group showing classes enlisted by the 17th Cavalry ...	146
Group showing uniforms worn by the men of the 17th Cavalry	146
The final parade of the 17th Cavalry	148
The Mess Plate, 17th Cavalry	150
Group at Ferozepore	170
The regiment on parade at Ferozepore	172
Snapshots at the farm	174
Snapshots at the farm	176
Types of 17th Cavalry stud-breds	178
Types of 17th Cavalry stud-breds	180
Types of 17th Cavalry stud-breds	182
Types of 17th Cavalry stud-breds	184
Types of 17th Cavalry stud-breds	186
Types of 17th Cavalry stud-breds	188
Snapshots with the East African Squardon	194
Map of East Africa	198
Group at the Indian Cavalry Polo Tournament, 1921 ...	206
Regimental Polo Team with Inter-Regimental and Indian Cavalry Polo Cups	208
Pigsticking snapshots	232

HISTORY

OF

THE 17TH CAVALRY, 1858–1922.

The Regiment of Irregular Cavalry, subsequently known as Robarts' Regiment of Cavalry, Robarts' Horse, the 17th Bengal Cavalry, the 17th Bengal Lancers, and finally the 17th Cavalry, was raised at Meerut on the 21st November 1858. It was raised from four sources :

(1) *The Meerut Military Police*, a corps that had been raised by Captain Tyrwhitt, from Sikhs, and from Mahomedans of Meerut and the adjoining districts. The following incident, related by Malleson, occurred in its career :—

"One of the most enterprising and daring of the rebel leaders was Sah Mull, zamindar or Bajrul, a man who had conquered, and who had since maintained a kind of semi-independence in the town of Barauth, capital of the district of the same name, in the Meerut Division, from which Sah Mull issued to carry fire and sword into the neighbouring villages. Mr. R. H. W. Dunlop, Collector of Meerut, proceeded against him with a small mixed force. Sah Mull led his men to the attack but the rebels, their flanks turned, broke and fled. In the pursuit Sah Mull was overtaken and killed by a young volunteer assisted by an Indian trooper, and his head was stuck on a pole and carried as a standard for the rest of the day. For his part in this affair Jemadar Boodh Singh (referred to above and afterwards in Robarts' Horse) was specially mentioned for gallantry and given a reward of two hundred rupees for killing the rebel chieftain.

One hundred and eight sabres of this corps were transferred to Robarts' Horse on the 14th November 1858."

(2) *The Rohilkhand Auxiliary Police Levy.*—The story of the beginnings of this corps, which subsequently achieved fame as de Kantzow's Horse, is told in a little known but extremely interesting book about the Mutiny. "The personal adventures and experiences of a Magistrate during the rise, progress and

suppression of the Indian Mutiny," by Mark Thornhill, some time Collector of Muttra. (John Murray, 1884.) The following extracts give the story:—

"Anticipating the departure of the Kotah contingent (a body of semi-mutinous troops that the Government at Agra could not make up their minds to disband in June 1857), I had collected a force of my own. It was supplied by the great landholders; each sent in a party of so many men. Wonderful savages they were, lazy, dirty, stupid, and armed with as miscellaneous a collection of weapons as if they had plundered a museum. The way they performed their duties would have broken the heart of a disciplinarian. They had no conception of order or obedience. As guards, even as messengers, they were quite unreliable. They would sleep at their posts, or if the fancy took them, would desert them. A letter delivered to one, however urgent, would be passed on to a second or to a third. It would be delayed, whilst the man who ultimately took it, ate, smoked, or visited a friend by the way. Of such mobs, no doubt, were composed the armies of the native princes that we encountered in the early days of our rule. No wonder that with such mere handfuls of troops we so easily defeated them.

The horsemen,* however, were much better. They were men of a superior class, generally connected more or less nearly to the landholder who furnished them. They were well dressed, well armed in the native fashion, and mounted on really beautiful horses. I collected a large troop of these men. They were afterwards transferred to the Government, and under the appellation of de Kantzow's Horse, did good service towards the end of the disturbances."

Again, Mark Thornhill writes:—

"In the collection of the transport (for a movable column that was to go out from Agra in the cold weather of 1857-58 to pacify the Muttra District) I was a good deal concerned, as most of it came from the Muttra District. The facility with which, at such a time, it was obtained, impressed me greatly with the wealth and vast resources of India. Day by day, week by week, carts, bullocks, camels, ponies, came in by scores, by hundreds. The end of the great parade† was soon nearly filled with them. They were continually sent off to the East and yet the supply never diminished, nor, what was more surprising, did the country show the slightest indication of the drain thus made on it.

---

* These were the men who afterwards formed Roberts' Horse: not the ragamuffins previously alluded to.—[Ed. S. & C.]

† The "great parade" was the parade ground, across the river from Agra Fort, where the battle of Agra was fought.

Horses were less plentiful and the want of them occasioned the Government a good deal of inconvenience; for they were, required for the new cavalry and were with difficulty procured. Learning this, it occurred to me that the horsemen I had obtained from the various landholders might now be made useful. I mentioned the matter to my brother, he approved, and interested Colonel Fraser. The men were paraded, inspected, and an officer, Lieutenant de Kantzow, appointed to drill them into order. This was the origin of that body of cavalry whose services, as de Kantzow's Horse, were frequently mentioned in the dispatches of the ensuing campaigns, and have even, I believe, found a place in the histories of the mutiny. Very pretty they looked (de Kantzow's horsemen) for they were beautifully mounted, and wore gay dresses of white, with red sashes and turbans—dresses, I may remark, which they soon learnt the wisdom of exchanging for the less conspicuous uniform of khaki, that is, dust colour.

The first affair in which de Kantzow's Horse were concerned was that of Fatehpore Sikri in the winter of 1857-58. A force of all arms had moved out from Agra to restore order in the surrounding country, and hearing there were some rebels hiding in Fatehpur Sikri, they were summoned to surrender. The troops had advanced to the gate of the mosque, while my horsemen (I had better now call them de Kantzow's) were sent round to the opposite side of the ruins to cut off the fugitives. The gateway is magnificent.* Situated on the brow of a low hill, it rises one hundred and twenty feet above it. The gates were closed, and no notice being taken of the summons to open them, the guns were brought up and two shots fired; the first went wide, the second, better aimed, smashed open the door—at the same time, I am sorry to say, carrying away a portion of the delicate stone feathering that ornaments the arch. Some shells were next thrown in to clear out the enemy, and then Sikhs and English soldiers charged up the stairs, and to their disappointment found the mosque empty.

This mosque, one of the most magnificent in India, surrounds a courtyard, in which is the tomb and shrine of the saint Golam Chisti,† by whom the building was erected. The shrine, a beautiful building of white marble, had originally contained much treasure in the way of silver lamps and other decorations. These had been carried off to Bhurtpore nearly a century before by

---

* The Buland Darwaza, carrying Akbar's famous inscription "Said Jesus" on Whom be peace! "This world is a bridge, pass over it, but build no house there. He who hopes for an hour, hopes for an eternity. The world is but an hour; spend it in devotion, the rest is unseen."

† A lineal descendant of the Chisti family still lives in the mosque.

Sooraj Mull. The present ornaments were of little value, but the Sikhs commenced to plunder them. They tore up the Koran, broke to pieces some old sandalwood chests, and picked out the mother-of-pearl from the canopy. While the Sikhs continued to desecrate the mosque, de Kantzow's men had intercepted the fugitives, bringing in two or three. This was the end of the affair of Fatehpore Sikri. Thereafter de Kantzow's men were employed at Muttra, until the time came for them, on the 20th February 1858, to join the force of Sir Thomas Seaton, who was about to operate in Rohilkhand."

Marching at the rate of twenty-five miles a day, they arrived at Mynpuri on the 24th and at Fatehgarh on the 26th February. On the 7th April was fought the action of Kankar in which de Kantzow, who had two horses wounded under him, greatly distinguished himself.

He had previously it may be mentioned, distinguished himself by saving the treasury at Mynpuri from the mutineers of the 9th Native Infantry; his conduct on that occasion being acknowledged by the Viceroy, Lord Canning, in an autograph letter stating that de Kantzow had "given a noble example of courage, patience and temper."

The Rohilkhand Levy was left in April as part of Colonel Hale's force at Shahjehanpur, which place on the 3rd May was attacked in overwhelming force by the leader known as the Faizabad Moulvi with eight thousand men and twelve guns. Colonel Hale's force, consisting only of four companies of the 82nd Foot and four guns in addition to the Irregular Cavalry was driven into the Jail. On this day de Kantzow opposed the rebel cavalry who were swarming over the plain eight thousand strong, and offered to charge with his two squadrons, those in his immediate front who were one thousand strong, headed by the mutineers of the 12th Irregular Cavalry. Colonel Hale's force then sustained a siege and an incessant bombardment till the 8th May, when the colomn under Brigadier Jones (known as "The Avenger") arrived.

Continued fighting followed, and in the action of the 15th of May de Kantzow sustained two dangerous sword wounds and again had a horse wounded under him. The Commander-in-Chief, Sir Colin Campbell, arrived on the 18th of May when an action was fought, and a fortnight later the Moulvi was shot dead while forcing his way into Powain. In June the corps was attached to the Rohilkhand Division and remained for a short time in Fatehgarh.

There now appeared in the field the pensioner Khan Bahadur Khan, the Nawab of Farrukhabad, and Wilayat Shah, and a small force was despatched to protect Powain, in which was included the cavalry commanded by the gallant de Kantzow, scarcely recovered from his wounds. He marched to Shahjehanpur on the 23rd of June and reached Powain on the night of the 28th—the country was swarming with the enemy and he was engaged throughout. At Powain the Levy had to display untiring activity against the rebels, who mostly mounted and with a strength of twenty thousand men and sixty to seventy guns, were swarming in the vicinity.

In December, de Kantzow crossed to the right bank of the Sardah River in boats, and occupied Putthen, thence operating with the Rohilkhand Field Force towards Pilibhit, and in driving the rebels across the Nepal border during the early months of 1859.

On the completion of the pacification of Rohilkhand, the Levy which had already been embodied into Robarts' Horse as noted above, marched to Cawnpore where it joined the Headquarters of the regiment there on the 1st October 1859, with a total strength as stated by de Kantzow of three hundred and twenty sabres. The total casualties from all causes sustained by the Levy since the 27th October 1857 amounted to between two hundred and fifty and three hundred men, and about the same number of horses.

Lieutenant de Kantzow received the thanks of the Government of India for his services. He is referred to by Malleson in his history as "truly one of the heroes of the Mutiny." He afterwards reverted nominally to the 48th Native Infantry, but was really posted to the 8th Central India Horse, and ultimately entered civil employ. He retired as a Colonel and died at Brighton recently.

(3) *The third source* from which the regiment was raised was from transfers received from other Bengal and Punjab Cavalry Regiments, among whom were the following distinguished soldiers :—Naib-Risaldar Kumruddin Khan, 3rd class Order, of Merit gained in the Siege of Lucknow, Jemadar Mahbub Khan, 2nd class Order of Merit, for great gallantry in action with 3rd Sikh Cavalry, Sowars Nur Gul and Sher Muhammad, both with the 3rd class Order of Merit, gained with the 3rd Sikh Cavalry in the Siege of Lucknow.

(4) *The fourth source* from which the regiment was raised was enlistments by Major Robarts. He enlisted one hundred and five Afghans at Meerut.

The regiment first appears in the Army List of the 1st of January 1859 as a regiment of Irregular Cavalry. It was composed as follows :—Major and Regimental Captain C. J. Robarts,

43rd N. I., Commandant, from 24th November 1848. Lieutenant C. A. de Kantzow, 48th N. I., 2nd-in-Command, from 2nd November 1858.

Risaldar Raja Ram.
Risaldar Kamruddin Khan.
Jemadar Muhammad Umer Khan.
,, Mahbub Khan.
,, Budh Singh.
,, Salwant Singh.
,, Mytab Singh.

Establishment—1 Wordie-Major, 1 Nakub, 1 Persian writer 3 Risaldars, 3 Ressaidars, 5 Naib-Risaldars, 6 Jemadars, 6 Kote-Daffadars, 8 Daffadars, 6 Nishanbardars, 6 Trumpeters, 6 Pay Sowars, 488 Sowars.

This strength, however, was probably only a paper one including the Rohilkhand Levy which had not yet joined, as in the next two army lists the corps is shown as consisting of three troops only, with a total strength of one hundred and sixty in April and one hundred and ninety-nine in July. In the latter month, however, the regiment was made complete in officers with the addition of Lieutenant T. J. Watson appointed Adjutant from the 24th November 1858, and Lieutenant T. B. M. Glascock from the 31st May 1859, and Assistant Surgeon W. H. Adley from the 15th April 1859.

In September the regiment marched to Cawnpore, where it arrived on the 28th. In July the regiment was designated Robarts' Regiment of Cavalry, and on the 1st October its name was changed to Robarts' Horse, and the Rohilkhand Levy under the Kantzow joined, with a strength of two hundred and twenty-eight sabres,* bringing the regiment up to its proper strength of six troops and four hundred and twenty men and horses.

In December 1859 a detachment of ninety-six sabres was sent to Etawah under Jemadar Budh Singh, and early in 1860 a detachment of one hundred and fifty sabres marched to Kalpi under Lieutenant Glascock, and another to Mahona under Lieutenant Clifford.

In May 1861 the Staff Corps of the three presidencies were formed, the Bengal Army being styled "H. M.'s Indian Forces on the Bengal Establishment," and the officers, "The Bengal Staff Corps." Consequent on this change the designation of the

---
* De Kantzow states, 320 sabres. The surplus were probably discharged.
† Standard bearer.

Captain (afterwards Colonel) C. J. Robarts, First Commandant, 1858—1873.

Lieutenant (afterwards Colonel) C. A. de Kantzow, who raised de Kantzow's Horse which was incorporated in what afterwards became the 17th Cavalry.

regiment was again changed and it became "The 17th Bengal Cavalry (late Robarts' Horse)."

As de Kantzow joined the regiment with his Levy on the 8th October 1859 and reverted to the 48th N. I., and to civil employ in December of the same year, it will be seen that he only served a few months with the regiment; just sufficient time, in all probability, to hand over his Levy to Robarts. No doubt, however, the tales of his reckless daring were told and retold to the recruits of Robarts' Horse by the men who had ridden with him in Mutiny days, so that the regiment may be said to be an heir to his tradition, and an inheritor of his fame.*

Except for this limelight, thrown on one of the figures of the Mutiny, the stage on which the early history of the regiment was played is very imperfectly lighted. Robarts took no part in the Mutiny. He had predicted its coming, and in disgust that his prophecy was not attended to, he took furlough to Europe, and thereby escaped the fate of the other officers of his regiment, the 43rd Native Infantry, who were murdered by their men. But although he played no part in those stirring times, his was a career that had been marked by destiny and the history of the old regiment, as we see it across the years, seems chiefly concerned with his fascinating personality.

Rich, handsome, versatile, and perhaps not over-burdened with the fears and conventionalities of lesser men, the figure of Charles James Robarts, looking down from its frame in the Mess ante-room from the spacious times of 1858 on the about-to-be-amalgamated generation of 1922, with a certain cynicism, is the figure of a man, and a leader of men, of whom the regiment may well be proud as its first Colonel. His name was noted for promotion at Army Headquarters; it was a name to conjure with among the swashbucklers whom he enlisted, and was a by-word in the bazaars where "Robarts' Robbers" were quartered......Colonel Burton says of him :—

Colonel C. J. Robarts, who died at Dehra Dun on the 6th January 1873, was in many ways a remarkable man. He was the son of Mr. T. J. Robarts who was in charge of the East India Company's factory at Canton; and entered the Company's service, his first commission being dated 12th June 1839. His family was connected with Robarts, Lubbock and Co., of London, and he was a man of large private means. He had served in the Afghan War of 1840—42 and in the Sikh Campaigns of 1848-49. He possessed considerable literary ability and was a very good Oriental scholar: being able to converse in darbar with the

---

* See note on de Kantzow, Appendix 1.

various races of men composing his regiment in Urdu, Persian, Punjabi, Pushtu, etc. He enlisted into Robarts' Horse men of the wildest Afghan tribes, without any enquiry into their character or conduct, and was on very intimate terms with them. During his command discipline was of a primitive character: and his regiment was regarded with some fear by the civil population of the cantonments and districts in which it was quartered. He was a very fine judge of a horse and kept a large racing stable; on his death it was difficult to decide what horses were his own and what the property of the regiment and his heirs alleged that the regimental Chanda owed his estate Rs. 30,000 to Rs. 40,000, for horses in the ranks owned by him.

The greater part of his property went at his death to his adopted son, Abdul Gyas, whose mother belonged to a noble Afghan family: and who subsequently lived at Dehra Dun and raced and finally dissipated it. This family was recalled to Afghanistan by Abdur Rahman about 1890; but was ruined, and ejected to India, by him ten years later. Two nephews of Abdul Gyas were enlisted in the 17th Bengal Cavalry at Rawalpindi in 1901: and died without descendants, at Bannu, in the regiment, in 1907.

In "Forty Years of a Sportsman's Life" there is the following reference to Charles James Robarts, as well as an opinion on the Silladar Cavalry—not endorsed by Army Headquarters alas!

"The period during which I was stationed in India was a very interesting one from a military as well as from a sporting point of view. In the end of the sixties, those three superb regiments, Probyn's Horse, Robarts' Horse and Hodson's Horse, were still in their prime. There are probably few soldiers acquainted with those regiments who would declare that their disbandment—for such it practically was—worked wholly for the good of the service. Having seen more than a little of the regiments and noted their unrivalled smartness and efficiency, I have never doubted that it was sheer folly to do anything but encourage the system. Colonel Robarts never took the trouble to keep exact accounts of what he spent on his regiment. He was a rich man, and his generosity in the patriotic work of making Robarts' Horse the first cavalry force in the world knew no bounds. When he was called upon to render an exact account, he could not do so, and he was therefore never repaid. It was no secret that the Government remained his debtor to an account not far short of twenty thousand pounds."

Beyond this, there remain only the oral traditions still current in the 17th Cavalry to preserve the memory of Robarts.

Owing to the kindness of Risaldar-Major Ghulam Mohiuddin, Bahadur, and late Risaldar-Major of the late 17th Cavalry, whose father knew Robarts well, it is possible to write some of these traditions down, and so preserve them for posterity; any errors there may be in this appreciation, however, must be imputed to the writer only, for he has added from other sources to the particulars supplied by the Risaldar-Major Sahib.

"Robarts Sahib was a Nawab and he lived like one"—such is the verdict of those who knew him. He fed about two hundred people in his compound every day: he kept hounds, horses and hawks: he kept an Oriental establishment in the old style, having adopted an Afghan lady as his mother and her son Abdul Gyas as his own son and heir.

A letter from Robarts, dated Lucknow, the 26th December 1859, to de Kantzow (who must have been about to leave the regiment) shows something of the man. It does not need a fortune-teller to deduce from the slapdash writing, that its author was warm-hearted, artistic, impulsive.

Lucknow, 26th December 1859.

My Dear de Kantzow,

I am well satisfied with what you have done in the case of those Afghans as indeed in everything else since my departure. In the "Mofussilite" I see an extract from the "Bombay Standard" with reference to Mayne's New Force, but a man with whom I was talking to yesterday about it did not appear to think that a Brigade would be organised—but I suspect he knew nothing about it and like many others merely talked for the sake of talking. I shall leave this the day after to-morrow, 28th, so as to be at Cawnpore on the 29th. Please take care that no more letters are despatched by the Cawnpore Post Office to this.

I have had very bad luck with my horses, but the fact is they were not fit to go.

You see the China Force is in orders. People here seem to think that Dighton Probyn or Watson—General Grant's famous outpost officers will go in command of the Indian Cavalry. Love to Watson and Adly.

Yours very truly,
C. Robarts.

That is all. The voice that speaks to us from the Lucknow of those days is a very ordinary one; we seem to have heard a snatch of conversation about the common affairs of every day.

It is for this very reason that it speaks to us with such an intimate sense of reality.

Let us try to reconstitute that reality for ourselves, and see what Charles James Robarts was really like. Now every voice and every gesture in the world have their place in time and a certain interval elapses before they are transmitted from lip to ear, from hand to eye. Following out this idea, let us take an observer with a telescope, watching a big gun fire, then imagine the same observer observing the same phenomenon from the moon; obviously gun-flash and report would be still further delayed in time. Extending this principle through the infinities of space, we see that at some point in the universe the roar of the sabre toothed tiger or the thunders of Trafalgar are still actual and living facts. From the general to the particular. Robarts is still living. At some point in space it is now, say, a morning in December 1861, and Robarts is commanding his regiment at Cawnpore. Let us try to look on that time with the inward eye of imagination.

It is a cold December morning. The mists of dawn wreath the ground, the thirsty looking grass in the compound is glinting with dew, and a couple of sleek *minas* are watching Major Robarts' *chota hazri* tray which has been placed by his bedside on the verandah. With a bound, Robarts is up and splashing in his bath. Meanwhile there is great stir in the colony that inhabit his compound. A couple of orderlies and several syces are superintending the harnessing of a heavy and magnificent *barouche*. Another orderly is riding out towards the lines with a couple of Robarts' chargers: the one caparisoned in all the panoply of parade order, with heavily bossed bit chain reins, saddle cloth, and crested breastplate, while the other carries a plain hunting saddle and double bridle. These horses are being taken to the lines. Grass-cutters are going out to their work, syces are clearing up their stables, *bheesties* are carrying water, sweepers are raising the immemorial dust of India, the hawkers are bestirring themselves, a couple of dancing boys from Kohat are combing their hair, and an old drummer is stupifying himself, as his custom is of a morning, with liberal doses of *bhang*. Meanwhile Robarts' toilet is complete. The dressing boy gives a wipe to his neat top-boots, the bearer helps him into a loose civilian *surtout*. Robarts winds a small blue silk Meshedi turban round his long black hair, and jumps into the *barouche*. A *hukka bardar* puts a lighted *hubble bubble* at his feet, there is a bustle among the dog-boys and hawkers, the coachman-orderly whips up the horses and the cavalcade starts for the lines followed by a couple of

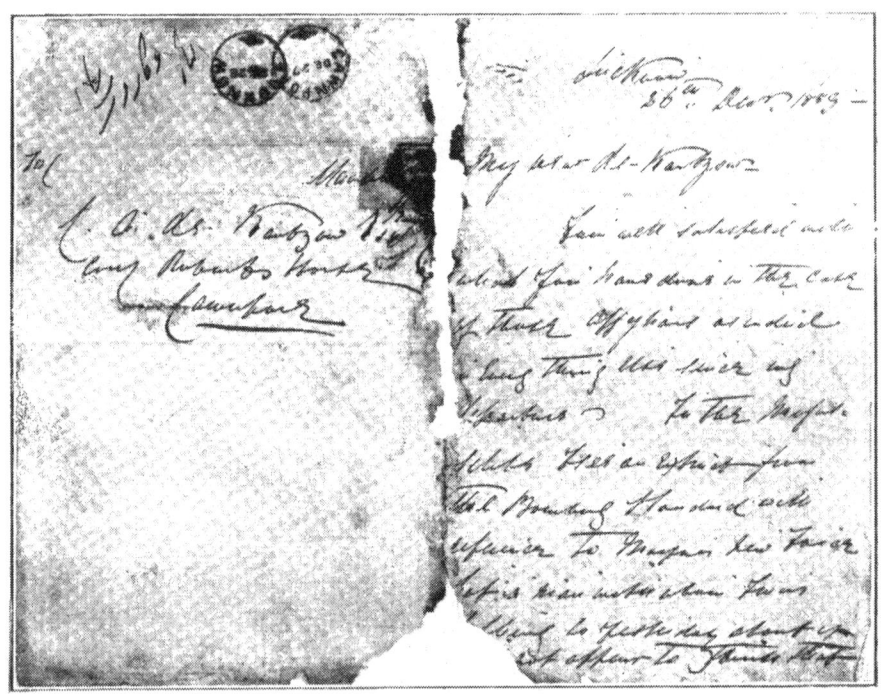
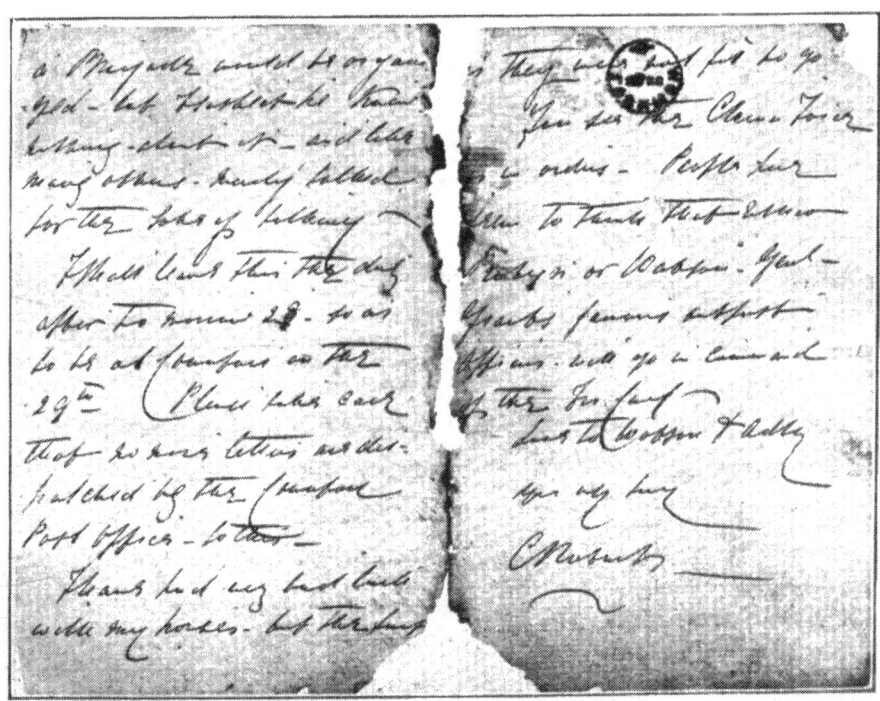

Facsimile of a letter from Roberts to de Kantzow.

long dogs and a falconer with Robarts' favourite gerfalcon at his wrist.

Arrived at the regiment, Robarts looks down the ranks with the eye of a master, in more senses than one. A master first because he was one of the best Cavalry leaders of his day ; and again a master because he actually owned about one-third of the men and the horses in the regiment. The horses he had bought, without any very careful account of what was Chanda property and what was his own. As to the men, many of them were his *bargirs*,* and dependent on his bounty. And all ranks knew that his word was law. There is no such absolute autocracy in these days as the Commandant of an Irregular Cavalry regiment. The only modern counterpart is, perhaps, a submarine at sea. Robarts' Horse was Robarts' Horse in fact as well as in name ; his regiment in life or death. Sikhs, Jats and Rangars were there, de Kantzow's men; heavy bearded Afghans ; Afridis from the uplands of Tirah ; Pathans with the blood of Israel in their veins, whose ancestors had been a race of Kings : every man jack of them soldiers whose families had lived and died by the sword. The routine of drill was not for them : they would have maddened a sergeant-major, but they were a terror to their enemies.

"Good morning, Hoggan,—who wants to come hunting with me this morning?" This to his Adjutant who has ridden up and reported the regiment two hundred strong.

" Everyone, Sir," says Hoggan.

" They can't all come. Choose five men a troop, will you ? The rest can drill under Watson."

For a moment or two Robarts watches his regiment—the six *nishan bardars* with their *guidons* fluttering in the morning breeze —the serried lance pennons—the officers with glinting swords choosing out the men who were to go hunting. Presently some thirty troopers leave the ranks. Robarts makes a sign to the orderlies with the Rampur hounds, the gerfalcon flutters at the hawker's wrist, and the whole party jogs off, past the lines, and across some open fields to a patch of *arrah* where a hare has been seen.

Behind them, a trumpeter is sounding the " march." By nine o'clock, the party is back in the lines with a jack and a

---

* *Bargirs* = without, *i.e.*, a man without *assami* or money for the purchase of his horse and equipment which was paid for by another. A sowar was called a *bargir* when his *assami* was paid by another person usually an Indian Officer, and the person paying it was known as a *bargirdar*. In some regiments, but not we hope in the 17th Cavalry, the *demi-monde* of the bazaar occasionally were *bargirdars*. Robarts owned several hundreds of *assamis*, as well as several hundred horses. A more complete note on the whole Silladar system appears in a separate article.

couple of hares. Stables are already in full swing, for work began early and finished early in the old Irregular Cavalry.

At the table by a horse hospital, spread with a coarse cloth, stands the Adjutant, with some native officers, drinking green tea out of small cups in the Turkey fashion. Robarts joins them. A *chillum* is brought, and he takes a few puffs, before attending to the business on hand. A troop horse is rope galled, one of his racing ponies is lame, a mare is in foal : these matters are attended to with a care impossible in the *babu*-ridden days of objection statements and vouchers in triplicate............Then the party walk round the lines. Here Robarts sees a newly joined subaltern, who in an excess of keenness is instructing a patriarchal Pathan how to groom his horse. This sight rouses Robarts to fury. The subaltern is sent to the right about immediately. This is Robarts' regiment : no English officer is wanted down in the lines, interfering between the commanding officer and his men. The place of English officers is on parade, to command the men in the field, not to harass them in the lines : Robarts hated seeing British officers (except the Adjutant) in the lines. Then the *barouche* appears again, and Robarts lumbers back to his morning meal of *pilau* and small beer and Kabuli grapes, procured by his relatives at great expense.

Into his private life we may not look. He passes out of our sight behind the veil of the *zenana*. That he was happy there, there can be no doubt, for he never returned to England and lived for fifteen years with his adopted family. Who his wife was the present writer does not know, but he can remember the nephews of Abdul Gyas, Robarts' adopted son, when they enlisted at Bannu. These lads were treated with the greatest respect by all ranks, but they were both consumptives and died at Bannu. Abdul Gyas was last heard of in 1910. He was there a very old man, living at Cawnpore in complete seclusion, as the dependent of a Nawab. He is probably dead now. May he rest in peace.

Later in the day, Robarts again mounts his *barouche*, and drives up to the regiment, to transact whatever business there may be with his Naquib and Persian writer. There is no formal office. The Commanding Officer rarely signs his name : he gives orders instead, which are rapidly taken down *verbatim* in the running Urdu script (a species of shorthand) and afterwards read aloud to the person concerned. The scriveners write standing, with a reed pen dipped into a jar at their girdle. They hold the paper in the palm of their left hand and they salaam after an order has been dictated. Reports and returns were in their

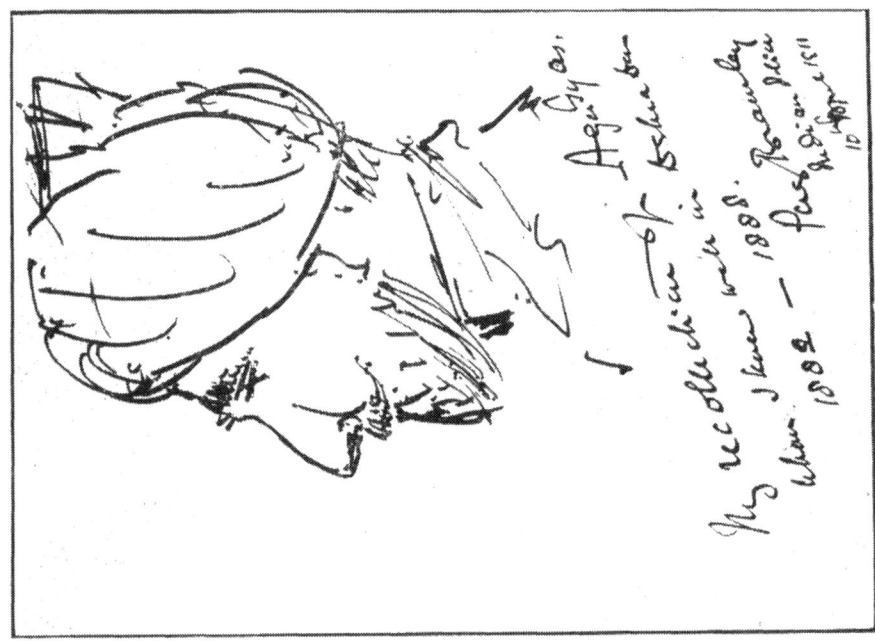

Abdul Gyas (the son or adopted son of Colonel C. J. Robarts).

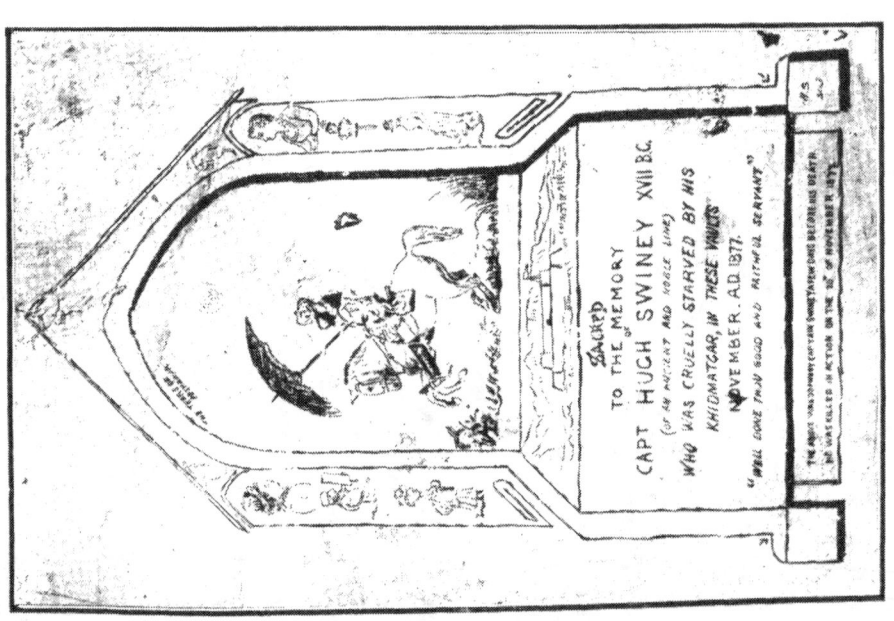

Copy of an inscription executed in Fort Mackeson by Captain Swiney shortly before his death.

infancy (as far as the army was concerned) in those days. All important decisions were communicated to, or taken by the Commanding Officer in open Durbar.

That morning however there is no Durbar. Robarts chats to Assistant Surgeon Adly, sees some recruits that Risaldar Kumruddin Khan has brought and settles a dispute between a Sikh and Pathan, who have been fighting. Now Robarts judged his men, as Orientals love to be judged, by emotion, blended with commonsense. His judgments were summary, tradition alleges that he carried a handkerchief in one hand and a club in the other, ready to weep with the afflicted or castigate a delinquent. After listening patiently to both sides of the quarrel as set forth in Punjabi and Pushtu, he gives club to one of the protagonists and Risaldar-Major Raja Ram's big *lathi* to the other, and makes them fight it out all over again, nor allows them to desist until both parties have dropped from sheer exhaustion.

Then he goes off to see his racing ponies, which were kept in the lines as there was no room for them in his bungalow. No story of Robarts would be complete without mention of his racing stable, yet the present writer has no materials on which to build. A few Arabs he had, and perhaps a thorough-bred or two, but the majority must have been country-breds, perhaps of the then renowned Parrat stock.

On his way back to his bungalow, an orderly from Brigade Command stops his carriage and hands him a letter. The man is dressed as follows: a red turban, and a blue double-breasted **kurta** (alkhalak) with a red kummerband of Kashmir shawl: round this is a belt from which is suspended the curved sword (*talwar*) which is his only weapon.* His loose khaki pyjamas are tucked into black jack boots: the latter have big brass spurs. He rides a shaggy Biloch mare, with a long mane and swish tail, that whinnies and frets at the halt. In her mouth is the barbarous native snaffle with spikes in the mouthpiece: a tight standing martingale is fitted. The saddle is a *charjama* (literally a four-cloth) composed of pads secured to wooden frame-work. Beneath, is a blue saddle cloth edged with red.

The letter announces that the regiment will leave Cawnpore in February and March for Segowlie on the Nepaulese frontier.

Back at his bungalow, Robarts strolls round to see his horses and hounds and the *Langar Khana*, where an evening meal is

---

* At this time only the front rank carried lances; the rear rank sabres. Later (1865) ten carbines per troop were issued to the rear rank. In 1869 the whole of the rear rank had smooth bore carbines, and in 1876, Sniders. It is not known when the front rank were first armed with rifles.

being prepared for his numerous friends and retainers. Here we must quote a paragraph or two from a recent letter of one who cultivates the Robarts' tradition.

"He had dogs of different species. Some of them were long tailed hounds, bullies, and spaniels, and some of them were domestic animals. They were about two hundred. Ata Muhammad of Ludhiana District used to superintend them, and sound the bugle at their times of meal. They were very carefully taught to abide by discipline and used to take their meals calmly. Their dishes were arranged in line and it was a very pleasant scene for spectators. He was the same Ata Muhammad who was afterwards appointed Trumpet-Major. Under his guidance the dogs used to go out in the evening in big *gharries*. Colonel Robarts had plenty of servants, grooms and other staff of his own and for this purpose he had kept one *Langar Khana* from where his employees used to take their daily meals. Sometimes men from the ranks and syces of the regiment were also known to have filled their bellies from his *Langar Khana*.*

Afterwards, there is Robarts' own dinner, some puffs at a cool *hookah*, desultory attention to his correspondence, and as twilight is falling, his phæton (a lighter edition of the *barouche* of the morning) comes to take him to the bandstand and brandy *pawnee* of Cantonment life of those days. And so to bed.

Alas, this sketch is dependent only on oral tradition helped out by imagination.†

Such is the peculiar oblivion which India visits on all but her most favoured servants that the real Robarts, who was born only a century ago, has already become a legendary figure. In 1862, in the memory of our fathers, Robarts was in his prime, yet to-day, in the regiment he raised and commanded for fourteen years, all that is known of him is contained in the foregoing description. Perhaps in some archive at Simla, or in the papers of those who served with him (their number alas has grown sadly small) or perhaps (possibly indeed) in some snuff-scented docket of papers kept in the household of his descendants, now scattered God knows where between Kabul and Ludhiana, there may be some records, diaries or letters, which would tell us something of the races he won, and the lady he loved and the regiment he commanded. We do not know. Of the memory of Charles James Robarts we have here put down all that we could salve from dust, oblivion, and the white-ants

To resume our history: we must now chronicle the marches and counter-marches of two decades. Little, alas, of human

---

* Cook house.
† See note on Robarts, Appendix 1.

interest, has been left on record of this time. By a glance at the map, we can trace the routine of twenty years, of service in as many seconds

On the 28th of September 1859 the regiment arrived at Cawnpore from Meerut. On the 1st of April 1863 the regiment arrived at Segowlie, on the Nepalese Frontier. In January 1866 the regiment was at Rungeah, in the Bhutan Duars on the Bhutan Expedition, which terminated in March of that year. In May 1866 the regiment was at Barrackpore. In January 1869 it marched westward again into Hindustan, being cantoned at Sitapur. Next year during the cold weather 1869-70 the regiment spent a fortnight in Lucknow during the visit of H. R. H. the Duke of Edinburgh. In 1871 the regiment marched *via* Delhi (where it took part in a camp of exercise in December of that year) to Sialkote, arriving March 1872.

During this year the regiment was resaddled, saddle cloths were abolished, and accoutrements of new pattern were issued to sowars. But the greatest change was one of personnel. In January 1872 Colonel C. J. Robarts proceeded on leave to Dehra Dun, and never returned, dying at Dehra Dun on the 6th January 1873. The command of the regiment was given to Lieut.-Colonel D. W. Ryall in an officiating capacity on 31st January 1872 * and to Lieut.-Colonel J. W. Graham on the 2nd January 1873.

In 1875 the following changes were introduced by Colonel Graham. Blue lungis for all ranks, with gold bars according to rank, instead of red lungis. Gauntlets for British officers, white pyjamas for Indian officers, and chevrons for non-commissioned officers.

In the previous year (1874) *Seedimuls* had been introduced to hold the bit, independent of the headstall, and the following changes made in the dress of British officers:— Blue forage caps and sling sword belts were introduced pouch belt ornaments were changed to silver from gilt.

In November 1874 the medals for the Bhutan Expedition were received and distributed, after an interval of eight and one-half years from the conclusion of the operations. In January 1876 one Squadron went to Jummu in Kashmir on escort duty with H. R. H. the Prince of Wales. On the 2nd of February 1876 the regiment marched from Sialkote for Peshawar, *via*

---

* Colonel Ryall known as "Paddy" Ryall, had been recommended for a V. C. in the Mutiny. He was transferred to the 14th B. L. and retired in 1881 and was later promoted Major-General.

Jhelum and Rawalpindi, arriving at Sialkote, 25th February 1876. The next four years were spent on the Frontier.

On the 12th of November 1876, the garrison of Fort Mackeson of which a detachment of the 17th Bengal Cavalry formed part, had a skirmish with Jawaki Afridi raiders. A few days later Captain H. D. Swiney who was on reconnaissance with a Staff Officer of the Pehawar District received a sword cut, severing the arteries of his arm. The Indian Doctor was on the spot but was unable to apply the usual remedies, so that Captain Swiney bled to death. He was a very valuable officer, greatly loved by all ranks. He was also a talented artist as the picture he drew over the mantelpiece of a room in Fort Mackeson testifies, he was also a fine rider, being able to pick up a lance laid on the ground, at full gallop.

Lieut.-Colonel F. W. Graham retired in April 1878, Lieut.-Colonel T. J. Watson being appointed Commandant.

Next year 1879 the Afghan War broke out and the regiment moved up its Headquarters from Peshawar to Bhusawal, with detachments at Jamrud, Ali Masjid, Landi Kotal, Landi Khana and Dacca. The regiment at this time picketted its horses in the manner customary throughout Afghanistan, to long ropes secured at either end to heavy pegs. While camped on the Jamrud plain the whole of the horses stampeded one night and were only collected with much difficulty.

In February the regiment marched to Jalalabad and on the 24th March 1880 into Kabul. On the 9th of April 1880 it was inspected at Kabul by General Sir Frederic Roberts, its strength then being four British Officers and four hundred and twelve Indian Ranks ; Major Newnham in command.

On the 13th August, the regiment was back in Peshawar and in November 1880 marched south to Bareilly, arriving on 22nd of January 1881.

In 1882, (Gladstone being then Prime Minister of England), it was decided to break up four Indian Cavalry regiments, and to increase the strength of the remainder from three to four squadrons. The 17th Bengal Cavalry was one of the regiments chosen for disbandment, probably owing to the fact that the methods adopted by Robarts during his thirteen and a half years of command had made it too difficult for his successors to inculcate that discipline which is one of the first requisites of a regular regiment. The men, however, were noted for their fine physique and fighting qualities at this time and the horses were of an excellent stamp. It must, however,

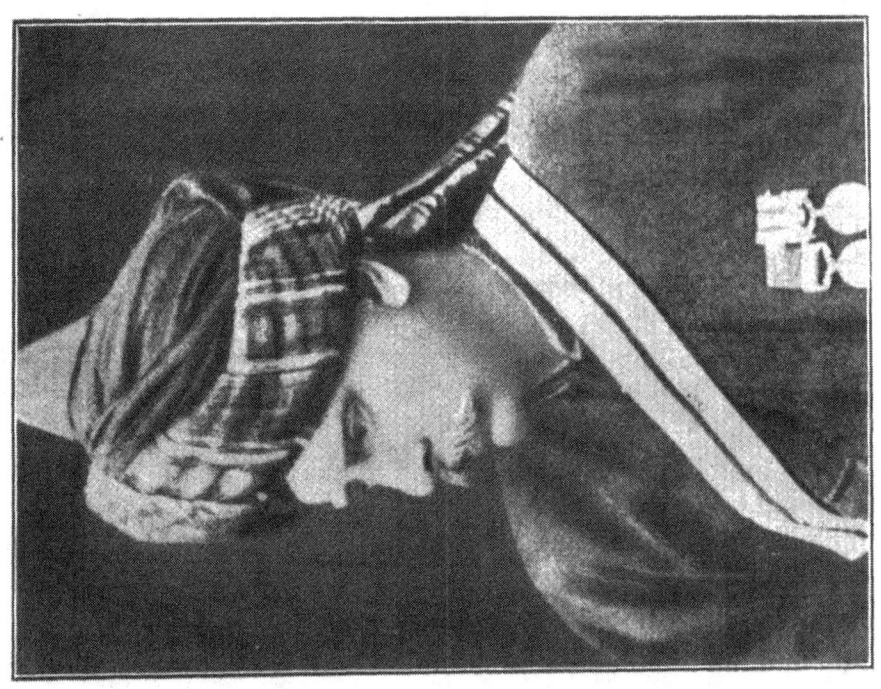

Colonel T. J. Watson, Third Commandant, 1878–1882.

Colonel F. W. Graham, Second Commandant, 1873–1878.

have been difficult to follow Robarts in command of Robarts' Horse. At any rate, a choice of the doomed regiments had to be made, and so, whether for the reasons suggested above, or for other causes, the 17th Bengal Cavalry was disbanded (for the first time) on 13th of June 1882 after an existence of nearly twenty-four years.

Colonel E. J. Watson, the last Commandant, was a man of most irascible temper, if tradition is to be believed. It is related with what truth the writer does not know, that when the regiment marched into a certain cantonment, all the officers except himself and his adjutant were under arrest. On the other hand, one who was present at Bareilly under Colonel Watson's command, has a different and more agreeable story to tell, which can be reproduced in his own words, and may well form the concluding note of the history of the old regiment.

"It was in the year 1882 that I got myself enlisted in the old regiment as a recruit. I used to get twenty-seven rupees per mensem besides good conduct allowance. In those good old days one could comfortably live on six rupees as everything was cheap. Ghee, flour and vegetables could be had at such cheap rates that nowadays one day's expense for meals would be fairly equal to four days expense of those days. Cotton goods and woollen goods have also advanced abnormally in cost. The parade hours were the same as nowadays, and I believe there is no alteration in the hours of going to school as well. Regimental deductions were made in far less degree than at present. There were three squadrons and six troops in the regiment. It was commanded by Colonel Watson, with Mr. Trotter as Adjutant. Colonel Newnham then Major, was the squadron commander of the first squadron. It consisted of Hindu Jats, Brahmans and Punjabi Musalmans. I was in the second squadron, commanded by General Lawrence, then a Major and it consisted of Peshawaries, Yousafzais and Mohmand, Pathans and the fourth troop had Sikhs. The third squadron had Hindustani Musalmans and Jats. Colonel Watson was very fond of long jumps and his putting the stone was simply surprising, as none in Bareilly Cantonment could throw while competing with him. His son used to learn wrestling from Sowar Pakar Singh and Sowar Bude Khan, the famous wrestlers in the regiment. The members of the regiment were highly interested in musketry and tent-pegging. All the ranks were chiefly credited for their neatness. The lines and horses were always kept clean."

On the 8th of September 1885 (after an interval of three years and eighty days) the order constituting the new regiment was promulgated. The new regiment was to be composed of two squadrons of Punjabi Mahomedans and one squadron of Pathans from British Territory and one squadron of Pathans from Independent Territory and was to be raised at Mian Mir. We quote from Colonel Boudier's history of the regiment published in *The Star and Crescent* for September 1914.

The uniform of the regiment was ordered to be the same as that of the 12th Bengal Cavalry, *viz.*, blue with blue facings; arms, the sabre and carbine; saddlery and equipment, the Mackenzie equipment modified. This equipment had been invented by Colonel A. R. D. Mackenzie, 3rd Bengal Cavalry, who was afterwards made a K.C.B., and who was until recently still living in Simla. The facings were, however, changed immediately to the present white.

Transfers were invited from other regiments of Bengal Cavalry, and certain regiments were also directed to supply, on payment, old horses, totalling one hundred in all, for training the recruits.

The 17th Bengal Cavalry was raised in Mian Mir, the headquarters of the Lahore District, then commanded by Major-General Murray, C.B., who had originally raised the 14th Bengal Lancers.

The following British officers were posted to the regiment from the 18th September, and joined at Mian Mir during October:—

Col. E. H. E. Kauntze	Commandant from 7th B. C. (formerly with the old 17th B. C.)
Col. R. W. Sartorius, V.C , C M.G ...	2nd-in-Command from 6th B. C.
Lt -Col. W A. Lawrence	(Formerly with old 17th B. C.)
Capt. C. D. Muir, C.I.E.	From 6th B. C. (seconded as Commandant of the Viceroy's Bodyguard.)
Capt. R. F. Trotter	From 7th B. C. (formerly with old 17th B.C.)
Capt. W. F. Montresor	From 5th B. C. (formerly with old 17th B. C. for a short time.)
Lieut. E. J Medley	From 7th B. C., Adjutant.
Lieut. E. B. Burton	,, 15th B. C.
Lieut. M. Z. Darrah	,, 11th B. L.
Lieut. H. Bower	,, 6th B. C.
Surgn -Major W. E. Griffiths ...	,, 21st P. I.

The following Indian officers were transferred to, or promoted into, the regiment during 1885, the order given being that of their joining:—

Risaldar-Major Rustam Ali Khan. ...	From	16th B. C.
* Risaldar Mahmud Khan	,,	7th B. C.
Resaidar Bhai Khan	,,	9th B. L.
Resaidar Muhamed Akbar	,,	13th B. L.
Resaidar Karm Khan	,,	1st B. C.
* Resaidar Taj Mahomed Khan ...	,,	7th B. C.
Jamadar Sarbuland Khan	,,	6th B. C.
Risaldar Izzat Khan	,,	6th B. C.
* Jamadar Mahomed Amin Khan ...	,,	7th B. C.
* Jamadar Saadat Khan	,,	6th B. C

* Had served in old 17th Bengal Cavalry.

About one hundred and fifty men were received as transfers from other regiments, the greater number of these were Punjabi-Mahomedans, from the 9th Bengal Lancers who were mostly discharged during the succeeding year. Some fifty horses were also received from other regiments, but though useful for training recruits, the majority of them were cast very soon.

The composition of the regiment was—

"A" troop	...	Adam Khel Afridis.
"B" troop	...	Afridis of Tirah and men of Bajour, Buner, Orakzais and Farsiwans from Ludhiana.
"C" troop	...	Yusufzais from Peshawar District.
"D" troop	...	Khuttucks, Mohmunds and Khalils.
"E" troop	...	Ghukkars and Rajas.
"F" troop	...	Ghukkars and Rajas.
"G" troop	...	Tiwanas.
"H" troop	...	Pathans from the Hazara border (*i.e.*, Abbotabad District).

The raising of the remaining men and horses was commenced quickly, and was largely carried out by three subalterns Burton, Darrah and Bower, as Colonel Kauntze with his Adjutant had to remain at headquarters to superintend the organisation of the regiment, while Colonel Lawrence was given the task of starting the accounts on a sound footing. In November Lieutenant Burton was sent to Peshawar to enlist the two Pathan squadrons, and Lieutenant Darrah to the Shahpur and Jhelum districts to enlist the Punjabi Mahomedans, while Lieutenant Bower purchased those remounts that were not bought in Lahore.

The horses bought in Lahore were purchased by Colonel Kauntze himself, at the rate of about twenty a day from the horse dealers, Afsul Khan and Wazir Khan. Kote-Dafadar (late Risaldar-Major and now Honorary Captain and Sirdar Bahadur). Hamzullah Khan made all arrangements for the reception of the horses so bought, under the orders of Captain and Adjutant Medley. Medley had a herculean task in licking a regiment of recruits and young horses into shape and succeeded admirably. The recruits all learnt to ride on blankets, as there were no saddles to give them, and in Hamzullah's opinion the good riding of the regiment at that time is largely attributable to this fact. On the march to Ferozepore in March 1886, the greater number of horses paraded in blankets, there being no saddles available. Later these were purchased from Messrs. Cooper Allen & Co., and were of such excellent quality that they were still quite serviceable when replaced eleven years later. Tents from the Elgin Mills were also of good quality and serviceable thirteen years later. The swords supplied by Messrs. Joseph Bourne, of Birmingham, were not good.—[*Ed. S.& C.*]

It was decided that the regiment should be stationed at Ferozepore, and the building of new lines there was accordingly commenced under the superintendence of Risaldar Major Rustam Ali Khan. The lines were built entirely at the expense of the Native ranks of the regiment, the amount per head ranging from two hundred and fifty rupees for senior Indian officers to twenty-five rupees for Sowars. On the regiment leaving Ferozepore these lines were handed over, free of charge, to the relieving regiment.

Later, the lines of all Indian Cavalry were taken over, first by combines of certain regiments, and finally by Government who bases its claim to ownership of the lines of the Indian Cavalry regiments (which were built as we have seen entirely at the expense of the troops themselves) on the grounds that for some years it (Government) had assumed responsibility for repair and upkeep of the lines, in return for a monthly payment of four hundred and fifteen rupees from each regiment.—[*Ed. S. &.C.*]

The sum of one lac of rupees was given as a loan by the Government of India to assist in raising the regiment. This had to be repaid by fixed monthly instalments.

The regiment was completed to full strength both in men and horses by the middle of January. Thus less than three months were occupied in raising it. This period might with advantage have been extended, but in spite of this the men were, on the whole, of very fine physique, and the horses, though somewhat small, of a good hardy stamp, which worked well.

In order to assist in the raising of the regiment, the following direct commissioned Jamadars were taken early in 1886. They each made a deposit of five thousand rupees as *assamis* for twenty men and in addition to this they were each also largely instrumental in raising a half squadron :—

Mahomed Hassan Khan ...	... Utmanzai.
Malik Hayat Khan ...	... Tiwana.
Kadir Khan	... Son of Afridi Khan of the Khyber Rifles, and father of the present Risaldar-Major Babadur Sher.

The following Indian officers were mainly instrumental in raising their own half squadrons:—

Risaldar Izzat Khan ... "A" Troop.*
Risaidar Taj Muhamed Khan ... "C" Troop.*
Risaldar Karm Khan ... "H" Troop, with the Assistance of Mahomed Hassan as mentioned above.

The following direct commission Jamadars were also taken:—

Mahomed Usman transferred to the 7th Bombay Lancers, about seven years later.

Ghulam Hassan, who did not prove a success and was allowed to resign his commission after a few months.

To complete the Indian officers of the regiment, the following promotions and transfers took place in 1886:—

Risaidar Bhai Khan was promoted Risaldar.
Jamadar Sarbuland Khan was promoted Resaidar.
Jamadar Saadat Khan was promoted Resaidar and Wordie-Major.
Dafadar Rahbudin from the 6th B. C. was promoted Jamadar.
Kote Dafadar Kazi Latif from the 5th B. C. was promoted Jamadar.

The constitution of the different troops then was practically the same as it was in 1922 except that the men were (especially in the Pathan squadrons) of a much bigger and heavier type; indeed, as lately as when we were at Umballa, the average weight of several squadrons was close on ten stone.

In March 1886, the regiment having attained its full strength was inspected by General Murray and marched to Ferozepore on the 15th. It will be understood that with a regiment composed mainly of raw recruits and untrained remounts (many of which were entires), this march was somewhat difficult and that some confusion occurred. Indeed, I believe that on the first morning the wordie-major† paraded the regiment early in the small hours and put every man in his place in half-sections, so as to have them ready at the time fixed for the start.

The rest of the year, and a good part of 1887, was occupied in training the men and horses. The regiment was, of course, armed with the old Snider carbine, which was a heavy, clumsy weapon, but this was not replaced by the Martini-Henry until 1892. Good results with this weapon were difficult to attain, and the difficulty of training was increased by the fact that the firing was done at old iron targets which could not be moved into the marker's butts, so correct marking was very difficult; paper targets on trollies were only introduced in 1889.

---

* At this time a squadron consisted of two troops which corresponded to the half squadron organisation abolished in 1921.—[Ed. S. & C., 1922.]

† Saadat Khan subsequently Risaldar Major.—[Ed. S. & C.]

In December 1886, Lieutenant Burton was detailed as a special service officer with the troops in Burma, where he remained throughout the campaign, doing very good work and being mentioned in despatches.

In March 1887, Lieutenant Darrah was appointed to the Burma commission, and was shot a few months later in an attack on a stockade at Pym-ul-win (Maymyo). His death was much deplored in the regiment; he was an exceptionally good officer, of very fine appearance and physique, and much loved by all ranks.

In 1887, Lieutenant Bower was awarded the Royal Humane Society's medal for having saved, at the risk of his own life, one of his coolies who, while marching in Kulu, had been swept away in the torrent of the Chandra Baya, or Chenab, owing to the breaking of a rope bridge. This was a very fine act, and would have been impossible for anyone who was not a most exceptionally strong swimmer, as anyone with experience of mountain torrents will easily understand.

During 1886 and 1887 the following officers were appointed to the regiment :—

Lieutenant W. S. Mardall, Royal Marines, 23rd March 1886.
Lieutenant G. Browne, Border Regiment, 18th April 1886.
Lieutenant J. F. Stewart, Scottish Rifles, 11th May 1886.
Lieutenant E. W. Boudier, R.A., 14th April 1887.
Lieutenant C. P. G. Griffin, 4th December 1887.
Kote Dafadar Hamzulla Khan was promoted Jamadar, 1st August 1887.

At the end of October 1887 the regiment marched to take part in the cavalry manœuvres held at Lawrencepore in December, under Major-General Luck, who had just been appointed the first Inspector-General of Cavalry—an appointment then much needed to bring the cavalry in India up to the standard required in modern warfare. As regards this camp, however, the regiment went in much too great strength, as it took five hundred and seventy-five men and horses, as against three hundred and five taken by the 16th Bengal Cavalry which was raised at the same time. To make up this number, recruits who had hardly done any riding, and partially trained horses (some just out of hospital after gelding) were taken, which meant, of course, that many of the latter were broken down. Nevertheless, on the whole, the regiment did remarkably well at the camp, and the men, in spite of their short service, were found to ride well and fearlessly over any country, and to be quite fit to take their place in line with older regiments.

While on the subject of this camp it may be of interest to note the change which occurred in cavalry drill shortly after the creation of the Inspector-General of Cavalry in India. Up till then, though Indian cavalry were just as capable of galloping and charging as at present, the drill was the old "Pivot" drill, consisting largely of what were known as "standing movements." This contradictory term meant movements from and to the halt, mostly changes of front or position, which, though elaborate, and many very pretty were hardly the best training for cavalry in their true mobile rôle. In 1887, "squadron columns" had been introduced, but were not of very much practical use, as squadrons were formed of only two troops (sized from the centre), of any strength instead of having front ranks of fixed numbers. I have certainly seen a squadron on parade with two troops of fifty-six files each or rather more. It was not until the winter of 1888-89 that four troops per squadron were organised, and it took about five or six years longer before the system was fully introduced into the lines as well as for parade work.

Another change that the Lawrencepore camp was instrumental in introducing into the regiment, was khaki uniform. Hitherto all regimental work had been done in blue uniform both hot weather and cold. Anyone who knows the temperature of Ferozepore during the hot months, will understand that this was hardly joy. Even in 1887 the men only had got one khaki *kurta* for use at camps-of-exercise. But shortly afterwards we started wearing white *kurtas* for hot weather parades. Khaki *kurtas* came into more general use in the regiment in Umballa some eight or nine years later, but several more years elapsed before the khaki short coat was also adopted.

The year 1888 was not a very eventful one for the regiment. Its only move was the first of its annual visits to Lahore in December for a camp-of-exercise, lasting about a month.

On the 19th December 1888 Colonel Kauntze retired and Colonel Lawrence was appointed Commandant. In the previous April Colonel Sartorius had availed himself of a privilege he was entitled to as one of the old general list; he went on two years' furlough to Kashmir on eleven hundred rupees a month. After this he joined for two days before taking another six months' leave, which completed his time with the regiment, and he then got an additional six months' leave on thirteen hundred rupees a month. They don't do one as well nowadays !* He was one of the finest soldiers, and the most powerful man in

---

* These sums represented much more in those days than they do now.—[*Ed. S. & C.*]

the Indian Army, and in addition was quite a good painter, and could sing and play more than a little.*

In 1889, Lieutenant Bower commenced a career of adventure which has brought him to the front unusually quickly. In June he accompanied the celebrated sportsman Captain Cumberland, late of the 30th Foot, on a shooting expedition in the Pamirs and Central Asia. He got some good specimens of Ovis Poli, and in addition to doing some survey work for Government, was deputed to capture Dad Mahomed, who had murdered an English trader, Mr. Dalgleish, on the Leh-Yarkand Road. This was accomplished after some months travelling in Chinese Turkistan. The murderer was traced to Samarkand by two of Lieutenant Bower's men, and was arrested by the Russian authorities; he subsequently committed suicide (perhaps not exactly voluntarily) in prison.

Up till this year the transport of the regiment had consisted of rats of ponies, of the type of the usual ekka pony, with just an odd mule or two that had been picked up cheap. All were the actual property of the men, often just picked up anywhere by the Indian officers as required. In October of this year a pony *chunda* was started, and a committee was formed to value and take over any of the existing animals that were fit for work. Many of these were, of course, cast very shortly afterwards and replaced by better class ponies in the first instance and later on by mules. As a slight digression it may be mentioned that in those days when polo height was, of course, a small 13-3, we used to have a regimental game once a week, in which a mixture of all the Indian ranks used to turn out to play. The result of this was that just a few very fair ponies were found in the regiment—almost entirely among the Farriers' ponies of course (these not having at that time been brought with a view to polo). But for several years at Ferozepore we had quite a good polo pony (who rejoiced in the name of "Bucephalus" and did his best to savage anyone trying to mount him) who had commenced his career as a grass-cutter's pony. In those days polo ponies were very much cheaper than at present; they were nearly all country-breds of which class good raw ponies could generally be picked up from two hundred and fifty to four hundred rupees. The Arab came into general use in the nineties, and the Waler some ten years later. My own first polo pony I bought as a trained pony, that had just played in the Infantry Tournament, for the large sum of two hundred and fifty rupees, but even for those days that was unusually cheap.

---

*A separate notice of Colonel Sartorius appears on page 36.—[Ed. S. & O.]

GROUP AT FEROZEPORE.

	Griffiths (I. M. S.)		
Mardall.	Boudier	Muir.	Trotter.
Lawrence.	Griffin.	Burton.	Montressor

GROUP AT AMBALLA.

Warre-Cornish.	Wikeley.	Wall.	Hudson.
Boudier.	Marshall (I.M.S.) Muir.	Montressor.	Mardall.

He was comparatively speaking the best pony I have ever owned, as I won a race or two on him, and sold him after three years for a hundred or two more than I had given for him.

During this year the system of purchasing remounts for Indian Cavalry by Remounts Committees was started. Hitherto each regiment had bought their own as now, but it was thought that the competition of officers of different regiments at Horse Fairs, etc., tended to raise the price, and accordingly committees were formed in each Province, consisting of an officer of the Remount Department and two Indian Cavalry officers. Regiments indented on this committee for the numbers they required. This proved most unsatisfactory from the point of view of the regiments—the horses were, as a rule, not good, and prices, if anything, ruled higher than when regiments competed at fairs; it was dropped again after a few years.

Up to the middle of the eighties, Bengal Cavalry regiments were mounted entirely on country-breds, but about this time some regiments began buying walers. We got up our first batch from Calcutta in 1889. The "Bounder" of those days was a very different class of animal to those procurable now, as he was coarsely-bred, much more addicted to "buck-jumping." His only recommendation, as a rule, was that of being up to more weight than a country-bred.

During the winter of 1889-90, H. R. H. Prince Edward, Duke of Clarence, made a tour in India, during the course of which he visited Lahore and the Muridki Cavalry Camp. The regiment as usual went up to Lahore for two or three months of the winter, and the second squadron under Major Muir was detailed to act as escort to H. R. H. at Government House during his visit to Lahore. All the Indian officers of the regiment were also presented to the Prince at a reception in the Montgomery Hall. The regiment afterwards proceeded to Muridki to take part in the parades and other ceremonies in honour of the Prince. An autograph letter was received by the Commanding Officer from the Commander-in-Chief congratulating him upon the appearance and performances of the regiment on this occasion.

In August 1890, Lieutenant Bower returned to India from his travels in Central Asia and was attached to the Intelligence Branch in Simla.

In October, Captain Burton went on a year's furlough, and proceeded viâ Bushire to Ispahan, where he joined Captain Vaughan, 7th Bengal Infantry, who was travelling in Persia.

They travelled from Ispahan to Khar and Tabbas, and thence to Samnan and Teheran, having skirted and surveyed, by a plane-table and a running traverse, the borders of the great salt desert of Persia. Captain Burton then proceeded to Europe *via* Resht, Baku, Batoum and Constantinople.

In December the regiment again marched to district manœuvres at Mian Mir, lasting about two months.

In April 1891, Lieutenant Bower, accompanied by Surgeon Thorold, of the Indian Medical Service, commenced his great journey from Kashmir to China, through Leh and over the great Thibetan plateau. He was also accompanied by Sowar Munir Khan of the regiment, a very powerful, trustworthy man.

Dafadar Fazaldad Khan, third squadron, was awarded the Macgregor Memorial Medal for Indian soldiers for this year, for survey work in Burma. He afterwards became one of the most skilful surveyors in the Indian Army, and eventually received a commission in the 13th Bengal Lancers.

In October 1891 the regiment proceeded in relief to Loralai in Baluchistan, marching *via* Multan, Dera-Ghazi-Khan, and Fort Munro. The fourth squadron was detached to occupy the outposts at Forts Murgha and Maratangi. In May 1892, Captain Burton, Lieutenant Wall, Jamadar Hamzulla Khan and 20 sabres executed a reconnaissance to Gumbaz and Bar Khan, returning *via* Rankan and Rakhni. Major Montresor and Lieutenant Hudson executed a reconnaissance towards Peshin, returning *via* Zhob.

In August, Captain Mardall, with sixty sabres, proceeded as escort to the Political Agent, Zhob, while on tour on the border. They rejoined after two and a half months in excellent order, and the Political Agent wrote expressing high praise of the manner in which the duty had been carried out and of the conduct of the men.

During the summer Captain Bower returned to India after his remarkable march, for which he received the thanks of the Government of India. He was again attached to the Intelligence Branch in Simla, and was awarded the gold medal of the Royal Geographical Society and the Macgregor Memorial Medal—a special gold medal.

In May 1893 the Murgha and Maratangi outposts were handed over to the Bombay Cavalry regiment at Fort Sandeman, and the Gumbaz post was taken over in exchange and occupied by a squadron under Lieutenant Wikeley.

On the 23rd October, Colonel W. A. Lawrence proceeded on leave to England and did not again rejoin the regiment, Major Muir officiating for him as Commandant.

On the 6th December the regiment, on relief by the 16th Bengal Cavalry, marched back to India, having been ordered to Umballa.

At the time when the regiment was there, Loralai was not a good station. All the water was obtained from open "karezes," with the result that there was much fever and other sickness, and though our meat-eating men stood it much better than regiments who had been stationed there before us, a good many deaths occurred during our two years there—the bodies of these were disinterred on our return to India and carried by their relatives to their homes to be re-buried there. From the officers' point of view, the one redeeming point about the place was that very fair shooting was obtainable, but otherwise it was an unpleasant station. Though over three thousand feet high one found it very hot in government quarters, consisting of one room, fifteen feet square and a bath-room. The roofs were composed of iron, covered with some six inches of earth, and there were no punkah. Now there are good bungalows there and a proper water-supply, so the station is much improved.

In other ways Loralai is not a good cavalry station, as the whole Bori Valley in which it is situated, consists of stones, so cavalry is only required there for escort duty up the road to the Zhob Valley. While there we had to shoe the horses all round, and used extra heavy shoes obtained from England; these may have saved the horses' feet a little, but there were many objections to them, and I do not advocate their use.

While at Loralai our furlough men marched to their homes *viâ* the Gumal and Tonk, as a rule, but in 1893 one party travelled *viâ* the Chuha-khel-Dana Pass, which at that time was very little known, and during the march the party was attacked by raiders and one man and horse were killed.

The march from Baluchistan was again carried out *viâ* Dera-Ghazi-Khan, Multan and Ferozepore, and the cold, until we reached the Punjab, was very severe. Umballa was reached after a march of five hundred and seventy-seven miles on the 27th January 1894, on which day there was a Proclamation Parade there in honour of Lord Elgin's assumption of the office of Viceroy of India.

During the nineties, a new era had been commenced as regards the mounting of the regiment, which at our arrival in Umballa was on the whole very good. Hitherto, as already mentioned, the horses, though good and hardy, were almost entirely country-breds, and of a small stamp. We now began buying a large proportion of walers, and, like most Indian cavalry regiments, went through a phase of getting as big horses as we could. As one of the late Inspectors-General of Cavalry expressed it to me once, " Indian cavalry at that time thought that the heavier their men were, the longer must be the legs of their horses." A very mistaken policy, of course, for though our horses at this time were up to much more weight and were generally much better than formerly, they required more food when doing hard work, and probably would not have stood active service so well. But it was not until the present well-bred " Bounder " came into the waler market about the beginning of this century, that any of us realised that we were making a mistake, and that the 14-3 horse (whether waler or country bred) was most suited to Indian cavalry. I will remember that as adjutant we were very proud of finding in about 1895 that the average height of our horses was just over 15-2.

Incidentally it may be of interest to mention that our first batch of Arab polo ponies was purchased so as to meet us on our arrival in Umballa in January 1894. Their average price landed there was four hundred and sixty-five rupees, and though we found later that they were rather lower-priced ponies than it was really advisable to buy, very good ponies could be got in Bombay at that time for between five and six hundred rupees.

Another thing in which there was a great difference before 1897, was the price of grain. All the time we were at Ferozepore the rate for gram was generally about thirty seers to the rupee, and if it ever went below twenty-five seers at the most expensive time of year, there was much grumbling. When we got to Umballa we found that grain was over thirty seers to the rupee, so a six months' contract was made at thirty-one seers and at that price the men actually lost a little for some months; indeed, they really lost a good deal, for as soon as the current rate got more expensive than the contract rate, the bunniahs repudiated it.

In October 1894, Captain Bower was deputed on special duty to China to watch the course of the Chinese-Japanese war, then in progress. He returned to India on the conclusion of peace, after an absence of eight months.

In 1895, the Chitral Campaign took place. Captain Burton who had gone up in charge of the Government Transport Mules on the establishment of Indian cavalry regiments, was appointed Field Intelligence Officer with the Chitral Relief Force, with which he served throughout the campaign, and was mentioned in despatches for the excellent way in which he carried out the work.

GROUPS AT RAWALPINDI, 1901 and 1902.

Henderson. Smith. Wikeley. Shakespere. Warre-Cornish. Wall.
Burton. Marshall. Muir. Atkinson. Boudier.

       Hewitt.   Shakespere.   Wikeley.   Wilson.
Smith. Barnes (I.M.S.). Atkinson. Burton. Boudier. Hudson.

Early in 1896 a commencement was made in re-saddling the regiment with saddles obtained from Messrs. Cooper Allen and Co. Every horse was measured with trial saddles and an average struck of the sizes required.

In May 1896, Captain H. Bower was appointed D. A. Q.-M.-G. for Intelligence with the Indian Contingent despatched to Suakin under Brigadier-General C. C. Egerton, which returned to India about the end of the year.

A spontaneous petition presented by the Indian officers, non-commissioned officers and men of the regiment was placed before H. E. the Commander-in-Chief, asking that the regiment might be employed on service. A reply was received by the Commanding Officer that H. E. much appreciated the spirit of loyalty and keenness for service expressed in the petition, and that a note had been recorded regarding it.

On the 8th May 1897, Captain Burton left with Captain Vaughan, 7th Bengal Infantry, to travel in Persia, returning in November. They had travelled from Bagdad to Karmanshah, and to Sehna in Persian Kurdistan. The routes from Karmanshah to Khoramabad, and thence to Dehbala, and on to Kut-el-Amara on the Tigris, and to Dizful and Shuster were also traversed.

On the 11th May 1897, Risaldar-Major Izzat Khan, accompanied by Sowar Rahmat Sher* as his orderly, proceeded to England with the escort of Indian Cavalry sent to take part in the Diamond Jubilee celebrations of Her Majesty Queen Victoria. They were decorated by Her Majesty with the Silver and Bronze Jubilee Medals, respectively.

During this year the whole of the North-West Frontier tribes broke out and the following were employed with the different Field Forces:—

> Lieutenant Steel was attached to the 13th Bengal Lancers during the Mohmand Expedition.
>
> Lieutenant Warre-Cornish was attached to the 9th Bengal Lancers. He distinguished himself by executing a reconnaissance up the Bara Valley previous to the advance of the 1st Division, Tirah Expeditionary Force, from Mamanai to Ilm Gudr.
>
> Lieutenant Henderson was detailed to take charge of the regimental government transport on mobilisation, and later produced in charge of the transport of the Headquarter Camp of Sir W. Lockart during the Tirah Expedition, and subsequently joined Sir Bindon Blood's force operating in Buner.
>
> Lieutenant-Colonel Muir was appointed A.-A.-G. to the 1st Division, Tirah Expeditionary Force, and subsequently to the Khyber Force under Sir W. P. Symons up to June 1898. He was mentioned in despatches and recommended for a Brevet Colonelcy.

---

*Risaldar-Major, 1921.—[Ed. S. & C., 1922.]

Lieutenant Wikely was appointed Orderly Officer to Sir W. P. Symons commanding the 1st Division, Tirah Expeditionary Force, and was subsequently with the Khyber Force up to June 1898.

Jamadar Kaim Khan, three Dafadars and eight Sowars, Adam Khel Afridies, were employed on ordinary duty with the Tirah Expeditionary Force and the Khyber Force up to June 1898.

Dafadar Gul Mir, 'A' Squadron, was shot in the knee during the operations in Mardan, Tirah, and died of his wound. In addition to the above a number of N.-C. O.'s and men were employed on transport and other duties with the troops mobilised during the frontier operations. It is worthy of note that in spite of the disturbed state of the frontier, and of the fact the Afridis were involved in hostilities with Government, the whole of the furlough men returned punctually with their horses and mules on being recalled on account of the general mobilisation. Moreover, during the whole of the frontier disturbances, in which relations of many of our men were concerned, their conduct was exemplary, and they gave no trouble of any sort with the regiment.

In June 1898 two cases of glanders occurred among horses that had returned from service, and as a third case occurred in August, the order for the regiment to take part in cavalry manœuvres, near Delhi in December, was cancelled.

At that time Mian Mir was always a very feverish place. (In the autumn of 1887 the 5th Bengal Cavalry had close on two hundred men in hospital and could only send three squadrons to the Lawrencepore Camp, many of these going several marches in carts), and this year 1898 was such a bad one during October and November, that all parades had to be suspended for a month.

In October, Major Bower was appointed to raise the Chinese Battalion at Wei Hei Wei, and granted the rank of Lieutenant-Colonel, and seconded.

The following changes among officers occurred during the year :—

Lieutenant J. T. Ferris, 5th Dragoon Guards, was posted to the regiment in January. He was transferred to the Central India Horse in March and died on his way to Bombay a few months later.

Lieutenant R. C. Smith, Gloucesterhire Regiment, was posted to the regiment on the 7th of July.

Lieutenant-Colonel Trotter was transferred to the 13th B. L. on the 1st of October, Brevet-Lieutenant-Colonel F. G. Atkinson being transferred to the regiment in his place.

Lieutenant Wikeley was promoted Captain on the 5th February, and Lieutenant Warre-Cornish became Adjutant.

Risaidar Manneh Khan retired on the 8th of July.

Jamadar Ahmed Khan was promoted Risaidar, and Kote Dafadar Aslam Khan, Jamadar.

GROUPS AT RAWALPINDI, 1903.

Mohamad Amir. Ahmed Khan. Usman Khan. Hamzullah Khan. Sher Ali Khan.
Mir Alam. Ismail Khan. Aslam Khan. Dost Mohamed.
Young (I.M.S.), Hewitt. Smith. Boudier.
Saadat Khan. Atkinson. Medley. Wikeley. Hudson. Dodd
Said Akbar. Sultan Khan. Kirkwood. Bahadur Sher. Rukan Din.

Raja Sultan Khan. The Riding-master.
Rough-riding class trained by the 9th Lancers, Rawalpindi.

In April 1899, as 'A' Squadron was still having a good deal of illness resulting from the fever of the autumn, it was sent into camp at Shahdera for a month, which proved most beneficial.

In March, Lord Curzon, Viceroy of India, paid a visit to Lahore. 'D' Squadron under Captain Boudier escorted him from the station to Government House on his state entry, and a troop under Lieutenant Steel remained at Government House as escort during his stay.

It is worthy of note that this spring, in a shooting expedition, Captain Burton went with Captain R. G. Burton, Hyderabad Infantry, in to the Nizam's territory; they shot 12 tigers!

In August there was an outbreak of cholera in the regimen and it was sent into cholera camp on the Ferozepore road. There were twenty-eight cases and nine deaths (one, a Dafadar) among the fighting men, and thirty-nine cases with twenty-three deaths among the followers.

The following changes occurred among the officers during the year:—

Lieutenant-Colonel Muir was promoted Brevet-Colonel on the 7th of July.

Captain W. D. Hayward was appointed to Medical Charge of the regiment from 23rd January to 18th December.

Second-Lieutenant W. H. I. Shakespear was posted to the regiment, on the 5th of April.

March 1900 was a very important date to the regiment, as on that day it entered into possession of its grant of land on the Chenab Canal, on which to start a Horse Farm.* Thanks to the excellent start it made under the management of Colonel Atkinson, it proved to be a tremendous success, so that to it, equally with the improvement in the breeding of "Bounders" already referred to, was due the credit for the splendid way the regiment was mounted eventually.

Another important change was made in the regiment in April, when it was converted into a Lancer Regiment and its title changed to the 17th Bengal Lancers. The pennons were, as they remained to the end, blue and white, but no change was made in the uniform of officers till some years later.

During the year the regiment was indented on for assistance for the South African War. Early in the year fifty horses were purchased from each Indian cavalry regiment at an average price of six hundred rupees including saddlery and line gear. A few months later depôts were established at certain centres at which remounts for the British cavalry regiments were trained, so as to be ready for the latter on their return from the war. Our quota for this purpose consisted of forty-eight non-commissioned

---

* A full account of the regimental Horse Farm appears in a separate article.

officers and men under Jamadar Malik Dost Mahomed, with Jamadar Kaim Khan as Wordie-Major, who were despatched to the depôt at Umballa. This detachment was found to be rather a burden on the regiment, as of course they did not take their own horses with them, so it was necessary to reduce the leave of the rest of the men.

This year again the regiment suffered considerably from cholera and had to move out into cholera camp twice—in May and again in September, though the outbreaks were not as serious as in the previous year, as altogether only six sowars and a certain number of followers died of the disease.

One very unfortunate result of the cholera, however, was that the regiment, which had been warned early in July to hold itself in readiness for service in China with the Cavalry Brigade to be sent from India, was for fear of infection taken out of the proposed Brigade and the 16th Bengal Lancers substituted for it, and in consequence thus lost its first chance of active service. On account of the bad time it had been through, the regiment was however transferred to Rawalpindi, where it arrived on the 19th November, in relief of the 13th Bengal Lancers; the 11th Bengal Lancers succeeding it at Main Mir.

Major-General Sir G. Morton, Commanding the Lahore District, issued the following farewell order on the departure of the Regiment :—

"In bidding farewell to the 17th Bengal Lancers the General Officer Commanding desires to place on record his appreciation of the services rendered by the regiment during its stay in the Lahore District. The conduct and soldierly bearing of the regiment has fully maintained the reputation always borne by the 17th Bengal Lancers, and the fine spirit displayed by all ranks during two trying seasons of cholera had much to say in combating the disease. Sir Gerald Morton wishes the 17th Bengal Lancers every success and will follow its future career with much interest."

Kot-Dafadar Usman Khan, Left A. Half Squadron, was this year deputed from the regiment as its representative with a detachment of the Indian Army sent to Australia to take part in the Federation Ceremonial.

Risaldar-Major Izzat Khan, Sardar Bahadur, retired on the 1st December 1900. This Indian officer was a splendid specimen of the Afridi soldier; with little education he had raised himself to the highest position he could attain, solely by his natural ability and fine character. A born leader of men, he raised and commanded the Adam Khel Half Squadron with great ability and in such a way as to make it one of the best in the regiment. He was much

GROUPS AT RAWALPINDI, 1904.

Barkat Shah.
Mohamed Amir. Dost Mohamed Khan. Mohamed Amin Khan. Hamzullah. Mohamد Akbar.
Ahmad Khan. Aslam Khan. Atkinson. Kirkwood. Wilson.
Sumner. Boudier. Henderson. Mardall. Wikeley. Smith. Barge
Usman Khan. Sajid Gul. Dodd. Rahmat Sher. Sultan Khan. Mustapha Khan.

Men of the Regiment.

liked and trusted throughout the regiment, and was always of great assistance to the different commanding officers under whom he served.

In February 1901, the regiment took part in cavalry manœuvres on the Lawrencepore-Attock plain, with a cavalry division under the command of Colonel Muir, who was Director of the manœuvres.

In October, Major Medley rejoined from furlough taken after vacating the appointment of Commandant of the Troops at Gilgit. He had travelled from Gilgit over the Barogil Pass, and through Siberia and Central Asia to Europe.

On the 20th October 1901, Captain and Adjutant F. T. Warre-Cornish committed suicide in his bungalow. He was deeply beloved by all ranks and his death was a great blow to the officers present with the regiment. Extracts from his letters are given in another place.—[*Ed. S. & C.*]

On the 1st March 1901, General Sir C. Egerton, C.B., D.S.O., commanding the Punjab Army, dined at mess with all the officers, British and Indian. Indian officers had occasionally dined at mess with their own officers for some years past, but this was the first occasion on which they had been present at a dinner like this in honour of a General.

During January 1902, the regiment took part in manœuvres of all arms on the Yusufzai plain. It crossed the Kabul River at Jahangira in boats and returned to cantonments the 4th of February.

On the 12th of March, Lieutenant-General Sir Bindon Blood, commanding the Punjab Army, dined at mess with the officers of the regiment, the Indian officers also being present.

On the 20th of March, Jamadar Ismail Khan and two men proceeded to South Africa on field service. On the 4th of February, Lieutenant Henderson was appointed to one of the concentration camps in South Africa, and being seconded vacated the appointment of Adjutant.

On the 20th December, the uniform of the British officers was changed from Cavalry to Lancer pattern.

The following changes among the officers occurred during the year :—

Colonel Muir was appointed Colonel on the Staff, Delhi, on the 12th of April.
Colonel F. G. Atkinson was appointed Commandant.
Captain R. C. Smith was appointed Adjutant on the 7th of April.
Major Burton was appointed officiating Commandant, Military Police Battalion, Port Blair, on the 7th of April.
Lieutenant D. R. Hewitt was posted to the Regiment on the 1st of May.
Lieutenant D. D. Wilson was posted to the Regiment on the 29th of July.

Lieutenant A. Vincent Watson was posted to the Regiment on the 13th of November.

Lieutenant Bailey was transferred to the 32nd Pioneers in October.

Risaldar Khan Karm Khan retired on the 1st of June.

Jamadar Raja Gauhar Rahman resigned on the 13th of May.

Jamadar Ismail Khan was seconded 20th March.

Resaidar Ahmad Khan was promoted Risaldar.

Jamadar Nikab Gull was promoted Jamadar.

Dafadar Bahadur Sher was promoted Jamadar.*

Sultan Khan was gazetted to a direct Commission in the rank of Jamadar on the 14th of May.

Dafadar Sikander Khan was promoted Jamadar on the 1st of July, and pensioned on the 9th of December.

Saiyid Akbar Shah was gazetted to a direct Commission in the rank of Jamadar on the 23rd of December.

In January 1903, as a result of experience gained in the South African War, the regiment was equiped with bandoliers and the wearing of ammunition pouches was discontinued. In April the regiment was re-armed with Magazine Lee-Enfield Rifles, Mark II.

On the 19th May, Colonel Atkinson, who had been thrown by his horse on to a mud-wall and who had broken his elbow, proceeded on five months' sick leave to England.†

On the 12th October the Presidency distinctions of the Indian Army were abolished, and the cadres were renumbered throughout consecutively. The regiment accordingly received the title of the 17th Cavalry.‡

Major-General W. A. Lawrence was appointed Colonel-Commandant of the regiment.

On the 1st October, Major Boudier was selected to command the 2nd Ekka Train of the Somaliland Field Force for the operations under General Sir C. Egerton. He was accompanied by Dafadar Paskandar as temporary Risaldar, and by seven men.

On the 8th of May, Major Burton was appointed Consul at Muhammerah in the Persian Gulf. In December, Lieutenant Shakespear was appointed to the Political Department. He was afterwards posted as Consul to Bander Abbas in the Persian Gulf and later to Muscat.

Lieutenant P. McC. Young was appointed to officiating Medical Charge of the regiment on the 10th of April.

Lieutenant J. A. Barnes, officiating Medical Officer, was transferred to the 26th Punjabis.

---

* Risaldar-Major, 1922.—[Ed. S. & C., 1922.]

† Colonel Atkinson was watching recruits' parade: an orderly brought him a fluttering paper; his horse shied and threw him on to one of the riding school walls.

‡ This renumbering caused much heart-burning among Indian Army Officers.—[Ed. S. & C.]

SNAPSHOTS AT RAWALPINDI, 1901 to 1905.

The Orderly Dufadar and a mounted orderly.

The Drill-Major.
Mohamed Hussan.

In the autumn Major Burton vacated his appointment in Persia and rejoined. He had travelled through the Bakhtiari mountains to Ispahan, to Susa Dizful, Shuster, Ram Hormuz, Bander Mashur and Fellahieh by routes till then unsurveyed.

Since the South African War wits had been busy trying to devise methods to enable cavalry soldiers to carry infantry rifles. The equipment finally adopted was called the Patterson Equipment. It consisted of a revolving clip fixed to the near shoe case to hold the small of the rifle butt, and of a steel slot fixed to the rider's belt into which a steel stud on the barrel fitted. The equipment was most ingenious, but it was totally unsuited either for war or for hard work. So after a short time the whole equipment became unserviceable and for several years the regiment remained without any proper means of carrying the rifle.

About this time various devices were also invented to secure the lance to the saddle when dismounted. The regiment adopted a hook on the wallet with a ring on the lance shaft; the butt of the lance being slipped into a ring on the girth.

In October 'B' Squadron under Major Wikeley and Lieutenant Dodd was sent on detachment to Kashmir for escort duties in connection with the visit of the Viceroy,* and in the same month a Dafadar and seven men were sent to Teheran for duty with the Legation there.

On 10th November 1904 the regiment marched in relief to Bannu, arriving there on the 26th of November. On the 31st of July 1906 Colonel F. G. Atkinson was appointed to the command of the Bangalore Cavalry Brigade, Lieutenant-Colonel E. B. Burton succeeded him as Commandant on October the 15th. Captain R. C. Smith (now Lieutenant-Colonel R. C. Barry-Smith) vacated the Adjutancy after four years tenure and was replaced by Lieutenant D. D. Wilson on the 7th of April.

It will be convenient here to pause in our narrative, and look back a little on the men and memories of the regiment during the twenty-four years that had passed since it was re-raised in 1882.

Colonel E. H. E. Kauntze, the first Commandant of the newly raised regiment, had served in the Crimean campaign in 1856. Except for this service, however, he lived practically all his life in India. Retiring in 1888, at the age of fifty-two, he continued to reside in the country until his sixtieth year. He went home in 1896 and died in London in 1910. He was cautious in counsel, kind in speech, and the father of the regiment.

---

* The officers received mementos and an autograph letter of thanks for the way the escort was carried out. The N.-C. O.s and men received one hundred rupees.

Of Colonel Sartorius, much might be written, for he is still remembered with affection and respect. The following biographical notes have been supplied by one who knew him well :—

"Reginald William Sartorius was son of Admiral Sir George Rose Sartorius. He had two brothers: one in the British Infantry who like himself was given the V. C. and the other in the Bombay Army. He (Reginald) got the V. C. in the Abyssinian Expedition of 1868, also the C. M. G. He subsequently appeared with his aged father, who had distinguished himself in the Napoleonic wars, and his V. C. brother, at Her Majesty's Levée. After returning to India he was given several staff appointments and was on the staff of the Prince of Wales (Edward VII) when he visited India. He was a man of immense strength: over six feet high and very powerfully made, with dark eyes and hair and a high colour. When a young man he was strikingly handsome and retained his good looks to a great extent till late in life. He was a powerful swimmer and a good yachtsman; looking indeed very sailor-like at all times. He could hold out a heavy cavalry sword or the half butt billiard cue by the point between the tips of his first and second fingers. He was of cool and imperturbable courage and did not know what fear was; and maintained an unmoved and haughty countenance, treating Generals and Inspectors of Cavalry with the utmost contempt. At the Lawrencepore Cavalry camp of 1886 when on outpost duty, he turned into a four post bed borrowed from a village, and refused to stir when General Luck visited the outpost line at night. When in camp in the winter he had several skins of water put outside his tent at night; these, hard frozen, were poured over him for his morning bath. He smoked a Persian pipe with a tube several yards in length, and was a great eater and drinker. In the hot weather, after playing tennis, he had a quart of hock, two bottles of soda, and a mass of crushed ice, poured into an immense jug, to refresh himself. When he condescended to drink whisky and soda he poured it Threicia Amystide in the Thracian fashion, right down his throat without closing his lips, so as to cause it to splash in a distant and cavernous manner. He was in the 14th Bengal Lancers with Lockhart, Palmer, Welchman Becher, and other well-known men, and joined the 17th Bengal Cavalry in 1885 as a full Colonel and second squadron commander, refusing at first to do so, till told he could obey orders or leave the service. However he continued to look upon his presence in the regiment as second-in-command in a good humoured and jesting manner, and on the efforts in training of the young and enthusiastic British officers with amused

Colonel R. W. Sartorious, V.C., C.M.G.

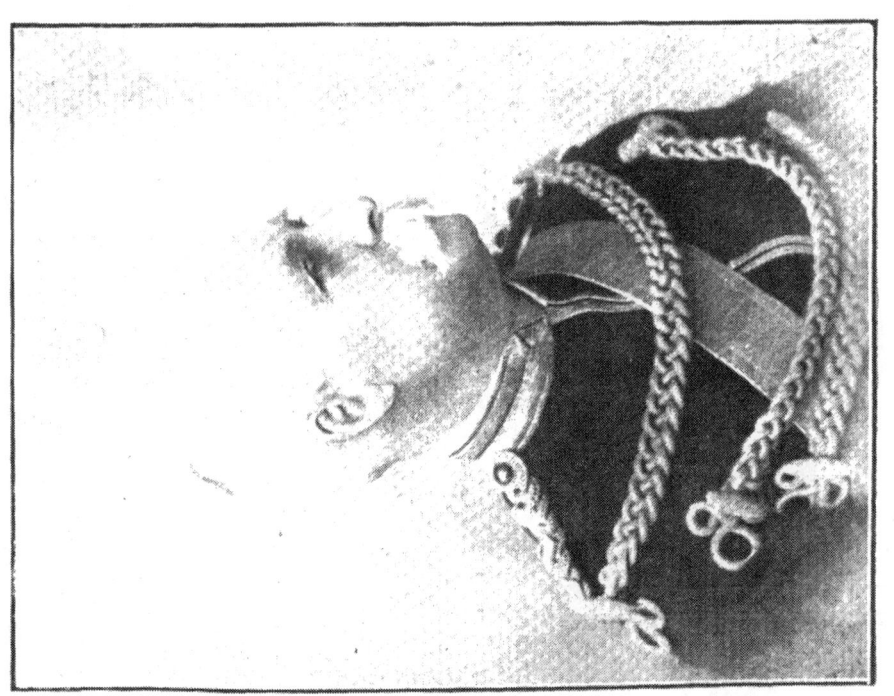

Colonel E. H. E. Kauntze, Fourth Commandant, 1885—1888.

and tolerant approval. He busied himself for a time in devising uniform, and invented the celebrated 17th Cavalry mess waistcoat. He wished also to devise a full dress tunic, but this was not allowed: so he contented himself with one of the regulation pattern, plus two extra gold cords across his chest. He was a strong and reckless rider, but cared little for the details of drill, his idea of that art being to get the regiment in line, sound the gallop and go across country in that formation over anything in the shape of walls, houses, or ravines, at a furious pace for some miles: returning, when able to stop, in the same manner to the starting point. Reginald Sartorius was a good artist in water colour, and a man of considerable taste. He passed much of the last ten years of his service on leave in Kashmir, where he amused himself with sketching, boating and swimming. He also built several house boats for himself and others: and was said to be the first person to do so in Kashmir. Some of these were elaborately and tastefully carved. On retiring to England about 1890 he took to yachting and was elected a member of the Royal Yacht Squadron. Many years after he left the regiment he was remembered with affectionate admiration by all ranks. At his death in 1906, at the early age of sixty-eight, there passed away a knightly figure more suited to a less drossy and degenerate age."

Colonel W. A. Lawrence, fifth Commandant in succession from Robarts, and Colonel-Commandant of the regiment from 13th May 1904 to its amalgamation on 15th January 1922, was a son of Colonel Richard Lawrence and a nephew of the immortal brothers, John and Henry Lawrence. He was greatly respected by all ranks. He joined the regiment in 1881, was transferred to the 14th Bengal Lancers in 1882 and subsequently to the 10th Bengal Lancers and was re-appointed to the regiment in 1885. He commanded it from 1888 to 1895.

Colonel C. W. Muir, C.B., C.I.E, was a son of Sir William Muir, the Lieutenant-Governor of the Punjab. He joined the regiment in 1885 and commanded it from 1895 to 1902, retiring in 1907. Colonel "Charlie" Muir had spent much of his early life in the Viceroy's Bodyguard. He was a man of charming manners and a very distinguished appearance, and was well known as one of the finest riders in the Indian Cavalry. He rode with a peculiar, but graceful, Indian seat, chiefly by balance, and was able to take an Arab straight off the Poona race-course and play it at once in a chukkur of polo. He was also an exceptionally good whip, a very fast runner, having won many cups, was always very well dressed and extremely active for his years. He was a great friend of Lord "Bill" Beresford and no less an authority than the regimental Moulvie declares that he was one of the finest officers who have ever served with the regiment, and the Moulvie ought to know, as he has seen all the officers of the 17th Cavalry come and go. During the Great War, Colonel Muir went out to France as a D. A. Q.-M.-G. to a Division in the field, at the age of seventy.

Colonel F. G. Atkinson, C.B., commanded the Regiment from 1902 to 1906. Francis Garnet Atkinson was transferred from the 13th Bengal Lancers, where he had made his name in the Shabkadr charge. Here his soldierly instincts had seized a fleeting opportunity. Although unable to swim himself, he took two squadrons across the Kabul River in flood, arriving just in time to save a perilous situation for our arms by a bold and completely successful charge. His knowledge of the vernacular was imperfect, and he was a man of fierce and irascible temper as far as the natives of the country were concerned, but his coming introduced something into the regiment it had previously lacked, namely, a great respect for authority and that sense of discipline, without which all the other virtues of a soldier are as tinkling brass and sounding symbals. On his arrival the 17th Cavalry was inclined to be "jungly". He brought it abreast of the times, in training and education. Possessed of great commonsense and of a good knowledge of human nature, he laid the foundations of that organisation which was afterwards developed by successive **Commanding Officers**. But it was in remounting the regiment that he did his best work. Possessed of an exceptionally good eye for a horse, he was able during his tenure of command to transform the regiment from an indifferently mounted one, to one that would bear comparison with any other Indian Cavalry regiment in the service. The farm was also started under him, and it is owing in large measure to the sound organisation at its inception under the direct control of Colonel Atkinson that the farm became such a prosperous concern when a kind Government took over and dissapated the fruits of the results of the labours of many years.

One more there is, whose life has been an inspiration to many and whose memory must be here recorded. Francis Thackeray Warre-Cornish joined the regiment in 1895 and committed suicide, when delirious with fever, at Rawalpindi, on October 20th, 1901, in the small bungalow by the race-course: the first bungalow on the right hand side of the Peshawar road after leaving the Cavalry Mess on the left. He was at the time in the prime of life (he was thirty) in the midst of success (having won the Bengal Cavalry Chase and the Kadir Cup that year), in the anticipation of leave home, and surrounded by the love and affection of all who knew him. Soldier, sportsman, and artist, it is no exaggeration to say that whatever he did, he did well. There was nothing second-rate about "The Cracker" as he was

Colonel C. W. Muir, C.B., C.I.E., Sixth Commandant, 1895—1902.

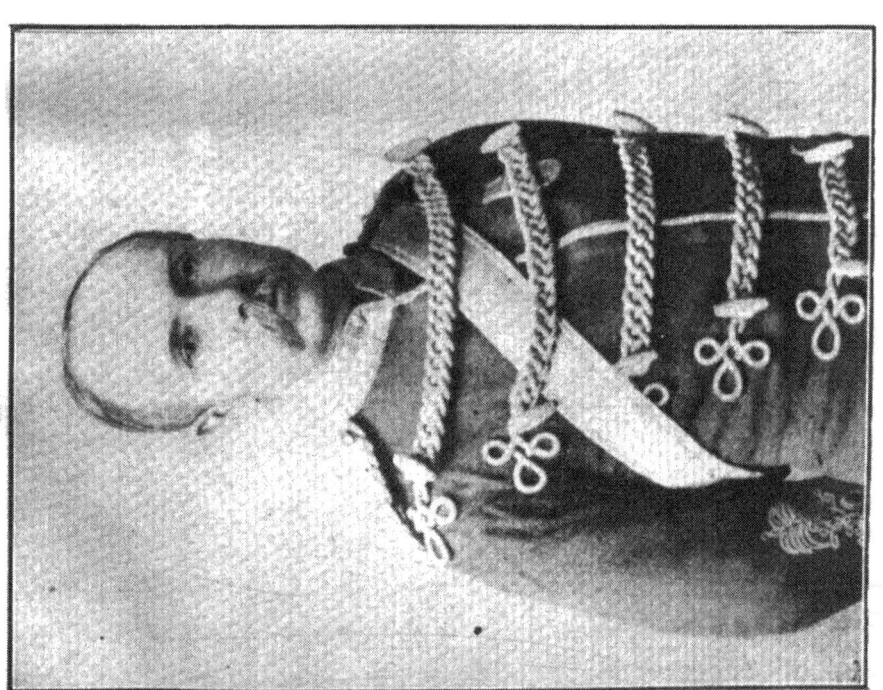

Colonel (afterwards Major-General) W. A. Lawrence, Fifth Commandant, 1888—1895.

affectionately called. As a soldier, he has left his mark on the regiment. As a sportsman he is known to fame. As an artist, in word and picture, the following extracts from his letters home (Letters and Sketches of F. T. W. C. privately published at Eton by Spottiswoode and Company, 1902), will speak for themselves. No apology is needed for the length of these extracts. Francis Warre-Cornish was " born articulate ;" we will let him tell us of life in Indian Cavalry in the days that are now past and gone, in that gay and inimitable style of his which was part of his rare " gift of converse with nature and with men." They give a good picture of a good man in a good regiment, and tell much intimate history that would otherwise have disappeared into oblivion.

UMBALLA: *2nd September,* 1895.

The Bengal Cavalry are only open to Sikhs, Pathans, and the warlike clans of Rajputs and Punjabi Mahomedans, who would consider that they demeaned themselves by going on foot. They, or their yeoman fathers, have to pay the price of their chargers on enlistment, and yet the colonel of a regiment need only pick out the very best recruits—such is the demand to enter the service of the Sirkar.* There is something rather fine in commanding these grim Pathans who ride " with the Koran strapped to their saddle-bow," or six foot Sikhs with their curled beards. However, do not suppose that I am at all carried away by any romantic nonsense, as it is just as honourable or more so to command a company of Somerset clods or little Liverpool and Birmingham rats.

* * * * *

UMBALLA : *6th November,* 1895.

.........It was rather trying saying good-bye to the regiment, all the men of my company wrung me by the hand, many of them saying all sorts of nice things to me..........

* * * * *

17TH BENGAL CAVALRY: *20th November,* 1895.

Now that I have joined (the Staff Corps), though feeling utterly homesick and wretched at leaving my British marching regiment whose glorious militarism is unspoilable even by modern regulations—I am very happy that it is the 17th B. C.—Colonel Muir, who had applied for me before, is a very good man to be under and has four more years of command. He is covered with medals and is thought a good deal of, having been on the staff most of his service.

---

* Government.

It would take a good deal to explain the extraordinary newness of my private life. The entire military system is different. On Monday I was introduced to all the native officers at Durbar—stout, fierce gentlemen who shook me by the hand and asked the Colonel if I played polo and had passed the higher standard. This weekly Durbar under a tree is all they have instead of orderly room—there being practically no crime to deal with.

I am simply chucked into the regiment without any work on the Barrack Square.........my squadron is at "squadron training;" I prance about on one of the troopers' horses beside Mardall, my Squadron Commander, and learn what I can.

UMBALLA: *27th November*, 1895.

Still Umballa is full of people and making horrible Indian attempts at being gay, instead of going in for fireside teas with hot scones after polo or field days. To-day there is a *café chantant* at the club, to which after duly dining out I am going. However there are lots of nice ladies in Umballa, and what with polo and soldiering "it is very jolly." I have lots of work, but rather of my own making, as I have to learn things by myself, and at present I don't seem to be getting much "forwarder" with it. Yesterday we went out to do " screening practice " starting at nine and coming back at dusk. I rode about with Colonel, who expounded and explained a great deal to me without my becoming much wiser. It was very jolly for me who had nothing to think about, " raiding " the country with our swarm of wild Afridis and Pathans..........

UMBALLA: *4th December*, 1895.

......The 17th B. C. are very popular in the station and we are going to give a dance, which I suppose means ruin to us. I must hastily change for afternoon parade with a squadron of villainous-looking Afridi recruits.

UMBALLA: *11th December*, 1895.

I ought to send sheets of descriptions of our glorious Bengal Cavalry, but I have no time for composition even for you and have given up books from the Library and thoughts of drawing till the hot weather begins.

Here is my day for to-day :—
Six thirty get up, Chota Hazri.
Seven thirty, go to Horse lines.
Eight o'clock, C. O.'s parade (instead of recruits' drill as usual).

Colonel (afterwards Brigadier-General) F. G. Atkinson, C.B., Seventh Commandant, 1902—1906.

Major-General Sir Hamilton Bower, K.C.B., 17th Cavalry, 1885—1908.

We did not get back from practising brigade drill over a jolly country of grassy sand hills about five miles off till after eleven. Breakfast eleven fifteen, "Stables" from eleven forty-five to twelve thirty, after which I having no squadron to command or accounts or grass funds or horse hospital to manage, and not being adjutant or quarter-master, should have done work for the day. But I am generally given some job or other, to-day a board or Court of Inquiry on a lost Afghan medal, of which I was president with two native officers as members. This I have just held in my quarters in mufti, instead of wearing a sword and having two or three court orderlies who are let off parade, as in the British service. At two thirty I go to recruits' dismounted parade in mufti, the recruits being also in Pathan white undress.

UMBALLA : 12*th*—19*th February*, 1896.

......The Bengal Cavalry polo tournament requires much arranging. I have to arrange for the tents, for the camp and hiring furniture for them, also for forage for about one hundred and forty ponies. Everyone says they have too much to do to attend to arrangements.

It is beginning to grow hot. To-day I heard a hot weather or brain fever bird practising very hoarsely in a mango tree.

UMBALLA : 25*th March*, 1896.

I get my out of door work done before breakfast now and get back from stables about eleven o'clock when it is nice to have letters to read over an enormous breakfast. After a cold weather like an Aldershot summer with polo in addition, we have now got inspection fever. Good regiments say they never have this disease, but always do......

There is a horse fair at Umballa City, five miles off, and this afternoon we are going to drive in the brake to it. In Native Cavalry regiments the officers do all the buying of country-breds at fairs themselves, with the help of the Native officers who do the bargaining. Umballa however is a bad horse district— the produce being small and very coarse—thanks to that misguided man Burdett-Coutts with his horrible hackneys, which with the equally under-bred Norfolk trotters were some time back largely imported as stallions. Enemies of racing should know that the only horse worth breeding from, in any country whatever, is the blue-blooded thoroughbred of England and Arabia and that a Derby winner at twelve years old much more resembles the portrait of the Godolphin Arabian than he does his own in the Duke's dining room taken as a three years' old. Forgive this long treatise.

UMBALLA : 23rd *April*, 1896.

On these sort of outings (pigsticking) one doesn't feel the heat in the slightest. The Saharanpur people find it difficult to get up early, and we began late. They had an elephant with ice and drinks, and kept saying : " You soldiers never will drink anything nowadays." We only killed one pig in the morning after a fair run and a very good fight; McLachlan getting the first spear. The Saharanpuris had to catch a four o'clock train and we four had a quiet beat in the evening. We found an immense boar in the marsh we were beating and had a fearful job to stick to him among the reeds : Greathed and I both underwent total immersions in bog holes, adding considerably to the weight of our clothes by black water. At last after losing him several times he broke away with four of us on the top of him, but he went over such a terrible country of " kunkur pits " that he gained on us a good deal. Then Bright had a terrfic fall in a blind nullah and was left, and my pony who had been blown in the struggle in the bog began to get left behind. So we ran for about four miles, and this distance in the hot weather is enough for any horse or man. At last he turned to bay in a reedy nullah (or dry stream) where it was hard to get to him, and the fight began between this gallant pig and the three of us. He kept struggling on down the nullah, but whenever one of us got ahead of him and faced him he charged in the gamest way. It is fatal not to keep moving with a pig at bay, but our horses were so done, it was impossible to. Our spears failed to stop his charges. He came right through my mare between her forelegs and out at her hindlegs, but without upsetting her, but giving her a horrible cut behind the knee. Then he ripped Mac's charger in the breast. Finally unable to make my pony move, with the courage of ignorance I got off and was of course at once charged; my spear only partially stopped him and he pushed his way up and ripped my breeches above the knee, only giving me a scratch. This spear and one that Greathed had got into him before and broken pretty well did for this glorious boar ; which was as well, as McLachlan had broken his spear, so mine was the only one left. A few blows with the leaden end of one of the broken spears finished him. He was in such a splendid rage all the time I don't think he could have felt the agony that the spears must have caused him.

Bright managed to get back to the camp all right, and I don't think four men ever sat down to tea and jam and remains of different sorts, before catching the train back to cantonments, more thoroughly satisfied with themselves and each other. My pony is doing all right.

SKETCHES BY WARRE-CORNISH.

After much drill learns to know his right hand from his left.

The Polo at Lahore Tournament, 1896.

The Afridi going to shoot his elder brother.

Becomes a Bengal Cavalry Sowar.

UMBALLA : *30th May* 1896.

We have a whole squadron of Afridis, who are a fine independent tribe who live on each side of the Khyber Pass and give continual trouble. These men I think are the best hillmen ; blue and gray eyes and light hair are very common with them, and red and yellow complexions generally heavily pitted with small pox...... We also have a squadron of Punjabi Mahommedans who are of Pathan origin. The Punjab must be a good country, as it has produced the Sikhs and has I think improved the Pathan settler or Punjabi Mahommedan, as well as being excellent for horse breeding. One of the troops of my squadron are Punjabi Mahommedans, and I like them the best. They are nice " lengthy " men with lots of bone, but thoroughly gloomy and solemn in manner. I wish they would hiss when they groom. It is so refreshing to hear the 15th Hussars at " stables " after the unbusinesslike way our men clean their horses.......

LAHORE : *23rd December* 1896.

We have come up here at frightful expense with what would be a very strong team, were it not that Burton who is about our best man, is ill. There were only there teams that had any chance (Patiala having scratched) of winning the cup—the Guides, the 11th Hussars and ourselves. We drew the 11th Hussars in the first round. At home to prevent ties they widen the goals at the end of the match and go on playing till one or the other side gets a goal. This is considered dangerous out here, as the ponies are fagged at the end of the game and liable to fall— falling being more serious on Indian ground than English turf. They therefore invented the " subsidiary goal, " which is like a rouge at football. We were one goal all, all through the game, and we seemed to be having so much the best of the game that we never thought that the extra subsidiary that they got could win them the match. Poor Burton was knocked over half through the game and said he couldn't see for the rest of the time. He had slight concussion, and is in bed to-day, but I hope will be all right in a day or two. He was not in a fit state to play in a tournament ; if he had been well we must have won.

UMBALLA : *3rd March* 1897.

We had a great week of it during our polo tournament We ran on into the final and met the Central India Horse, who beat us by one goal and had to ride their best ponies all the while. They had a marvellous native officer playing " number two " for them— as light as a feather, and with what marvellous suppleness and quickness of eye that makes some natives such good cricketers— who played most horribly well, and really won the tournament for his team. He played a thoroughly foul game, but personally I don't blame him, as a man who " crosses " another always stands a good chance of being knocked over, and I like a rough game. I tried hard to knock him over once, when he came across my bows, but of course he eluded me though I had time to mutter in his ear " Thy mother " the rest of which sentence I do not even know—it is never mentioned. My great " Powla " was brought to the scratch by means of hot water and belladonna and played splendidly. I had a race up the ground on him and got a goal, and the sound of clapping from the fashionable side of the ground, and yells and screams from the remaining three sides, which were packed with our men, I shall remember all my life.

24th March, 1897.

Last week I slipped away for a really enjoyable day's "pigging" at Patiala—the Maharajah mounting all his guests. We killed eight boars, and it is delightful to find what nerve one has on other people's horses. There were too many people out, many of whom had never been out before, but what made the day a really enjoyable one, was a gallop enjoyed by only three of us—Pretun Singh, a Sikh nobleman; Scott, the Maharajah's trainer; and myself, although I had to be content with a stern chase after the other two—very pretty to watch. A pig at bay is a grand animal, and this one gave us a great fight. Pigsticking is a far less subtle sport than fox-hunting and there is no beauty about it, but it is very good for one.

11th August, 1897.

I had an hour to write to-day, but have been interrupted by rather a dear old bore of a duffadar, who is being discharged on pension. He has been taking leave of the regiment for the last two days, and I have given him a "chit" or character, and shaken him about six times by the hand, and promised to get him a revolver (for his relations) if I could find one cheap, but to-day he brought his son, who is a recruit in the regiment, saying he left him in my charge as his squadron commander and much more sentimental bounce, as to how he had groomed his horse and cleaned his kit better than any man in the squadron, and how he was still *tagra* (strong and fit) and would always be ready to fly back and fight for the Sirkar....................

UMBALLA : *15th August*, 1897.

The daily round of work in the humble capacity of adjutant of a native cavalry regiment in a half empty station in the hot weather is to me full of interest and dignity than any other life

SKETCHES BY WARRE CORNISH.

The Grass "Jaggra" (quarrel and argument).

"Protector of the Poor. I am starving." (The Buniah's lament.)

The Bravest of creation—game to the last.

Buying Remounts.

could be in a non-military capacity; yet if there were to be a war in Afghanistan and the regiment did remain here I should feel that I was leading an ignoble and shameful existence. So the outlook for those of us in "compulsory garrison" is not very cheery.

Umballa though excessively hot and steamy is looking most lovely. In "the rains" our parade ground from being a sandy waste is transformed into a great plain of springy turf beyond which and belts of distant forest one sees the Himalayas—a wonderful steel-blue colour—only thirty miles off with huge rolling clouds clinging to the tops of the hills.

MIAN MIR : 4th May, 1898.

My ideas of life are now sufficiently fixed to be trusted. It is quite contrary to my creed as a soldier to be well off.

As things are my prospects are obvious to me so long as all goes right; five years drudgery as adjutant (I hope one year's furlough may be taken out of this) ought to give me a pretty good hold on the regiment, and as I am well placed in the list of officers......I ought after a period of being one of those impostors —a staff officer—to obtain what I think ought to be more enviable than any other capacity for a soldier—the command. It must be a fine thing to be able to set one's stamp on six hundred men—although nowadays a commanding officer with ideas of his own and a pride in his regiment is apt to be much worried by inspections and impostor staff officers, "usually ignorant and uneducated men" as * says.

There are only three of us at present. Burton, self, and young Henderson returned from Peshawar. It is dull and very hot here. The nights are cooler and the days hotter than at Umballa. I appear at the riding school every morning at five fifteen, work begins at five thirty, I and the "rough riders" get back to stables at seven thirty after the last troublesome remount has been made to go over the bar, or change his legs or rein back, and the last sulky recruit punched and beaten into the correct "position" in the sword exercise. Owing to the dearth of officers I am nominally commanding a squadron, so I have to go to their "stables" for an hour, and listen to useless questions about leave and grass and strayed grass mules, etc. Then to horse hospital, of which I am in charge. Between eight thirty and nine back to office, usually to find * already there. This is the worst part of the day. Every malcontent in the regiment seems to want some thing out of me at this time; * never asks me a question that I can answer. He knows everything himself and

---
* Obviously Burton.

if he raises a question it is probably to expose some horrible rottenness somewhere. I don't think there is anything that * doesn't know. He knows his work, which few do; he knows every-one of his men and all about their relations and ancestors and family feuds. He has been all over the world. He endeavours to conceal vast stores of knowledge of books. He is a linguist, a discoverer, a sportsman. Government has begun to appreciate him, and he had a very good appointment on the Tirah staff but was down with fever in Persia.

To finish my day (and my letter as quick as possible) by twelve o'clock I manage to be at breakfast—a rather nice and dawdling meal in the hot weather. Quails' curry, iced milk and mango fool are the sort of things one lives on. Then sleep till two or two thirty and very little time remains to do Pushtu, write letters or pursue one's studies in "military education," which the staff officers are always urging, before it is time for me to put in an appearance on my way to polo at evening recruit parade. Polo, or in my case long reining and schooling various animals with a view to polo, on non-polo days, takes one till dark, and after dinner one is much more inclined to smoke and drink till midnight than to go to a bed with hot sheets on it.

MIAN MIR: 21st *September*, 1898.

Last Sunday the Colonel and I had a good day's work in our "*rukh*," where all the regimental *saises* are hard at work haymaking. We found it extraordinarily cool in the breeze, and were out all day. On hearing of our arrival the sowars at the different grass guards prepare us the most excellent meals of eggs and chicken and rice, and even produce boxes of Huntley and Palmer's mixed biscuits and are quite hurt if we don't eat. As there is always a great deal to find fault with them, especially the state of their horses, they put one in rather a false position.

REMOUNT DEPOT, SAHARANPORE:
18th *October*, 1898.

Meerut is such a delightful old station. I used to tell you I loved the Punjab. I hate it. Umballa was called the Punjab, but it is really the North-West Provinces country. Meerut is even more sporting than Umballa......In the Punjab people talk about staff appointments, classes of instruction, musketry; in the North-West Provinces* they talk of horses, pig, snipe, duck and tigers. Marching in the Punjab, not even a military interest can be taken in the country, the fine Punjabi Mahomedans and Sikhs plough

---

* Now called the United Provinces of Agra and Oudh.

their fields in appallingly dull surroundings. One looks out of the train between Meerut and Saharanpur on waving grass where black-buck and antelopes feed regardless of the railway, and by jungles and rivers with water in them (the great rivers of the Punjab are all sand), and snipe-bogs. One feels one is really in India. It made me sweat (like Mr. Jorrocks) to see the heads of mighty boars in the messes at Meerut and to think of the sport one loses in dull old military Punjab .... In fact in the N.-W.P. one has a glimpse of the India of old John Company when Sahibs were Sahibs and not overworked and tied down officials, or officers pushing and elbowing each other for staff appointments. Really all this must be almost as interesting to you as a discussion between two Anglo-Indians at their club on the relative merits of Hazaripore and Ahmednagar.

MIAN MIR : 1*st November*, 1899.

I must try to give you more of an idea of my work and surroundings; soldiers' work is always hidden away, unlike that of the volunteers, who are always getting photographed and paragraphed. Our hours are becoming earlier, but we still have parade of some sort at eight o'clock which, in the case of regimental parade, means being there at half past seven......I generally breakfast about quarter past ten hurry back to stables for an hour or so. At stables I simply walk about while the men are grooming and discuss various matters with the Native Officers, and look at the numerous minor accidents which continually happen to the noble animal the horse, besides "gentling" and "making much of" the more shy or vicious of the species, to get to know them. I then generally go to the horse hospital if there is nothing else on, which to me is a most interesting and instructive place. This brings me to twelve or half past when I go to my quarter master's office......I generally get lunch at two. At three there is, except on Thursday, a foot-parade, sword and lance exercise, etc., or saddle parade or judging distances, or some minor business. The men work all day...... They are I think much like British soldiers or any others, except that they talk and laugh much less than the former and are much more interested in their work. In spite of this they are, of course, very much inferior to British cavalry, except perhaps in the matter of courage. The trans-frontier men are always going on leave to settle a blood-feud, and spend their furlough hiding behind rocks with a gun in wait for their enemy, so they ought to be accustomed to bullets.

MIAN MIR: 11*th April* 1900.

I have just returned from a most enjoyable and interesting trip to Amrisar, whither I went last Saturday with thirty picked horses and the same number of six-foot men to wait upon His Excellency the Viceroy. The excellent Steel having taken my parting advice to discard his pincenez and wear only a single eye-glass without a string, fixed rigidly for hours and hours in an unwinking optic, has been such a success as A.-D.-C. that he is now a fixture in the Viceregal house-hold, and dared to inform the Viceroy of my existence, and the latter having said something about bringing me to Amritsar, this explains my leaving my work here for such a frivolous task as commandant of the Viceroy's travelling escort.

Little Amritsar was looking perfect after "Croydon." With no one to worry me I selected a cool grove in the midst of shining cornfields, for my truly noble escort of giants and thorough-breds, and with grass in abundance, furnished (I believe and hope) by the municipality, we spent the whole of Saturday burnishing and polishing and singeing and trimming. At ten P.M. the special steamed into the tastefully decorated station, where on priceless Amritsar carpets stood the local magnates in various makeshifts for frock-coats, headed by the Lieutenant-Governor and his lady.

After a longish hush, during which introductions of the local magnates were taking place on the priceless carpets, the party appeared on the steps of the station. My words of command had been well got up before hand, my salute if slovenly was unnoticed, so that it did not matter how dazzled and "stounded" I became at the sight of Her Excellency. In the big ostrich feather black hat and beautiful gray dress that she wore, her movement and grace as she entered the carriage I shall remember for the rest of my life. A.-D.-C.'s in evening-dress and wideawakes or bowler-hats—(a great relief from the frock-coat makeshifts)—brought shawls and cushions. Steel in my patrol jacket being on duty took his place on the back seat, bang went the door, crash came my stentorian word of command, off trotted the giants, and the cortege started through the illuminated and crowded streets, "Hermia" behaving perfectly with six inches between herself and torches on one side and the carriage wheels on the other, and I occasionally getting a glimpse of a profile which caused me immediately to turn my eyes away *éblouis* with the beauty of what they saw. Ha! if some assassin, some Ghazi or fanatic had barred our way, how I should have hurled "Hermia" at him, and as I grappled with the ruffian on the ground, the feeling of the carriage passing over my body would have been an ample reward for her whom I had saved.

That morning H. E. drove to the golden temple through the narrow streets amid showers of rose leaves. The golden

SKETCHES BY WARRE-CORNISH

"Whip it up — Whip it up ——"

"Feed."

temple looked very bright for the occasion. The Viceroy could not quite order the hideous municipal Albert-Memorial-like erection to be pulled down, but he pronounced it to be hideous. There was a formal lunch, to which I was invited. After a long wait in the drawing-room, their Excellencies sailed in and the guests hurriedly ranged themselves round the room, prepared for introduction. I received a most cordial "So glad to see you, I know all your people so very well." After this I was most popular and smiled upon by all who had a slight acquaintance with me.

At lunch I sat next Baring, a captain in the 10th Hussars, whom I had heard a great deal about from Steel. I only found out then that he was a brother of Maurice Baring. Having been some time in the Egyptian army he was much too much interested in the Bengal Cavalry (of which he knew nothing), to have any other topics. He seemed to me to be a perfect specimen of an English soldier-sportsman-aristocrat moulded to a type. The lunch was most excellent and cheery, while above all the discordant cackle of conversation floated the deep mellow tones of Lady Curzon's beautiful voice. A photographic group became necessary after lunch. Some of Her Excellency's beauty seems to be radiated on all that surrounded her, the A.-D.-C.'s by a gradual process have become so many Apollos, Steel in my patrol jacket is quite an Adonis, the guests, especially our fine-looking L. G. are looking their best—even Cyrano—but there—as I stood over Her Excellency's ostrich feather-hat let us pray and hope that my negative may not be (as usual) a failure.

In the afternoon I listened to H. E.'s fine speech to the old Sikh burghers in the town hall, full of sentences bringing tears to the eyes, words such as "Sikh daring," "Sikh loyalty," "stalwart Sikh Regiments, from Hong Kong to the sources of the Nile," but he rather forgot that many excellent Muhommedan gentlemen were among the big men of Amritsar. He gave them a good rating about their taste for English modern designs instead of for Indian ones in all questions of art and decoration.

Before dinner I was found by Steel, hurriedly brushed and pulled together by him in his quarters and whispered with him in a passage for about half an hour, while on one side came the scratching of H. E.'s pen and on the other side of the passage came once during our wait a low mellow call of "Ayah" causing Steel and me to shrink away abashed at our too close proximity to Her Excellency's toilet. Several coughs from Steel at last produced a cessation of the pen-scratching, and

I was ushered in and sat down on a sofa and made quite at home, and after saying " oh " and " yes " for five minutes during which the Viceroy in the most wonderful way ran through and connected up my relationship with Eton, Richmond, Gerald and Margie and Douglas Freshfield and said that he must certainly read "Sunningwell," I was dismissed from the presence. The party then drove to the station, where I left my escort and ventured on to the priceless carpets. Amid the handshaking of the local magnates, I received a most friendly " So very glad to have seen you here and I hope we shall meet again." There were no delays, and the train glided away. I must end this too long letter.

MOTI BAGH (THE GARDEN OF PEARLS), PATIALA:
18th *April*, 1900.

Yesterday we had a very jolly morning's hawking with half a dozen merry Sikh gentlemen. The early mornings before the hot wind gets up are divine, the horses all thoroughbreds, the Sikh gentlemen all sportsmen, all handsome and merry, roaring with laughter at the most childish jokes, and probably feeling on such fresh mornings how jolly it is to be Sirdars. I too felt how jolly it was to be a soldier, to be a pauper with tumble-down quarters with no furniture or carpets in them, and yet occasionally to shake the hand of a Viceroy, or ride a Maharajah's horses. Hawking is the most picturesque and exciting of sports, but like all good sports full of disappointments. However, after several failures on the part of the peregrines, just as I was indulging in reverie on the futility of all sport we found a couple of partridges in a very open bit of country, crouching, poor things, under a bush invisible to my wretched cantonment eyes, but easily seen by the jungle ones of the *shikari* with a hawk, close to me. I watched the *shikari*, to see him throw the hawk off his wrist just at the right moment, and the flight began. Foxhounds are earthly beings, where a boar goes a man, if he smokes and drinks moderately, can follow on a good horse, but to ride a falcon one must fix one's thoughts on the heavens. But the sight of those two brown specks rapidly vanishing out of sight caused oblivion of all earthly stumps of trees and holes and blind nullahs. Riding after a hawk is capital practice for " leading on points "—(by the way, wasn't it the colonel of a Guards' battalion who was told a few months ago to lead on a certain hill and caused a disaster by leading on another one ?— nothing easier :—being an infantry man and accustomed to driving his men from behind, he probably kept turning round to them, giving himself a crick in his neck, and worrying his officers. At each of these neck-crickings he of course unconsciously applied his infantry knees to his charger's sides in such a way as to turn him slightly from orginal direction; back he looks at his hill, one hill more or less like another to barrack eyes and the whole regiment has to bring up their left or right shoulders and is led to disaster...... all through his infantry knees)—as looking on the ground or anywhere except at the spot where the brown specks disappeared would be fatal, causing one to be thrown out at once, and possible losing of the hawk. Following the line of direction to the edge of some jungle, there sat the hawk under a bush with his prey. Afterwards it was pretty to see how the *shikari*, of whom she had no fear whatever, coaxed the hawk from the dead bird. Hawks although perfectly tame have apparently no intelligence whatever, and are made to leave their prey for the falconer's wrist by a hoax, which although invariably enacted they never see through. A very nice Major Angelo in the 9th Bengal Lancers who is inspecting officer of Imperial Service troops is here on duty. This morning Loch and I went with him to see the Patiala regiment of Imperial Service Cavalry. This was most interesting to me. Instead of having only one's own experience, regimental customs and the inadequate drill book to go upon, it would be of immense use to one, if one could only go round and see other regiments and all their systems—but I am growing shoppy, the result of revising during these "passionate noons" at Patiala my great work "Thoughts on Riding School" translations of which my poor roughriders—the ushers of my school—have to read to them. I don't get much in the way of sport now and I do get rather mad with the tennis and battledore-and-shuttlecock players at Lahore and Mian Mir, and feel that boars are good for me now and then. So I came here.

MIAN MIR: *26th April*, 1900.

I had a glorious time at Patiala. We pigsticked on four mornings and coursed and hawked on the other mornings. We slew eleven boars. I had altogether seven gallops, one only of them being perfect, the others glorious but not quite heavenly. I took Hermia down with me. In the perfect gallop I was on her. It was the biggest boar of the eleven, I had three Sikh gentlemen to ride him with. The riding was all in "dak-jungle" which in my opinion is the most sporting form of country there is pigsticking. The only way of going through it is to leave everything to the horse, ducking one's head under branches. Every now and then the boar has to cross a hundred yards of open ground, but as far as possible he sticks to the trees. When he is getting tired he stops under thick bushes and waits sullenly, while you gallop on in terror at having lost sight of him. There is generally not much doubt as to where he stopped, but woe betide your poor horse if you stand still near the boar's hiding place; when he has got his wind a little and sees that his pursuers have discovered him he rushes out with a fierce " wugh-wugh " and continues on his way. Now he begins to think, if he is a good one, of fighting as his last resource. He slows down a bit under some bushes and as you gallop alongside of him comes in side-ways at you. Your horse is going so fast that you can generally avoid him but now is the time for the spear. In my perfect run Hermia regarded the boar with perfect indifference, she and the monster were going their fastest, the spear touched the boar behind the shoulder as he came in at an angle. I galloped on to get Hermia's precious hind legs out of the way of the boar, to see him after one huge effort to continue the battle, sink to the ground and give up the ghost. The touch with the spear had gone straight through his vitals. Great were the congratulations of the Sikh gentry—" lovelee mare, Sahib " " killing pig with one spear very first class thing, " etc., etc.

MIAN MIR: *28th June*, 1900.

I have returned from a very enjoyable morning. We marched out the regiment yesterday evening to historic Shahdara on the banks of the Ravi, and bivouacked there for the night. There was not a breath of breeze and the mosquitoes and sandflies cried " sleep no more " till five in the morning when the air seemed just as hot and frosty as the dusty evening; a regiment of dispirited men and horses began to remove clothing and saddlery on the banks of the Ravi, which from the melting snow in the mountains, has begun to come down in flood. Five minutes later the oily and warmish waters of the Ravi became a mass of struggling horses and shouting men, their listlessness and depression turned into the highest pitch of energy and high spirits. It was thoroughly jolly. One wants to practise the management of a horse in the water. Hermia and Helena in turn behaved like angels of course.

MIAN MIR: *12th July*, 1900.

I enclose a sad letter from Colonel Muir. I am too unhappy to write about it.

(The explanation of what follows is in the extract from the Colonel's letter written July 7th, 1900, which must be quoted.)

BARNES COURT, SIMLA: SUNDAY.

Crushing luck......Till yesterday the new despatch of troops to China was fixed: the 17th Bengal Cavalry, the 3rd Bombay Cavalry and I think C Battery R.H.A.

SKETCHES BY WARRE-CORNISH.

"Exercise"

Since I left Mian Mir on Friday evening, it appears there has been a case of cholera in Mian Mir. I have not heard it was connected with us in any way. But the medical authorities pronounced they could not recommend a regiment from an infected station for service. And so we have been cut out and the 16th Bengal Lancers substituted. I hear this batch of troops is off at once.......

Yours,

C. W. MUIR.

While I was up at Dalhousie I heard from him at Simla that there was every chance of the regiment going to China. Sir Gerald also seemed very sanguine about us. Colonel Muir was actually congratulated after Church on Sunday by General Ellis and told that he would get orders for the regiment to mobilise at once. That day the postmaster at Mian Mir died of cholera and his death was reported by telegram to the Principal Medical Officer. They had just been frightened by cholera breaking out among the second coolie corps.......So the 16th was substituted for us.

I am too unhappy to write about it. If I did, I should say things which would seem morbid. Meanwhile my leave has to be eked out, and I suppose it sounds very enjoyable.

NOWSHERA: *7th August*, 1900.

I have just come from the most delightful, exhilerating, romantic, exciting and very slightly dangerous excursion I have made since Barki three years ago. The Adam Khel Afridis held aloof in the Tirah war, and although as independent are more dependable upon than any other section of the Afridis. We enlist a troop of them, and four of our native officers all belong to the same sub-section of them and are related to each other. The Risaldar Major is one, but he having become rich and old in Government service has wisely left a country where it is unsafe to be thought to be growing too powerful. His cousin, a delightful old Risaldar of the regiment, was my host. He with the Risaldar Major and a large following met me in Peshawar and showed me the city. The next morning I rode round many villages in the Peshawar valley, where we enlist a troop of Pathans, and spent the heat of the day at the Risaldar Major's village which he has chosen as his asylum, and which is a sort of half way house for all our Adam Khels going over the border on leave of furlough. That evening various sowars on furlough turned up from the country round with baskets of grapes and peaches. After my evening meal of pillau and chicken stewed in ghee (clarified butter) and chupatties and curds and water and fruit, all eaten with one's fingers, various lads of the village —of the worst character—came out and sang the most excellent songs, including of course "Zachmi Dil." One tremendous ballad of some fifty voices was all about the Cabul war and how Cavagnari was murdered, and thoroughly seditious I thought. Next morning at half past five old Ahmed, I and a duffadar on horses, with a mule for our kit, started for the frontier towards the Kohat pass. At about eleven in terrific heat we arrived at the house of a holy man on the border, who gave us all we could desire—namely, a full meal, a bedstead on which to sleep, a well from which to drink somewhat evil-smelling water, and constant relays of old men and ragged boys to fan me. The Mian Sahib or holy man enjoys great wealth I find, as all our good Adam Khels give him two or three rupees whenever they go to or come from their homes. This being the frontier, a couple of sowars with a ragged boy bearing four Martinis on his shoulder turned up to meet us from the village of Kui—our destination.

At five in the evening we started again over the border and along the low hills east of the Kohat Pass. Soon we reached the village of Kandas where eighteen Afridis all armed, and counting with the four above mentioned sixteen Martinis, met us as a Royal Escort; all were brothers or cousins of our men actually in the regiment; all were perfectly delightful in the cordiality of their greeting and the romance of their appearance. The chief Malik of Kandas was a great man who had given great assistance to Government at various times. He was related in some way to my friends, and of course had to be visited in his stronghold. In spite of his good repute he was the most alarming-looking man I saw during my stay, and I would not have trusted him for a moment outside his own yard. He was a fairly big man, but I felt quite shrivelled up beside him; and the cruelty and cunning and fury in his face was perfectly horrible, concealed as it was by the heartiest manner and almost violent proffering of hospitality to us all for the night. However we managed to tear ourselves away from him and his relations and as Ahmed was loud in his praises of him I suppose he looked worse than he was. The Malik's old father had lately been murdered by the men in the opposite village, and he had recently become Malik and had greatly improved the position of his family. It was bright moonlight by the time we reached Kui, the journey with that cheery escort having been perfect enjoyment. The Adam Khel Afridis' villages are much the same as the Bara and Khyber Afridis,—namely, a series of towers each inhabited by a separate family of grandfathers, father's sons, uncles and cousins, and each tower as a rule in a state of blood feud with another; you may be sure I did not venture to pry about outside the bachelors' yard. A tremendous crowd of male relatives and friends and their children were gathered in the bachelors' yard to meet me, and great handshaking had to be gone through. A great show was made of my washing and changing and brushing my hair, while struggles went on behind me for the privilege of fanning me. Old Ahmed personally attended the eating of my dinner, which was excellent. The water in his well was delicious after all the other wells I had drunk from, perfectly clear and cold. The well was inside the yard, the working arrangement of it hidden by a thick creeper. Whenever I wanted to drink during the meal a fresh supply was brought up so that it might be quite cold, and each time the bucket was let down the wheel made the most fascinating creaking, very soothing to hear. There was a lantern in the middle of the yard, under which my bed was spread with perfectly clean bedclothes; all round me were the charpoys of the bachelors who when I thought it fit to sleep would sleep too. I felt that the view from the top of Ahmed's tower by moonlight would be enchanting and begged to go up to the top. Decided reluctance was shown at first, and objections were made that they couldn't take a lantern on account of their enemies. However Ahmed was quite willing to do what pleased me, so we climbed up and were rewarded by a perfect view, the hills above us on one side, the Peshawar valley on the other, and all along the hills the towers of the other families of the village. The one tower with whose people they were at enmity was at least a thousand yards off, and the lantern was brought up and they made conversation about murders and bloodshed, carried on with no thought for the enemy. The feeling of perfect security inside that yard sleeping with Afridis all round one, who if outside and if unchecked by any reasons of prudence would think it quite correct to rob or murder a stranger was most delightful, especially as in spite of these attributes they are entirely fascinating and lovable.

Next morning I woke under the concentrated gaze of the whole community assembled to see what I looked like by daylight. Immediately the extraordinarily kind ministering to my wants began. Ahmed brought tea and grapes from Peshawar. My hair was almost brushed for me and clothes put on for me. We then all went for a stroll near the village, away from the direction of the enemy. They have had no rain, and small interest is taken in agriculture except when the convenience of the seasons forces it on them; my friends had therefore no work to do of any kind.

The enemy happened to be very weak at the time I was there. Ahmed had about forty men of sorts including old men, *jawans* (young men) and lads, all capable of bearing arms, while the enemy had only sixteen or eighteen. It was the turn of the enemy to kill one of Ahmed's family to keep the vendetta going, but so long as they kept in fairly large numbers they could go where they liked without fear. Then we came back to receive the visits of various friendly Maliks. The difficulty of making conversation with these magnates was great, but they were delightful to see. All bore a strong resemblance to wolves: all were thin, old, tall, big-boned and splendid, and none of them had the look of treachery and fury that the first Malik I had seen had. Their beards were dyed red except that of one fellow.

Before my *dejeuner* at twelve o'clock Ahmed had contrived to overcome the enormous difficulty of the Englishman's bath, which I took in his tower. Before the arrival of the Maliks I had been reading the enclosed terrifying passages in a book on recruiting, and had during the morning been asked by a villainous youth how much my revolver had cost and how much ammunition I had with me. One of the Maliks had also roared with somewhat frightening laughter about my having lifted the purdah from his country, and when at the end of my bath, during which a heated discussion had been going on outside, a shooting match was proposed for the afternoon, in spite of my own particular friends I could not help questioning myself as to whether things would pan out successfully. In the afternoon all the visits had to be returned, the whole party going the round of the village. The welcome at each house was delightful. Whenever we went we sat down in a ring and talked and laughed. My extremely indifferent Pushtu must have been rather irritating to the Maliks. Then came the shooting match, which, was a great honour for me, cartridges being so precious...... some wonderful shooting, was done at a piece of cotton cloth stuck in a rock four hundred yards off but a rest for the muzzle of the rifle in the shape of a charpoy made it easy. Then the Maliks and I had a match with my revolver, which, as they knew nothing about, firing in such a foolish way as without the rest, I won amid much applause.

In the morning at about half past four we emerged from old Ahmed's strong-hold, twenty of us, and started our march back to India. Nothing could have been more romantic than this start under the morning star, the *jawans* (or young men) swinging along in single file, with a scout out in the direction of the enemy's tower, Ahmed and I riding in the middle.

Of course nothing happened during the march, when just as we were about to cross our very banal border, as we turned a

SKETCHES BY WARRE-CORNISH

"Stables."

corner, a man was suddenly revealed who walked off at right angles down into a ravine with the most uncomfortable lope, looking at the ground. He was one of the enemy, which one could well guess from the expression on old Ahmed's and all the others' faces. The man knew he was at their mercy evidently, but did not expect them to shoot. Ahmed said it was not their turn, also that if they were to do more than the usual retaliation business, the whole tribe would be down on them. some others said that if I had not been there they would have killed him, which I don't believe. They could not understand how he could have given them such a chance. At the border we met fresh horses; the man who had brought them from another village coming along in the night had seen a ghost—a horse without a rider—in his path. He was much impressed by the vision but much laughed at. At this point there were terrific handshakings and the old Ahmed and I bore on our way on this side of the frontier where the pax-Britannica and the villages without towers seemed intolerable to me : the dear cheery escort went loping back towards their mountains.

I don't know whether I shall ever be able to go there again, but I have the keenest regret that I am not still in that country now. Whatever may be said against them, I found the Adam Khels in their own home to be kind to each other and to all children, hospitable and honest to their guests. I had a loose bag of rupees and sixty rounds of ammunition. These things, when I took off my coat, were left about anywhere among the crowd of frequenters of the yard, I was convinced the whole time that they were perfectly safe; which they were. Their children are perfect darlings and in great numbers. Of their women all I saw was their tall forms in horrible blue clothes hurrying away when I approached.

I am rather proud that no one not even the political officer has ever visited the village before. I must go to bed.

MIAN MIR : *6th September*, 1900.

Poor old Mian Mir is looking very well now and the weather though feverish is delightful. The evening light is wonderful after the rains, everything green and brilliant but rather steamy.

I have many club polo ponies to train and a wonderfully tame class of young horses, who are beginning to practise a performance I call "Baden-Powelliana." These occupy my evenings after evening stables and recruits' parade or musketry.

At the end of the day of pleasant work, as, with straw hat and pipe I watch the mite of a sowar's son who is my "riding boy' giving Hermia the evening exercise, with half a dozen polite and jocular native officers surrounded by their children and dogs, I pity all staff-officers in their hills—who when they leave their offices have nothing to occupy their selfish sympathies but their frivolous wives

Amongst all the grumbling and struggling to "get on," how easy it is never to appreciate the pleasant Eastern "Soldaten-leben."

RAWALPINDI : 28*th November*, 1900.

Thank goodness everything has gone off as well as possible during the week we have been here. On Monday there was a fine parade for the Commander-in-Chief (the usual nonsensical ceremonial business with march past of Infantry and Cavalry, Horse Artillery, walk, trot and gallop past). The 17th created a favourable impression, being very much better mounted than the 13th B L. whom we relieved, and we heard that the Chief was pleased with our gallop past, which was like a whirlwind compared with that of the 4th Dragoon Guards.

We are in good hands here, as our "Colonel on the Staff," who is our immediately superior general officer, is a Colonel Burton (no relation to Major Burton in the Regiment) who once commanded the 17th for about six months. He looks on everything with a favourable eye and said that our escort to the Chief was the best he had ever seen of Native Cavalry. This consisted of my rough-riding Sergeant-Major (to use an English equivalent) mounted on "Helena," and four equally beautiful young men on bay walers.

Have I ever told you anything about Rukn-ud-din*, the above peerless rough-rider ? For three years we have worked together with batches of recruits and young horses and he has been *perfect*. He cannot be tired or spoilt. His cleverness and grasp and retention of everything he hears and reads are as great as his horsemanship and his good looks. He has been through tremendous troubles. Some nine years ago when he was quite a young soldier he was embroiled in the most stupendous love-affair. He constantly was on leave, from which he would return bandaged and bruised. The whole of the country round his village were at war with him. He was tried for and acquitted of murder by the District Officer, but had to pay heavily, and borrow to pay for marrying the wife of the murdered man against the will of her parents. He told me that the whole trial hung on the evidence of his present wife, who was tortured and beaten by her relations

---

Subsequently Rissaldar Rukn-ud-din.

to make her betray him. For his sins he has to pray morning and evening as regularly and devoutly as any old man has to, and he regards his having no son and only daughters as a punishment*, and he goes on paying and paying the relations. However, he is evidently perfectly happy in his married life and curses the social laws of his country. The story is altogether rather a dark one, but his state of civilisation is about that of King David whom he resembles in many ways I am sure. I only wish I could bring him home some day and show him to you.

Well—I must tell you much more about Pindi I suppose. In spite of the "brass hats"—conundrum—asking staff officers, riding about in the morning with nothing to do, I know it is a place I shall become extremely fond of. Regiments have to be very much on their "P's and Q's" here. It is the Metz of India, with every regiment ready for Cabul at a moment's notice—five batteries (including mountain batteries), the 4th Dragoon Guards, the Somersets, the Queens, and the Rifle Brigade with two Native Infantry Regiments and the 17th compose the garrison. The cantonment is kept in perfect order. The Mall down the middle of it has well-watered strips of lawn on each side with a tan gallop down one side. Large tubs of palms alternate with the lamp-posts along the strips of lawn, so that by day it looks Kew Gardens and by night like Piccadilly.

One cannot gallop across country except in one direction, but this is made up for by a prospect of constantly varying rides. I have been so absurdly occupied with riding about on the parade *maidan* that I have not made out which direction in the line of hills above us points to Cashmere, and which to the Hazara country, which I can reach in one day's ride, and by over the Indus into the country of those jungly Pathans I visited called the "Gadoon" in another day and so into Buneyer—"happy fairways" which I look on with as much interest as a child who imagines mountains inhabited by elves and fairies.

My afternoons and evenings now will have to be altered between polo and work after dark and work up to dark and the Club after dark, where the brass hats (now in tweed caps and clothes of sporting cut) discuss who is likely to get made officiating-something—somewhere, and whyso-and-so didn't get command of the—(probably because he was of a retiring disposition, or he didn't approve of General so-and-so's wife's style). The Chief saw our remounts yesterday and seems to be in a good humour with us generally. I am dining with the Somersets to-night.

---

* Since then Rukn-ul-din has had two sons, but too much praying has led him into much trouble.—(Ed. S. & C.)

They are dining the Chief (Sir Power Palmer) and I am rather looking forward to it.

RAWALPINDI : 1*st January*, 1901.

The officers of the Staff Corps are presenting a petition to Parliament praying for the period of service as a subaltern to be reduced from eleven to ten years—so on the result of this depends my answer to your question as to when I shall be a captain. Under present circumstances it will not be till March 1903, so that I shall still be a gray-headed subaltern by the time I come home. The petition I imagine will have no effect...... I have somewhat priggishly declined to have anything to do with the appeals of some mutinous fellow who calls himself " Quidnunc " who sends forms of petition to all officers to sign. It seems somewhat contrary to ordinary ideas of discipline and to the advice to soldiers given by St. John the Baptist......

RAWALPINDI : 30*th January*, 1901.

We have been having numerous trying field days for majors passing their "tactical fitness for command" examinations. These majors are most merciless with their cavalry and send us off on terrific flank movements, horribly trying to horse-flesh, and on the proper execution of which the bread of their wives and children often depends, after giving immense assistance to these majors by his perfectly accurate information, returns from these days in a state of the profoundest dejection at the way his horses have been treated and the total ignorance of everyone in authority as to the conditions under which the Bengal Cavalry are raised and kept going. Government will have to modify the conditions, they make with sowars for the purchase and keep of their horses if they want the excellent old Bengal Cavalry system to keep up under modern conditions of soldiering, and the enormous amount of worry and wear and tear and dragooning that the men are subjected to.

LAHORE STATION : 11*th February*, 1901.

I shall lose another mail, so must stop before biking down to Mian Mir to stay with the 11th B. L. Hermia, I trust arrived this morning; have not been able to attend to her training properly, and I am afraid a desperate little " thruster " called Pritchard in the 2nd B. L. who has won the race twice running is sure to beat me

(Hermia won the Bengal Cavalry Chase ridden by Warre-Cornish who was 10 lbs. overweight.)

RAWALPINDI: *27th February*, 1901.

My stay with Biddulph of the 19th B. L. in his hawking camp on the Jhelum was a most enjoyable experience. He is one of the best known characters in the Punjab. He is the greatest authority on hawking in the Empire. He is an artist. His drawings of birds are wonderful. I expect that no one has ever drawn peregrines so perfectly. His constant drawing of delicate feathers has given him a very good touch and all his black and white is exquisite. He is also a boat-builder. His Pathan squadron believe that there is no Sahib like him. He is spending a year's leave in India with his hawks and easel and boats.

I floated down the river Jhelum for a whole warm winter's day to reach his camp. I had long shots at geese flying overhead without success until my boatmen with extraordinary fowling skill brought me into a Briggs-like situation, round a bend in the river, in which I was almost as bewildered as the geese, but succeeded in knocking over two. We dined luxuriously at sunset off fresh-caught fish and wild duck killed by peregrines, and went early to bed. We rowed across the Jhelum next morning in the dark with two ponies in one boat, and seven shikaries with hawks on their wrists or perching on their heads. Duck were our quarry, and we did not find them till the sun was well up, which made the peregrines somewhat lazy. When we drew near to the duck who were feeding in a long creek well away from the river, two hawks were sent up in the air to " wait on." These at once inspired such terror into these wildest of wild duck that they remained swimming about till we got up quite close to them, and between them and the river. They had to go on swimming up the creek, which grew narrower and narrower. Whenever they attempted flight down came the hawks upon them with the most thrilling stoops. The duck were wonderfully quick and nearly always succeeded, after short flights across the dry land on each side of the creek, in gaining the water behind us, and the hawks are too great cowards to stoop at birds flying over water. The climax came when we reached the end of the creek, where we had five or six hawks " waiting on," and all the ducks were compelled to take to their wings. There must have been at least a hundred ducks, but the hawks, although constantly chasing and stooping, only killed a total of eight.

The exciting thing was that the ducks and the hawks were absolutely heedless of the human beings, and flew as close to us as though they had been tame fowls.

After breakfast at noon I left "Biddle Sahib" petting his hawks, and had a long canter through charming country to Jhelum cantonment to catch the night train there; and am once more with my nose on the grindstone.

RAWALPINDI: 6*th* *March*, 1901.

To-morrow is rather big with events for me. The Commander-in-Chief is here, and when he and his wife go for their morning ride they are going to stop to see a performance of my lying down horses. It will probably be forgotten about, or the big man will have some business, but the following is going to be the performance if he comes. Shots and yells are heard and the recruits got up as an Afridi lashkar (commando) are seen fleeing from some thirty horsemen. The horsemen then return and pass by some men in the guise of zamindars (yokels) making hay. They open their ranks and extend a few horses' lengths from each other, and the horses all lie down, the men lying down with them. The zamindars then quickly cover them up with grass—so that they look like so many heaps of hay. The recruits "lashkar" having rallied come marching to the spot to the tune of *Za-him Dil* * played on a native pipe, carrying banners and led by a clown mounted on a mule. They halt within a few yards of the inoffensive-looking grass heaps, the clown feeds his mule on some of the grass and falls foul of one of the zamindars, another clown. A terrific kicking and scratching match begins between these two, which is the signal for carbines to be poked out from among the grass heaps. Rukn-ud-din who with Hermia is lying concealed in one of the stacks blows a whistle, and there is a deafening discharge of musketry. The horses spring up with their riders on them, the recruits flee for their lives firing into the air and yelling Afridi yells,—— the sowars galloping in disorder after them and firing their carbines from horseback. This is an entirely new and original piece, and if only it succeeds (the men may be nervous and the horses refuse to lie down) who knows how but that in these days of royal splendour I may not soon be travelling homeward with my troupe to perform before King! This performance is to be given in the afternoon after the Native Cavalry tent-pegging is over.

MEERUT CLUB: 28*th* *March*, 1901.

I am here on a sporting outing. The "Kadir Cup" is the most tremendously sporting thing in the whole of Asia. † Soldiers and civilians from all parts, with hard

---

* A Pathan air of great beauty and pathos.
† This was before the Inniskilling Dragoons started the "Muttra Cup."

jady-looking horses come here for this great pig-sticking event which is run off in heats, the man getting "first spear" at the boar being left in for the next heat. The peerless Hermia, to describe whose perfections words are wanting, has carried me successfully through three heats. To-day I only had one heat—the semi-finals. I had the best of luck, as the pig was just the sort to suit Hermia and me—a big boar, who went striding away, scorning to "jink." Hermia being far the fastest in my heat was up to him easily first, and instead of—what so often happens with small pig—his "jinking" back, and so letting in the riders in rear, he went boldly on, and Hermia positively devoured him in her stride, so that my spear went right through him and broke off, killing the boar outright. Considering that the merest prod is sufficient for the competition, it was most satisfactory to get such an effective first spear. To-morrow I am in for the final with three others; but although Hermia is glorious, I am afraid I have not much chance unless greatly favoured by luck. The remaining three are all veterans.

This place is thirty-two miles from Meerut. You can't think how glorious the N.-W. Provinces are after the arid Punjab. The "Kadir" is a vast sea of high reeds, bushes and grass on either side of the Ganges. It abounds with pig, hog, deer, leopard, hares and partridges. On the edge of this "Kadir" are the ripening cornfields where the pig revel all night, and there are great clumps of shady trees and villages and copses of jungle.

I ask nothing better, in the hottest of weathers, than to camp under one of the clumps of trees with three or four hard-legged horses and a party of gypsies with their dogs to go about with me and beat, and every now and then to enjoy the feeling of being "alone" with the boar.

A great pal of mine, Pritchard in the 2nd B. L. (who you may remember I beat in the chase) persuaded me to come down here, and I am glad to say is in for the final too, so the Bengal Cavalry is well represented.

I am afraid I cannot make you realise the romance and beauty which is given to this delicious country by the boars that roam over it.

RAWALPINDI : *3rd April*, 1901.

I will continue the narrative of last week written from that delightful mango-grove in the midst of the 'Kadir.' Of course I could not sleep all night with the prospect of the final heat and the state of Hermia's legs in the morning, before me. The crops are splendid this year, and the pig are scattered all over the country feeding on ripening corn, and there are few of them in the 'Kadir'—the grassy bed of the Ganges which a humourist of the camp described as "very 'ummucky". While the line of the coolies with three men in for the final (Pritchard had to scratch, his horse left in for the final having been cut by a boar the previous day), and our umpire and the twenty elephants marching behind as moveable grand stands for the spectators were moving over the country, we espied a mighty boar some eight hundred yards away, and the umpire started at top speed in his direction. Almost immediately Hermia plunged head over heels into a blind nullah, and the horse of one Clementson (last year's winner) nearly came down, and gave himself a bad cut in recovering himself. The umpire of course did not start us and we missed this chance of running off the final after a good boar. Not very long afterwards, in very high and unyielding reedy grass, we were given the word to ride, after a very small and fast pig, who jumped up quite close to us. From the first we all went as fast as the pig. Wardrop in the artillery had a few moments of him when he 'jinked' towards me. Hermia (her head tied down with a "standing martingale") was as handy as a polo pony, and again with the other two close on my flanks she devoured the pig, and I got the spear (the merest prick,) and the pig being so small was allowed to go on his way with no more harm done to him than that to a skip-jack thrown back into the water. The umpire Allen*, a well-known Collector, *i.e.*, District officer—satisfied with the proofs of my victory in the form of a small amount of blood on my spear, shook hands with me and congratulated me on winning the Kadir Cup. Immediately about half a dozen sportsmen with kodaks leapt down from elephants' backs and insisted on taking snapshots of the lathering Hermia and her proud owner, who I suppose for once did not wear that expression of settled gloom when confronted by the photographic lens.

After the Kadir Cup final comes the "Hog-hunters' Cup," a race over four miles of rough country marked out by elephants and taking in a branch of the Ganges as an obstacle. It was rather a shame to run Hermia in this, but I had entered her the night before, so had to run her. Allen that sterling civilian of shy retiring disposition and heart of lion) I am glad to say led the whole way and won easily, beating several flyers who might have been ridden harder over the rough ground. I stuck pretty hard to Allen for three and a half miles; but I am inclined

---

* Afterwards Collector at Bareilly when the regiment was stationed there, and a well-known pigsticker.

to think that Hermia is too quiet and intelligent an animal to be very stouthearted like the more highly-strung mad sort, and she is by no means thoroughbred. Anyhow in spite of the good training she was in, she was minding the whole thing dreadfully and getting very distressed, when she came down in a small nullah. My pal Pritchard in the 2nd B. L., a great character in the Kadir, was going strong and catching up the leader when he passed over me, but less than a quarter of a mile further on he too came down badly and broke his collar-bone. There were altogether six falls in this race. My tumbles with the Windsor drag have always been of the greatest use to me. In these three days of hard riding I had three falls and came off with hardly a bruise.

I expect you will have got thoroughly bored with this long account. I travelled back as nurse to Pritchard, and stayed a day with his regiment to see their recruits and remounts at work, and their horses and lines. Arriving at Pindi I found a heap of telegrams and letters, very gratifying to receive. The Colonel was so delighted that he sent my wire informing him of the victory to the Commander-in-Chief and the Lieutenant-General commanding the Punjab, who are both Bengal Cavalry men. Some of the congrats were very nice to get. One from one Collins, Adjutant of the Black Watch, whom I had only met since Gibraltar hunting days, was 'congratulations from an old friend', another 'congratulations from the 11th Field Battery *" wired by the Major commanding it. Another—a letter from a Wykehmist civilian............congratulated me on winning 'the blue ribbon of Indian sport' and asked if it had ever been won by an old Wick before............I must stop this and go to bed. For these two days after my holidays I have suffered from extreme laziness. The weather is perfect mornings and nights, but a hot dusty wind blows all day. Best love to all.

RAWALPINDI: 21st *August*, 1901.

The chances of setting out to where there is actual fighting even with General Lyttelton's help, grow more and more remote. It is a most wretched and contemptible thing to be a soldier by profession and to have missed this war.

RAWALPINDI: 28th *August*, 1901.

Mail day has come, as usual, on a bad day for me (that is a day filled up with work) in reality a good day. I might have been in a mood during a long afternoon indoors to write a

---

* This was the Battery in which Stewart served as a Subaltern.

letter, but too often finishing one's day a half past one (begun at six) utter sleepiness comes o'er one after lunch, involving walking up cross and liverish for recruits' musketry at five and wakefulness at night.

This being haymaking time the mornings after breakfast are spent as shown;

The Grass Jaggra (quarrel, discussion or endless argument).

RAWALPINDI: *18th September*, 1901.

The weather is most perfect. Mornings glorious, noons hot but bright and still, without dusty winds.

Failing S. Africa, there is now only a winter of camps and hoped for tournament-polo before home coming. Four years of adjutant's work has produced in me a perfect loathing for all office-work and everything and everyone connected with the army outside my own regiment, while I feel I would gladly go on passing recruits and remounts into the ranks for the rest of my life.

RAWALPINDI: *25th September*, 1901.

The recruits are in a most satisfactory state of progress, and I seem to have succeeded in establishing in myself a state of serene fearlessness of persons on the staff and critics of that sort, which is best kept up by avoiding them as much as possble. The cold weather is beginning to bring down people from the hills, and Burton is scared by the appearance of 'determined-looking military women driving in the Mall in dog carts'. I am at present commanding the Regiment, the Yorkshireman being on leave, Burton away buying horses, and Wikeley having suddenly taken ten days' leave for the purpose of getting married.

RAWALPINDI: *9th October*, 1901.

This is a mail day evening, but my mind is such a dull blank that I cannot write a word. I am afraid my snipe bog is a feverish spot, for last Saturday I rode up into the Murree hills forty-two miles and stayed with the Somersets, spending Sunday riding quietly back again, and have been very fit in consequence with no thought of fever. There was a horse show at Murree on Saturday afternoon, and the peerless Hermia added a few small sprigs of fresh laurels to her previous bunch by winning the jumping competition and the prize for "all horses," and returned with two rosettes on her bridle, and two nice little cups.

I hope Khanna snipe-jhil will soon become more healthy—but next Sunday I go to see some young horses at a place thirty miles from here called "Wah"! (because the Emperor Jehangir made this exclamation when he saw its pleasant streams and hills), and the week after that a small "Ghukkur" rajah in the hills near here is getting up a boar hunt with dogs for Henderson and me.

* * *

The storm-clouds were gathering, and the days of Warre-Cornish's life were numbered. Since his early childhood he had been afflicted with malaria, and lately he had been suffering from continual attacks, although, with "Courage of a day that knows not death" he continued his work as Adjutant, and lived in the lines to his last hour. On Saturday, the 19th of October, he had a guest from the Somersets dining with him, and was quite his normal self, talking about horses, etc., and making an engagement to try a pony on Monday afternoon. He left Mess about midnight in the best of spirits. Next morning, Sunday the 20th, he got up early to see two squadrons off to Squadron Training Camp. The cold of the early morning was great. The Native Officer incharge of the Squadron observed his voice was weak and low, his utterance strange, and his motion on horseback as he returned by the racecourse unnatural.

Warre-Cornish called to give a regimental order to the Doctor, whom he eluded with regard to his own fever. On this occasion he spoke little, but coherently, and did not mention his prostration. He discharged his horse, and started to walk to his bungalow, a distance of some three hundred yards. It was then eight o'clock, and the sun was very hot. It is thought that it was at this time he became delirious. He went to his room, knelt down by his bed, put a revolver between his teeth, and fired two shots in rapid succession. Hudson, who was next door, rushed in and found him breathing his last. Medical evidence showed that death must have been almost instantaneous. Letters which awaited him that morning had not been opened.

Colonel Burton, in writing to Mr. Frank Cowie, I.C.S., says:

"I was away in camp and did not see Cornish for some time. But on Saturday night I came into Rawalpindi on business and dined at Mess. Cornish was there and looked as usual; he had a young fellow of the 13th Light Infantry dining with him. I heard him talking as usual,—about the training and riding of horses, etc. The next morning Cornish saw off two squadrons marching out to camp. My native officers, to whom he spoke, tell me that he looked very ill; he evidently had fever on him at the time. The sun was very hot, and the poor lad must have been off his head, and, either accidentally or in delirium, shot himself. He was the day before engaged and interested in his usual pursuits. I have before seen him very bad with fever at that hour of the day, that is, after the sun gets hot, and have several times told him I would get him put on the sick list if he did not take more care of himself. I have been put on his Committee of adjustment. In going through the boy's papers I find nothing whatever to lead anyone to suppose that he had any motive for making away with himself. You know young Cornish well: how high-spirited and courageous he was, and how, lately, everything seemed going well with him—successful in everything he undertook, and likely to attain eminence with service. There are few officers of his standing who had a wider reputation or were more sincerely regarded, or for whom a brighter career was prophesied. I don't know how we shall do without him.

Poor "Cracker"! He would have enjoyed our time at Bareilly. And in the war he would probably have commanded us. We seem to get so near him in these letters that we want to know a little more. Why exactly did he kill himself? Delirious, granted: but what was it that he had shut down below consciousness and suppressed, what was it that he had bravely fought down in normal moments, and that came to the surface in his delirium and took him by surprise and overwhelmed him? The people about him did not really understand him, or respond to his spiritual needs. This much is obvious. Was it then a sudden disillusionment about that "peerless roughrider" for whom his love had been "passing the love of women," or a bitter regret at having missed service in South Africa, or a disappointment about the Indian Cavalry, or did he feel in some flash of fever, that the artist-soul of him would die in India? We stretch out our hands to him across the grave. All that we can say has been well said by his parents; "'Deep seated in our mystic frame' is the belief that a life spent thus in humble service and a death in the midst of duty is full of blessed issues for the soul that is prepared—however strangely that death may come."

* * *

On leaving Rawalpindi in November 1904 the Regiment was very well mounted, thanks to Colonel Atkinson.

Capt. F. T. Warre-Cornish, whose letters form such a large portion of the subject matter.

Major F. C. C. Yeats-Brown, D.F.C., who wrote the 17th Cavalry History.

During 1903 and 1904 the following promotions, etc., occurred:—

> Second-Lieutenant Dodd was posted to the regiment.
> Second-Lieutenant Kirkwood was posted to the regiment.
> Major E. B. Burton was appointed officiating 2nd-in-Command of the 16th Cavalry, from the 3rd of May to the 29th of October.
> Captain R. W. Henderson proceeded on service with the Tibet Mission in charge of the Bhurtpur Imperial Service Transport Corps.
> Jemadar Barkat Shah retired on pension.
> Kote-Dafadar Mohamed Akbar Khan was promoted to Jemadar.

From Bannu, in January 1905 the regiment took part in the Pezu Manœuvres; heavy rain had fallen up to January and the weather then became very fine and cold, the cultivation around was heavy and the ponds were filled with water. At Ghazi Khel there was a severe frost and ice had to be broken in the ponds to get water for the horses. These, however, refused to drink before two in the afternoon. This cold destroyed the gram crops of the Punjab and damaged other crops as far south as Agra.

In April the following grants of land on Jhelum Canal were made for long and meritorious services:—

Risaldar-Major Sardat Khan	139 acres.
Risaldar-Major Mohamed Amin Khan	84 ,,
Risaldar Ahmad Khan	84 ,,
,, Mohamed Husain	84 ,,
Dafadar Sangar Khan	56 ,,
,, Mohamed Mir	56 ,,
,, Sikandar	56 ,,
,, Datta Khan	56 ,,
,, Habibulla	56 ,,
Trumpeter Fateh Din	56 ,,
Sowar Fateh Khan	56 ,,
,, Allahyar Khan	56 ,,

During this year the Regiment was in the unique position of having four Colonels and Lieutenant-Colonels and four Majors. Three of the latter were graded as Squadron Officers.

The following appointments occurred during the year:—

> Lieutenant D. R. Hewitt was appointed to the Remount Department.
> Lieutenant K. Barge, Cameronians, was posted to the regiment.
> Major E. W. Wall was transferred temporarily to the 25th Cavalry (Frontier Force) as Squadron Commander.
> Captain F. W. Summer was appointed to the Medical Charge of the regiment, vice Lieutenant F. C. MacC. Young (Officiating Medical Officer), transferred.

Risaldar-Major Saadat Khan retired on pension after 32 years' service.
Risaldar Mohammad Amin Khan was appointed Risaldar-Major.
Risaldar Ismail Khan retired on pension.
Jemadar Mualam Khan retired on pension.
Risaidar Ghulam Mohiuddin was promoted Risaldar.
Jamadar Malik Sher Ali Khan was promoted Risaidar.
Kote-Dafadar Sajid Gul was promoted Jemadar.
Kote-Dafadar Rahmat Sher was promoted Jemadar.
Kote-Dafadar Mustafa was Khan promoted Jemadar.

During 1906 the following appointments occurred:—

Captain R. C. Smith vacated Adjutancy and was succeeded by Lieutenant D. Wilson.
Lieutenant-Colonel E. J. Medley retired on pension.
Major W. S. Mardall was transferred to the 31st Lancers.
Colonel F. G. Atkinson was appointed Commander of Bangalore Cavalry Brigade.
Lieutenant H. S. Stewart, Royal Field Artillery, was appointed to the regiment.
Lieutenant-Colonel E. B. Burton was appointed Commandant.
Lieutenant F. C. C. Yeats-Brown, Unattached list, was appointed to the regiment.
Risaldar Ahmad Khan retired on pension after 32 years' service.
Jemadar Said Akbar Khan resigned his Commission.
Risaidar Malik Dost Mohamed Khan was promoted Risaldar.
Jemadar Usman Khan was promoted Risaidar.
Dafadar Zikerya was promoted Jemadar.
Kote-Dafadar Gauhar Ali Khan was promoted Jemadar.

In 1907 a Cavalry Camp was held at Gumbila, near Bannu, which the Regiment took part in. The Inspector-General of Cavalry visited the Camp and inspected the Regiment.

During March the building of the new Cavalry lines at Bannu was begun under regimental arrangements. Colonel Burton personally superintended the construction, and the lines as a consequence were very well built indeed. Mounted on his old chestnut mare (whom he objurgated in outrageous terms) clad in white Jodhpores, and carrying a stout silver-headed malacca cane, Colonel Burton slowly carried out his daily tour of the new lines. He was followed on another horse by the Indian officer in charge of the lines—Mahomed Amin or Hamzullah. A cringing contractor ran between the two. Behind came a daffadar and two sowars—these had large plumets with which all new erections were carefully tested. No argument was allowed. If any deviation from the perpendicular was detected, the daffadar and his satellites seized the walls with hooks and poles and the labour of the preceding day fell to the ground to the sound of the lamentation of the contractor, explaining his poverty and lamenting his loss. The hard work and patience of Colonel Burton was worthy of a better cause than the mud shantis allowed to the sowars.—[*Ed. S. & C.*]

During the year the Legation Guard sent to Persia was relieved by a second detachment. This duty was very popular with the men of the regiment, as they invariably return full of money. In December four men of 'A' Squadron deserted with their rifles; two were killed by the tribesmen near Zarnam Gorge, north of the Kurram River. Eventually two rifles were recovered and the half-squadron was fined Rs. 2,000.

The following appointments occurred during 1907 :—

> Captain R. W. Henderson was appointed Adjutant of the United Provinces Light Horse.
>
> Risaldar-Major Muhammad Amin Khan was gazetted to the Second Class of the Order of British India.

In April 1908, Risaldar-Major Mohammad Amin Khan Bahadur, accompanied by his Orderly Sowar Mohammad Azam, proceeded to England as one of the Indian Orderly Officers to His Majesty the King-Emperor, and on leaving England, he was presented with the medal of the Victorian Order.

Major-General Fasken inspected the Regiment before its departure on relief for Bareilly, and after the inspection he directed the following order to be published to all ranks :—On this, his last inspection of the regiment at this station, he wishes to say that he had always heard good reports of this regiment before coming to Bannu. That the regiment has, before him, always done its work well both on parade and the field ; and that he is particularly pleased with the willing and cheerful way in which all ranks have carried out his orders, especially on manœuvres. He considers the bearing of the men as above noted a credit to the officers, British and Native.

At midnight of the 23rd-24th December, the regiment received orders to send two hundred men to patrol the Bannu-Kohat Road, between the 25th and 40th milestones from Bannu, to intercept raiders. The detachment marched at 1-00 A.M. and reached the 25th milestone at 6-00 A.M. and put out patrols up to the 45th milestone by 11-00 A.M. The regimental mules with baggage left at 3-00 A.M. and reached the furthest patrol before nightfall. The detachment bivouacked three days and then returned on the fifth day to Bannu.

The relieved Teheran Legation Guard rejoined in January. They had been attacked by tribesmen on the road between Sheraz and Bushire and had lost rifles and ammunition. The Guard were fined five hundred rupees for the rifles lost and also one rupee for each round of ammunition deficient, besides receiving other summary punishment.

During this year Colonel H. Bower rejoined the regiment after eighteen years of consecutive absence.

The following appoinments occurred during 1908 :—

> Lieutenant L. H. Wilcox, Army Service Corps, was posted to the regiment.
>
> Lieutenant E. G. Atkinson, Unattached list, was posted to the regiment.
> Lieutenant A. H. R. Dodd was appointed unpaid Attaché to the Chief of the Staff's Branch at Simla.
>
> Colonel H. Bower was promoted to Brigadier-General and was appointed to command the Assam Brigade.
>
> Captain A. K. Hudson was placed on half-pay.
>
> Lieutenant D. D. Wilson was promoted Captain.
>
> Risaidar Arbab Mohammad Amin Khan resigned the service and was posted to the Police.
>
> Risaidar Malik Sher Ali Khan retired on pension.
>
> Jemadar Zikirya Khan was promoted Risaidar.
>
> Jemadar and Wordi-Major Rukn-ud-din was promoted Risaidar.
>
> Sahibzada Ata Mohammad Shah was gazetted to as a Direct Commission in the rank of Jemadar.
>
> Kote-Dafadar Tikka Khan was promoted Jemadar.

On January the 15th, 1909, the regiment left Bannu on its long march to Bareilly. At Rawalpindi there was a halt for two days, and all the retired Indian officers of the regiment were invited to meet it at Rawalpindi, where they were entertained as regimental guests. The regiment reached Bareilly on the 23rd March, having executed the march at a rate of about fourteen and a half miles a day, including halts. No casualties occurred among the men or horses.

A new departure was made at Bareilly in introducing a six horse-power Rushton Oil Engine with a flour mill and grain-crusher to take the place of the old bullock mills owned by the buniahs.

On the 28th of December the regiment marched to the Gurgaon Cavalry Camp. This Cavalry Camp was the largest that had ever been assembled in India in modern times, as fifty squadrons attended it. The drill struck us all as being rather clumsy and slow, but this was probably due to the fact that no officer in India had previous experience in handling such large bodies of cavalry.

A camel sowar with his camel.

The 17th Cavalry Pipers.

In November, Colonel Burton was granted leave out of India. He got his leave extended and never rejoined. Major E. W. Boudier was appointed as officiating Commandant in his place.

The regiment during this year was re-equipped with the Mark III Lee-Enfield (short) rifle and at the same time the old-fashioned pattern of long rifle buckets to carry them were issued. Thus, after many years of discomfort, we were at last got rid of the mounted infantry cranks of the South African War in the shape of patent equipment and short buckets designed to make the man and rifle inseparable.

The following appointments occurred during 1909:—

> Lieutenant Wilcox was transferred to the 17th Infantry on the 9th of October.
>
> Lieutenant J. A. W. Foottit was posted to the regiment on the 9th of October.
>
> Captain D. D. Wilson vacated the Adjutancy on the 8th of April and was succeeded by Lieutenant A. H. R. Dodd.
>
> Lieutenant H. S. Stewart was promoted Captain.
>
> Risaldar-Major Mohammad Amin Khan Bahadur retired on pension after 34 years' service on the 16th of October. He was the last of the original Indian officers appointed to the regiment in 1885.
>
> Risaldar Hamzullah Khan was appointed Risaldar-Major, on the 16th of October.
>
> Risaidar Usman Khan was promoted Risaldar on the 16th of October.
>
> Jemadar and Wordie-Major Bahadur Sher Khan was promoted Risaidar on the 16th October.
>
> Jemadar Mohammad Akbar Khan was pensioned on the 1st of October.
>
> Kote-Dafadar Wazir Khan was promoted Jemadar on the 1st of October.
>
> Jemadar Tikka Khan was appointed Wordie-Major on the 1st of December.
>
> Captain F W. Sumner, I.M.S., was transferred to Civil employ in April and posted to Bijnor.
>
> Lieutenant W. E. Brierley was appointed officiating Medical Officer on the 14th May.

The following appointments, etc., occurred during 1910:—

> Lieutenant K. Barge was appointed A.-D.-C. to Lieutenant-General Sir J. Wodehouse, Commanding Northern Army, in March.
>
> Lieutenant V. C. Duberly, Royal Field Artillery, was posted to the regiment on the 20th of June.
>
> Major E. W. Boudier was promoted Lieutenant-Colonel on the 5th of July.
>
> Captain B.A. Steel was appointed to Army Headquarters as unpaid Attaché.

Captain R. A. Steel was promoted Major.

Major R.A. Steel was appointed Assistant Instructor (temporary and unpaid) at the newly-opened Cavalry School at Saugor, in October.

Risaidar' Aslam Khan was pensioned on the 30th of November.

Jemader Sultan Khan was promoted Risaidar on the 1st of December.

Kote-Dafadar Daim Khan (son of the late Risaidar Kaim Khan, and grandson of Risaldar-Major Izzat Khan) was promoted Jemadar on the 1st December.

Lieutenant K. Barge was appointed Extra A.-D.-C. to H. E. the Commander-in-Chief in November.

Major R. A. Steel was appointed to the staff of H. I. H. the Crown Prince of Germany during his tour in India from December 1910 to February 1911. For his services in this appointment he was given the Order of the Red Eagle. During the tour he was accompanied by Dafadar (now Risaldar) Malik Alam Sher Khan, I.D.S.M., and Sowar Khushal-Khan.

During this year an Indian Officers' Mess was tentatively organised for the use of the sirdars while the regiment was in camp. It was a development of the system of supplying them with morning tea whenever the regiment was on the march or at manœuvres. This departure proved so successful, both at Squadron Training and at the Gurgaon Cavalry Camp, that it was decided to form it on a permanent basis, and later in the year a Mess-house was built in the lines at Bareilly. In cantonments it has remained more of a Club than an actual Mess, but from this experiment has sprung the idea of Indian officer's club which are now organised in all units.

During this year an Equipment *Chanda* was started in the regiment. This maintained and provided all the men's saddlery, arms and other equipment, excepting the actual personal clothing of the men and horse clothing and line gear. The equipment "price" was fixed at one hundred rupees and the subscription at five rupees. Subsequent experience necessitated the subscription being raised.

On the 9th November the regiment marched to Delhi to take part in the Coronation Durbar, arriving there on the 23rd. The regiment took part in the lining of the streets on the occasions of the State Entry, the laying of the All-India King Edward Memorial, the Imperial Durbar, the Garden Party in the Fort, and the State Departure, as well as in the Royal Review, where it formed the Divisional Cavalry of the 7th (Meerut) Division. On the 13th of December H. M. the King-Emperor inspected the camp of the Regiment, and on the same date all the Indian officers were presented to His Majesty. On the 15th of December the regiment furnished a Field Officer's escort (under Major Wall and Captain Henderson) for Their Majesties on the occasion of the Police Review. In commemoration of this the Commanding Officer was presented with signed portraits of Their Majesties to be placed in the Officers' Mess. All the retired Indian officers of the regiment came to Delhi to see the ceremonies as guests. The regiment commenced its return march on the 18th December and reached Bareilly on the 2nd January.

In March 1911 the regiment sent some horses to compete in the United Provinces Horse Show at Meerut, and took the first prize for country-bred horses with a horse bred at the regimental Farm; the 11th K. E. O. Lancers, 12th Cavalry, and 18th K. G. O. Lancers were also competing in this class.* The regiment took first and third prizes for troop horses in the same show.

The following appointments, etc., occurred during 1911:—

> Lieutenant W. E. Brierley was promoted Captain from 1st of February.
>
> Risaldar-Major Hamzullah Khan was gazetted to the second class of the Order of British India on the 1st January, with effect from the 4th of May 1909.
>
> 2nd-Lieutenant C. G. Y. Skipwith, Unattached List, was posted to the regiment on the 3rd January.
>
> Lieutenant A. J. Lee, I.M.S., was posted to officiating Medical Charge of the regiment on the 30th of January, during the absence of Captain W. E. Brierley.
>
> Colonel E. B. Burton was promoted Brigadier-General and appointed to the Command of the Secunderabad Cavalry Brigade on the 2nd of May.
>
> (Colonel Burton thus severed his connection with the regiment, after serving in it for twenty-five and a half years. He was the last of the original officers appointed when the regiment was re-raised in 1885.)
>
> Lieutenant-Colonel E. W. Boudier was appointed Commandant from the 2nd of May.
>
> Captain R. C. Barry-Smith was promoted Major from the 20th of May.
>
> Lieutenant K. Barge was appointed A.-D.-C. to H. E. the Commander-in-Chief from the 31st of May.
>
> Lieutenant A. H. R. Dodd was promoted Captain from the 27th of August.
>
> Lieutenant I. D. Guthrie was posted to the regiment on the 8th of October.
>
> Risaldar-Major Hamzullah Khan was promoted to the first class of the Order of British India in the *Honours Gazette* at the Delhi Durbar, with effect from the 2nd of May.
>
> Brigadier-General E. B. Burton was created as Companion of the Bath in the *Coronation Gazette* in June, and was invested personally by His Majesty at Delhi.

The Trumpeter-Major of the regiment was one of the Herald's Trumpeters at the Durbar. To commemorate this the

---

* All regiments with horse-runs of their own.—[ED., *S. & C.*, 1922.]

officers were presented with the Silver Trumpet and Bannerol used at the ceremony.

The coat worn by the Trumpeter was presented to him by the Committee and was purchased from him by the officers to keep with the Trumpet.

> Risaldar-Major Hamzullah Khan, Sardar Bahadur, retired from the service with thirty-five years and eight months' service on the 31st of December, and was granted the Honorary Rank of Captain.

A new pattern full dress *kurta* for British and Indian officers was introduced before the Durbar, as it was felt that the simple blue serge *kurta* which had been worn up to that time as the Indian pattern full dress was not suitable for such an occasion. The pattern adopted was designed by Captain Stewart, and was a great improvement on the old pattern which it superseded.

In November 1912 the regiment again took the road to Delhi. This time it was not for a pageant but for manœuvres. These manœuvres took some time and over two divisions took part in them. The Commander-in-Chief as well as General Officer Commanding the Northern Army was present.

In October this year Brigadier-General Burton replaced Brigadier-General Peyton as General Officer Commanding the Meerut Cavalry Brigade. He had specially asked to be transferred from the Brigade he commanded to the one in which his old regiment was.

The following promotions and appointments occurred during the year:—

> Risaldar-Major Ghulam Mohiuddin Khan was promoted to Risaldar-Major from the 1st of January.
>
> Risaldar Zikarya Khan was promoted Risaldar from the 1st of January.
>
> Jemadar Rahmat Sher Khan was promoted Risaldar from the 1st of January.
>
> Dafadar Malik Alam Sher Khan was promoted Jemadar from the 1st of January.
>
> Lieutenant K. Barge was promoted Captain from the 18th of January.
>
> Lieutenant T. W. Kirkwood was promoted Captain from the 21st of January.
>
> Major E. W. Wall was promoted Lieutenant-Cononel from the 30th of January.
>
> Captain W. E. Brierley was appointed Substantive Medical Officer of the regiment from the 11th of April.
>
> Risaldar-Major Ghulam Mohiuddin Khan was gazetted to the second class of the Order of British India on the 14th of June.
>
> Captain R. W. Henderson was promoted Major from the 15th of October.
>
> Captain W. F. Brierley proceeded to East Africa on special duty with H. H. The Maharaja of Datia on the 24th of October.

Captain J. W. Barnett, I.M.S., was appointed to officiating Medical Charge of the regiment from the 2nd November to the conclusion of the manœuvres.

Major-General Hamilton Bower was created Knight Commander of the Bath in recognition of his service in the operations against the Abors on the North-Eastern Frontier of India.

The regiment was under orders to march to a cavalry concentration near Sitapur at the end of December, but this was cancelled on account of the failure of the monsoon and consequent scarcity. Accordingly new orders were issued directing the regiment to proceed by rail to Allahabad in relief on the 15th of December, with one squadron on detachment in Calcutta. The move of the Headquarters of the regiment was, however, eventually postponed, first to the 21st December, and then to the 3rd January, on account of the occurrence of two cases of plague among sowars, one of whom died and one of whom recovered. As a precautionary measure all the men who were present in Bareilly were inoculated for plague.

Prior to this, however, 'A' Squadron had already proceeded to Allahabad by rail on the 19th of November, and on the 22nd 'C' Squadron was despatched by rail and route march to Dacca, to take part in the manœuvres there before relieving the squadron of the 12th Cavalry on detachment in Calcutta. This squadron was made up to a strength of one hundred and fifty with no recruits or remounts by twenty-six men of Left " B " Half Squadron. The officers who proceeded with it were Major Henderson, Lieutenant Guthrie, Risaldar Sultan Khan, and Jemadar Sajidgul Khan, Jemadar Mustafa Khan and Jemadar Guahar Ali Khan.

Immediately on arrival at Allahabad 'A' Squadron under Major Barry-Smith was sent to brigade manœuvres in the Mirzapore District for about three weeks.

The following promotions, etc., occurred during the year:—

Major J. M. Wikeley was promoted Lieutenant-Colonel on the 5th of February.

Captain A. H. R. Dodd was appointed Station Staff Officer, Meerut, on the 15th of March.

Lieutenant F. C. C. Yeats Brown was appointed Adjutant in place of Captain Dodd.

Lieutenant V. C Duberly was promoted Captain on the 29th of July.

Lieutenant-Colonel E. W. Wall was transferred to the 3rd Skinner's Horse as Commandant from the 1st of October.

Lieutenant-Colonel J. M. Wikeley was appointed Second-in-Command from the 1st October, but remained seconded. Major B. A. Steel being accordingly appointed Second-in-Command, *pro tem*, in his place.

Second-Lieutenant R. P. I. Cochrane was appointed to the regiment as officiating Squadron Officer from the 28th of October.

Captain T. W. Kirkwood passed the Preliminary Examination in Russian in October and proceeded to Russia to study the language.

Major R. A. Steel was appointed Military Attaché at Teheran on the General Staff on the 15th of December.

Captain D. D. Wilson, having qualified for the Staff College at Camberley (for the second time) was given a nomination by H. E. the Commander-in-Chief, and proceeded to England to join in December.

Captain K. Barge was appointed officiating Adjutant of the Imperial Cadet Corps from the 1st March to the 3rd October.

*   *   *   *   *   *

Colonel Boudier's history of the regiment founded on Colonel Burton's Digest of Services ends with the above extract and a paragraph may be quoted from the *Star and Cresent* regarding its compilation. "This" (history) "has involved a great amount of work and research, and has been kindly supplied by the Colonel. Whatever turn of fate befall the regiment in the future that is blind to us, this history will not have been written in vain if it helps us to emulate our predecessors in peace and war and helps us to be worthy of the fame we shall surely win when swords are again unsheathed."

Before adding to the above the account of Bannu and Bareilly let us turn for a moment, with the eyes of recollection to the two men who commanded us in those full and happy years that preceded the war. Colonel Burton commanded the regiment from October the 15th, 1906 to 1911 and as he comes within the memory of many of us still present, and tradition clings round him as a mantle of affection, a rather fuller biography of him has been attempted.

Edmund Boteler Burton was in many ways a remarkable man. He suffered under one disadvantage: he was born wise and of mature age. Like Athena, he seems to have come into life girded with knowledge and discrimination. As a subaltern he was in the prime of his powers, and had he commanded the regiment then instead of fifteen years later, the regiment would have reaped as much benefit as it did subsequently, and there would not have been that undercurrent of bitterness in Burton's mind (which he tried to hide under the cloak of cynicism) of talents unappreciated and services unrequited. He had a quite unrivalled knowledge of Silladar Cavalry accounts and administration, and a Napoleonic grasp of detail. All who knew him testify to how much they learnt from him. His administration was however in many ways a relic of the past. He never attended regimental office, nor allowed other officers to do so, as he said it bothered the Adjutant. It was in his house that he conducted all the business of the regiment, sitting there all morning like the Ruler of an Indian State. Everyone was welcome, whether he came with a complaint, petition, or mere routine business. For those who were transacting the latter this procedure was naturally rather exasperating: the Adjutant and Quartermaster had sometimes to wait a long time before they could get papers signed, while prosy old gentleman held forth to the C. O. about nothing in particular. Poor "Professor" (the most conscientious of men) as Adjutant was sometimes driven to the verge of desperation. Every day a long list, neatly written in the Colonel's handwriting, of delinquencies on the part of the Sanitary Staff, of reminders for returns due, and of suggestions for training, used to come to him from the Colonel's house at about breakfast time, and it was often three o'clock before the "Professor" could dispose of his business and eat his well-earned lunch. The Colonel, incidentally, fed at eleven o'clock and eight. He was an abstemious eater, and drinker, and liked a small bottle of claret with his evening meal. He never smoked. He was most methodical (almost old-maidish) in his domestic habits, and all his shirts and handkerchiefs were numbered serially. His servants were inclined to be slatternly, but he used to abuse them roundly, and summoned them to his presence with a Thunderer whistle, which he had made four times the usual size by the regimental armourer, so that he was able to sound a blast on it loud enough to wake the dead. In later years (as C. O.) he abandoned the Mess, and lived entirely in his own house, where he was a charming host, and the officers of the regiment frequent guests. The present writer remembers vividly his first interview with "the old man" who was afterwards to become his counsellor and friend. It was a chilly-bright January morning and the previous day the writer had consumed a bottle of sloe gin to keep himself warm in the tonga from Kohat: consequently he was not feeling as bright as the morning might warrant. He was told where to report his arrival. "Just walk straight to in the Colonel, he will be delighted to see you" the Adjutant had said. Some hirsute and alarming-looking Indian officers sat on the verandah. Inside there was no sound but the scratching of a pen. Summoning his courage, the writer knocked and asked if he might come in. A gruff voice acquiesced, and there was the Colonel in a dressing gown. The usual remarks were made about not disturbing him. "You are not disturbing me at all" he said very ceremoniously. Then silence, which gradually became almost unbearable. After a minute, or was it ten (?) the same cold ceremonious voice said "Please don't let me detain you". That was all. The bald powerfully intellectual head bent over its writing again, and an astounded boy, fresh from the orderly room of a Rifle regiment, crept out through the chick, feeling like a minnow that had somehow swum in among the struggles of a Leviathan. When one got to know Burton better, however, one discounted the Napoleonic manner, which was really only a form of shyness. No kinder or more loyal man to his subordinates ever existed, and it was because everyone throughout the regiment knew this, that they worked as hard as they did for him.

The neatly written list of orders and awkward questions already alluded to, was by no means confined to the adjutant. The Colonel kept a night-light burning by his bed, and in the early morning watches (when the memory of errors and the anticipation of troubles-to-come is sometimes poignant) he used to note down on appropriate slips, and in copper-plate calligraphy, the past and potential sins of the Officers Commanding squadrons, in charge of the Grass Farm, Horse-hospital, etc., etc. Sometimes, to ensure delivery perhaps, he used to *write a postcard* to the officer in the next-door bungalow. Naturally under this system, junior officers never bothered to remember anything. The Colonel worked all day, and sometimes far into the night.

He was well educated in oriental languages, having no doubt inherited some of that facility that was so remarkable in his relative, the famous Sir Richard Burton, and he thoroughly understood the mentality of the various classes of men who composed the regiment. His rather " cranky " or peculiar ideas, when looked into, appeared sounder and sounder, the more one studied them and the better one became acquainted with Indian Cavalry. He invented a regimental system of grooming horses, whereby each sowar groomed a specified portion for a specified time. Having enlisted most of the Pathan wing himself, he had a peculiar hold over the men, and in spite of the fact that as his age increased his temper shortened, and he was inclined to speak to them in a way that would have been resented in any other officer, he retained, up to the end, their respect and affection. He called all the Indian Officers " tum ", while showing them all the respect due to their rank ; and he used to beat the men with a big stick, and afterwards give them sweets. He had a passion for making horses walk fast, and used his legs to great effect to this end. On the March from Bannu to Bareilly he trained the regiment (for mile after weary mile along the Grand Trunk Road) to walk at the rate of about five miles an hour, and there is no doubt that after our thousand miles of training no unit in the world could have beaten the 17th Cavalry at walking.

Colonel (afterwards Brigadier-General) E. B. Burton, C.B., Eighth Commandant, 1906—1911.

Colonel (afterwards Brigadier-General) E. W. Boudier, Ninth Commandant, 1911—1917.

Among other peculiarities, he had learnt *a graduated scale of salaams* from the Rajah of Faridkote, which enabled him to return every salute according to the rank of the person greeting him. For an equal the hand would be carried to the head in the usual way, while for those of inferior rank the salute would gradually diminish in extent, until the acknowledgement of a sweeper's salutation would be a mere gesture near the waistband.

He will be generally remembered by those who served with him, by his expressions, such as "A thin horse is always dirty" and "God stamped the character of a Pathan on his face". A long life spent in cutting the tails of squadron horses and looking down the heel pegs to see if they were in line, had tended to make him view soldiering through the wrong end of a telescope. A large part of his great energy was spent in superintending the operations of sweepers or attempting to correct the irregularities and absurdities of silladar cavalry baggage mules, ironically described by him as the "best transport in the world".

It is not with a view of exaggerating his peculiarities that these idiosyncracies in a great character have been mentioned, but in order to give a life-like portrait of the man who more than any other C. O. perhaps has moulded and stamped the individuality of the regiment with his own high and chivalrous spirit. Burton had a great character. He would have been a great man, if opportunity had come to him while he was young.

Colonel E. W. Boudier commanded the regiment from 1911 through all the trying period of the early part of the War, until July 1917 and although his biography belongs to a later period in our history it is put down here, close that of his friend and contemporary, Burton. Edward William Boudier, like Burton, was a man cast in no common mould. His charming personality endeared him to all ranks of the regiment and he was able to carry out by love what another man could not have done by terror. His one thought was the regiment in which he had passed the whole of his life, and in which (except for his family) all his interests lay. All ranks, high and low, felt that come what might, their interests would be looked after. The regiment was a mutual benefit society, in which each and all, provided they behaved themselves, were entitled to enjoy such advantages as the resources of the office or his personal influence could obtain. Even the matrimonial affairs of a *bhangi* might engage his attention for an hour or so, rather to the disgust of his Adjutant, it must be admitted He was an extraordinarily industrious man, and after spending many hours in office (from eleven o'clock till half past three was no uncommon session for a hot weather afternoon) he was able to return home and attend to an immense amount of domestic correspondence. He was very happy in his home and kept quantities of dogs and horses and about one hundred servants. All who knew him have pleasant memories of Mrs. Boudier's charm, and of the cheerful household, with its unpunctuality, romping dogs, round games after dinner, and spirit of perpetual youth. Colonel Boudier was a great lover of horses, and one of his great pre-occupations was to help officers to mount themselves well for parade and for polo. Another hobby was the Horse Farm, and he kept in his own writing long complicated lists of everything connected with it. His eye for a horse was such that he very rarely bought a bad one.

He played the game of life as he played polo: a thoroughly sound unselfish game: not at all theatrical, but always thinking of his side, so that he was worth more than more dashing players to his team. In his last years in command, what with the regiment failing to go on service and his broken leg, he appeared to have aged considerably, as was only natural, but he never lost heart, and has now, we are happy to say quite regained his health. As an instance of his grit, when be had broken his leg and was lying in great pain on the Bombay-Worli Road, he dictated an answer quite calmly to an official telegram while waiting for the ambulance. He was *never* tired, *never* cross (and let those who know their regiment realise what this means), *never* disconcerted. He smoked constant cigarettes, liked weak whisky and soda, going to bed late, and bridge. He would have been in his element in France, commanding the regiment in the early stages of the war, but Fate decreed otherwise. It was his custom to drink the old Peninsular toasts " Our swords," " Ourselves," " Our horses," " Our men," " Our religion," " Absent friends," " Sweethearts and Wives ". He used to exclaim " Wah !" when surprised, and had a peculiar way of screwing up his face as he wrote. He had a happy and contented regiment which would have gone anywhere or done anything for him (only he would never have asked it to do anything that was not strictly in reason!) and he was known to all the British Officers as " Bong," which was an abbreviation for a phrase which exaclty discribes him— *le bon Commandant.*

BANNU, 1905—1908.

Soldiering was the order of the day at Bannu: throughout the cold weather we were generally on manœuvres or squadron training camp. In the summer the heat steadily rose in intensity, until by August it was almost beyond endurance. In the winter it was very cold, with a biting wind. A more unpleasant place, with more disagreeable inhabitants it would be impossible to imagine.

At that time the broad guage railway only ran as far as Khushalgar on the Indus. Thence to Kohat there was a metre guage that was slower than the tonga it replaced. In the hot weather there was a nightmare drive from Kohat to Bannu, across barren foothills that absorbed heat all day and exuded it all night. Ponies were wretched "tats," that jibbed and required ropes tied to their forelegs before they would start at all. After a night of jolts, refusals, and sticking in sandy nullahs, one arrived in the environments of Bannu, and was immediately apprised of the fact by encountering the damp atmosphere of the hot-house after the scorching heat of the previous miles. A network of water channels was laid all over cantonments and the city, to irrigate the sugarcane, and incidentally to give the city a name notorious throughout the frontier for its atmosphere of a conservatory and for the morals of a monkey-house. Drab bungalows loomed out in the dawn light: on their roofs lay officers, under hardly-flapping punkhas, who at the only moment they could sleep were turned out to go on parade.

Parade was at five fifteen. Then came a bath, stables, breakfast, office, sleep (if possible), then the miserable hot-weather-afternoon awakening, polo, long and short drinks in the Mess where one sat under the punkha until it was time to go to the other punkha on the roof and prepare for another night, another day, another night. One thought of little but when one's turn of leave would come. The cold weather was more vital and the days spent in squadron training camp at Laluzai are pleasant memories. Imagine a stony plain, an amphi-theatre of jagged hills, a clear sky, a bright sun, a keen wind, two squadrons under canvas. Parade was at nine o'clock after breakfast. At eleven drill was over and there was an interval during which one read one's letters or the paper, and indulged perhaps in a glass of Madeira and a slice of cake. Stables were at noon: then a little office work brought one by pleasant gradations to lunch. Then there was a gallop into cantonments for polo or afternoon parade. In the evening a lecture, or football with the men. And so to one's bath, after which putting on Gilgit boots and a thick *posteen*, one went out into the moonlit night, that had the nip of frost, and which smelt good. The mess tent was cosy from an open brazier, over which one warmed one's hands. Outside, except for the lights burning in the guard tent and the hourly cry of the sentries "Number One all's well,"

"Number two all's well" and so on to the eighth sentry—except for this the camp is hushed and dark. Rest has come to the little world of canvas. The men are telling each other stories perhaps, huddled two and two under their blankets, and the horses are standing still, very still in the moonlight, thinking intently about nothing at all, or puzzling out some fancy of their troop horse brains.......

Life in cantonments was strenuous, but fairly diverting. The other regiments at Bannu, namely, the 31st Punjabis and the 51st Sikhs were great friends of ours and there were many cheery guest nights (the guests being chiefly ourselves) in the big "Piffer" Mess. In December 1908 we gave a dinner party to all the ladies of the garrison, to celebrate our departure. Vodka, caviare, jeroboams of champagne and other delicacies were ordered from Bombay, and a very successful function it was. Some eighty sat down to dinner. After dinner there were mounted sports, jumping through flaming hurdles, and the like. Then there was a dance. The junior members of the regiment went as an Afridi lashkar, and were a great and instant successes. Next day, the regimental polo team left by tonga for Peshawar, where they were to play in the 'Xmas week tournament, their first appearance in public.

It was a narrow cramping life at Bannu and everyone heartily rejoiced to see the last of the frontier, with its quite illusory chances of seeing real active service, and its very certain discomforts and lack of sport.

THE MARCH FROM BANNU TO BAREILLY which began on the 15th January and ended on the 23rd March, was a delightful time : our hearts were high for we had turned our backs on the wilderness and were getting nearer every day to the promised land of the United Provinces : the land of pig and panther and duck-jheels and tiger forests and green polo grounds.

We passed close to the Attock Oil Fields (then undiscovered) and stayed two days at Pindi, when several old Native Officers came to see us, amongst them Buldeo Singh. Other halts were made at Ferozepore, Ludhiana and Rurki. The march was carried out at a very fast average pace, faster indeed than the horsemen of Alexander rode, when pursuing Darius. Occasionally we had a bad day, like the march into Narsingpur, when we toiled all day and far into a spring evening, getting *bhile* carts up a steep river bluff : it was long after dark that day before the men lay down beside their horses, too tired to pitch their tents.

The routine of marching was pleasant enough, however, one pressed amid falling tents, gurgling "oonts," and a general atmosphere of scramble. After girding one's loins in a kummerbund, and one's brow in a lungi, and swallowing a little smoky tea, one cantered on parade a minute or two before the " old man." ...The *bhile* carts containing the officers' kits were already loaded up (each officer had at least one *bhile* cart, hired at a cost of fourteen annas a day) with tents, trunks, and their *Lares et Penates* such as goats, hogspears, easy chairs, etc. The men's kits were already on the road, balanced on the "best transport in the world"—the silladar cavalry grass mules. A hay-net enclosed the goods and chattels and the "twenty pound" tent of two sowars and a syce : this was slung across a lean and cow-hocked mule, and surmounted by the syce, who holds a hen in one hand and the string reins in the other, and urges his steed onward at a tottering gait. Each tottering mule raises a cloud of dust behind it : out of this "pillar of cloud," in which the syces live and move and have their being, come cries and oaths and the occasional crowing of cocks who are endeavouring to identify their wives. The loads, being dependent on the delicate mechanism of balance which syces are deficient, frequently topple over or come adrift, so that the route of a regiment is always strewn with the debris of its luggage. But the syces are never dismayed. With a wonderful skill at string expedients, they tie the loads together again, and continue their five-mile-an-hour totter. It took the Great War to make the Indian Government realise the defects of this transport, dating from Moghul days. Amid the crush of thrones, vanished also the silladar cavalry system of transport, and now only the dhobi's donkey remains to show how we used to carry our kit. It was an impossible system for organised war but for marches on manœuvres it was ideal. The silladar baggage mule carried twice as much baggage as an S. and T. mule, he carried much faster and much farther. Silladar baggage mules cost less, ate less and had a longer working life than Government mules. The syces laughed at all attempts to march them in "first" and "second lines of transport" under baggage guards. They moved straight from one camp to another, the fastest animals leading the rest strung out on rear.

Arrived in camp, we settled down the horses, and began stables. Meanwhile, if it was a short march, the transport was beginning to arrive. Directly our day's work was done, we went out, with a few Indian Officers and men, with rifle, shot-gun, or long-dogs. One incident of Blackbuck shooting, has been recorded in verse by Steel.

AN INCIDENT OF THE MARCH FROM BANNU TO BAREILLY, 1909.

Our Jim behold, he's shot his Buck,
He rubs his hands and cries "What luck"!

"The biggest buck that ere was born,
I'll sit me down and 'nāp' his horn."

Full fifteen minutes by his side,
Our Gamble sits and swells with pride.

Meanwhile the crafty antelope,
Has closed one eye and feigns to mope.

Hot foot across the rolling sand,
There pad the Faithful, knife in hand.

One almost *hears* long Ooran Shah—
"Bismillah hé Allah Akbar."

But counting chickens ere they're hatched,
Is how our Jim and Co are catched,

For vension's Venison when it's *cooked*
(A fact they've rather overlooked.)

One gurgle as the *ounts* subside —
The glazing optic opens wide,

Then Hey for freedom, gram and corn,
The blackbuck *gambols*—Jim's forlorn.

The tahsildars and other village officials with whom we came in contact on the march, made an interesting study, for we had dealings with officials of every creed and complexion, and of every disposition from the servile to the truculent.. We saw every kind of man: we ran the gamut of village officials. One saw India, in fact, during those eight hundred miles of marching in a way that few of our legislators ever see it: its vast resources its immense diversity its child-like heart: its great tendernesses and astounding cruelties. It is difficult to sum in words the result of these experiences. Suffice it to say that one must travel, and travel slowly, and off the beaten track to see India as she is. Settlement Officers will corroborate this, yet they are confined to a single district, where as we traversed a distance equal to that between London and Rome.

India is a country of camps: only thus can she be seen at her best. Her cities are generally squalid, and her cantonments are always hideous, but the Indian country-side, even in the Ganges plain, has a glamour all its own, especially for the sportsman. Snipe and teal and venison were our daily fare on the line of march, and we had delightful evenings on the jhils we passed, waiting for the evening flight of geese, or watching the companies of duck, that whirred and swept by, and turned at the glint of a rifle barrel, with a shimmer of white underwing against the sunset. It was a pleasant life.

FANCY DRESS GROUP AT BANNU.

Kirkwood.   Wazir Khan.   Atkinson.   Barge.
    Steel.   Wilson.
        Yeats-Brown.

GROUP AT BAREILLY.

Foottit.   Atkinson.   Duberly.   Guthrie. Brierley.   Wilson.
    Stewart.   Wall.   Yeats-Brown.   Barry-Smith.

BAREILLY.

Arrived at Bareilly, we settled down there as if it was to be our permanent domicile. In the Mess, we had little kit but plenty of cash. We brought out furniture from England without misgiving and spent thirty thousand rupees, without a tremor, and we made ourselves thoroughly comfortable, with gardens, jumping lanes, and even, in one instance, a pond was constructed with the idea of stocking it with a special sort of mosquito-eating goldfish from Bombay.

Our ponies rapidly began to improve in condition, as all ponies do who change from the meagre diet of bhoosa to the dhub grass of the United Provinces.

We were a happy family, and settled down contentedly to polo, pigsticking, racing and shooting after our time of duress on the frontier. To be quite frank, I don't think we regarded soldiering as our *profession* in those days. There may have been some of us who did: officers who envisaged the world-struggle that was impending: sowars who ate the bread of the Sirkar in the hope of distinguishing themselves in battle—but to say that this was the general spirit of the regiment would be to say the thing which was not. We were too happy to bother. We knew that a war would come some day (*cf.* 'Star and Crescent' for April 1912. "The cold weather which is past will be numbered among our happiest days in India. There is one thing more for which we hope. It is that one day—(not too far distant)—will come a time when polo, pigsticking—and parades also— will be left on one side for the realities of service. In the next war, if it ever comes, and if we go, our star shall surely climb its zenith "), but although the chances of service were always on the horizon they did not bulk very largely in our lives. Officers and men were serving simply because they liked the life—and who would not when *atta* was sixteen seers to the rupee, and a polo pony, syce and all, cost twenty rupees a month to keep?

Of soldiering, however, as well as sport we had a plenty. In the cold weather of 1909-10 we attended the Ghaziabad manoeuvres. We left Bareilly directly after our Christmas pigstick, and spent the New Year on the dusty road to Delhi. Our first training camp was at Gaziabad, where we formed the 2nd Brigade with our old friends the 11th Lancers and the Alwar State Lancers. Later we manoeuvred, "under field service conditions" (no tents, no sodas, etc.), against the Muttra division, made a night march, and fought an indecisive battle. Great importance was attached to those manoeuvres, and Generals at that time were exalted or "ungummed" as the result of a field day. We experimented with telephone equipment, we got our noses almost scorched off through wearing *lungis*, we rode out for days on long distance patrols, we "gin-crawled" round the mess tents of our force, and we came away at last about as wise as when we went. Such at any rate, is the writer's impression. The Staff wrote reams about the lessons they had learnt.

Our sports at Bareilly such as racing, pigsticking, and polo are being treated in separate articles, so there only remains shooting and soldiering to describe. One word, also about hunting. Writing in February 1911 Colonel Wall records that " We had some grand hunting on spare afternoons when at Fatehgunj West and accounted for three or four hares and a fox or so every time we went out. Our pack was very much what is known as *bobbery* and consisted of some half dozen greyhounds and the same number of terriers of sorts. As far as hunting went, Joey's two were the prize packet: "Tatcho." black greyhound, a haunter of cook houses and the scourge of the *khansamah*, and "Bubbles," a fox terrier, a rare good 'un to find and put up a hare. Other notable performers were "Taffy" usually known as "Stuffy" and the bull-dog "Brimstone" who though obsessed by his own beauty, is full of keenness and did his best "...
...Besides these, there were Raja Sultan Khan's hounds and "Nell," and "Dougal," and "Maidstone," "Johnstone," "Tombstone," *et hoc genus omne*. As for shooting and soldiering, a couple of extracts from the *Star and Crescent* will give a fair idea of how we passed our time in Bareilly.

The first is by Kirkwood, and is dated November 1911.

"A LITTLE TRIP TO MEERUT."

Knowing the ferocity of the British officer in mounted combat, I shuddered when I heard that I was to go to Meerut to compete for the best officer at arms in our division, more especially as the adjutant informed me that I was in for no less than sixty-four bouts. My wife, who fully expected me to be brought back on a stretcher, implored me not to go without taking "Bareilly"[*] with me to patch up the wounds.

The preliminary canter was held close to the riding schools, where we all assembled to chose the victim who was to go to Meerut. Poor "Shirt,"[†] after one particularly *strenuous* bout, had to be carried by two men to a chair, greatly to the alarm of the sympathetic audience, amongst whom was our new General. The

---

[*] "Bareilly"—Major (then Captain) W. E. Brierley, I.M S.
[†] Major (then Captain) H. S. Stewart, 17th Cavalry.

Mounted Combat.

Men of the regiment.

choice was difficult, and finally fell on the Quarter-master, the other officers, I suppose, rightly considering he needed a few days' rest from his arduous duties!

Rukn-ud-din represented the Indian officers.

At Meerut, I went to stay with the 18th, and the first person I met there was Gatacre ‡ of the 11th up for the same game. He and I worked through the same riding class some years ago, and it was a great pleasure to see him again looking so fit. He had had a very nasty fall just before the Indian Cavalry Tournament last year and had hardly ridden since then.

There were two events to be competed for, Tent-pegging and Mounted Combat, win counted four points, second two and third one. We were allowed only one horse for both events. With all due respect to whoever was responsible for this rule, it was not a very sound one, especially as two are allowed for the finals at Delhi, and it meant the man whose horse was good at tent-pegging failed at mounted combat and *vice versa*; the two events requiring totally different qualities.

This was very apparent in our competition, as the best man at tent-pegging was nowhere at mounted combat, while the best man at mounted combat failed at tent-pegging. We started off with tent-pegging for British N.-C. O's. My courage rose when I saw the feeble exhibition made by them—our turn came next, there were eight of us, of which six took their two pegs, so we had to have another run. Eventually Gatacre and I were left in, both having taken all four pegs, Gatacre was given more marks for style, so he was first with four points and I was second with two.

The Indian Officers four in all, were the next to perform. They were rather disappointing, especially as they were given bigger pegs than we were and they were allowed to use their tent-pegging lances, while we had to use the regulation lance. Rukn-ud-din had splendid style, but unfortunately only took two pegs out of four and was not placed.

The British officers then went off to do mortal combat. We each had to get through seven fights, my horse lasted out the first fight all right, after that he refused to go in. Medlicott of the 3rd Skinners Horse who had not been placed in the tent-pegging, won all his fights and came out easy winner. It is very hard for the judges to see every point, and in consequence the best man

---

‡ Brevet-Major Gatacre won his Brevet and a great reputation for gallantry while attached to the 4th Hussars in the early days of the war. He was killed in October 1914 at Mont des Cats. He won the Kadir Cup in India. In one combat during the war he killed eleven Germans with his own sword.

does not always win, but in this case there was no doubt about it. In my fight with Medlicott he got three points into me before I could wink, partly, I own, due to my horse, but he would have beaten me easily, however good a horse I was on.

Gatacre and I were not placed in this event, so it ended in Medlicott and Gatacre getting four points each and they were to decide it by tent-pegging with a sword on Wednesday. The result I have not heard.

On Tuesday morning the British N.-C. O's and Indian-Officers fought their mounted combat. What struck me at once was that their mode of fighting was of quite a different standard to the British Officers. The Indian Officers were better than the British N.-C. O's, the latter made a very tame show.

Rukn-ud-din did splendidly at this and played the game with tremendous dash, circling round his opponents and dashing in with a point whenever the opportunity came. He drew for first place with the Indian Officer of the 18th Lancers. They fought it out, and Rukn-ud-din was beaten on time. This was their third fight together, as the first time they drew and had to fight again when Rukn-ud-din lost.

So far the results in other divisions that I have heard of, show the Indian Cavalry officer winning. One of them is my brother * who won for the Quetta Division. It will be grand if all the Divisions send Native Cavalry representatives. The 18th Lancers were very good to me at Meerut. They were very interested in our polo team, and seemed to think we must all be full of money to enter in for the Durbar tournament, on that point, however, I quickly disillusioned them.

* * * *

The extract connected with shooting, although it belongs to a somewhat later time than 1911 gives our youthful attitude towards life so neatly that it must be quoted *in extenso*. At the time of its publication Sir John Hewett was the Lieutenant-Governor of the United Provinces and that physically lion-hearted sportsman but somwhat timid official Mr. P. U. Allen, of pigsticking fame was Collector of Bareilly.† The author is Major W. E. Brierley, I.M.S., then known to us as the peerless physician who followed our fortunes for so long, in cantonments, camp, hunting field,—"Bareilly", to whom more than to any one perhaps, we owed our good health through hot and hectic hot weathers.**

---

* Major (then Captain) Kirkwood of the 23rd Cavalry.

** Except perhaps the officers Mess cook, "Robello" who kept us all well fed, and was so fond of the regiment that he was going to follow it to France, to meet the Gallic chefs on their own ground.

† See page 64 and also the special article on "Bareilly pigsticking."

Yeats-Brown.   Stewart.   The Mess Camel

Wilson.   Boudier.
Horses Watering.

Atkinson. Barge. Yeats-Brown.
Horses Feeding.

HOW WE SHOT THE L.-G.'S JHIL.

The following incident occurred not a hundred miles from Bareilly and not a hundred years ago.

October was drawing to a close and already in the station rumours of big bags of duck and snipe were being freely circulated. I bethought me, then, that if I wanted to shoot the neighbouring jhils before our gallant line regiment had entirely cleared them, I had better be up and doing. I was spurred on to seek for snipe and duck by this fact also, that the fare supplied at the Mess under the auspices of a cheese-paring Mess Secretary had of late been far from ample or nutritious.**

Accordingly I arranged with two gunners that the following Sunday we would shoot a certain *jhil* which has always had a good reputation for holding snipe. We took the train early on the morning in question, and were pleased to find the Collector on the train going out to shoot somewhere also. We communicated to him our rendezvous, and were surprised and shocked to see how ill he took the news. His face at once assumed an expression of deep concern. We begged him to tell us what sudden trouble had intruded itself on his mind. Brokenly, he told us that the *jhil* we intended shooting had been specially reserved for the Lieutenant-Governor that it was even now manned by a posse of police, who had had orders to evict any one who ventured to shoot there. As, however, we were already on our way, he could not find it in his heart to ask us to turn back; so he would like to compromise between his supposed duty to the Lieutenant-Governor and his duty to us, by asking us to leave a few birds for the Lieutenant-Governor whose visit there was expected almost immediately.

We expressed our sorrow at being about to unwittingly interfere with the enjoyment of a high official, but at the same time urged our claim for consideration in this act of discourtesy we were about to commit, to wit, that we had not been warned in the station that such a shoot was contemplated. We eventually separated with mutual protestations of good will and promises on our side to bear the Lieutenant-Governor in mind during the day.

Arrived at our destination, our troubles began. The troubles had perhaps best be tabulated :—

1. At the station we soon found that the terror of the police prevented any coolies from turning out to help us. We finally started for the *jhil* with one coolie and left our lunch to follow when

---

** Robelle was engaged shortly after the publication of this article.—[Editor *S. & C.*]

the station master had succeeded in finding coolies to carry it. We did not know then what a difficult task this would prove for him.

2. We arrived at the *jhil*, still with one coolie whose attention was entirely confined to looking after my dog who proved herself the veriest novice at the art of *shikar*. Result.—Many birds hit and but few recovered, none of the party showing a marked desire to do their own retrieving. My dog suddenly disappeared which, at any rate, had the good result of putting our one cooly at liberty to pick up the birds, and we began to get on a little better.

3. Attracted by the greed of gold, we finally succeeded in attaching to ourselves two more coolies. We now began to get on quite well. Unfortunately just when the situation was looking brighter, we espied a posse of those dreaded police bearing down on us, and could only prevent the coolies from bolting by levelling our guns at them, and threatening them, if they did so, with instant demolition.

4. The police arrived and a long argument ensued. A paper was handed to us on which was a request that no one should shoot in a certain area of country measuring some hundreds of square miles, because it was in the bounds of possibility that the *Lát Sáhib* might drop down there for an hour or two's shooting some time or other. In common with the greater portion of the U. P., our little patch of ground was included in the prohibited area.

5. There now followed a lengthy altercation with the police officials who bore down on us from various points of the compass. We pointed out the merits of our case and that the blessed providence of our calling in life rendered us immune from the wrath of the *Lát Sáhib*.

6. Time was now two thirty P.M. and no sign of lunch. Tongues were hanging out all round and a cooly was sent to the station to ask the reason of the delay in the dispatch of tiffin. Shooting was frequently interrupted by the various dependents of the *Lát Sáhib* who showed considerable pluck in getting in front of our guns.

7. Time, three thirty P.M. No lunch. A climax reached by the accidental wounding of a chaukidar who had been too zealous in interfering with us. Result.—An armistice proclaimed, and we proceeded to consult with the Darogah and to arrive at an understanding, if possible. We were entirely successful in this, and in addition succeeded in getting the Darogha to send a party of chaukidars for our lunch.

GROUPS AT BAREILLY 1909.

Stewart.   Zikryia Khan.   Barge, Sumner, Mohamed Akbar,
Rukan Din, Ghaur Ali Khan, Usman Khan, Mustapha Khan Kirkwood, Wilson, Dodd,
Aslam Khan, Barry-Smith, Hamzulla Khan, Burton, Mohamed Amin Khan, Boudier, Dost
Mohamed Khan.
Yeats-Brown.   Ata Mohamed Shah.   Atkinson.   Sajid Gul.

Atkinson.   Stewart.   Brierley.   Kirkwood.   Steel.   Wilson.   Dodd.   Barge.
Barry-Smith.   Boudier.   Burton.   Wall.   Wikeley.

8. Time, four P.M. Lunch at last. Quickly partaken of and refreshed and freed from the attentions of the *Lat Sáhib's* friends who had now given the matter up as a bad job, we set to work to add to our bag—already considerable one. By the time the shades of evening were falling too fast for further shooting, we had had one of the best days after snipe, I have ever had, We got seventy-six couple, and the great majority were full snipe. I think we may be said to have remembered our words in the morning to the Collector. We kept the Lieutenant Governor in mind practically throughout the day, and we had a kindly thought for him even in the birds we shot, for many were allowed to escape wingless or legless, and no doubt would live to furnish excellent marks for the Lieutenant Governor's deadly aim when he should make his projected visit. So passed a day full of lights and shades.

* * * *

As a result of the above article, the *Star and Crescent* was called upon to register itself as a magazine and find security. Later, during the war, some genius in some bureau, looking through old files perhaps, thought that a journal that had jested about a Lieutenant-Governor was a fit subject for propaganda news about the War. Consequently reams of communiqués were addressed to the Editor (who was several thousand miles away) and were relegated by the Mess clerk to a large zinc box, where the Editor found them, a solid ton of propaganda, in 1920.

Beyond squadron training, hunting, and helping flustered old Majors to pass their "Q" examinations, the regiment did nothing particular until November 1911, when it marched to Delhi for the eagerly anticipated Royal Durbar.

Our camp was beyond Kingsway station, in a desolate and dusty spot. The Mess had decided, not without trepidation, to admit ladies to our board, and as a consequence we were treated to some minor but most amusing quarrels; amusing, that is, for the bachelors: for the participants they were sometimes, alas, the cause of tears.

Soldiers were badly treated at the Durbar, and we expressed ourselves as follows: "Mere soldiers, like the Jews of old were kept in bondage." It was a benevolent subjugation no doubt, but it was arduous none the less. And murmurs were heard as the Pharaohs of the Civil Service whizzed down the guarded streets on their big Rolls Royces. Before the Durbar opened, all was expectancy and suspense. The thermometer was low, and the hopes of the civilians were high. The fire of the Star of India burnt in their bosoms and sustained them in their chairs for hours during rehearsals, while the troops were at attention. A fever got hold of the Egyptians and the poor Israelites knew no rest. Afterwards however when there was the stimulus of our Sovereign's presence, the long parades were as nothing, neither did we grudge the time that had been spent in making every function perfect; so that the pageants of the King-Emperor should be the most brilliant that the world has seen.

One thing was very noticeable, and that was the air of impermanence about the city of canvas that was to endure for a fortnight only. Jerry-built shanties were to be seen everywhere, and the afternoon sun shone through the lath and plaster of some of the most massive triumphal arches. No doubt it was impossible to make use of the old buildings at Delhi, with all their historical associations, but certainly His Majesty's gracious speech at the Durbar would have been even more impressive if it had come from the marble throne of the Moghuls in the Diwan-i-Am, instead of a pavilion of wood and gilt and white-wash. However as this may be, there could be no doubt in the minds of any spectator, of the immense personal success of the King-Emperor, whenever he appeared to his people.

A quiet march home followed the excitements of Delhi, and the polo team took a turn at the wheel while the rest of us took a holiday. We celebrated our return to Bareilly by a gymkhana race meeting and after this we enjoyed a month of excellent station polo, an amusement which is becoming rarer and rarer in the modern strenuous training season. Then came Umballa and our success there. The final was played with a strong wind blowing across the ground, which made combination difficult and made the issue more doubtful perhaps than it would have been on a better day and a better ground.

"Joey" was brilliant and his ponies were beautifully trained. "Prof" also played splendidly in the final game and worked like a Trojan as he always does. "Hender" was ubiquitous and certain on the ball in spite of a severe blow on the nose in the first chukker of the final. "Kirks" neat wrist strokes were very noticeable and his big fast stud of ponies gave him some great runs down the field.

But we say must no more of polo, for we encroach on Atkinson's article. Yet one thing must be added, else it will remain unsaid. The success of the 17th Cavalry as a polo regiment was due to a variety of causes : it was due for instance, to everyone in the regiment being keen on the game, and to their buying good animals, to their being encouraged to keep a number of ponies and to feeding them well. It was also due to players being ready to work

AT THE DELHI DURBAR, 1911.

Trumpeter-Major Shah Wali Khan as a Herald's Trumpeter.

17th Cavalry escorting Her Majesty Queen Mary at the Delhi Durbar, 1911.

hard at the game, and give up other things for its sake. But given these things, we would still have lacked something that would have kept us in the second rank as a polo regiment. That something was the confidence that "Joey" gave us since 1909 onwards and that he will, we hope, continue to inspire in the amalgamated regiment. Never was a "crack" player better liked or more trusted. He was the most unselfish of players in spite of his high handicap. It was confidence in his judgment, in his play, in his opinion about a pony or a player that made the team "pull together" and times without number, was the deciding factor in a hard-fought game.

Once again, in the winter of 1912-13 the regiment took the road to the Imperial City, this time to engage in a perfect orgy of manœuvres.

"Since we last went to press" it is recorded in *The Star and Crescent* for June 1913" the sport and the soldiering in which the regiment has taken part has provided much notable matter for record, and it is for this very reason that we have not recorded it. Our time has been so fully occupied with work and play, and our hands so constantly grasping either sword or polo stick or spear, that the pen has necessarily been somewhat neglected of late.

At the beginning of October there was a very cheery autumn polo tournament which must be recorded in these annals as one of the bright spots in the monsoon of nineteen hundred and twelve. After this vivid hot weather interlude, came a somewhat hurried squadron training, and the eighth of November found us on the road to Ghaziabad to take part in the Northern Army manœuvres.

Dilli dur ast is an old cry, but to many of us who enjoy camp life, Delhi is not half far enough away, and we confess to being sorry when the peaceful march is ended. On this occasion the shooting was quite up to the average, the best bag being fifty-three couple of snipe to three guns, at Gujraula. At Opheyra and other halting places we had some rattling gallops with the long dogs.

A great pilgrimage was in progress as we passed through Garmukhtesar and a thousand little huts of grass had sprung up on the banks of the Ganges and at least a thousand Brahmins had assembled to offer sacrifice and prayer to the sacred river. All through the dusty day, the slow procession of bullock carts carried fresh reinforcements to the hundred thousand worshippers of Gunga-mai,* mother of all Hindus. It was a strange and

---
* The river Ganges.

impressive sight, this caterpillar of devotees that crept by, half-scoffed at and half-unheeded by us, who followed the way of service by a directly opposite, though (who shall deny it?) just as straight a road. However that may be, the road led to Ghaziabad, and our guns had to be put by, and our long dogs sent back to Bareilly. From the blessings of Peace, in the calm of moving camps; and Plenty, in the shape of a free breakfast table of game, we plunged into the sternness of a Concentration and the hustle of a War which may have been "mimic" to the general public but was quite a serious matter for some of the mimes.

We began on the twenty-first of November, and did "flag-enemy" to the brigade during several fielddays, during one of which His Excellency the Commander-in-Chief was present and watched the work of the regiment. A few days later, 'B' Squadron was detached to Loni and 'C' Squadron to Shahdara to form the cavalry of two other brigades. On the sixth of December the Inter-Divisional Manœuvres proper began, and we did a long march across country to Bagpat. War broke out on Monday, the ninth, and we were up in the freezing hours before dawn stumbling into kunker pits and searching for our men in the darkness and dust. At the very second that hostilities were timed to start, 'C' Squadron began to gallop for a tactical position on the river forming "Eastland's" boundary. The remainder of the regiment followed at a few minutes' interval, and although surprisingly good order was kept, to many men in rear ranks of a troop or squadron that hell-for-leather helter-skelter for the crossings of the Jumna must have seemed a nightmare of fallen blankets and flying hoofs. We accomplished our object, however, which is the main thing in war, and reached the far side of the ford and had intrenched ourselves and our maxim guns before the enemy arrived.

To go in detail into all the operations which followed is a task beyond me; to tell the truth as the situation developed so my memory dissolved, and I have no clear recollection of any but the opening phases. One thing however I am sure that many young soldiers can sincerely say, and that is that manœuvres on field service scale are infinitely preferable to the ordinary picnic.

On the final day, Henderson's squadron was detailed as escort to Major-General Pilcher, C.B., commanding our side. They had a really hard day's galloping cross country to keep up with the dashing leader of our army, and earned a warm recommendation from him. We have tried to avoid smug self-

THE RECRUITS AT BAREILLY, 1911.

Tikka Khan.   Dodd.
(Woordie-Major)   (Adjutant).

satisfaction in these pages, but we cannot refrain from mentioning that two of our patrol leaders were sent for to be thanked by Headquarters. There is no harder work than that of a patrol, and no work in which the qualities of a cavalryman are more essential.

We returned to Ghaziabad on the fourteenth of December and marched back as quickly as we were allowed to go, reaching Bareilly on Christmas day.

Bareilly presented various cold weather attractions. The annual week provided for us three days' good racing on a scale never hitherto attempted here.

On the third of February Lieutenant-General Sir James Willocks came to Bareilly to present colours to the Leicester Regiment and to give the Order of British India to two Indian Officers, one of whom was Risaldar-Major Ghulam Mohuy-ud-din Khan, to whom we offered our most cordial congratulations not only on receiving this well merited distinction, but also on the very cordial manner in which Sir James referred to his services.

An inspection by the G. O. C. of the Meerut Cavalry Brigade, Brigade Field Firing, and " Q " Examinations kept us all busy until March, when practically everyone, under the rank of field officer, suddenly vanished for ten days' leave, leaving the Colonel and Hender to run the regiment.

Some of us indeed had already vanished: Steel had gone to Delhi for some special staff work prior to his departure Home; Dodd had left us—(though he has not gone far we are glad to say)—to take up his new duties as Station Staff Officer at Meerut; Kenneth Barge had gone to Dehra Dun as Adjutant of the Imperial Cadet Corps, Kirkwood was on his way home, and Brierley had been engaged in killing gigantic rhinoceroses, buffaloes and lions in Somaliland throughout the cold weather. Only nine of us remained, and of these nine Duberley, Atkinson, Foottit and Guthrie went down to Delhi to win the Radha Mohan Cup for the second time—a most remarkably good performance, considering that the team had hardly played together at all and were not well mounted. Three of us (Stewart, Skipwith and Yeats-Brown) went to Muttra to take part in the Muttra Pigsticking Cup, a thoroughly sporting event where hard riding was at a premium and 'first spears' at a discount. We were very hospitably entertained by the Inniskilling Dragoons.

All things have an end, and in 1913 we began to realise that our days at Bareilly were drawing to a close

We give a full extract from the *Star and Crescent* of December 1913.

"Solomon's temple we are told in the Book of Kings, rose without sound of hammer or axe, but except for this notable instance it is doubtful if any enterprise has ever been undertaken in the East without infinite fuss and noise. Certain it is that the move of the regiment to Allahabad will be attended by various minor anxieties. Already the hammer's voice is heard in the mess compound, and soon, when the days of our move to Allahabad are still nearer, we shall be left forlornly among our packing cases, to seek our dinner where we may. All this is inevitable, of course, and Kenneth Barge, who is to command the advance party at Allahabad, will certainly make everything comfortable for us there. But meanwhile the fever of departure is in the air. Before it has really gripped us, let us consider reflectively the summer that has passed, and record in these imperishable pages our life in cantonments and in camps since June. Amongst the officers of the Regiment many a change has taken place.

Brigadier-General Burton, C.B., retired from the command of the Meerut Cavalry Brigade on May the 31st, 1913, and is now enjoying a well-earned rest after many years of service to India and his country. We cannot here allude to his work in Persia or on the Staff, but as a regimental officer his name will live with that of the regiment. Many men less gifted than he, have risen to the highest ranks of their profession, but no man can wish for a finer record than his. To have helped to raise a corps of six hundred men, to have commanded those men in the prime of life, and to have retired with the esteem and the affection of every man, both high and low, who served under his command, is no small matter. Than this, in time of peace at any rate, no better life could be hoped for or desired.

Lieutenant-Colonel Wall has left us also, having taken over command of the 3rd Skinner's Horse on September 1st, 1913. We cannot write as we would wish of an officer still in service, but now that Colonel Wall has left us, we may be permitted to say that, however sorry we are ourselves, we heartily congratulate the 3rd. Rumour (may be idle) asserts that the C. O. of the 3rd has since Mutiny days had a gold mace carried behind him on ceremonial parades : whether true or not, this at any rate is certain, that the present C. O. will carry with him—every where and always—a heart of gold.

Other appointments include that of Lieutenant-Colonel Wikeley (who we hope soon to see with us again) as 2nd-in-Command of the regiment, and of Major R. A. Steel as Military

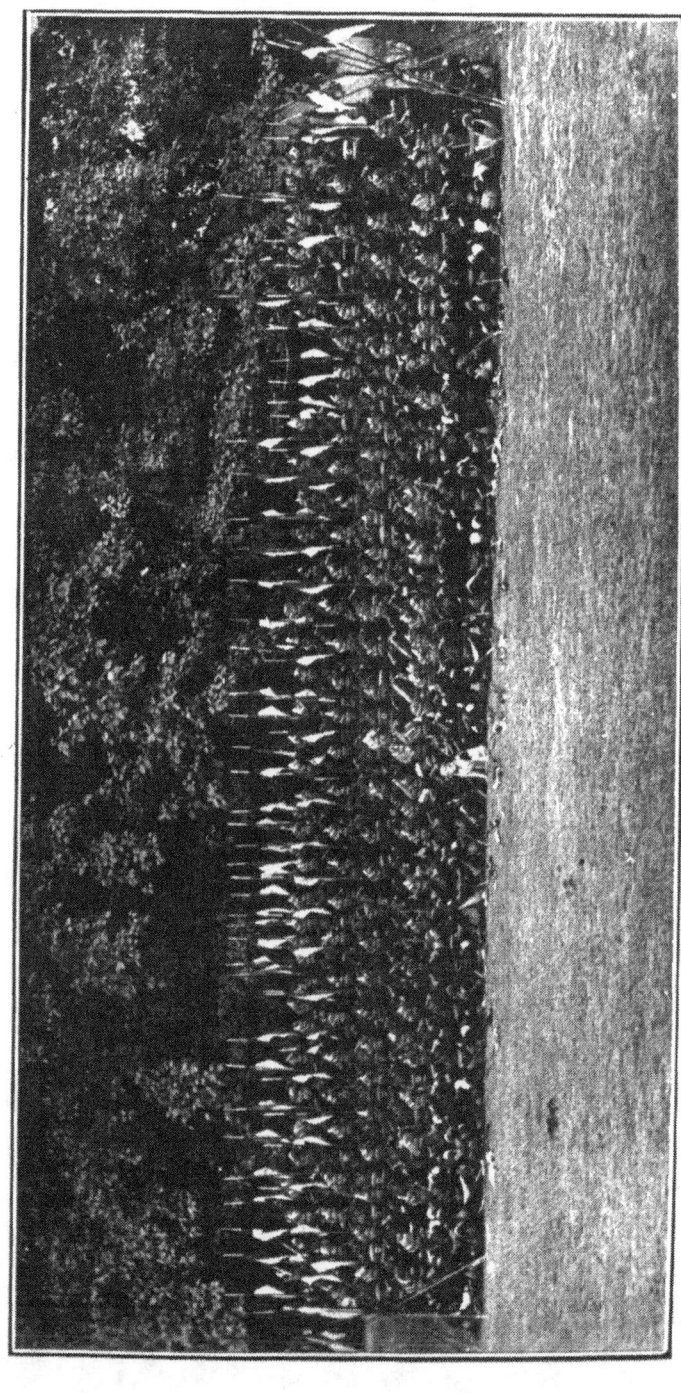

"C" SQUADRON AT BAREILLY, 1910.

Stewart. Ghaur Ali Khan.
Ghulam Mohi-ud-din, Sultan Khan.
K. D. Sarwar Khan.   K. D. Diam Khan.
Salutri Rahuuan Beg,
Trumpet-Major Sher Wali Khan.
"Brimstone."

Attaché at Teheran, a responsible position nowadays in the Near East, and a post where his talents should find their full scope. Major R. W. Henderson has taken the road to Dacca, and appears to be enjoying his march thoroughly. Thousands of natives flock into the camp daily to admire his horsemen, and no doubt the memory of " C " Squadron will live long in the minds of the Bengalis . . . " A " Squadron under Major R. C. Barry-Smith has preceded us to Allahabad, to take part in a training camp at Barkatcha, so a very exiguous regiment is left behind. Captain K. Barge is back with us for a short time, but only for a short time unfortunately, as he returns in March to Dehra Dun, where he teaches the young idea of India's nobility 'how to shoot' and how to ride and play polo and behave themselves generally. A more charming existence could not be imagined, nor a more able exponent of that existence than Kenneth . . .

Atkinson is at present attending the Cavalry School at Saugor, as also are Jemadar Daim Khan and Dafadar Arbab Mahomed Husain: from all accounts the world seems treating them very kindly.

I do not think that there are any other incidents that call for especial note! We have most of us brought several ponies and some of us have sold two or three, but this is nothing new. More up-to-date is Stewart, who has brought an immense Motor Car with one cylinder. She has an iron constitution and actually attempted to take six of us, to say nothing of the cartridges and the sodas, to a *jheel* some thirty miles away. Unfortunately the clutch slipped under the strain; and we had to discuss our lunch by the roadside instead of by the *jheel*, while Stewart and a good samaritan and motor cyclist discussed " Miss Cadillac's " chassis. Beyond this our shooting excursions have been few, although I heard last night that Brierly had returned from a Saturday to Monday trip with a few teal, and also a writ for assault served on him in consequence of alleged intimidation of an engine driver who is supposed to have started a train without ascertaining that all was right behind. Knowing the Rohilkund and Kumaon Railway, however, I can hardly believe the engine-driver can have been so precipitate.

Although we have done little shooting, we have had a fair season's pigsticking—not so good perhaps as that of 1912, and certainly not so full of thrills and excitements, yet good enough to live as a treasured memory against the days when we shall be far from the great spaces of the Ganges basin. May those days be distant! May it be long before we pigstick in recollection only . . . and yet, when that time comes, and memory recalls the slain boar and dead horses and friends of the past, how vividly will they come to life again!

If we are lucky, we shall find good sports and good friends again, but we have said good-bye to Bareilly pigsticking and to the friends of three seasons' hunting.

To turn to polo should provide several paragraphs for these notes, but I prefer not to be a prophet (and a Jeremiah at that in my own country, and will therefore await the result of our endeavours in the I. P. A. Championship at Calcutta.

Suffice it to say then, that we are all very keen, and that if our ponies are not very well schooled, they are at any rate very well fed......We entered for various tournaments in Naini Tal during the hot weather and for the Meerut Autumn Tournament on November 7th, but did not succeed in getting through the first round in any, so our endeavours since the Radha Mohan Cup call for no special comment. One noticeable feature of the September week at Naini was the narrow escape from drowning of which Duberly was the subject. His boat upset, he tried to swim ashore, got caught in the weeds, and was only rescued at the last, or at any rate at the penultimate, gasp. However, all's well .....

Paper-Chasing was rather a neglected sport at Bareilly until the Worcestershire Regiment very sportingly got up a meet towards the end of November at the Sandhills at the back of the Sadar Bazar. An excellent afternoon's racing was provided over a good pigsticking country consisting chiefly of nullahs. Wilson on "Seacroft" won one of the events, with Cochrane on "Mohawk" second, and Skipwith on "St. George" third. In the pony race the regiment was well placed again, Skipwith winning on Cochrane's "Geordie" and Cochrane getting second on his own "Dorothy." The Indian Officers' race fell to Risaldar Rukn-ud-din Khan on his gallant little charger.

Encouraged by the success of this meeting, Barge organised another point-to-point at the same place on Saturday, December 6th. The first race was for horses, the property of N.-C. O's and men of the 17th Cavalry and a field of ten turned out, all determined to do or die. From the pace at the start it seemed as if some of the runners would achieve the latter alternative, but fortunately there were no serious mishaps. Six finished in the following order :—

A. L. D. Fateh Khan, R. D.	.. ..	Half Squadron.
Trumpeter Zaman Khan, R. D.	... ..	Half Squadron.
A. L. D. Mohamed Akram, L. D.	.. ..	Half Squadron.
A. L. D. Mohamed Nawaz, R. D.	.. ..	Half Squadron.
Sowar Alam Khan, L. D.	.. ..	Half Squadron.
L. D. Zaidullah, B. B.	.. ..	Half Squadron.

GROUP AT BAREILLY, 1912.

Duberly. Guthrie. Sultan Khan. Rukan Din. Kirkwood. Steel. Dodd. Dost Mohamed
Rahmat Sher. Usman Khan. Ghulam Mohy-ud-din. Zikryia Khan. Khan.
 Barge. Bahadur Sher. Mustapha Khan. Boudier. Ghaur Ali Khan. Henderson.
 Stewart. Alam Sher Khan. Skipwith. Tikka Khan. Ata Mohamed Shah. Wall. Sajid Gul.

The first and third horses had both been hired out as pig-stickers last season.

The next race was for ponies: catchweghts, 11st. 7lbs., and was won by Cochrane's "Geordie" (ridden by Skipwith) with Captain Hogan's "Bart" (Bush) second, and Cochrane's "Dorothy" (Owner) third. The third race was for horses: catch-weights, 12st. and was won by Stewart's "Kim" with Captain Ludgate's "Hobson's Choice" second, and Barge's "Hegara" (Owner) third. "Hobson's Choice" was recently sold from the regiment because though a good horse he was impossible in the ranks. He was cleverly ridden by Risaldar Rukn-ud-din. The next race was for ladies and produced three runners who were placed in the following order:—

    Miss Dyer's "Magpie."
    Mrs. Boudier's "Hall Mark."
    Mrs. Kirby's "Surrender."

This was a most sporting event, as the owners all rode their own horses. "Surrender" was first past the post, but was disqualified, having had the misfortune to miss a flag. The last item was for Indian Officers and was again won by Risaldar Rukn-ud-din, this finishing a most enjoyable afternoon.

Soldiering is a difficult subject on which to enlarge, but a few words may not be *mal apropos*...In May we competed for the Empire Day Cup, and although we were not successful, a great enthusiasm for musketry prevailed throughout the hot weather, with the result that there are now hardly any third class shots in the regiment. In June there was the usual practice in swimming horses and night marches combined with a tactical scheme. During one of these operations the resourceful leader of "D" Squadron is supposed to have lost his way, whereupon he climbed a small hill and rallied his troops by trumpet call, just as they were preparing for a silent dawn attack! Beyond such little incidents, our daily rounds and common tasks occurred smoothly and in their appointed time during red-hot May and white-hot June, and suffered but little interruption during the aluvial months of August and September. Lately we have taken part in several brigade field days, and have also been out into bivouac for a night for a Brigade Signalling Test (wherein the Regiment was reported as "very satisfactory")—but, on the whole, our lot has been an easy one.

"B" and "C" Squadrons went into Training Camp at Harunagla on October 17th, and moved thence to Fatehgunj for the inspection of the Regiment by Major-General Edwards, C.B., which took place on October 31st and November 1st. After this "B" and "C" Squadrons returned to Bareilly and "A" and "B" went out to Fatehgunj. "A" Squadron, however, was soon ordered to the manœuvres at Allahabad, and "C" Squadron had to start for Dacca, leaving a rather clipped wing of the Regiment at head-quarters.

A Postscript is necessary owing to the lateness of publication.

Twice has the move of the Regiment been delayed by an inexplicable case of plague, but now we will undoubtedly start for Allahabad on January 3rd, 1914.

Before these pages are passed in proof, we hope to be able to congratulate Mrs. Boudier on having surmounted a very bad attack of enteric fever. For a few days we were very anxious, but now we hear that the dangerous symptoms have happily passed, and the whole Regiment will wish her a speedy convalescence.

The team representing the regiment in the Indian Polo Association Championship was composed of Atkinson, Barge, Skipwith, and Yeats-Brown, Brierly having been of necessity omitted as he had been detailed to accompany Prince Yusuf Pasha of Egypt on a four months' shooting tour in India.

Our first game was against the 12th Cavalry, whom we defeated by eleven goals to four. We then met the Viceroy's Staff and after a good and (for the first six chukkers at any rate) a closely contested game, we were defeated by nine goals to four. During this game Joey received a blow on the side of the face which affected his appearance, though certainly not his brilliant play, for some time after. Poor "Kipper" met his death in the same game; his pastern being broken by a hard backhander. The Viceroy's Staff eventually won the Championship easily.

In the Ezra Cup we first beat the Calcutta team, to whom we gave four goals, by five to four. The final goal was scored by Skipwith just as time was called. We then met the Travellers, and beat them by four to three after a hard game. The Travellers were giving us three goals and at one time it seemed they must win, but Joey played magnificently and kept out their determined attacks. In the finals we were defeated by the 12th Cavalry, whom we had beaten by eleven goals to four in the Championship Tournament. In this game we missed several easy shots in the first two chukkers, and although we hit the ball across their back line twenty times at least, we rarely succeeded in sending it through the goals, so that we lost by five goals to three, after a thoroughly good and enjoyable game."

Men of the 17th Cavalry jumping, Bareilly Horse Show.

Yeats-Brown on Tot jumping in the Bareilly Horse Show.

"Point-to-point" at Bareilly.

* * * * * *

Here also is Kennath Barge's description of Allahabad, taken from the same issue of the *Star and Crescent* (December 1913).

" Before leaving Bareilly the other day as our regimental advance agent, (!) our editor told me that I must send in my long promised article at once. One gets tired of writing personal experiences, and I am quite sure the subscribers do not want to read mine. As I sit at a little table in an enormous ante-room totally unfurnished only lit by a ha'penny dip, I don't think I can do better than tell you about Allahabad as far as the regiment is concerned, and how I think we shall like it.

Before I go on, this article is not intended for those with the regiment to read, as they follow on here within a week, and can form all their own opinions about the place. But it is written for those who have left the regiment. We have never been so far south as this before and I don't expect many of them have been stationed here. Then again it may be of interest to seconded officers. And there are the fond parents and relations (by-the-bye, I hope they all subscribe to the *Star and Crescent*) of those who are destined to simmer through many hot weathers in a station which registers just about the highest temperatures of any place in British East India! And lastly there might be those who are not relations—but there is no one at present who looks like being engaged, so perhaps no one comes under this category! I have just shouted "Qui Hai" and it has brought me back to where I am. I feel something like a dwarf inside the caves of Elephanta, the sound of my voice was echoed through all the walls of the mess. The 12th Cavalry who we are relieving have taken all their furniture away. And ours has not yet arrived from Bareilly.

Any one who gets a Indian bungalow owner to do what is wanted in the way of repairs at once, is worthy of a gold medal. The day I arrived the bungalow owner and his brother came and greeted me with profuse *salaams*. I took them round and showed them exactly what I wanted in the way of plastering, colourwashing, painting, etc. They told me what I wanted was nothing, and that the next morning an enormous staff of artisans belonging to each of the required trades would appear, and all the rooms would be finished within three days. The next day from their description, I expected to see the bungalow like a human ant-hill, but not a sound issued from any of the lofty rooms. Feeling full of wrath and wondering what I would do to the owner when I got a hold of him, I suddenly was faced by him and his brother, both smiling and *salaaming* still more profusely They had only come to know if I had not perhaps changed my mind about the colours required! After shouting out a "No" that rang through the bungalow they waddled (for they are very fat) off as fast as they could to call forward this enormous staff of workmen.

Needless to say no one came. That afternoon they sent a letter to say, when we had been making all these arrangements none of us had counted on the "Mohurrum" which was the next day—and of course no one worked on this day, not even the Hindus. But they promised that they would swell the ranks of their artificers on the following day, so that the whole building would be finished in two days. Well I could do nothing but wait. On the morning after the Mohurrum I went eagerly into the mess expecting to hear the swish, swish, of hundreds of brushes on all the walls—again I found empty rooms. But no on making a thorough search of the bungalow, squatting behind a pillar on his hunkers was a very old man smoking a hookha and coughing as if he was going to break to bits. Alongside him was a *gumlah* full of colour-wash (the wrong colour). On asking him where the rest of the men were he said he expected his brother and could do nothing without him. In the meantime after he had unwrapt an enormous *chudder* and coughed and croaked as if he only had a few more days to live, I got him to mix the right colour. This fatigued him very much and he had to rest again as his brother had not arrived. I expected to see a real spritely man who would put a little ginger into the show, when all at once I espied coming up the avenue a still more decrepid and much older man than the one alongside me. "Ah!" he said, "my brother comes at last, now the work will go on space!" The new arrival told me that this was the day after the Mohurrum, and that no one in Allahabad worked on that day; but these two noble brothers knowing the urgency of the work had sacrificed themselves and were going to do wonders. Well they jabbered to each other like monkeys explaining to each other what had to be done, and eventually after much struggling they got a ladder into the room. One of them ventured up the ladder very slowly, while the other held it at the bottom and shouted directions. The net result of the day's work I should say was about fifteen square feet. I have written round a snorter to the owner. I suppose he will say that this enormous staff will be trebled and that the work will be finished in one day. When the Mess does get finished it will be very comfortable and I am sure all will like it, we also have three good quarters in the Mess building.

SNAPSHOTS AT BAREILLY.

Stewart.
"D" Squadron at Stables in Camp.
Jemadar Khan. Dost Mohamed Khan.
Risaldar Malik Dost Mohamed Khan.
Kote-Dufadar Fasal Shah.

The Regimental Syces making hay at Bareilly.

The lines are well shaded. The stables, though a good pattern, seem rather dilapidated. The men's houses are much bigger than one usually finds in Indian cavalry lines. Our bungalows, the Mess and the lines are all close together and we have quite a good little one and a half mile race-course opposite the lines, which makes an excellent exercising track for our polo ponies. Never in India have I seen such a spread out station as Allahabad. Why, the polo grounds are four miles from here. But I must say when you do get to them you are rewarded for they seem to me excellent. Well no, perhaps I am too sanguine, one certainly is excellent, it is soft, can always be watered and kept green. The other one looks to have a good surface but is rather too hard and dry. But I must say it will be a very long trek down to polo in the hot weather afternoons. Motor cars or motor bicycles are practically essential nowadays in Allahabad. From one side of the station to the other is over seven miles.

Talking about the hot weather, they tell me the *punkha* is kept swinging for eight months in the year in Allahabad. That is a little more than we have been used to. But we should not grouse, for we must remember we had a very good station in Bareilly and cannot hope to get a good station like that every time. One of the great points in Allahabad is that we get our *Pioneer* the day before it comes out!

I dined in the Club the second night I arrived here, and found it most comfortable. They gave me a really good and well served dinner. And it may interest the gourmands to know that during the cold weather they get Karachi oysters twice a week!

I was much struck with the buildings in Allahabad. The High Court, and some of the schools and the new University are very fine buildings indeed. The judges in Allahabad are always renowned for being great sportsmen, they generally have one or two who play polo.

This year we are going in for the Championship Polo Tournament at Calcutta. I think that we should certainly continue "playing" in it while we are here, as it is a very inexpensive tournament to go in for, as the Calcutta Turf Club give us five hundred rupees towards expenses if we enter. The Maharaja of Panna is going to start polo in his State which is only about a night's journey distant. We must encourage him to bring a team to Allahabad, and I know he would also like us to take a team to Panna some time.

The ground for cavalry round here is abominable and our parade ground is much too small, though quite good to knock the ball about on ! It is nice to have an old friend of the regiment—General Cowper—here, and I feel quite sure he will find some good ground for us to manœuvre on.

It is a pity that we have one squadron detached at Calcutta, as for both work and polo it is a great disadvantage.

Taking it all round and from what the 12th Cavalry say Allahabad is quite a good station. They have enjoyed their time here very much and I am sure we will too—I quite forgot I won't be here. (D.V.) I shall be away in February for four years."

* * * * * *

Let us follow the fortunes of the regiment at Allahabad during the hot weather of 1914 as recorded the pages of the *Star and Crescent*. No more recent account could give the story of how the War broke, on us so simply, and so dramatically as the acting Editor (H. S. S.) writing in September and again December 1914. Unconsciously perhaps, he draws the contrast between the rains in India and in the thunder-cloud that was breaking over Europe.

" Way back in the distant days of Bareilly at the time when the idea of a magazine originated, its creator was by way of being a philosopher as well as a scribe. His philosophy always started with the assumption that he had a good dinner, after which feeling at peace with all mankind he would meditate on the great world in general, which we only hear about, and the little world in particular in which we live. Hence he called his communications, to the readers of the *Star and Crescent*, " After-dinner Thoughts."

The Editor has now become an Adjutant and even he has ceased to consider the period after dinner as suitable for writing articles. In fact he is now at least a follower if not altogether a believer in the old motto " Early to bed, early to rise." Hence the time now seems auspicious to change the title of these notes, which up to date have caused each acting Editor in turn to protest that his brain was not suited to after-dinner thinking.

In this number this article has been called what it really is : The Editor's Note-book. It may seem somewhat unnecessary to so labour the point of a change in name, yet the strength of a magazine such as ours lies in preserving traditions and any changes, even minor ones, should be made with hesitation, and explanation.

SNAPSHOTS ON THE MARCH AND IN CAMP.

Group at the Cavalry Camp at Gurgaon.

BREAKFAST ON THE MARCH.

Stewart.   Yeats-Brown.   Foottit.
   Guthrie.   Barnet (I.M.S.).

We were all sad at leaving Bareilly and at one time it seemed as if we might stop there another year, but that was not to be, and finally, after many delays, on January 3rd the last party of the regiment left for Allahabad by troop train. In India with its continually moving official population our recollections of old stations remain more connected with persons than with localities. In India we are like the Bedouins: wherever we pitch our tent is our home. Judged by this standard Bareilly is now a strange land, for we were the last to leave the Garrison which marched in, in 1909.

Life in Allahabad is marred by the keeping of a detachment in Calcutta. Having three British officers there makes the Mess small in numbers and in the hot weather leave is difficult to get. It will be rather a nuisance if this has to go on for several more years, but who can say what the future has in store. Allahabad is essentially a place of long distances: the polo ground is over four miles from the Mess, and the other local centres are proportionately distant. The discomforts of having long distances to travel does not tend to alleviate life in the hot weather.

This has been more trying than usual in the way of heat, and to make it worse the Mess has been so dull that for the first time for many years it has not been possible to even raise a rubber of bridge after dinner. Now we are well into the rains. And good rains they have been up to date. Let us hope that they will continue and that grass will again become plentiful and grain cheap.

We congratulate Colonel Wall on the luck which he brought to his new regiment, as evidenced by their victories in the fields of sport. May his term of command of the Skinner's Horse continue to be auspicious.

Colonel Wikely is back in our midst again, but we feel he must soon get a command outside. His gain will be our loss.

Brierley has been doing great things with the Prince of Egypt. Now he is back in East Africa looking after his coffee plantation. The Mess will be glad to see him back again.

"Joey" is now a prominent member of the European Polo world. We expect great things of him when he comes back.

Shakespear has been making a name for himself these days. The *Englishman* says:—

"The young officer whose name is best known in connection with the exploration in Central Arabia is Captain Leachman; his exploits, however, have been thrown into the shade by Captain

Shakespear, Political Agent at Koweit, who left Koweit last February and has now appeared at Port Said, thus crossing North Arabia from east to west. His story, of course, will be looked forward to with the greatest interest." Perhaps he will consent to tell some of his adventures in his paper.*

Rissaldar-Major Ghulam Mohi-uddin has retired on pension after completing thirty-two years' service.

Polo has been going on all through the summer and the number and class of the chukkers compares very favourably with what we used to get in Bareilly. A team of Barry-Smith, Duberly, Foottit and Cochrane went down to Jubbulpore at the end of March. They did not have much luck in the tournament, but Cochrane's pony Sparrow Hawk won him a very good race and he at least came back with more money than he went with.

Pigsticking in Allahabad has not as yet been patronised by any of the regiment except Cochrane. From what the Editor hears, a radical change in the food and in the management generally is required before there will be much fun in going out. At present the expenses daily average about twenty rupees and the food provided is absolutely uneatable. Another year we must all start pigsticking again.

Racing is not in a flourishing way in Allahabad at present. The only thing we can say about is that the course is being slowly got ready for the spring meeting, and that " the occasional dull sound of wood on flesh " merely marks a stage in the education of the staff.

As we go to Press, the news is to hand that we have declared war on Germany, and that now all the world is at each other's throats. Papers and periodicals now make it a rule to depict war as an awful thing and to pray for its aversion. Let us, however, be honest. This paper is the organ of a corps anxious to dip their swords in the blood of their enemies. To us the news of war is good, not ill.

A final paragraph is necessary. Our orders for the great war have come: our lances are sharp and our hearts are light. For short time again the sword becomes mightier than the pen: so the Editor like others must now lay down the latter and draw the former.

*.   *   *   *   *

---

* Alas, like Leachman a few years later he was cut off in his prime. A biographical note appears on page. . ,

However after all the regiment got no forther than Bombay. Let us again quote from the "Star and Crescent" written in December 1914.

"The nations in their harness" had met in Europe, but we as a regiment were doomed by Fate to see no active service. The following account will re-tell the tragedy that befell us.

The wisdom of the gods was great when they denied to mortals knowledge of the future: for man born of woman could not continue the struggle for existence with hope crushed, knowing that no effort could combat revealed fate. Hope springs from the uncertainty of life and the effort to succeed is the result of hope.

Way back in those hot days in the middle of July when the proofs of our last number were fresh from the press, the inhabitants of the world were living in blissful ignorance that they were on the verge of a greater war than any that has been recorded on the pages of history; of a war that would affect the fortunes and destinies of those as far removed from it and each other as the negro warriors of Africa and the plutocrats of America. And we of the 17th Cavalry in common with the rest were engaged in our own little plans, immersed in our own little doings, thoughtless of the affairs of nations, busy with the trifles of the moment like the ants when the spade of the digger is about to commence the destruction of their homes. Little thought had we of the misfortunes and humiliations that the regiment was to pass through.

In June we had heard with sorrow of the murder of the heir to the Austrian throne, yet peace seemed so firmly established on the earth that the vocation of the soldier seemed to belong to a barbarian age that was fast passing away. Then like a bolt from the blue came the Austrian ultimatum: what followed is a matter of history.

In India the nature of the struggle for world-empire did not for the moment penetrate the public mind. The possibility of its soldiers taking part in the struggle seemed remote. In all regiments the officers and men except those required to carry the hot weather duties were away on leave. Our officers were distributed over half the globe—from East Africa to Moscow, from Naini Tal to Ostend. The first warning of military activity was an order on July 31st stopping leave for the Indian ranks altogether and directing that British officers were not to be allowed to proceed beyond twenty-four hours' recall. Then nothing more happened till August 8th when all officers on leave in India were ordered to rejoin their regiments.

Hot weather life in Allahabad is at ordinary times very dull. In war time of course anywhere in India seems to be buried in the desert, but in Allahabad the war news as received is—(thanks to the courtesy of the " Pioneer ")—posted up on the Club noticeboard, so there is always something to talk about. Even when news is scarce, rumours are plentiful. We all knew that certain divisions were mobilising, but no one knew their destinations—these were secret. Great discussions took place in the bar. A few maintained that the troops were for Europe, but the majority derided these views and asserted that Egypt was the destination. Heated arguments by amateur strategists continually took place. The general opinions were: that the Germans would be either bankrupt or starved out in a few months, that the Germans would never get past the Belgium fortresses of Liege and Namur, that the French would wipe out the Germans before the British arrived and so on. Those holding contrary opinions were derided. And so the month of August passed away.

The night of Sunday, August 30th, was indeed an eventful one for the 17th Cavalry. Little thought had any one as he went to bed what sort of news would shortly wake him up. A little after midnight came a "clear-the-line" message : "The 17th Cavalry will call up all reservists, recall leave and furlough men for service with the Indian Expeditionary Force ' A.' Division will send detailed orders mobilisation."

Only several evenings before had come a report from Calcutta saying that surra had broken out in the squadron there; it seemed like the tortures of Tantalus. How could a regiment with surra go on service? We all saw visions of the China bad-luck being repeated, and although preparations went forward nobody's heart was really in them. Yet for the moment all appeared to be well, or at least as well as could be expected, for down came a second telegram—"Calcutta squadron 17th Cavalry will not accompany regiment on service. 27th Light Cavalry will supply instead a squadron of Punjabi Mohamedans." This was of course bad luck on "C" Squadron, but we thought, perhaps, they may get a chance later and anyhow the regiment is getting off.

Much had to be done and few were present to do it, but telegrams kept rolling in bringing news of the absent. The first news was a cheery wire from "Kirk" in London telling us to expect him. This surprised us indeed ; we had not imagined that he would be able to get out of Russia. On the 4th we heard from Kenneth Barge saying that he was resigning from the Imperial Cadet Corps. Then came official news that Y. B., Joey, Skipwith and Kirk would rejoin at the base and that the others would rejoin in India.

Preparations went on apace, Stewart was made the regimental purchasing agent and he made constant journeys to and from Cawnpore: drab serge uniform for the regiment was arranged for, great consignments of articles of every sort were ordered, mobilisation equipment was taken over from the 16th Cavalry, the field kits of absent officers were ransacked out of boxes and packed up for them, examinations of men and horses for disease were made, and so on. Finally the last of the reservists and leave men turned up and on September the 20th we were able to wire "mobilisation completed."

Then began a weary wait, which was suddenly terminated on the afternoon of Saturday October 3rd, when telegraphic orders for the entrainment of the regiment on Tuesday morning were received. What a rush there was on Monday to settle things left to the last minute by individual officers; but everything was got through and on Tuesday morning we steamed out of the Allahabad Station. A three-day journey in a troop train is no joke, and every one was glad to see Bombay and the ships in the harbour as the trains pulled into the docks on the evening of the 8th. It seemed like a fairy tale come true to be taking regiment to Europe: disallusionment was yet to come.

The original arrangement had been to embark on the morning of the 9th, but we now learned that we would go aboard on the 10th and that the date of sailing of the convoy had been postponed. This was welcome news, the idea of a day's holiday was appreciated by all. The regiment went into camp on the Marine Parade, but there was no arrangements there for officers, so we had to crowd in hotels as best we could. Then came the morning of the 9th of October: we will never forget that morning as long as we live. The journey in the train had brought out three cases of latent glanders. Where we caught this disease will always remain an unsolved mystery. Yet there stood the horses!

The brigade "Vet" was sent for, and he brought the S. V. O. of the division. Then there was a great discussion and the S. V. O. said that this would not stop us, but that he would "mallien" the regiment and that we would have to leave any re-actors behind. Then our troubles began, the suspense was awful. The horses were all picketed in the blazing sun and they all had high temperatures as a consequence. A more unsuitable spot for malliening could not have been chosen, but there was nowhere else to go. We waited patiently all Friday and Saturday but there was no "mallien" in Bombay. Suddenly on Saturday night without warning anybody or taking temperatures properly the Vets began the malliening. How we watched those miserable horses next day hoping against hope, that none of them would show re-actions, but all was in vain—the head Vet suddenly changed his mind and reported that the regiment must be tested a second time before it was fit to go abroad. Telegraphic orders were hurriedly sent and the 29th Lancers who had been mobilised to go as Divisional Cavalry of the Poona Division were put into the Lucknow Cavalry Brigade to go in our place.

Life in Bombay is, I am sure, rather dull at the best of times. For one thing the climate can only be classed as abominable; however living there on a field service kit is what the Yankees call "the limit." We are glad, however, to be able to acknowledge the kindness with which we in common with all officers proceeding to the front have been treated by the members of the Bombay Clubs. The privilege of using these Clubs did much to aleviate discomforts. We also desire to place on record our thanks to the Directors of the Taj Mahal Hotel for their princely generosity in entertaining officers in their hotel free of charge.

The regiment continued to remain in camp on the Marine Parade until October 26th. No official orders of any sort as to our ultimate destination were received, but at first we heard that we were to go with the Poona Division and then a fellow fresh from Simla brought news that we were going in a brigade with the Inniskillings and the Central India Horse in a new cavalry division. On October 26th, all arrangements having been completed, we marched out to Worli Camp. Here the Sappers had erected tin-roofed stables and here the second malliening was to take place. Life in Bombay we had thought dull, but life in Worli Camp was unutterably worse. The sooner it is forgotten the better. Yet hope still held us up. Everybody kept assuring us that we were going. On November 3rd, in response to an urgent telegram from the Q.-M. G, the Vets started their malliening again and all seemed going well when suddenly another series of bombs fell upon us. A young man from the 33rd Cavalry went off with our mobilisation kit. Brierley was ordered to join the 33rd Light Cavalry and our reserve Indian Officer was ordered to rejoin his regiment. Great consternation and visits to the Embarkation Office followed and to our horror and disgust we found out that 2nd Lancers were replacing us in the Second Cavalry Division—the orders had just arrived.

Kenneth and 'Bareilly' took the night train for Delhi, but it was then too late……At last we were up against facts and we found we were out of everything. All the consolation we could get was "remain ready at the port of embarkation." Great efforts again were made. Twelve walers and twelve arabs were bought in Bombay, twenty horses were wired for to the farm and eight were demanded from the depot. Alas all to no purpose for the Final Disallusionment was at hand. One day we heard quite casually that we were to go back to Allahabad. Apparently the order had been in the Divisional Office for some time, but they did not see any point in letting us know. Time dragged wearily on; our departure for one reason or another was delayed, but at last on December the 8th, the return journey began. The journey down was uncomfortable, but who minds that when you are off to the front: the journey back......well we shall try and forget it as quickly as possible.

And this is how the 17th Cavalry started for the great war and then returned.

Although it has been denied for the present that the regiment should as a regiment make for itself a reputation in war, yet while there is life there is hope. The struggle is with a people who are fighting for "world-power or downfall;" there will be room for us all before that downfall is assured. Already Steel, Wilson, Kirkwood, Yeats-Brown, Brierley, Atkinson, Skipwith and Guthrie are at the front, while Stewart, Jemadar Alam Sher and forty-eight men are on their way, and this is only the beginning.

* * * * *

In March 1916 the last number of our magazine was published, from this we make the following extract:—

It is just over a year since the last number of the Magazine was published and the Great War, which has changed the destinies of so many of our readers, has not left even the humble fortunes of the *Star and Crescent* unaffected.

It is felt necessary, to announce a modification in policy for at least the duration of the war. The Magazine will for the present become annual instead of trying as formerly to be a quarterly. The Editor reminds his readers that it is difficult in these days to get even enough articles for an annual and he appeals to them to send from the four corners of the earth some little accounts of their doings and what they have seen. An account of commonplace happenings which may seem very tedious and tiresome to the person concerned may be lively reading for his friends on the other side of the earth. And it is the duty of all when the hand of fate has scattered us over the globe to keep up our regimental *esprit de corps* and our regimental friendships. This can only be done by keeping each other informed of our doings and our fortunes. In the *Star and Crescent* we have the means for doing this. The officers of the regiment of to-day can give to this Magazine accounts of the war that will be read by us now with interest and re-read in the times to come with avidity by our successors when we have answered the great Roll-call in the world beyond.

When the Editor closed his Note-book last year the regiment was still in Bombay. The return to Allahabad is a subject which evokes no enthusiasm. Everybody, or rather those that were left, settled down into the old rut wondering if their luck would give them the chance of going to the war as a reinforcement.

Barge did not have long to wait, he with Ressaidar Rahmat Sher and fifty-four N.-C. O.'s and men left for Bombay on January 4th. Then on January 18th came a wire ordering us to send a squadron of Pathans to British East Africa. It was decided that the squadron should be a composite one of "A" and "B," and three days after the receipt of the wire Barry-Smith, Duberly and Mawdsley with Risaldar Usman Khan, Ressaidar Sajid Gul, Jemadar Wazir Khan and Jemadar Wazir Mohamed and a composite squadron of the right wing left for Bombay: they sailed from there on the 25th. And so there only remained Foottit and the Indian Army Reserve Officers in Allahabad.

I had omitted to mention about the I. A. R. previously, but we must here pay a tribute to them, for without their assistance it would have been impossible to carry on the work of the regiment at all after the departure of the squadron for East Africa.

The days in Allahabad grew longer and winter turned into spring and spring into summer. The Colonel had come back from Bombay, but his accident still prevented him from pursuing his usual activity. The regiment had had its establishment raised to seven hundred and fifty, also it had been drawn on for two lots of reinforcements. This resulted in such an increase in the number of recruits and remounts that the adjutant had work enough for ten men. It was the irony of fate that at such a time poor Foottit was left to battle alone. He could not even see any prospect of getting any leave. Then suddenly Yeats-Brown, Kirkwood and Stewart were sent back from France. The return of all three, however, was only temporary, for Kirkwood was immediately sent to Bombay, Yeats-Brown to Mesopotamia, while Stewart has gone to the Lucknow Divisional Staff. Cochrane who was nearly in despair of ever getting off to the war is now with the 12th Cavalry in Mesopotamia. Poor old regiment—the Colonel, Hender and Foottit are the only regular officers left with it. The I. A. R. officers have worked like Trojans, otherwise things would have been very difficult.

During the past year a radical change, but a good one, has been made in the system of training recruits and remounts. Each squadron now has its own staff of rough-riders and drill instructors and it is responsible for the instruction of its own men and animals. The idea has been a great success in every way and we have been able through it to utilise the services of all the officers and non-commissioned officers of the regiment for training purposes.

Polo, strange to say, goes on in Allahabad just as if it were peace time. We get our eight and nine chukkers regularly; and we were even able to get up a local American tournament with five teams. Of course it is not the same sort of polo that one got before the war in the cold weather, still it is good healthy exercise and provides a break in the somewhat monotonous existence in India in war time.

Marriage Bells have indeed been set jingling with a vengeance since the issue of our last number. Colonel Burton, Barge and Abercrombie (I. A. R.), have all entered into the happy state of matrimony. To one and all the Editor wishes to extend his congratulations and to wish to them all happiness and prosperity. Now on top of it all comes the news that "Joey" is going to marry Miss Cole. Prosperity and happiness to him also.

The Calcutta squadron after having been away two years has now been changed. 'C' Squadron has come to Allahabad for the first time. Its place in Calcutta has been taken by the Second Composite Squadron of the right wing which marched off at the beginning of the new year. 'C' Squadron was lucky and came here by rail.

'A' and 'B' Squadrons, as they were formed at the beginning of the war, are for the time being in abeyance, the right wing is for the present organised in two composite squadrons and a depôt squadron.

Guthrie, Wilson and Ressaidar Rahmat Sher have all been in the casualty lists as wounded and we congratulate them all that their wounds have been slight and that their recovery has been speedy.

Up to date the following men of the regiment have lost their lives in the war :—

    No. 61/1837 Reservist Abdul Rahim on shipboard on his way to join I. E. F. 'A.'

    No. 72/1886 Reservist Saidan Shah, I. E. F 'A.'

    No. 1974 Sowar Nazar Gul, L. B. Half Squadron, I. E. F. 'B.'

    No. 2255 Sowar Mian Gul, R. A. Half Squadron, I. E. F. 'B.'

    No. 2281 Sowar Pir Dost, R. A. Half Squadron, I. E. F. 'B.'

The Editor regrets very much to announce the death of Risaldar Major Mohamed Amin Khan, late of the regiment. The deceased Sirdar died suddenly at his home in Ludhiana. At the time of his death he was an Honorary Magistrate, Municipal Commissioner and Sub-Registrar. His nephew, Dufadar Mohamed Azam Khan, is at present on his way as a reinforcement to the Indian Cavalry Corps. He was of Afghan extraction, his father an Afghan Sirdar came to India with Shah Shujah.

Just as we are going to Press the sad news has been cabled from East Africa that Duberly is severely wounded and a prisoner and that Mawdsley is missing. We all feel very sad for them in their misfortune and hope that we will soon hear some good news about both of them.* Stewart and Ibbotson are leaving at once for East Africa."

    *   *   *   *   *

The period of the War is a miserable and muddled time in our Regimental History: a dull succession of duties and movements in relief: a drab tale of effort without excitement, and struggle without reward.

We moved back to Allahabad from Bombay in December 1914, and when, in January 1915, orders came for a squadron to go to British East Africa,** our joy was tempered by the certainty that the regiment, as such, would not take part in the Great War. We trained one hundred and eighty-four recruits and three hundred and seventy-six remounts during this year, and sent drafts of men and horses to Europe, Africa and Mesopotamia.

In 1916, as in the preceding year, the regiment was employed in training recruits and remounts and in despatching reinforcements to its own service squadron and other units overseas. Three hundred and ten recruits and one hundred and sixty-six horses

---

    * Both killed. See article on German East Africa, pp....

    ** Commanded by Major (now Lieutenant-Colonel) R. C. Barry-Smith. See separate article or German East Africa.

were trained during the year, chiefly by squadrons, instead of by the adjutant's staff, which was not big enough to cope with all the work suddenly thrown on it. Skipwith rejoined in July of this year, relieving the sorely tired Foottit, and the regiment received orders to move to Jhansi, in which place it arrived on the 10th of July. In October the strength was raised to eight hundred men, and the East African squadron returned at the end of the year. An account of their doings will be found in a separate article. In the meantime however the regiment had again been depleted by a detachment, a squadron strong being sent to Mesopotamia as a Remount squadron. Eventually we managed to get this composite squadron seconded which was an advantage as the personnel of it did not rejoin the regiment until 1921 at Dehra Ishmail Khan.

The chronicle of these long days of training do not make pleasant reading: there is really nothing to say about them. All honour however to Skipwith, who slaved and endured as adjutant through all this trying time.

A large number of officers passed through the regiment in the four years of war, and consequently the Mess was always full of all sorts and conditions of men, who came and went as the necessity for reinforcements arose. Small wonder that the Mess, from having been one of the most comfortable in India, became a sort of public-house.

Small wonder also that the Indian ranks began to look on the British Officer rather differently from hitherto: he was not the same infallible being that he had seemed to be when there were fewer of him. Not that all the war-time officers were bad: far from it: some were sportsmen, and leaders of men. But with a large and shifting population of officers an Indian regiment cannot be efficiently managed. It is, or at any rate the old silladar system was in its essence an individual affair: one man to command the regiment, one man to command the squadron. Indians do not either like or understand the modern idea that in the administration and command of units individuals count for nothing and that they can come and go without the efficiency of the unit being impaired. In this connection it is not out of place to remember that with the Asiatic soldier personal influence is its basis of the whole system of command.*

Our first batch of I. A. R. Officers was an exceptionally good one, sportsmen all and men of knowledge and experience of the East. Later, as the roll of officers increased in size it deteriorated in quality, as was only natural. Colonel Boudier's time

---

* Field Marshal Sir Charles Brownlow, G.C.B., writes, "with an Asiatic soldier personal influence is the beginning and the end of all power."

was finished in March 1917, and when he left, regretted by all ranks, Lieutenant-Colonel Barry-Smith assumed command.

During 1917, four hundred and eighteen recruits and one hundred and twenty-two remounts were passed into the ranks, and a fifth squadron was formed, consisting of the men who had previously sent to Mesopotamia as a remount detachment.

In October the regiment was ordered to move to Lahore and Jullundur. Subsequently the Lahore squadrons were diverted to Risalpur, owing to cholera. The other two squadrons went to Jullundur, but by the middle of November Headquarters had changed their mind and the whole regiment was moved to Lahore, and intensive training proceeded there with vigour, if not with enthusiasm. The regiment by this time had become a large and loosely knit school, or more accurately, "a crammers," for the passing of officers, men, and horses into the ranks. There were no Thursday holidays, and there were three parades a day.

During 1918, three hundred and twenty-two recruits and fifty remounts were trained, making a total for the war of twelve hundred and thirty-four recruits and seven hundred and fourteen horses. The rather pathetic entries in the Digest of Services for this year record manœuvres, drill and tactical schemes, at Kasur, near Lahore, during the month of February. Later, in the autumn, it was intended to do two months' squadron training at Muridki Camp, during November and December but this laudable project was interferred with by the influenza epidemic, then raging throughout India; and incidentally, we presume, by the news in November. As the Digest so truly observes: "This year was chiefly notable for the fact that an Armistice was signed on November 11th. In honour of this a grand victory celebration was held on November 27th."

Leaving the garrison of Lahore to their somewhat belated celebrations, it is pleasant to turn back to other spheres of interest. An article by Barge, written in December 1914, for the *Star and Crescent* gives us an idea of how our detachments sailed for France. It is entitled, "The Sowar at Sea."

"There must have been a lot of rain about these parts, said one of 'A' squadron to me" (so Barge writes), "when we were a day out at sea and land was quite out of sight! He had been pensively leaning over the rail, gazing upon this huge expanse of water. Never having seen the ocean before, he naturally thought that only a perfect deluge could blot out all signs of land!" Even when we were lying off Bombay prior to weighing anchor, some of the men would insist that they knew the sea was

GROUP AT JHANSI, 1917.

Back Row.—
Footitt.   Ibbotson.   Small.   Cones.   Lloyd.   Ballentine.   Wallace.

Sitting.—
Skipwith.   Barry Smith.   Boudier.   Hallowes,   Brierley.   Stewart.
(15th Lancers)

GROUP AT DERA ISMAIL KHAN, 1921.

Taken on the occasion of the last inspection of the Regiment by H. E. the Commander-in-Chief in India.

Said Raza.   Persse.   Ballentine.
　　　　　　　　　　　　　　　Stewart.
Ata Mohamed Shab.   Ahmad Ali Khan.   Wazir Khan.   Williams.
Wazir Mohamed.   Monkton.   Campbell Harris.   Sultan Sikander Khan.
　　　　　　　　　　　　　　　　　Rahmat Sher Khan.   Trumpet-Major.

just a huge river; for by looking across the harbour they could see the mainland. "There you see the other bank," they said, but they were not quite sure which way the river was flowing. So when they got out to mid-ocean the sowar was truly "at sea!"

I am writing these few lines on my way across to Aden *en route* for France, with the second reinforcement of fifty six men from the regiment. The men are all hale and hearty, and enjoying the novelty of the whole thing immensely. We have about twelve hundred troops on board, and only twenty-four horses, which are mostly officers' chargers, so there is very little work for the men as far as horses are concerned. I am adjutant on the ship and my time is well filled up as there are about twenty-two different detachments to look after. I keep the men well exercised by physical drill and sword exercise. I have not yet found a big enough space for lance exercise!

The rations the men get on board are excellent and ample. The men are very worried as to our chances of ever finding Aden. "Are you sure the Captain Sahib knows the way?" one of the men asked me. A brilliant fellow suggested there was a rail *puttli* under the water on which the ship was running. They will talk of "Aden being the next station," and "will be drawn alongside the platform?"

The constant change of direction of Mecca is causing them a lot of worry. But Rahmat Sher has made great friends with one of the ship's officers, and with his night-marching compass he sits down with his pal and they get a chart out, and between them they lay off the correct direction. He then assembles the men and gives them the direction for that day. Most of the men clustering round him have little compasses on the palm of their hands.

Rum on board is a medical comfort and only to be dealt out by the doctor's orders. Of course, all the Sikhs at once came to me and said they were ill, and would I give them rum! I have refused to give any of them rum, and many of them have told me that without rum they will die. I explained to them what little trouble they cause us if they do, and graphically described to them the way they would be slid over board, and what an excellent grave-yard the sea made—since that no more petitions for rum.

There were twenty-seven boxes of comforts—tobacco, cigarettes, books, cards, beetle-nut, etc., placed on board for the men from the women of Bombay. The gifts have been greatly appreciated. It is really very kind of them to have given so liberally.

We had one day a little rough weather, and some of the men were *hors de combat*, and many were not able to cook or eat their very liberal ration on which they started, with such zest.

One of my detachments consists of three Bengalee Babus in the Government Stationary Department. They are very good fellows, and all this life is quite new and rather rough for them. Their quaint remarks at times make me smile. "Sir, our heads, have been going round, and we, unfortunate fellows, have perforce been vomiting fluently." I have been making them do physical drill with the men, and they agree that by reason of this violent and soldierly exercise their health is greatly improved. The youngest Babu told me on the roughest day that for economy's sake he had eaten nothing, and thus saved his rations. He only drank water, but this he unfortunately lost through excessive vomiting! I found the senior Babu finishing a letter to be posted at Aden. He asked me if I would like to read it. I was so amused at it, I asked him if it might appear in the *Star and Creseent*. "Most certainly, sir, I should feel highly honoured."

It was as follows.—

My dear Benode Babu,

"I managed to send to Controller from Bombay just after our orders for embarkation were duly passed on the evening of the fourth. I on that date wrote to you one P.C., which must undoubtedly reached you by this time. I did inform you that we were perhaps going to France. Yes, the s.s. Coconada on which we are proceeding is destined for France. The adjutant, Captain Barge, who is practically in charge of us all, and looks to everything, is somewhat kindly disposed towards us, wretched fellows. In fact he listened to every grievance of ours on the boardship. Our ship left Bombay at about 11-30, Tuesday morning. She was towed by one more small boat which designated 'launch' where she anchored till about 2-30, Wednesday. It is since that time that we practically are on the rough high sea. An hour after the ship steamed off we all of three were attacked with what is called sea-sickness (*chuckár* as termed usually on board). For three days we could hardly feel any appetite for our food. We lay and slept all the time. The adjutant quite realised our situation and told me that 'Babu, you are getting lazy. I will give you a doubling exercise.' Since that time I tried to shake off my lethargy; and asked for some books to read which he very kindly allowed me to go through. I should mention to you that the adjutant is an activity incarnate as it were: he has no rest so to speak. He will come round several times a day, so it is not easy to deceive him. He asked me 'Babu, how far you progress,' and actually found out the page of the book I was at and gently reprimanded me, that I was a slow reader. I have been keeping notes of my voyage, and he was pleased to read a portion of these and encouraged me in so doing. I represented to him where I should land, and he wanted to see my orders. I told him every minute particular and he assured me that he would let me know after inquiry. Within five minutes I was called upstairs (in sea parlance this is termed by some other word). Again I told the same story to the senior officer of 'E' Force and also of my telegram to the Controller, and that our all most important stationery was left behind in Bombay. Without stationery we babus are of no profit. The officer, I believe will cable under the sea to Embarkation Commandant, Bombay, to expedite despatch of same by first available mail.

Now let me ask to you some advice of yours as to where should I bill on for our haltage for a day at Bombay, and at what rate? The authorities here on the ship allowed me second class, but you did show no consideration to myself. Neither you allowed me price of boots allowed to my assitants Rs. 10 each. You told me to bill on later. To whom should I bill on, please? To our office or the field office? If my service actually commences from the time I entertained, why should I not be allowed to ride in the train at rate of second class also? You, my senior babu *re* myself, have I mean to say not given me the fair treatment due to myself. Moreover, the T. A. you gave me fell short of actuals. I had to give both the assistants Rs. 3-5-6 each in excess of Rs. 50 given to them in the office. Just please inform me once, should I send the T. A. account to office? I hope you will write with the permission of A. C. and Superintendent. Of course, let me know whom should I bill on for my boots and actuals and halting expenses at Bombay.

It is unfortunate the adjutant will land us, poor fellows, at Egypt to which post I could not ascertain yet. If we could have got master like him we could complain little. He seems to understand our peculiarities. We are comfortably arranged now to take our meals in the orthodox Hindu style so far as practicable on the ship's board, mixing up with everybody. Everyone is sympathising. No Bengalees except us blessed three. We are with our dhoties here on board of the ship, the characteristic of the Bengalees. Charoo Babu and Probosh Babu are feeling comfortable as well. For the first three days the former somewhat was prostrate but now all right. Kindly tell Mukerjee Babu to write to my brother at Dacca, saying, I am undergoing the rigours of the sea but am all right. Inform A. C. to show this memorable letter to my friends by and bye.

Compliments to all in the office.

Yours sincerely,
(Sd.) R. B. MUKOTAJEE.

11th January 1915

The latter part of this letter seems to be more about the 'Babu on the Briny' rather than the 'Sowar at Sea.'—K. B."

* * * * *

In 1918 Stewart had the misfortune to break his leg in practice polo match owing to the kick of a vicious pony. This proved to be so serious that he was invalided to England. A little later in the year Barry-Smith who was returning from hunting sustained a serious accident in which he also broke his leg and had to be sent to England on leave on medical certificate. Kirkwood having in the meantime been sent to Siberia on the Knox Mission, no senior officers were now left with the regiment in India. Atkinson who had now rejoined from France was made a temporary Lieutenant-Colonel for a short time, but Army Head Quarters sent Major and Brevet Lieutenant-Colonel R. B. Worgan of the 20th Deccan Horse as temporary Commandant. Major Stewart returned to India in 1919 and shortly afterwards Worgan was transferred to the Wazir Force as a Brigadier-General, a rank that he had already held in France. He was a famous polo player and a fine soldier and was very popular with all ranks.

* * * * *

After the Great War, the regiment began to demobilise down to peace establishment In spite of this fact our men were constantly under arms as the following accounts will show. Squadrons were employed in the Punjab Disturbances, in and round Mangrotha in Baluchistan, and in the Afghan War.

PUNJAB DISTURBANCES.

In April 1919, during the Punjab Disturbances, the regiment was employed in guarding Government House and patrolling the city and the surrounding country. It was a critical time, as the following extracts from the Report of the Disorders Enquiry Committee will show:—"The *hartal* on the 6th (April) was complete. The crowds marching through the streets indulged in cries such as '*hae hae George mar gya*' (George is dead). They demonstrated against Indian gentlemen known to be friendly to the Government." "On the

GROUPS AT LAHORE, 1918 and 1919.

Sydenham. Harper. O'Dwyer. Pratt.
Withinshaw Gordon. Whyte. Lucas. Corkhill. Dixon. Wilson. Freston. Clews.
Ballentine. Persse. Skipwith. Atkinson. Williams. Garle. Griffiths.

Greenway. Dixon. Persse. Pratt. Williams.
Cochrane. Stewart. Barry-Smith. Barge. ta Skipwith.

10th the political atmosphere, already highly charged was made actually worse by the arrival in the afternoon of two pieces of news. News of ('Gandhi's') arrest reached Lahore about three-thirty P.M. on the 10th and soon afterwards came the news of the horrible outbreak of Amritsar."..." On the night of 10th April and for some days following, the city of Lahore was in a dangerously disturbed condition....For about two days the city was controlled by the mob."

On the 12th while a moveable column was making a demonstration towards the Fort, the attitude of the mob became so threatening that it was necessary to order a cavalry charge. This was not in any way pressed home; eventually Stewart who was commanding the cavalry halted the men and with his officers and his trumpeter chased a mob numbering many thousands out of the square in front of the Badshahi Mosque. The police at the same time opened fire up the streets leading into the square and several casualties were inflicted upon the rabble, many of whom stupified by drugs and drink, insisted on attempting to attack the troops.

The terror inspired by cavalry was very noticeable; a few horsemen at the trot were enough to cause a panic among a very large crowd. However the crowd cared little for the infantry; it was horses and not the fire arms that frightened them.

On April 15th a party of fifty sowars under Captain Persse joined the Kasur moveable column which marched to Amritsar (*via* Kharal and Tarantaran) arriving on the 23rd April and camping in the Ram Bagh. This column was employed in punishing offenders under the Martial Law Proclamation and also in reassuring loyalists. The detachment received the greatest assistance from retired Indian Officers in the villages it passed through, and returned to Lahore on April 31st. In addition to the above, detachments under Stewart, Atkinson, Williams, etc., were sent to Manhiala, Padhana, Jallo, Wagha, Sohuke, Narwa and other villages in the neighbourhood of Lahore to apprehend seditionists. The arrests on each occasion were carried out without incident.

MANGROTHA SQUADRON.

On 4th June 1919, 'C' Squadron, under Captain J. A. W Foottit with Lieut. J. S. Ballentine, Lieut. T. A. Freston, Risaldar Sultan Khan, Risaldar Tikka Khan, Jemadars Pir Dad Khan and Sultan Sikandar, was sent from Lahore for garrison duty at Multan. It remained there until August 14th 1919, when it proceeded across the Indus to Mangrotha to join the Multan Movable Column under Lieut.-Colonel Dyer, D.S.O.

The duty of this mobile column was merely on of demonstration, to prevent hostile tribes from coming down into the plains to raid. The heat was extreme, the provisioning of the squadron most inefficient, and the men suffered great discomfort and hardship with no very visible result. On 11th October the squadron marched to Vihowa, to give a stiffening to the Baluch Levies in posts in the neighbourhood. Shortly afterwards Captain Foottit went sick and was relieved in command of the squadron by Captain Persse.

Being dependent on no Field Ordnance Depôt, requisitions from the squadron and from regimental headquarters, produced little effect. In all probability the squadron would have starved, had not urgent representations to the proper quarter been made in Major Stewart's* most forceful telegrams. One lengthy despatch especially caused the squadron commander (Persse) not to lose heart, for it ended "every one concerned is being thoroughly gingered up." The "gingering up" resulted in some rations and stores being sent to the patient squadron. In spite of neglect the men worked steadily and well.

Patrols were regularly sent out, but nothing of importance occurred although there were frequent rumours of impending raids. The men lived chiefly on the very thin goats supplied to troops engaged in frontier warfare. There was no milk, no soda, no comforts of any description, no horse-shoes, no replacements of saddlery, and the water being impregnated with the salts of magnesium, chlorine and potassium, had the effect of giving the men a form of dysentary. The squadron returned to Lahore on the 8th of December, practically in rags, with saddlery tied on by string and rope.

PESHAWAR SQUADRON.

A composite squadron of Pathans left Lahore on the 6th of June 1919 for Peshawar. The officers were Captain E. G. Atkinson (Commanding), Captain S. H. Persse, Captain L. C. Clews, Risaldar Rahmat Sher, Risaldar Bahadar Sher, Jamadar Nizam-ud-din, Jamadar Said Raza.

The despatch of this squadron from Lahore, despite the fact that it was proceeding on service, will be most generally remembered in connection with the various comic and ridiculous incidents that occurred during its departure.

The Railway Transport Officer at Lahore was firmly of the opinion that camels should be made to travel in closed trucks like

---

* Commanding the regiment during the absence in England of Lieutenant-Colonel Barry-Smith on eight months' leave.

horses instead of in open high sided trucks, and all efforts to convince him to the contrary were in vain. Consequently various efforts were made to induce the squadron camels to enter the closed trucks provided on the train but in vain. The impending departure of the train and the approaching dusk soon brought matters to a crisis and brute force had to replace kindness and tact. But all to no effect, excited men and terrified camels with tied up legs hopped and jumped about the platform and the rediculous incidents that followed would have made the fortune of a cinema camera man. At last the poor camels were tied up in such a manner that they could no longer move either their heads or their limbs and they were carried on great timbers by parties of men and put bodily into the truck. This in no way ended the matter however, for just as the train was starting one burst his bonds and jumped out on the platform and tried to escape. At last after a great chase he was again secured and put back in the truck and the train started. This camel in struggling so injured himself that he had to be shot on arrival in Peshawar. Government had to pay the regiment for a new camel, and it is trusted the lesson was brought home to the R. T. O. This was not the only comic relief by any means as a large number of followers with their families were going to Peshawar with the squadron. Some of these were being discharged on account of reduction of establishment due to field service and they were taking their wives and families on the troop train to avoid the expense of purchasing tickets; this in itself was probably most irregular. These people, their kit and their packing into the train, presented problems which, owing to the fun of watching the camels, few were interested in solving however, to the accompaniment of the usual noise of the East, they packed themselves in. Shortly after the train started the squadron barber's wife for some unknown reason fell out of a carriage. This necessitated an unauthorised stop; finally she was picked up much frightened but not injured and again the train started. At this stage a *dhobi's bail* which had been smuggled on the train with other miscellaneous property considered that it would be great fun to jump out and run away; this meant another unscheduled stop, but it also was recaptured. Other incidents followed but finally the squadron did arrive in Peshawar, much to the relief of the squadron commander.

On the 10th June, the duties of divisional cavalry to the 2nd Division North-Western Frontier Force, were taken over from the 23rd Cavalry F. F. at Peshawar and the squadron was given a part of the Peshawar perimeter to hold.

On the 19th a few cases of cholera occurred. During this time the squadron had been employed in reconnaissance and patrol work only in the neighbourhood of Peshawar. On the 20th a relative of Bahadar Sher brought information of some raiders lying up in Mohmund Country. Captain Atkinson, with two troops started off in pursuit, and caught four raiders asleep in a house two miles along the Abazai Road. These men were arrested with their rifles, bandoliers and mussucks (the latter for crossing rivers). On the way back, another raider was captured with his rifle, bandolier and knife. For this good work a reward of five hundred rupees was given to the squadron by orders of the General Officer Commanding the 2nd Division.

This day proved to be an eventful one, for that evening orders were received for the squadron to take part in a "drive" from Jamrud to the Bara River. The squadron marched at nine o'clock on the night of the 20th June for Jamrud, arriving half an hour past midnight. After a short rest, it took up its position for the drive at three o'clock on the morning of the 21st. Altogether thirty-five prisoners were captured and a complimentary order received from the General Staff of the 2nd Division a few days later read: "Force Commander is very pleased with the manner in which the drive between Jamrud and Bara River was carried out."

On the 30th of June 1919, it being the festival of the "Id" news of the Afghan Armistice was also received, and the occasion was celebrated by the firing of a one hundred and one guns salute.

On the 5th of July, the squadron marched to Kacha Garhi; there were continual attacks by raiders here, and an attempt was made (on the night of July 10th) by Captain Atkinson and Risaldar Rahmat Sher, with twenty-nine picked men, all disguised as tribesmen, to surprise the raiders at their own game. Nothing came of this remarkable effort unfortunately, as no raiders were met. Escort to convoys was the chief duty at Kacha Garhi: it was extremely hot and there was no shade. On the 14th of July, the squadron marched to Ali Masjid, encamping near Lala China village; the duties consisted in escorting convoys up half way to Landi Kotal and down to Fort Maude. Constant sniping and occassional rumours of attack by an Afridi lashkar gave a certain liveliness to the hours of repose. On the 17th, 18th, 19th of July tribesmen attacked the Ali Masjid picquets and the camp was heavily sniped. There were no casualties in the squadron, but five tribesmen were killed in front of the squadron wire.

During these days of tension, it was curious to note how the British and Indian troops began to fraternize. It was a common sight to see men of the Loyal North Lancashire regiment feeding

Risaldar Rukan Din who is so often
referred to in the History

GROUP AT RAWALPINDI, 1920.

Dixon. Greenway. Williams. McCay. Ballentine. Monkton. Clews.
Atkinson. Barge. Barry-Smith. Yeats-Brown. Cochrane.

in our lines. Risaldar Rahmat Sher was a special favourite with the British soldiers, being known to them as "Jubilee Jack," owing to his having the Queen's Jubilee medal.

On the 24th of July, the troops paraded to see the Afghan delegate on their way to Rawalpindi; and on the 30th the horses and spare kit of the delegates passed through, the extraordinary appearance of which caused the troops great amusement. The troops were cheered by visits from their Excellencies, the Commander-in-Chief and the Viceroy on 26th of July and 11th of August respectively.

On the 13th of August heavy floods coming down the Khybar nullah almost washed away the squadron. Captain Persse who had fever at the time was carried three hundred yards down river but was rescued by Kote Dafadar Pir Mohamad. A quantity of squadron kit was unavoidably lost; and a number of deficiencies were made good. One of the results of the flood was that the tribesmen round Ali Masjid came in to loot. Every unit except our squadron suffered from these marauders: the men of the 17th Cavalry were too well known in the district for any liberties to be taken with them.

An immaculate gunner subaltern, who believed himself immune from theft owing to having two large Airedales, woke up one night to find some one fumbling with his tent fly. Asking who it was, his bearer (as he thought), answered that he had come for his marching boots. Thus re-assured, he turned over and went to sleep again. When he woke next morning, he had not a stitch of property, save his bed-clothes and tent. All else had vanished, and the Airedales were lying dead a few yards away, having been poisoned by the thieves.

At the end of August the squadron was inspected by Major H. S. Stewart (commanding the regiment) and the men were given a special dinner by him in honour of the event.

On the 5th of September, fourteen camels were captured grazing on Chora Kandao during the course of a reconnaissance. On the 13th of September practically every man and horse of the squadron was engaged in the operations in the Chora Valley which resulted in the blowing up of Yar Mohamed's Fort and the instalment of Malik Latif Khan in the place of Yar Mohamed The squadron was disappointed in being kept behind the infantry advance guard throughout the day and, in spite of the country being open and suitable for the mounted arm, no cavalry work took place.

On the 5th of October 1919, the squadron left Ali Masjid for Jamrud and Landi Kotal. Two troops were sent to Landi Kotal, the squadron head quarters and the other two troops remaining at Jamrud. During this month and the next the chief duty of the squadron was escorting camel caravans in the Khyber. On the 26th of October the squadron entrained at Jamrud, being inspected on the platform by Major-General Sir Charles Dobell, Commanding the Second Division, who expressed his thanks for the work done by all ranks, and said that he only wished that more opportunity had occurred to show their fighting qualities. After his shaking hands with the Indian Officers, the men gave him three cheers

The following day November 27th, 1919, the squadron detrained at Lahore Cantonment West and the lines were reached at one-thirty P.M., where the officer commanding squadron (Captain Atkinson) expressed his pleasure at the way in which the squadron had carried out its duty and thanked all for the part taken by them. Throughout the operations Risaldar Rahmat Sher had been invaluable to the squadron, not only by the information he obtained but by his personal example of energy and soldierly bearing

On December 23rd, 1919, Lieutenant-Colonel R. C. Barry-Smith returned from long leave and took over command of the regiment from Major H. S. Stewart who had been officiating Commandant in his absence. Shortly afterwards Major Stewart and Captain E. G. Atkinson were sent to join the Waziristan Field Force, where they remained until the hot weather.

In spite of wars, riots and detachments the regiment managed to get a good deal of hunting while in Lahore. The hounds had an extraordinary keen master in Casson of the 27th Light Cavalry and he showed excellent sport. Hutchinson and Pratt were very keen whips but the strenuous mornings in the ridiculous caps which formed part of the Hunt uniform were unfortunately responsible for the latter's break down in health. In the East there is only one headdress when out of doors in the sun and that is a sun helmet. The Lahore hounds were one of the great attractions of Lahore and it is hoped that they will long remain so.

Captain C. G. Y. Skipwith, Adjutant of the regiment, left for England on the 22nd of February 1920, and retired from the service on the 17th of September. His had been the tedious and trying task of training hundreds of men and horses during the latter stages of the war. Conscientious and hard working to a fault, popular with those junior to him, and never complaining of the hard luck that kept him tied to his dull yet indispensable duties in India when other men were achieving fame in the field, he was a man of promise, both as a soldier and sportsman. We do not think he would ever have been a *great* soldier: he had not enough luck, or enough bluff. But he would have been a great asset to the regiment had he stayed; and as a polo player it is no exaggeration to say that the success of the regiment in 1921 and 1922 was in some degree due to the ponies which Skipwith had trained and chosen during his time as Adjutant, and which were thus available and in play. It was generally regretted that he could not share in our success.

On the 8th of May 1920, the regiment moved by train from Lahore to Rawalpindi. It had previously been inspected by the G. O. C. of the Sialkot Cavalry Brigade, who reported as follows: " A thoroughly smart regiment, well commanded and well officered with great *esprit de corps*". Major-General Nigel Woodyat, the G. O. C. of the 16th Indian Division then stationed at Lahore had written : " A smart and well-turned out regiment that thinks well of itself, and rightly so." In Rawalpindi the regimental reports were no less complimentary: we will only quote two, that of the G. O. C.-in-Chief of the Northern Army, General Sir William Birdwood : and that of Major-General Sir H. Uniacke, Commanding Rawalpindi District. Major-General Uniacke wrote " A very fine regiment, well commanded and in every way fit for service. A fine spirit prevails among all ranks."

In November of this year General Sir William Birdwood, the General Officer Commanding-in-Chief of the Northern Army, in agreeing with these eulogistic reports added following memorable words :—" An excellent lot of Indian Officers, who have a high opinion of the 17th Cavalry." General Birdwood found the *mot juste* : the spirit that made our regiment famous was that inculcated by a notable succession of Indian gentlemen, who were not too proud to serve in our ranks, and who rose step by step in the noblest of professions, to the command of troops, and who enjoyed the full confidence of their English comrades.

General Birdwood's remark about the spirit of the Indian Officers, should be remembered as long as there is any memory of the regiment. The 17th had always been noted for its *sirdars*. They were backbone of the regiment, and to a great extent, set the 'tone.' The practice of insisting on a certain degree of social status as well as military efficiency before promotion to commissioned rank had excellent results. The *sirdars* of the 17th Cavalry were nearly always men of standing amongst their own people. If deviations from this normal rule occasionally occurred it was only in the case of such exceptional men that the underlying idea was not upset. Such men were only too keen to associate themselves with the sentiments and position of their brother officers. In the 17th Cavalry it had long been the regular practice for the Indian Officers and the regimental Moulvi to be invited to dine several times during the year in the British Officers' Mess. This helped to maintain that excellent understanding that had always existed between all ranks and made for the Indian Officers feeling perfectly at their ease when meeting Europeans socially. Another innovation which was introduced by the regiment is mentioned elsewhere, that was the Indian Officers' Mess. Now, in its modified form of an Indian Officers' Club, it exists in all regiments, but the idea originated in the 17th Cavalry. As class regiments no longer exist, a mess as it was run in the 17th Cavalry, where all the unmarried *sirdars* fed together, would now be difficult to organize.

The Risaldar Majors of the regiment and the regimental Moulvi deserve more than a passing mention. The notes that follow are all too brief yet they will do something at least to preserve the memory of men who should not be forgotten.

The regimental Moulvi, Khan Bahadur Qazi Abdul Hakim Khan had been with the regiment from the time that it was raised until its disbandment. His photograph forms the subject of our frontispiece. What he meant to the old regiment, the tradition of loyalty and true religion that he maintained, and the great trust reposed in him by all ranks, needs no retelling. These things are written in the heart of all who read these lines. May he long be spared, full of years and honour, to maintain the best traditions of Islam and of the Mohamedan soldier.

Risaldar Major Mohammed Amin Khan Bahadur, who retired in 1909, had served in the Kabul War and was a native of Afghanistan, when his father held the office of Qazi (or judge) of Kabul. He was a man of striking personal appearance, tall, distinguished, bulky, and absolutely upright, morally and physically. One of the finest Indian Officers who have ever served in the 17th Cavalry, he was regarded with the deepest respect by the officers and men with whom he served. Early in his service he broke his leg very badly, and ever after walked with a limp, but this did not affect his riding, and he remained active and a fine example of a horseman up to the time of his retirement. After leaving the regiment he lived in Ludhiana, where he was an Honorary Magistrate, Municipal Commissioner and Sub-Registrar. While still with the regiment he had been specially selected to go to England as one of the King's orderly officers. He passed away from this transitory world early in 1916 deeply regretted by his many friends.

Honorary Captain Risaldar-Major Hamzullah Khan, Sardar Bahadur—"The little red-bearded Captain" as a Staff Officer

AN INDIAN OFFICER OF THE OLD REGIMENT AND THE RISALDAR-MAJORS SUBSEQUENT TO RE-RAISING OF THE REGIMENT IN 1885.

Risaldar Kumrodeen Khan, Bahadur (the only Indian officer of the old regiment whose portrait is available).

Risaldar-Major Rustam Ali Khan, First Risaldar-Major, 1885—88, in the uniform of the 4th B.C.

Risaldar-Major Mahmud Khan, Second Risaldar-Major, 1888—90.

Risaldar-Major Izat Khan, Sirdar Bahadur, Third Risaldar-Major 1891—00.

Risaldar-Major Mohamed Akbar Khan, Fourth Risaldar-Major, 1900—01.

Risaldar-Major Saadat Khan, Fifth Risaldar-Major, 1901—05.

fresh from England described him at the Pezu manœuvres in 1907—was one of the most forceful characters that have served in the regiment. He had the intense vitality so often found in short men, an iron will, an eagle eye, and a brain that never forgot a fact or an enemy. He was an exception to the general rule and rose from humble beginnings to a position of great influence through sheer force of character. Had he been born in other times he might have carved his way to a throne and established a dynasty.

Of his sons: Abdulla Khan, as a Jemadar attached to the 22nd Cavalry won great renown in the attack and capture of Baghdad, by crossing the Biala river with a small patrol, and capturing a Turkish convoy practically single handed. Shad Mohmmed, a Dafadar Major is with the new regiment, shaping well at polo and a likely lad in every respect to carry on the high traditions of his family. Captain Hamzullah Khan lives in Peshawar City, and as God has still spared to him the active brain of his youth, he was able quite recently to dictate his early experiences in the regiment. May He long preserve him in health and prosperity.

Risaldar-Major Dost Mahomed Khan was a typical Punjabi gentleman. He was a fine rider, a first class tent-pegger and had a natural dignity which well-fitted his position. He retired in 1918 and is still in enjoyment of all his faculties, physical and mental, at his home in the Tiwana country. He was a worthy representative of a fine race.

Risaldar-Major Ghulam Mohy-ud din was the cleverest Indian Officer from the European standpoint that the regiment ever had. He read and wrote English fluently, had an excellent knowledge of accounts and business, and was thoroughly capable in the administrative affairs of a regiment. Colonel Boudier greatly respected him. Different from every other Risaldar-Major, individually he was invaluable to the regiment in which he served with distinction for years; and although after retirement his health is not as good as it was, he is still in full enjoyment of his mental powers and sees the world clearly and sees it still with a mind undimmed by years. May he long continue to enjoy his well-earned rest.

Honorary Lieutenant Risaldar-Major Zikerya Khan came from Afghanistan, where he had served as a young man in the Amir's Army. Enlisting in the 17th Cavalry he rose, though not without reverses and set backs, to the position of an Indian officer. Subsequently his promotion was rapid. If Ghulam Mohy-ud-din was the cleverest Indian Officer with books, Zikerya may be said to have been one of the most able men that there had been in the regiment. Like Ghulam Mohy-ud-din his talents were not those of a cavalry officer however. Tall and handsome, with an exceptionally fine presence, and endowed with the charming manners and easy conversational powers which are a characteristic of men of the Afghan race, he was a man who would have probably reached a great administrative position under the Moghal Empire. He was naturally tactful and difficulties dissolved and quarrels vanished before his agreeable method of dealing with men. He became Risaldar-Major at an exceptionally difficult time during the war, when the regiment was flooded with young British officers with no experience of Indians, and often possessed of an unfortunate manner in dealing with them. It speaks volumes for Zikerya's tact and ability to deal with men and affairs that things went smoothly. While Zikerya Khan was Risaldar-Major there was never the slightest difficulty, although the regiment was working at high pressure through hot weather as well as cold, and with a new staff of instructors, and a host of young British officers who did not know their men and did not know their work. And while the regiment maintained its efficiency unimpaired, Zikerya's popularity in no way diminished. In spite of his trying duties he maintained friendship with British and Indians of all ranks. After the war, he retired to Nowshera, where he now fills the position of Honorary Magistrate with distinction and is an ornament to the society of that place and a credit to the regiment in which he served so long and honourably. His son Pir Mahomed is serving in the new regiment as Squadron Dafadar Major and we hope that he will follow in his father's footsteps.

Risaldar-Major Rahmat Sher Khan, who was responsible for the internal administration of the regiment from 1920 to February 1922, when the regiment was disbanded, was a worthy successor to the illustrious line of Risaldar-Majors that preceded him, and was in his own way pre-eminent. During a time of war he was essentially a fighting soldier. The routine of peace did not appeal to him, and although he discharged his duties with efficiency, and was invaluable during the trying period of the Hijrat in 1920 in keeping intact the high tradition of the regiment for loyalty, at a time when the families of our men were going over bag and baggage to Afghanistan; and the Pathans were as a consequence tried to the utmost—although during these difficult times his example and his advice were invaluable,—yet it is as a fighting soldier that he will be chiefly remembered. Attached to the 19th Lancers in France, he earned golden opinions from everyone he served under, and later, during the Afghan war he was quite invaluable in obtaining informtion as to the movement of the enemy. It was largely owing to his efforts and example that

THE RISALDAR MAJORS SUBSEQUENT TO THE RE-RAISING OF THE REGIMENT IN 1885.

Risaldar Major Mohamed Amin Khan Bahadur, Sixth Risaldar Major. 1905-09.

Honorary Captain Risaldar Major Hamzulla Khan Sirdar Bahadur, Seventh Risaldar Major, 1909-12.

Risaldar Major Ghulam Mohy-ud-din Khan Bahadur, Eighth Risaldar Major. 1912-14.

Risaldar Major Dost Mohamed Khan Bahadur, Ninth Risaldar Major 1914-18.

Honorary Lieutenant Risaldar Major Zikryia Khan, Tenth Risaldar Major. 1918-20.

Risaldar Major Rahmat Sher Khan Bahadur, Eleventh Risaldar Major. 1920-22.

"A" squadron under Captain Atkinson earned in 1919 the reputation it did. His loyalty, his bravery, his military skill, had never been in question : the best of good fellows and the best of Indian officers; his memory will long be kept green by the men he commanded and the British officers under whom he served. He was " an example to all ranks of upright and trustworthy service " as the C. O. said in a farewell order on 17th February. He is now in retirement in his Afridi house at Kui, but he is ready as ever to draw his sword in good cause. He has a big following and no man ever better commanded the trust of his fellows. Should any of the old officers want good men then they have only to turn to Rahmat Sher. Long may his spirit shine a guiding star to men of his race and blood.

Four officers gave their lives in the War: Wilson, Shakespear, Duberly and Maudsley.

Denis Wilson was really and truly a *chevalier sans peur et sans reproche:* than this nothing truer or completer can be said of him. He served with credit in the South African War, getting the Queen's medal with seven clasps. After joining the 17th Cavalry he was made adjutant under Colonel Burton, and filled this onerous position with distinction and a delicate tact, that was never ostentatious but always efficacious. Just before the War he was at the Staff College, Camberly. and immediately after the outbreak of hostilities he was sent to France. As General Staff Officer to the North Midland Division, he earned golden opinions from everybody with whom he came in contact. During the attack of July 1916 in which he commanded an infantry battalion he was seen to be wounded, but continued to advance. Later he was reported missing and nothing has ever been seen or heard of him again. So passed away a very gallant gentleman.

W. H. I. Shakespear, a member of the family that has given so many useful servants to India for generations, was appointed to the regiment in 1899 and showed himself at once to be a man of no ordinary keenness and ability. As years progressed he wisely realised that his figure precluded the possibility of getting the full advantages of a cavalry soldier's life. So, having passed Higher Proficiency Examination in Urdu and in Arabic with comparative ease, he obtained an appointment in the Political Department. After serving in one or two uncongenial spots, he was eventually posted to the Persian Gulf. It was there that he found his *metier*. He was one of the very few, if their were any other Europeans who up till then had spent two hot weathers in Bandar Abbas without detriment to health. The two years passed there were more or less uneventful but they laid the foundation for future energies. A short tour of duty in Hyderabad, Deccan, and he was again appointed to the Persian Gulf, this time as Consul at Koweit. His real work was to look after the Sheikh there, keeping him happy and well-disposed towards us. The German pre-war project of the Berlin-Bagdad Railway was badly in need of a suitable outlet to the sea. Koweit, a small harbour towards the north of the Western coast of the Gulf, was selected as the very spot for them. But for once in a way we got there first, and the old Sheikh refused to have the Germans and their railway at any price. Shakespear found the life at Koweit as congenial as could be. He was of an extremely buoyant, cheery nature, full of resource and self-reliance. He made the most of the Sheikh, and even brought him over on one occasion to India: a visit which the old man enjoyed to the full and wished to repeat. Shakespear's European companions consisted of an unpleasant Scandinavian customs official, and an occasional captain of a coasting British India ship. Life was also sometimes tempered by a very occasional visit of one of the gunboats on duty in the Gulf. He was well known to the sailors as the man who sailed his little boat alone across the Gulf. After sailing, his real delight was to make journeys into Arabia and to stay with various Arab chiefs with whom he was a *persona grata*.

It was really owing to his acquaintance with Arab affairs, that "Shakes" met his death. He had in Koweit become acquainted with Ibn Saud (Abdul Aziz Ibn Abdul Rahman Ibn Faisal Ibn Saud) the Emir of Najd, a man who but for Shakespear's untimely death might have played the part in the great war which afterwards fell to King Hussain of the Hijaz. Shakespear had been appointed the accredited British Agent with this potentate, who is the Wahhabi Chief, and who in fact may be considered the "King of Central Arabia." Ibn Saud was opening the projected campaign by falling on another chief Ibn Rashid with whom he had long had a standing feud, and who incidently was the principal Pro-Turk in those parts.

"Shakes" with his usual readiness to take on anything at hand wished to take part in the battle. The infantry that he accompanied were not able to withstand the enemy attacks and were defeated and scattered. The last seen of poor "Shakes" was the figure of a desperately wounded man fighting like a hero.

Thus died in 1915 one of the cheeriest and ablest servants of the Indian Government. It is agreed that had he lived he had a great future in store for him.

The following extract from the "Heart of Arabia," by **H. St. J. B. Philby** gives us a full account of the tragedy.

"I was fortunately able to procure for the satisfaction of Shakespear's family somewhat fuller and more circumstantial details of the manner in which that very gallant officer came by his death—an irrepairable loss to his country and to his great friend. Ibn Saud.—from the lips of one who was actually with him at the time, Husain, a Master Gunner in the Wahhabi forces 'When Ibn Saud raised his standard, so ran his story of the events of January 1915, to go forth against Ibn Rashid, he had but one gun of which I was in charge. We arrived in the vicinity of Jarrab, and the Army was divided into two sections, Ibn Saud in person leading out the whole of the cavalry to seek out the enemy who was reported to be near at hand, while the infantry leaving the camels and baggage in the camp, march out of a different course along the Shaib. With my one gun I accompanied the latter and with me was 'Skaishpeer'—such is the common pronunciation of a name held in high honour in Arabia,—who had been begged by Ibn Saud the night before to betake himself to Zilfi, seeing that the issue of the morrow's battle was so uncertain, but had resolutely declined to do so and insisted on accompanying us. Of a sudden our scouts found the enemy advancing towards us and I immediately dragged my one gun to a commanding position whence to open fire. Without delay I began firing while Skaishpeer stood up on a little eminence watching the enemy through his glasses and telling me where to aim. I shouted at him not to expose himself and begged him to take off his topi—for he was dressed not as us but in his British uniform—but he heeded me not and went on telling me where to shoot. Before long he was struck in the thigh by a rifle bullet, but, unable as he was to move, he went on with his work directing my fire until the opposing forces met at close quarters. Then I stopped firing and the two of us sat down to watch the battle. In a short while I noticed that our force was being pushed back. 'Come', I said to him, 'it is finished; let us escape by the Shaib'; and with that I detached the removable parts of the gun, and, burying them in the sand started off in the direction I had indicated; he called out something about going in a different direction, but I waited not for our people were running for their lives." Well in the van of the rout Husain, looking back, saw the enemy cavalry charging down upon Shakespear who, wounded as he was, stood up to receive them, and fell fighting; he saw no more. Meanwhile Ibn Saud's cavalry had driven the enemy cavalry before them, but the Ajman, seeing how it fared with the infantry, deserted to pillage the camp and the battle was lost. Ibn Saud claimed a victory by reason of his cavalry success, but the honours clearly rested with the enemy, who was, however, not in a strong enough position to court a further trial and retired with the booty of the plundered camp. "Two months later," said Husain, "I went back to recover the buried parts of the gun and found the battlefield strewn with the corpses of friend and foe left as they had fallen, and among them I saw Skaishpeer *Cinna in quatil aims*—as though he had been killed but yesterday; by his side lay a Shammari, and close by a camel, and but a little way off, one of the Badu of our side. Wallah, they say that no less than three thousand men fell in that battle." This estimate of losses was, of course, greatly exaggerated, and is probable that the total casualties on both sides did not exceed three hundred, but judged by its results, the battle of Jarrab was one of the decisive battles of the Arabian theatre of war and the death of Shakespear, followed as it was by the abandonment of all attempts to use Ibn Saud for the furtherance of our campaign against the Turks, put an end once and for all to the hopes of Arab co-operation in the war, which were not to be revived until eighteen months elapsed, and were then revived in a different quarter with such remarkable results. It was left to Lawrence and the army of the Hijaz to accomplish what in other circumstances— with a little better luck, and a little more imagination on the part of the authorities responsible for the conduct of the Mesopotamian campaign—might have been accomplished by Ibn Saud and Shakespear. Under the star spangled vault of the Arabian sky he lies as he fell on the field of Jarrab—a true friend of the Arabs as every Arab knows in Central Arabia—and some day, perchance if a scheme recently initiated by his family proves to be practicable, the memory of his sacrifice may be perpetuated of the scene of his last endeavour by the simplest and best of monuments, a well in Desert Arabia.

Captain V. C. Duberly joined the regiment on the 20th of June 1910, on transfer from the Royal Field Artillery. He was a man of irascible temper and intrepid courage. He was a very fine horseman and took the greatest pains and trouble in training ponies. The system which he followed comprised methods which seemed theoretically incorrect as they involved considerable castigation, nevertheless with him these methods worked like a charm and his horses seemed to thoroughly understand them. His untimely death (details of which are given in the Appendix IV) was a very great loss to the regiment.

Lieutenant B. J. P. Maudsley only joined the regiment from the Unattached List shortly before the outbreak of the Great War. He was posted to the Calcutta squadron and never actually served with the regiment itself. On the departure of the 17th Cavalry for France he was recalled from Calcutta to join the depôt at

Allahabad, and shortly afterwards accompanied the squadron sent to East Africa. He was fine rider and promising polo player and much liked by all who knew him. His death with Duberly was a sad loss. He was the last officer ever permanently posted to the regiment.

The regiment lost in the last year of the war another officer who was not however killed in action. Lieutenant S. M. Ferguson died in the British Station Hospital at Lahore of appendicitis at the early age of twenty-one. He had served in France with the Seaforth Highlanders in 1916 and 1917 and had subsequently been transferred to the 17th Cavalry. He was a general favourite with all ranks and was deeply regretted.

It would be outside the scope of this history to describe the doings of officers in France (at one time we had a score there) Mesopotamia, East Africa, Russia, and Afghanishtan but a summary of the decorations received, and the mentions in despatches, will not be out of place.

In this list, "attached" officers have not been included, although several of them achieved distinction in various fields, because full particulars have been impossible to obtain. Particulars of such decorations as are known of are noted in the List of officers of the regiment in Appendix XI. The only "mentions" for work actually with the regiment by British officers were those received by Lieut.-Colonel R. C Barry-Smith for East Africa and Major Atkinson for the Khyber Squadron, 1919, and Waziristan, 1921.

The following officers and other ranks were mentioned in despatches, or received decorations during the Great War and the Afghan War:—

Lieutenant-Colonel R. C. Barry-Smith.	Mention—East Africa
Major (now Colonel) R. A. Steel.	C.I.E., C.M.G. Order of St. Lazarus and two other orders. Service chiefly in Directorate of Military Operations, War Office.
Major (now Colonel) R W. Henderson.	D.S.O. and mentioned in despatches twice for operations in Palestine. Brevet-Lieutenant Colonel.
Major and temporary Lieut.-Colonel D. D. Wilson.	Two mentions—France. Missing, 2-7-16.
Major and Brevet-Lieutenant-Colonel A. H. R. Dodd.	Brevet-Lieutenant-Colonel for services with Dunster Force.
Major T. W. Kirkwood	Mention—Knox Mission, Russia, awarded the O. B. E. and Rising Sun of Japan.

Major and temporary Lieutenant-Colonel K. Barge	D.S.O. and M.C. for services in France and four mentions in despatches.
Major F. C. C. Yeats-Brown	Two mentions—Mesopotamia. One mention—While prisoner of war. Awarded D.F.C. for service with Flying Corps in Mesopotamia.
Captain (now Major) E. G. Atkinson.	Mention—France. Mention—Afghan War, 1919. Mention Waziristan, 1921.
Captain C. G. Y. Skipwith.	Mention—France, 1915. Mention—France, 1916.
Captain I. D. Guthrie	Twice mentioned in despatches and M.C. for services in France. Bombing Officer to North Midland Division, Staff Captain, 36th Infantry Brigade, Brigade Major 36th Infantry Brigade.
Risaldar Major Rahmat Sher	Mention and I. D. S. M., Afghan War, 1919.
Risaldar Wazir Khan	Mention and I. O. M., East Africa.
Risaldar Alam Sher	Mention and I. D. S. M., France, with 18th Lancers.
Risaldar Wazir Mohmed	M. B. E. for work in India during war with the Remount Department.
Dafadar Khan Sahib	I. D. S M. in East Africa.
Sowar Mohamed Husain	I. O. M. in France.
Dafadar (now Jemadar) Ghulam Sarwar.	I. D. S. M. with 13th Lancers in Mesopotamia.
Dafadar Major Shad Mohd.	I. D. S. M. Afghan, 1919.
Dafadar Major Madat Khan	I. M. S. M. work in India during War.

Risaldar Dost Muhammad Khan was awarded a Sword of Honour for services rendered at Lyallpur during the Punjab disturbances.

Captain R. P. I. Cochrane succeeded Skipwith as Adjutant on the latter's retirement. At the beginning of 1921 however Captain Ballentine took over the duties when Cochrane was granted leave home. Ballentine was afterwards confirmed in the appointment and subsequently became the Adjutant of the new amalgamated regiment, after a highly successful term as the last Adjutant of the 17th Cavalry.

Rawalpindi is a big bleak station with many "fatigues" and orderly duties for the men, and courses and boards and examinations for the officers. Yet in some respects it is one of the best stations in the north of India. Its large population, and its cold winter climate save it from the deadly inertia that so often lies like a blight over cantonments. There is good polo there, some shooting, dances twice a week, and in the summer Murree is within the week-end radius, and Kashmir is not very far off. We enjoyed

THE TRENCHES IN FRANCE.

Barge. Atkinson-Wills (8th Hussars.)
Atkinson.

A GROUP IN INDIA

Jemadar Sajid Gul.   Jemadar Nizam ud din.
Risaldar Rahmat Sher.   Hutchinson.   Jemadar Ahmad Ali.
MacIntyre.   Taylor.   Risaldar Rukan Din.   Risaldar Bahadur Sher.

our time there, settling down to peace time soldiering and sport, happy among ourselves as a regiment, and fortunate in the General Officers under whose commands we were serving (Birdwood and Uniacke).

Soon, however, the voice of rumour spoke of our impending dissolution. We heard of various schemes for halving the number of cavalry regiments, for abolishing the silladar system, for changing the class of men we enlisted, for changing our identity and merging it with another regiment, for changing our interior economy. Everything was to be changed. At first we hoped that " something would turn up " to delay the scheme, or to divert the attention of its authors to other and to us more suitable economies, beginning with Army Head Quarters. But slowly, inexorably in spite of brief moments of hope, and protests from distinguished officers of Indian Cavalry, we saw the corporate life of our service ebbing away. It has been replaced by another service, and by other regiments, units of the regular Indian Cavalry: our irregular and delightful existence had run its course.

But we anticipate: our death was no sudden affair. From the first premonitions in the autumn of 1920 to our final decline on February 15th, 1922, we passed through various stages of recruiting and demobilisation and amalgamation. On the 30th of August, 1920, a composite squadron (from all four squadrons) under Major F. C. C. Yeats-Brown, D.F.C. was ordered to march to Abbotabad, in aid of the Civil Power. The Indian Officers were Resaldar Bahadur Sher, Resaldar Sultan Sikandar Khan, Jemadar Arbab Mahomed Hussain, Jamadar Malik Ahmad Yar and Jemadar Nizam-ud-din Khan. The squadron reached Mansehra by forced marches, to find that the trouble consequent on the seditious activity of a local moulvi had subsided. It remained in the district till the end of November, marching however to the Chattar Plain, Oghi, etc., under orders of the civil authorities.

The polo tournaments in which the regiment took part during this phenomonally successful year are described in another place. A word must be added, however, which the author of the monograph on the regimental polo will be sure to omit . . . Our success was due to the qualities of hand and head of the captain of the team. " Joey " Atkinson knew just what was wanted in men and horseflesh in order to win tournaments, and he achieved his end so tactfully that no one knew he was tactful—probably he would be the first to disclaim it. He could not of course have succeeded unless the officers had kept good ponies, had taken an interest in their training, and had fed them well. This last by the way was a habit far from universal in the old Indian Cavalry: officers got into the habit of making eight pounds of corn do the work of twelve in the lines, and thought that a polo pony could play on starvation diet. Also, everyone who hoped to play in the team took the trouble to practise hard, and to keep himself fit.

Another factor in our success was the attached officers, who were keen sportsmen and kept good ponies. We feel, indeed, that, we have scarcely done justice to the attached officers through all this narrative. Their's was often a difficult and a thankless position. Although they were of the regiment they were not *in* it. Many gave some of the best years of their life to the 17th Cavalry, only to find on reduction and amalgamation, that they had to make room for permanent officers who had been on leave or on staff employment while they, the attached officers, had borne the burden and the heat of the day in India. This was hard. To some extent it was the fortune of war and inevitable. But they have our sympathy none the less; and they may take comfort in the fact that they were "in at the death." After them came amalgamation and movements of officers within the new group system, so that whatever else the distinguished regiment now known as the 15th Lancers may claim to have, it cannot claim to have retained many of the officers or men of the late 17th Cavalry.

To return to "Joey." While he was Captain of the team, his decision was never once questioned. A dispute was something unknown. His suggestions were followed as a matter of course, when he made them, which was rarely. More often, things just seemed to happen. . . Now, anyone who knows the inner history of polo teams, no matter whether small or great, English International or the "station side" at Dustpore, will realize that this is no mean achievement. To manage a comic opera chorus must be easy compared with a polo team, with all its idiosyncrasies of players and ponies. "Joey" made the very best of the human and equine material at his disposal, and if there was still something lacking to bring us up to the level of our oponents, he often turned defeat into victory by playing above his own fine form and winning the match off his own stick. The tougher the struggle, the better he played. The moral is to the physical as three to one at polo, and often against a good side "Joey's" reputation made our opponents nervous before they rode on to the ground, while his dash completed their demoralisation.

In dash and brilliance, Kirkwood was "Joey's" equal, and being a bigger man was able to ride anything that was strong enough to carry him. He turned the scale in 1921 against the 21st Lancers in the finals of the Inter-regimental. Had he been playing in 1922 there is little doubt that we should have won again.

In the spring of 1921 we knew definitely that our days as a regiment were numbered, but owing to the fact that we were to be one of the last regiments to be amalgamated and converted to a regular basis, it was arranged that we were to see service on the frontier by being transferred to the Wazir Force.

Lieutenant-Colonel Barry-Smith's four year tenure of command expired in May 1921 and he had practically completed all preparations for handing over command of the regiment to Major H S. Stewart and leaving the country, when a telegram arrived from Simla detailing the latter to be a member of the Special Committee appointed to carry out the conversion of the Silladar Cavalry to a regular basis. Shortly afterwards Barry-Smith was given an extention of tenure for a year, but the matter was delayed so long that he had practically disposed of all his belongings before the news came, and consequently had to replace these again!

The Silladar Cavalry Conversion Committee did not disolve for over a year. Consequently Major Stewart never actually rejoined the regiment again, being given a staff appointment in Calcutta when the Committee finished their travels and labours. He was one of the great authorities in India on the organization and administration of the silladar system, a capable soldier and a great horse-lover and sportsman. He will always remain associated in our memories with the happy days of Pigsticking and Racing in Bareilly, a full account of which appears elsewhere.

On April 1st, the first squadron left Rawalpindi for Wana. It was "D" Squadron with the following officers : Major F. C. C. Yeats-Brown, D.F.C., Lieutenant V. H. Dixon, Risaldar Alam Sher Khan, I.D.S.M., Jemadars Ahmad Yar Khan, Ghulam Hussein Khan and Pir Dad Khan, the latter with a troop of his "C" Squadron men to complete the war establishment of the squadron. The squadron arrived at Mari Indus the following day and drew complete field service equipment including a pair of *chaplis* for each man, which were later found to be better than boots for the work the squadron had to do in patrols and reconnaissance. Crossing the Indus the next day, the squadron railed to Tank in two metre-gauge trains, and then marched up by easy stages through the intense heat. An action was fought at Haideri Katch the day the squadron left that place, about ten men of the Punjabi regiment stationed there being ambushed. Except for this, there was no incident during the fifteen days journey to Wana. The Fort there was still in a dismantled condition, but the men soon cleared up their corner and installed themselves with such comfort as the flies and dust allowed. Reconnaissances were carried out daily and the men had their first taste of Mahsud tactics on April 29th. An attempt was made on that date to round up a raiding gang at Tiarza Post; the gang got away, but there was a certain amount of desultory firing and one sowar, who had become separated from his companions, was fired on close to one of our picquets. He escaped wounded losing both horse and rifle.

In May Captain E. G. Atkinson took over command of the squadron and Lieutenant Dixon was replaced by Lieutenant Monckton. The squadron continued to do excellent work, impossible for infantry, in gathering information and supplies from out-lying villages, and in denying the Wana plain by daylight at any rate, to raiding parties of the enemy.

This plain is a desolate and stony upland, some four thousand eight hundred feet above sea level, circled by abrupt blue hills and traversed by a single stream, the Wana Toi, whose waters are led off in channels and *karezes* for irrigation. The villages on the plain consist of the usual mud forts of the frontier; here and there traces of the loot got in the disaster of 1919 were to be seen—beams from the Fort, an easy chair, a post box, some faded green baize probably off the billiard table. The Wazirs are a hardy and a handsome people, inclined to be treacherous, but heartily sick of the chronic unrest of their country. Their neighbours, the Mahsuds, on the contrary are of a different mind. They appear willing to fight for ever, and are the fiercest and most intractable tribesmen of the frontier. From Wana, looking east, you can see the Inza Narai, a low pass leading into their country. To the north, are the foothills of Afghanistan, leading to the mountains of Shakin and Ghazni by an ancient and well-worn path trodden by Tamerlane's men and a thousand other robbers through country of a haunting desolateness. Twenty miles north the scenery changes by all reports to grass land and fir forest and running water, but the vicinity of the Wana plain is a strange stern country, with little to recommend it, except retrospectively from a safe arm-chair. From there one may conjure visions of a great Imperial future in the cool green country beyond, where on the Razmak Plateau, among the mountains and the pines, Great Britain may perhaps some day build the last and best outpost on her far flung frontiers.

On the 30th of June, Atkinson very nearly caught the famous raider Angur He was out on patrol with a troop of the squadron, when he sighted a party of fifty men with two or three

Major subsequently Lieut.-Colonel, H. S. Stewart, Second-in-Command, who succeeded to the administration of the affairs of the regiment on the retirement of the Tenth Commandant.

Lieut.-Colonel R. C. Barry-Smith, Tenth Commandant, 1917—1922.

camels moving across the plain. Taking five or six men, he lay up for them in a deep nullah, while the other two sections and the hotchkiss guns he sent towards the hills to cut off their retreat. They were too late to do this however, and unfortunately also the hotchkiss jammed at the critical moment, so that instead of rounding up the whole lot, only three of the raiders were hit. Atkinson meanwhile had pursued another party of raiders, but coming under heavy fire was obliged to retire with his few men to a neighbouring village. Meanwhile the remainder of the squadron arrived at the gallop. The official report concludes: "Our casualties were *nil*. Enemy's three wounded known and one camel. I would draw attention to the risk and fine leadership shown by Captain Atkinson who made the most of the opportunity with the few men he had."

On another, somewhat similar occasion, another two couple of raiders were bagged and Lieutenant Monckton had his charger shot under him.

The rest of the regiment moved from Rawalpindi to Dera Ismail Khan on the 10th of April, and "B" Squadron was ordered to Tank on the 13th, with Lieutenant L. C. Clews, Risaldar Bahadur Sher and Jemadar Arbab Mahomed Hussein. The duties at Tank were similar to those at Wana, namely patrolling, reconnaissance and occasional escorting of a convey; but Tank was hotter, dustier and duller than Wana. Even Tank however, was preferable to "D. I. K." The latter, during the summer, was the very abomination of desolation.

Very soon after arrival at "D. I. K." the regiment was inspected by the Commander-in-Chief, Lord Rawlinson, who expressed himself as very pleased with its appearance on parade, and we received the following telegram from General Sir William Birdwood: "Army Commander much regrets your departure from Northern Command and wishes all ranks every happiness and success in future."

Dera Ismail Khan was not in the "Concession Area"—that is to say, the men were not entitled to field service allowances. The Staff lived in a perpetual state of fuss, and there was an utter lack of sympathy and understanding of which we will not trust ourselves to speak while we remain serving soldiers. Suffice it to say that the heat was staggering, the climate unhealthy, the country featureless to ride over, the bazaar a squalid Sodom, the club a pot-house with slatternly servants, the society uncongenial and that all the plagues of Egypt, from malaria-mosquitoes to obstinate boils troubled the wretched inhabitants of the hottest place in the world . . . Officers and men were unanimously delighted to see the last of Dera Ismail Khan and everyone in it.

The squadrons at Tank and Wana, while under more trying conditions as far as physical comforts went, had the satisfaction of seeing the enemy sometimes, and of being far from Wazir Force Head Quarters. They kept in better health and spirits than the troops at " D. I. K."

At the end of October 1921 the squadrons at Tank and Wana were relieved by squadrons of the 28th Cavalry, and the regiment entrained in five trains for Lucknow on dates between the 18th of October and the 2nd of November.

Directly we reached Lucknow fifty N.-C. Os. and men were demobilised, to bring the establishment down to the peace time strength of four hundred and sixty-one. During this same month general demobilisation began and continued until the beginning of February, 1922. The terms offered to the men were somewhat intricately worded : they came roughly to this, that a man would receive a bonus of three months' pay if he was to be demobilised as one of the " not wanted " classes.

Our two Pathan squadrons had to be made into one, to form the Pathan squadron of the new amalgamated regiment. All Tiwanas, Ghukkas, Punjabi Rajputs, Awans, in fact Punjabis of every description had to go. A new squadron of Rangers was raised from the Central India Horse and other regiments who had such men in their old establishments. A squadron of Sikhs came from the 37th Lancers, with whom we were amalgamating. Of the three squadrons in the new amalgamated regiment, only one (the Pathans) therefore, was composed of men of the 17th Cavalry. As a matter of fact the majority of these Pathans even were men who had transferred from other corps.

We saw our men go off with heavy hearts . . . Men whose fathers and grandfathers had served in the regiment, were now being sent away. At a stroke of the pen the ties of fifty years of sport and soldiering, and the fabric on which our lives had been built and the hope of our future years, had been brought to nothing. Our world had passed away. In the new regiment we might find new scope and new interest—that does not concern this narrative—but our old life together was over and done with.

The British officers had also been fading away. Colonel R. A. Steel, C.M.G., C.I.E., retired from the service in December 1921. It had of course been many years since he had actually done

GROUP TAKEN BEFORE AMALGAMATION

Back row.—Alam Sher Khan, Ahmed Ali Khan, Mohamed Aslam Khan, Ghulam Hussain Khan, Sultan Sikandar, Pir Dad Khan, Mohamed Raza Khan, Wazir Khan.
Second row.—Ballentine, Dixon, Persse, Wazir Mohamed, Turner, Foottit, Griffiths.
Third row.—The Maulvi Sahib, Stewart, Rahmat Sher, Barry-Smith, Bahadur Sher, Yeats-Brown, Atkinson.
Front row.—Ata Mohamed Shah, Arbab Mohamed Hussain, Ahmad Yar Khan.

GROUP SHOWING THE UNIFORMS WORN BY THE OFFICERS, 17TH CAVALRY.

Review order White (British).   Mess Dress Blue.   Review order Blue (British).
Drill order (Khaki). Review order Blue (Indian). Review order White (Indian). Field Service
Blue undress (British).   order (Indian).
[*N.B.*—Drill order Blue (Indian) and Mess Dress White unavoidably omitted.]

any duty with the regiment. Major and Brevet-Lieut.-Colonel R. W. Henderson, D.S.O., about the beginning of 1920 was transferred to command the 28th Light Cavalry; in him the regiment lost one of the most popular officers in the Indian Cavalry and a most capable soldier. Major and Brevet-Lieutenant-Colonel A. H. R. Dodd feeling that the prospect of promotion in the reduced cavalry service was hopeless, transferred to the Gurkhas; it had also been many years since he had done any regimental duty. Major T. W. Kirkwood, O.B.E., decided in 1921 to retire from the service to the general regret of everyone who knew him and proceeded on a year's leave. His retirement was not only a great loss to Indian Polo but also it meant the regiment losing a real regimental officer just at the time when they were needed the most.

Major Kenneth Barge, D.S.O., M.C., went to England at the end of 1920 for the purpose of becoming a student at the Staff College but his private affairs prevented his remaining in the service and he was in 1921 obliged to retire in order to look after them to the great regret of all his many friends He had a distinguished military career but had not done very much actual duty with the regiment since he left in 1909 to become A.-D.-C. to Sir Joceyline Woodhouse.

Captain I. D. Guthrie in 1921 completed his arrangements for an exchange from the Indian Army into the Enniskilling Dragoons and left us for good. He was another officer that the regiment could ill-afford to lose. He has since been transferred to the 10th Royal Hussars.

Captain W. E. Brierley, who so often figures in these pages under the name of "Bareilly", was another great loss. The Government having decided that regimental medical officers were to be done away with, in 1918 he left the regiment for the last time. Captain J. Hutchinson was another officer who we could ill afford to lose. He only joined the regiment in 1917 but he was most popular with all ranks and it was a matter of genera' regret when the loss of his father forced him to resign from the service to attend to his family affairs.

On arrival at Lucknow the regiment occupied the Government Mess house, an ugly and idiotically designed building near the Race Course, while the 37th Lancers occupied tents in the Mess compound. The combining of the two messes was a matter of some difficulty, for both messes were rather in debt. The debts of the 17th Cavalry Mess, although fairly heavy were well covered by substantial assets in silver, brakes, furniture, and crockery. Two minuses, however, do not make a plus in real life, as they do in Algebra; and it became finally necessary for the Trustees of 17th Cavalry Polo Club to purchase all the dead stock of the 17th Cavalry mess and thus provide that mess with funds to pay up its bills. As these bills were mainly due to necessity for replacing mess property damaged and destroyed by the numerous moves of the regiment, this arrangement was a very fair solution. The Trustees agreed to lend the property to the new regimental mess. Again, it had to be decided which belongings of the two regiments were most suitable for the amalgamated regiment, and which members of the two mess staffs should be retained. These and similar matters connected with the mess, the polo club, and various funds took some time to decide and much good humoured discussion. But there was none of the heart-burning we had been led to expect. The two regiments realised the necessity of carrying out their unpleasant task as smoothly as possible, and both the Indian and the British officers co-operated, to make the fusion of the two bodies take place with a minimum of heat.

General Sir William Peyton's inspection, on November 25th, 1921, marks the closing scene of our regimental history although we survived for three months afterwards. This old friend of the regiment came to see us before relinquishing command of the United Provinces District (that district which has been the scene of some of our happiest hours, through the *dâk jungle* and on the polo ground) and after the formal inspection was over, he sent for all the officers and said, speaking with obvious emotion :—" On relinquishing command of the United Provinces District I am glad to have been able to come to say good-bye to the 17th Cavalry whom I have known for twelve years. There is no regiment of Indian Cavalry for whom I have greater respect, and I say this with full knowledge, as you were with me for some years in the Meerut Cavalry Brigade and always did me well. I hope you will carry on your fine tradition of efficiency in the new regiment."

After this there remains little to tell. On the surface, things went on much as usual. Lucknow is a delightful station during the winter months. There were afternoons on the Martiniere polo ground which is one of the best in India; week-ends on the splendid *jheels* by Mohanlalgunj with their glittering water and wheeling companies of duck and geese, and the great turquoise vault of sky which is the chief beauty of the Indian country-side, and odd half hours at the ever-glorious Residency, and evenings at the Chattar Manzil, dancing to the "Queen's" band among the hand-painted arabesques of a vanished harem of Oudh. We settled into our houses, we started the polo team, began regimental training and rehearsal parades for the Prince of Wales' visit.

GROUPS TO SHOW UNIFORMS AND CLASSES OF 17TH CAVALRY, LUCKNOW, 1922.

Punjabi (Tiwana). Pathan (Khalil). Punjabi (Tiwana). Pathan (Afridi). Punjabi (Awan).
Stewart. Risaldar Major Rahmat Sher Khan.
Pathan (Khalil).

Indian Officers Field Service Order. Indian Officers Drill Order Blue.
Indian Officer (short coat) Khaki. Indian Officer Review Order. Indian Officer Drill Order Khaki.
Sowar Review Order White. Kote Dufadar Full Dress.
Indian Officers Review Order White. Sowar Field Service Order.
Indian Officer in plain clothes. N.-C. O. in plain clothes.
N.-C. O. Drill Order Khaki. Trumpeter Drill Order Khaki (dismounted).

The Royal visit took place from the 10th to the 15th December. A regimental team won the polo tournament that took place in the Prince's honour, and in the Gymkhana race meeting a few days later several regimental ponies distinguished themselves. Griffith's "Fanny" ridden by Atkinson won the polo scurry against some of the best polo ponies in India.

Lieutenant Malik Khizar Mahamed Hayat Khan Tiwana, son of the Hon'ble Nawab Colonel Sir Umar Hayat Khan Tiwana, was during this year gazetted to the regiment as an Honorary Officer. He was the only Indian who ever held a British rank in the 17th Cavalry with the exception of two Indian officers who were given Honorary British ranks on retirement.

There was a glut of officers at this time. We had about fifteen and the 37th Lancers about thirty, and as the men were due their Christmas leave and there was little work to do, many of the 17th went down to Calcutta to see the polo there and later to Delhi and Meerut. Our successes in these tournaments are described in another place.

Some time in December we were photographed, squadron by squadron, and as a whole regiment. This was the first, and the last time, during Colonel Barry-Smith's tenure of command that he had been able to get the whole regiment together. After the picture had been taken, some of the older officers rode back with the Colonel. We had expected a few words from him, on this, the last occasion we should meet together as a regiment. But his heart was too full to speak. Indeed there was nothing to be said.

Our friend Rahmat Sher, the oldest serving member of the regiment, except the Moulvi Sahib, left on February the 17th, and the following regimental order was published:—

"On the retirement of Risaldar-Major Rahmat Sher, I.D.S.M., the Commanding Officer wishes to bring to notice his meritorious service. By hard work and absolute integrity he has raised himself from sowar to the rank of Risaldar-Major, an example to all ranks of upright and trustworthy service."

By his retirement, the British officers lost a faithful friend, and the regiment a very gallant soldier. May he long be spared to guide his people—the trans-border Afridis—in the paths of wisdom and comparative virtue and may he live long enough to see another war because he loves fighting, and because those who have fought with him, would like to have him again by their side!

The regiment amalgamated with the 37th Lancers at Lucknow on the 15th February 1922 and the new regiment became the 17th/37th Cavalry, a name since changed to the 15th Lancers.

The following British officers of the late 17th Cavalry were posted to appointments in the new amalgamated regiment :—

Lieutenant-Colonel R. C. Barry-Smith—Commandant.
Major H. S. Stewart—Squadron Commander.
Major F. C. C. Yeats-Brown—Squadron Officer.
Major E. G. Atkinson—Squadron Officer.
Captain J. A. W. Foottit—Squadron Officer.
Captain R. P. I. Cochrane—Squadron Officer.

Attached officers.

Captain S. H. Persse—Squadron Officer.
Captain J. S. Ballantine—Adjutant.
Captain W. S. Griffiths—Squadron Officer.
Captain C. Pert—Squadron Officer.
Lieutenant V. H. Dixon—Squadron Officer.
Lieutenant E. P. S. Monckton—Squadron Officer.
Lieutenant J. A. Greenway—Squadron officer.

Of these Lieutenant-Colonel Barry-Smith, Major Yeats-Brown, Captain Cochrane, Captain Griffiths, Lieutenant Dixon and Lieutenant Monckton have since retired or resigned from the service.

The following Indian officers of the late 17th Cavalry were posted to the new regiment :—

Risaldar Bahadur Sher Khan (Khalil Pathan)—Risaldar-Major.

Risaldar Malik Alam Sher Khan, I.D.M.S. (Punjabi Tiwana)—Troop Commander.

Risaldar Ata Mohamed Shah (Kohistani Afghan)—Troop Commander.

Risaldar Inayat-ullah Khan (Babar Pathan)—Troop Commander.

Jamadar Arbab Mohamed Husain (Khalil Pathan)—Troop Commander.

Jamadar Mohamed Aslam Khan (Akora Khattak Pathan)—Troop Commander.

The final parade of the regiment at Lucknow, February 1922.

Jamadar Ahmad Ali Khan (Punjabi Awan)—Wardi-Major of the late 17th Cavalry, was appointed Indian Quartermaster.

Dafadar Mir Amanat-ullah (Koreshi)—Head Clerk of the late 17th Cavalry, was promoted Jamadar and appointed Head Clerk of the amalgamated regiment.

Risaldar Malik Alam Sher Khan, I.D.S.M., and Jamadar Ahmed Ali Khan were very shortly afterwards transferred to the Remount Department, and Risaldar Inayat-ullah Khan retired on pension.

The following Indian Officers retired from the service on amalgamation:—

1. Risaldar-Major Rahmat Sher, I.D.S.M., from 18th March 1922.

2. Risaldar Wazir Khan, I.O.M., from 11tk February 1922.

3. Risaldar Dost Mohamed Khan, from 1st January 1922. (Afterwards appointed A.-D.-C. to H. H. the Nawab of Rampur.)

4. Risaldar Wazir Mohammed, M.B.E., from 15th March 1922.

5. Risaldar Sultan Sikandar Khan, from 1st January 1922.

6. Jamadar Malik Ghulam Husain Khan, 31st January 1922.

7. Jamadar Malik Ahmad Yar Khan, 1st January 1922.

8. Jamadar Pir Dad Khan, from 31st January 1922.

9. Jamadar Alam Khan, 5th February 1922.

Lieutenant-Colonel R. C. Barry-Smith was the last Commanding Officer of the 17th Cavalry. He was *par excellence* a regimental soldier. Starting life in the Gloucestershire Regiment, he was transferred to the Indian Army and spent the remainder of his service in the 17th Cavalry. The regiment and its affairs were his principle interests in life and he will be long remembered by all who knew him as a high principled English gentleman who always did his duty and saw that other people did theirs. He successfully attained to the two goals that all regimental soldiers should aim at, having been both Adjutant and Commanding Officer of his own regiment.

On the retirement of the last Commandant the control and administration of the affairs of the 17th Cavalry devolved on the Second-in-Command, Major H. S. Stewart.

* * * *

We have done. We have been amalgamated and abolished. The 17th Cavalry has gone but we will not complain. Ghosts cannot complain. We have however taken the privilege of ghosts and have haunted for a spell the times of which tradition tell us the romance of Robarts, the old days on the frontier, the hopes of our youth and the scenes of our middle age. For an evening by the fireside, you who come after us, may follow the career—undistinguished perhaps,—yet not altogether forgotten in India, of one of the silladar regiments that have served the Throne.

We have traced our story from the red dawn of the Mutiny years to the angry sunset of post-war economies. From storm to storm, from the hatreds, hangings and loot of 1858 to the squabbling and pinchbeck policies of 1922, we have reviewed the daily life of the regiment. Whether on the polo grounds of the Punjab or on the fields of Flanders, whatever sky was above them, the regiment has had a heart for any fate. And, if, in the years to comes, in the turmoil of the awaking East, or the travail of a world at war, our men have again to draw their swords then the spirit—if not the body—of the old 17th may live again.

The Officers' Mess Plate, 17th Cavalry

ENVOI.

Few are the years of man and sorrow laden: so brief has been the life of the 17th Bengal Cavalry that its existence has merely coincided with that of its first leader*. No genial fortune was present at its birth: and since the storm of the Mutiny died away, few indeed are the campaigns incident to the expansion of the British power in which it has taken part. Now for the second time it has fallen. Yet what has not fallen with it, and to that which remains what duration can be assigned?

One hundred years have passed away since the eye of the philosopher discerned the spectre of Napoleon standing on the brink of and gazing into an abyss, strewn with the fragments of an earlier world. In that hundred years what great events have transpired. Can we not say with the orator Aeschines " what is there among the list of strange and unexpected events which have not occurred in our time? Our lives have transcended the limits of humanity: we are born to serve as a theme for incredible tales to posterity."

The English soldier has placed his King upon the throne of Akbar, and has entered the storied halls of Chosroes and Al Raschid. Kabul and Mandalay have resounded to his steadfast tread: *super et Garamantos et Indos proferet imperium.* Again the sons of Edward " untaught to yield, thronged to Crecy's laurelled field." Enduring martyrlike the vast and aimless slaughters of the Somme and Paschendaele, like the Roman he stood at length victorious on the Rhine and the Euphrates. *Quæ caret ora cruore nostro ?*

The English monarchy has withstood the dangers of a thousand years, and still rides the wave beneath which lie whelmed the houses of Romanoff, of Habsburg and Hohenzollern.

Yet the victorious Nadir upon the throne of Timour, ignorant of the assassin and the fated term of his life and labours, acknowledged that he was in His hands before Whom the thrones of kings and deep ocean of earthly glory are no more than the bubble floating on the surface of the wave. It behoves us then to remember the vicissitudes of fortune. The spider has woven her web in the halls of Cyrus, and the owl has sung her song on the watch tower of Afrasiab.

---

* de Kantzow.

APPENDICES.

REGIMENTAL MARCH OF THE 17TH CAVALRY.

"The Coronation March."

From

le Prophete (Meyerbeer).

STATIONS OF THE 17TH CAVALRY.

Meerut and Rohilkhand	1858—59
Cawnpore	1859—62
Segowlie	1862—65
Bhutan Expedition	1865—66
Barrackpur	1866—68
Sitapur	1869—71
Sialkot	1872—76
Peshawar	1876—79
Afghan War	1879—80
Bareilly	1881—82
Disbanded	June 30th, 1882
Re-raised	September 18th, 1885
Mian Mir (Lahore Cantonment)	1885
Ferozepore	1886—91
Loralai	1891—93
Amballa	1894—97
Mian Mir (Lahore Cantonment)	1898—00
Rawalpindi	1900—04
Bannu	1904—08
Bareilly	1909—13
Allahabad	1914—16
Jhansi	1916—17
Jullundur and Risalpur	(October and November) 1917
Lahore	1917—20
Rawalpindi	1920—21
Dera Ismail Khan	(April to November) 1921
Lucknow	1921—22
Amalgamated with the 37th Lancers	February 15th, 1922

APPENDIX I

THE FATHERS OF THE 17TH CAVALRY.

NOTES ON COLONEL C. J. ROBARTS AND COLONEL C. A. de KANTZOW.

ROBARTS.

Charles James Robarts was born on the 28th of August 1820, he arrived in India at Fort William and was admitted to the service on the 2nd of August 1839. He was then nearly nineteen years of age. He was first sent to do duty with the 40th Native Infantry at Dinapore, and was subsequently posted to the 43rd East India Light Infantry in the Army of the Indus and directed to join the Depôt Company of that unit at Bareilly. From there he must have joined his unit during 1840—42. During 1843 he proceeded to Europe on a year's leave without pay; subsequently he was posted to the 14th Irregular Cavalry. This regiment mutinied, while he was on leave in England in 1857, as he foretold that it would. He served in the First Afghan War, in the Sikh War 1848-49 and in the Bhootan Campaign and was awarded a medal for each. Apparently he refused to accept the Mutiny medal, and it is thought that his reason for so doing was to mark his resentment against the Indian authorities who had laughed at him for warning them that the mutiny was going to take place.

He was very eccentric, fond of having his own way and cared very little for Government orders. Possessed of an income of some £5,000 or £6,000 a year, he lived with patriarchal dignity amidst a mass of retainers collected from India, the Frontier and Central Asia, by the pleasing news of the mediæval hospitality which he dispensed. He was liberal to a degree and many were the officers that he helped out of a scrape never asking or expecting to see his money back. He also used to advance money to the men of the regiment without dreaming of any interest; all he wanted was to see them mounted on waler horses.

He was an early riser, a non-drinker and a non-smoker, an excellent pistol shot and one of the best judges of a horse in India. Although he never went to church, he was in his own quiet way quite religious, and despite the fact that he was an adept at strong language in many tongues, he seldom employed it.

He stood about five feet nine and was well built. His eyes were blue and his hair reddish. He always dressed very plainly and had a strong preference for grey coloured clothes, always affected a grey felt *topee* with a grey *puggari* and invariably wore Wellington boots. He disliked wearing uniform and avoided doing so whenever he possibly could. He had a peculiar idiosyncracy of sticking the corner of his handkerchief into his mouth and going about like this. He invariably rode Arabs himself, although owning many Walers as well. He usually kept some seventy animals in his private stables. He was very keen on hunting and always kept a pack of hounds. When he became so senior as to be in command of the stations where the regiment was quartered he used to tell the commanding officers of British units that hunting was better for subalterns than parade; he would then remove batches of the latter and take them off to the meet where they were mounted on his own horses.

He was extraordinarily fond of racing and won many races all over India. Amongst these were included the Viceroy's Cup and the Calcutta Derby. The records of those far off days are very fragmentary, even in the archives of the Royal Calcutta Turf Club; but it appears that Robarts raced under the name of "Mr. W. W." and that he was a very well known figure on the turf. In spite of his fondness for racing it is worthy of note that he never attended a lottery or indulged in any betting.

He was a great linguist, wrote well and often sent contributions to the papers and was a great Russophobist. As well as foretelling the mutiny, he also prophesied the Afghan War which broke out some five years after his death. He had inherited considerable wealth from his father but he must himself have been a man of considerable financial ability because, despite his lavish expenditure, his wealth continued to increase. He apparently was one of those lucky men who turn to gold whatever they touch. He was promoted Lieutenant-Colonel in 1862, Brevet-Colonel in 1865 and substantive Colonel in 1867.

Regarded with affection and respect by all who knew him he continued to command the regiment from the time it was raised until the time of his death. He was more than a commandant however. To the men of the regiment he was a feudal chieftain and they were his followers and retainers; for a more complete parallel one must go back to the commanders of the "Free companies of the middle ages."

de KANTZOW.

Charles Adolphus de Kantzow was born on the 27th of June 1835. He appears to have been originally posted to the 38th Bengal Native Infantry and subsequently in 1858 sent to the 48th Bengal Native Infantry. This latter transfer must have been about the time when his Levy was incorporated in Robarts' Horse. He was promoted Captain in 1865, Brevet-Major in 1866, Brevet-Lieutenant-Colonel in 1876 and substantive Colonel 1883. He was admitted to Colonel's allowances on the 14th September 1891.

de Kantzow, although only remaining with the unit known as Robarts' Horse for a few months after the incorporation of his Levy with that corps, must nevertheless be regarded equally with Robarts as the father of the 17th Cavalry. His Levy numbered rather more than about half the effective strength of Robarts' new corps; in fact, remembering how this Levy had been welded together into a unit in the field, it must already have acquired sufficient individuality to make it reasonable to almost regard "Robarts' Horse" as "de Kantzow's Horse" under a new name. The memory of a hero, such as de Kantzow had proved himself to be, must have remained cherished amongst the men that he had led during the stirring times of the mutiny long after his departure. Even in the presence of a dominating personality, like Robarts, de Kantzow's name and traditions must have left in Robarts' Horse an inheritance which could not fail to stamp itself on the unit of which so many members had served under his banner. The essential modesty of his character is well illustrated by the fact that the only portrait that he ever had taken was the one of his youth.* A copy has been published in this book but it is regretted that the lapse of time has caused it to fade somewhat. It shows a handsome young man in a semi-military dress which sets off his tall and sinewy form. One can judge his daring and romantic character from the cast of his countenance ; and in his eyes shine that romantic valour and boiling courage that led him to charge sword in hand single handed and to put to flight hundreds of mutineers. He was of foreign most probably Polish origin—one of a race whose military temperament specially draws them to the mounted arm. The Indian Army lost one of those born cavalry leaders, who are so seldom met, when de Kantzow (probably from disgust at the loss of his Levy) passed into civil employ.

His services during the mutiny were of a very distinguished nature and a statement describing them is appended.

---
*Taken in 1859 by Mr. Rushton, Superintendent of Telegraphs, who served under e Kantzow as a Volunteer in the Agra Militia Cavalry.

War Services.

He served with the 90th Native Infantry during operations against the Bassee-Khel Afridis on the Peshawar frontier in 1855. He was present at Mynpooree during and subsequent to the mutiny of the Native troops at that station in May 1857, receiving Her Majesty's approbation and an autograph letter of thanks from H. E. the Governor-General for the admirable services rendered by him at the eminent peril of his life on that occasion. He was present with thirty-nine sowars in the action on the sixth of June 1857 at Bowgong against detachments of the mutineers (of the 7th Light Cavalry, 13th, 48th and 71st Native Infantry) from Lucknow. On this occasion, he in a hand-to-hand conflict, killed the rebel leader, being himself wounded on the forehead with a sabre cut. He served at Mynpooree in command of an Irregular Force and subsequently as a volunteer in the action near Agra on the fifth of July 1857 against the Neemuch mutineers. On this occasion he had a horse killed under him. He served as volunteer in all the minor operations against rebels in Agra District up to the nineteenth of August 1857 and also as Commandant of a detachment of cavalry at Agra. He was in action near Alyghur on the twenty-fourth of August 1857 and in the subsequent operations carried out by Colonel Montgomery's Column. For these operations he was mentioned in despatches.

He served as a volunteer in the action of the tenth of October 1857 at Agra against the Mhow and Delhi mutineers, and as Commandant of the Muttra Horse in Colonel Cotton's movable column during operations against Fatehpur Sikri and elsewhere in Agra and Muttra Districts. He raised and organised the Fatehpur Police battalion and served as Commandant of the same under General Sir T. Seaton, K.C.B., at Bangaon, where he had a charger and a troop horse wounded under him. For these operations he was mentioned in despatches. He was present at Shahjehanpur commanding the cavalry, in the action of the 3rd of May 1858, and in the defence of the Jail under Colonel Hale, C.B., where he had a charger wounded under him, and was mentioned in despatches. He was present in affairs subsequent to relief by Brigadier Jones, C.B., including the action of the 15th of May 1858. During these he was very dangerously wounded by a sabre on the face and the right arm.

He was made Commandant of the Oudh Auxiliary Levy raised by him for the defence of Powaine, and was present during the period from June to November 1858, at the attack on the enemy's outposts at Ahmednagar and at the defence of Powaine. He received the thanks of the Government of India on each occasion

He served with his Levy against the rebels of the Shahjehanpur District, across the Sarda, during the move on Pullee, and during the expulsion of the rebels from the fort and the town and in the pursuit of the enemy into Oudh. He was again thanked by the Government of India.

He served with Brigadier Dennis' Column in Khyreeghur jungles and in two actions with rebels in January 1859. For this he was mentioned in despatches. He served with his Levy in clearing up the jungles, etc., until the end of the operations. For this he again received the thanks of the Government of India.

He received the special thanks and gracious approbation of Her Majesty for excellent services rendered to the State during the period from 1857-58.

He was officially and specially reported to Government when leaving Rohilkund in 1859 for "valuable services rendered by the force under his command in Rohilkund," and honourably mentioned by the North-West Province Government to the Government of India.

[*The following is an extract of the " Pioneer," dated February 17th, 1927, subsequent to the printing of the History.*]

THE LATE COLONEL C. A. DE KANTZOW.

Colonel C. A. de Kantzow, who died at Brighton recently, was a prominent figure in Delhi forty years ago. He was a son of Baron St. George de Kantzow and was born in 1835. When eighteen he was nominated to a cadetship of the East Indian Company and joined the Bengal Army. After serving in the Indian Mutiny he held various civil appointments. During the Bengal famine of 1874 he had charge of the transport of grain to the seriously afflicted districts of Bihar and later he was superintendent of the bazars of Delhi. He served in this country for thirty-eight years and retired forty years ago.

APPENDIX II.

SKETCHES OF LIFE IN THE 17TH CAVALRY, 1886 TO 1894.

I.—FEROZEPORE—MARCH 1886 TO OCTOBER 1891.

"*Naya pul karib taiyar hai, Sahib.*"—Thus spoke old Mahmud Khan, second senior Indian officer and commanding the then "B" troop of the regiment, which is returning from one of its annual cold weather outings to Mian Mir, and having camped successively at Kana Kacha, Luliani and Kasur, spent the previous night at "Ganda Singh Wala" and is now crossing the Sutlej by two bridges of boats and three sand banks on its march in to Ferozepore. To its right the new masonry bridge nearly two hundred yards long over the Sutlej (the first of the Punjab rivers to be bridged by a combined rail and road bridge) produces the Rissaldar's remark, which is manifestly correct, as the bridge was opened (in a good old Ferozepore sandstorm) a few months later, in April 1887.

After crossing the river the regiment halts for a few minutes on the left bank, and all ranks spend the interval in watching the toy train, that has just wound along the "*Kacha*" at the side of the road from Ferozepore, being taken across the river. The engine is too heavy for the bridge of boats, so the semi-open carriages are uncoupled and joined by long pieces of wood with hooks at the ends, to be pushed across by coolies, while the passengers have to alight and walk.

From there the road winds past the Fort and Arsenal, along a wide shady road, just touching the fringe of the city, till it reaches the sandy *maidan* some three-quarters of a mile in length, which brings the regiment (headed by two *surnai* players and a drummer), to the newly constructed lines with their tiny trees trying to grow in that arid soil.

On arrival at the lines, while waiting for "stables," the officers stand about, talking and chaffing among themselves, and with the Indian officers. Good old Izzat Khan (one of the best of the lot) begins by pointing out that during the absence of the regiment he has had his house colour-washed pale blue because Burton Sahib had told him it looked untidy, whereupon the latter retaliates as soon as the Rissaldar's back is turned by "posting" his *dak* in the tops of the Indian officer's boots, which are considerably too wide, owing to his calves not being big enough to fill the space required for the passage of his heels. Attention is also drawn to the growth of Izzat Khan's son Kaim, who is told that he will soon have to enlist in the regiment. The time of waiting is also diversified by the appearance of the Bengali Head Clerk, Suraj Narain, to complain to the Commanding Officer that the Adjutant had called him "you d—d man," but before he has done more than begin his complaint, he is hustled away by the Indian officers and nothing more is heard of the "insult." On the arrival of the patients in the Horse Hospital, shortly before stables, the condition of the sick is reported by the head *salutri*, Rajab Khan. He was the last of the old race of *salutris*, a class of men who carried on their calling from father to son without any training at a Veterinary College. They began as boys by being first bottle-washers, then assistants, and lastly they developed into full blown *salutris*, ready in time to step into their parents' shoes.

After "stables" all the bachelors proceed to the mess just behind: a very fine house belonging to the Rajah of Faridkote with quarters for three officers and a swimming bath. In the latter most of us disport ourselves twice daily; before breakfast to wash off the dust collected in our morning's work and again before dinner. To-day three of us amuse ourselves by an attempt to duck Bower, but he is much too strong a swimmer, and, keeping shoulders as well as head above water, puts a big hand on each of our heads in turn, and sends us all to the bottom while he goes scatheless. Just as the first of us are completing our toilets, Medley (the Adjutant) turns up with the news that as we had missed polo this week (only played twice a week then, and chukkers of ten minutes each) he has arranged a regimental game for this afternoon, for which we must all turn up.

Accordingly four o'clock sees us all assembled on the polo ground. Its beautiful *pat* surface remains in good condition for a chukker or two, after which it cuts up. There is a heterogeneous collection of ponies, all country breds; one of the best of them is Bucephalus, a man eater which can only be mounted when a cloth is placed over his head, and which briginally was bought as a grass-cutter's pony. The Indian officers, especially the direct-commissioned boys (Muhamad Husain, Muhamad Usman and Hayat Khan), the Mir Munshi Ghulam Muhy-ud-din,* and even some of the clerks, who are mounted on ponies take part. With this crowd participating one cannot say much for the quality of the game, but it is marked by *camaraderie* and good tempered chaff of all ranks, while it gives us British officers practice in hitting the ball and in riding each other off.

---

*Afterwards Risaldar-Major.

From the polo ground we adjourn to the Station Library, (which at that time took the place of the present day club) for drinks and to meet the small station world ; and later we all go again to the swimming bath. There we are joined by officers of other regiments, as well as old Allsop, the District Superintendent of Police, who can float like a porpoise.

Then to celebrate our return to Cantonments we dine at the R. A. Mess across the road, where we are entertained by many whose names are well known (or were at the time). Colonel "Joe" Hornsby, a character, and one of the best whist players in India, Major Lyster, Von Donop (afterwards Master General of Ordnance), Murchison, "Tommy" Lambert (now a Brigadier-General), Malleson (who later went into the Indian Army and became a Major-General).

The evening winds up with a "sing song," in this one of the chief performers is our grey-haired Montresor who shines in the Guards' song of the "Quirass" and in his favourite "Ticklebury Brown." He is more than seconded by his brother "Joey" of the 107th the Royal Sussex with a much more extended repertoire, which includes "The Boar." He has a very good voice. Trotter who is a versatile genius also contributes to the "harmony," by playing a few bars on various instruments, including the violin, the ocherino and the bagpipes!

And then to bed, and thus ends a day in good old Ferozepur.

II.—THE LAWRENCEPORE CAMP.

"*Too ti too...000*"—"Oh D—! there's reveille!"

"*Sahib, char taiyar hai*"—"Oh Lord how beastly dark and cold it is!"

"Hullo young man, time to be up"—this last summons is from Colonel Kauntze, our Commanding Officer, who is always up first and who after dressing, amuses himself by poking his head into each officer's tent in turn to see that they too are rising.

The above occurs in the autumn of 1887 on the march from Ferozepore to the cavalry camp at Lawrencepore. This is the first camp in which the recently raised 17th Bengal Cavalry has taken part, and the first to be held under an Inspector-General of Cavalry in India—General Luck who has just received the appointment.

Colonel Kauntze still adhered to the custom of marching before dawn. This practice was very unpleasant on a cold winter morning in the Punjab (when as often as not there was ice in the basins in our tents) and even then it was nearly obsolete. During the preliminary parading and marching off, one's fingers and toes felt frozen. However after half a mile we had a dismount, followed by a mile on foot leading our horses, and then a trot of a mile. This thaws everything, including our tempers and brings us to sunrise, and what a sunrise it is! To our right runs the long range of the Pir Panjal, which when we start looms merely as a dark mass hardly discernable against the stars, but which now turns to a pearly grey with the first light. At dawn the peaks at first show cold and white, but become rose coloured as the rising sun lights them up with its rays, and finally the sun rises over the summit and shows us clearly the grandeur of the mountain chain of the Himalayas.

Our early start brings us to our camping ground by eight o'clock or soon after, the horses are watered, the tents are pitched, and the grass-cutters, as soon as they have got rid of the loads on their ponies go off with them to descend on the country side like a swarm of locusts; they cut grass between the fields or anywhere they can find it, according to the custom which the irregular cavalry of India had practiced from time immemorial.

While everything is thus being prepared for "stables," the officers adjourn for breakfast, and during this interval I cannot do better than introduce our small party. A very small one compared with the number of officers with a cavalry regiment now-a-days, and peculiar in its way as it is composed of three full colonels, one captain and three subalterns, two of whom are probationers.

The first is of course Colonel E. H. E. Kauntze, the first commanding officer of the re-raised regiment. He has a beautiful seat on a horse in spite of his snow white hair and moustache, and is the most fluent speaker of down country Hindustani that I have ever met.

Next to him comes Colonel Reginald Sartorius, who won the V. C. and C. M. G. in the Ashanti War, and who is one of the finest and most powerful men in the Indian Army. He would perhaps have made better sailor than a soldier. (I have yachted with him in Kashmir). But at any rate he has one necessary attribute for a cavalryman, he can both move himself and make the regiment do the same. I remember on one occasion at Ferozepore when he was officiating in command of the regiment, he appeared at morning parade on his huge charger and began circling about at some distance from where the regiment was drawn up. The adjutant waited, thinking he was not ready, until he thundered out "Mr. Mardall," and when the latter galloped out and explained why he had not reported the parade at once. Good old " Sartor " told him "I come on to parade at the gallop, I expect the adjutant to report to me at the gallop, and I sound the gallop!"

To show what a hard man " Sartor " was, I may mention that both mornings in bivouac he had his morning tub by the means of a *bhisti* emptying a *mussak* of icy cold water over his head while he squatted on the ground in pyjamas; as his squadron officer I felt bound to follow his example, but can't say I exactly enjoyed it, though at that time he must have been about fifty while I was less than half that age.

The last of our colonels is W. A. Lawrence, a nephew of the mutiny Lawrence, who is possessed of great knowledge of Indians and was much loved by them.

Our captain is R. F. Trotter, who had served originally in a Hussar regiment and had run an excellent circus for them. He is a man of great character, and a very powerful horseman who can ride anything.

The only subaltern who actually belongs to the regiment is W. S. Mardall, who started in the Marines, and who was later eventually transferred as a Major to the 31st Lancers which he commanded until his death at Kohat.

The first of the probationers is Lieutenant J. Fernley Stewart, who had a somewhat varied career. He commenced his army life as a Highlander and from there he came to the 17th. In 1888 he went into the commissariat department later returning to cavalry (he was I think posted to the 14th B. L.), and afterwards he joined the Judge-Advocate-General's Department in which I think he remained till he died as a Major.

Then comes E. W. Boudier, lately joined from the artillery, and a future commanding officer of the regiment, in which he served for close on thirty years.

And lastly (but not till half way through this camp) the " Bold Griffin " joined us, with his famous racing mare " Sally " and a riding boy. The life of the latter with the regiment was short and unfortunate, as on the second day after his arrival, to use Griffin's own words "I heard a noise outside my tent in the early morning, and on looking out found the commanding officer and the adjutant flogging my riding boy for transgressing the sanitary rules of the Camp." I think I must give one more anecdote of Griffin: when he had been about eighteen months with us the commanding officer had him up and asked him what steps he was taking to acquire a second charger, to which his characteristic reply was—" Well sir, I think my mare ' Sally ' is in foal to a Norfolk Trotter !"

There was not much shooting on the Grand Trunk Road north of Lahore, but on most afternoons, some of us wandered out with a gun. Occasionally we succeeded in bringing back a bird or two for the pot. On the day about which I am writing however, the regiment was challenged to a cricket match by the Mission School at Gujrat. We accepted, although none of us were much to talk about as cricketers, and our eleven was completed with Indian officers who had never touched a bat. The match was played on a spare portion of the camping ground, with a path for the pitch; this being the only bit of true ground that we could find. The result was rather disastrous for us, as the boys, who won the toss went in first, and had only lost about three wickets by the tea interval. After this we took an innings and were all out for a very small score before dark. That is to say the British officers were, as funnily enough all the Indian officers who had been playing suddenly found it necessary to go off to "stables" after tea, and they did not return.

On arrival at Rawalpindi we were met by the post orderly with two telegrams for "A" Squadron—one for Colonel Sartorius announcing the arrival of a daughter, and the other for Risaldar Izzat Khan informing him that he was a grandfather; the latter infant being the future Jemadar Daim Khan of the regiment.

Now to pass on to the camp itself; this took place at Hazro on the edge of the Hatti Jheel, three marches beyond Rawalpindi, and was a very strenuous one. It took a good deal out of our young horses, mostly of whom were little more than re-mounts, as parades were either on marsh, or on sandy stony ground towards the Indus. The 17th was brigaded with the 12th Cavalry and the Guides Cavalry with Colonel MacNaghten of the 13th Bengal Lancers as Brigadier. The other Brigadiers were I think Colonel Benson of the 17th Lancers and Colonel Wardrop of a Hussar Regiment. There was not time for much in the way of amusement, but we did manage to get a few games of polo, the outstanding figures in which that I remember being D'Aguilar and one or two others of the 17th Lancers, George Richardson and Money (both Captains) of the 18th Bengal Lancers, Stuart Beatson of the 11th, one of the brothers Peyton, and Smith of the 12th, all well known polo players both before and since.

The Camp lasted from about the end of November till about the 21st December, finishing as a grand *finale* (at which Lord and Lady Roberts were present) with two nights in bivouac with no tents at all and a series of battles between the division and a skeleton enemy formed chiefly by the K. D. G's. under Colonel **Napier.**

"Charlie" Muir, our future commanding officer and then seconded with the Viceroy's Bodyguard, also paid us a visit during this camp.

III.—LORALAI, 1892-93.

Loralai, a post in the Bori valley between Harnai on the railway and Zhob, was undoubtedly the worst of the Bengal Cavalry stations at the time of which I am writing. It was a cheerless looking valley, a few miles long by about one wide, surrounded by nearly bare stony hills. The valley itself was literally covered with stones so thickly that a horse could not put his foot down without hitting three at least. To cope with these conditions we had to get out extra heavy horse shoes from England. It was also an unhealthy station then, as the water supply was brought into cantonments in open "*karezes*," which formed excellent breeding grounds for mosquitoes, while sandflies also abounded. The officers' quarters consisted of mud erections providing each officer a room fifteen feet square and a bath-room; the roofs were of tin with about four inches of mud on the top. The lines were government ones and fairly-good, but almost treeless; indeed the only trees to be seen in this desolate spot were in the cantonment gardens, and in the neighbourhood of the so-called "city" situated about half a mile away.

On the Thursday morning of which I am writing I, as adjutant, am deprived of my "Europe morning" by having to take a squad of recruits at musketry: rather an unpleasant job when the usual strong dust wind blowing down the valley makes shooting difficult, as well as making a *Poshtin* over one's uniform a necessity.

Musketry over, I return to the lines cold and hungry but before I can get my breakfast I have also to superintend a *post mortem* on a horse that died in the night of colic. This is rather prevalent, owing to the fact that the only fodder available is *bhoosa*, which is difficult to thoroughly clean in such a dusty windy place.

However this ends my labours for the day, and after hurriedly changing into shooting kit, I join Montresor and Burton at the mess for breakfast, as we are going up the valley for a day's shooting. There is a certain amount of this to be got; the one compensation for the other discomforts of the place. Here I may interrupt my story to mention that the mess is a station one, which we share with a Baluch regiment and a Mountain Battery. On my arrival this particular morning I find every one chortling over the complaint book; a remark of Wikeley's has called forth a scathing reply from our C. O., Colonel Lawrence, who is doing Mess President. In the innocence of his heart, Wikeley had entered a remark that he did not think meringues worth eating without cream, to which he received the retort that—"even if an angel from heaven came down to supply this Mess with Manna it would not satisfy some of the officers. How does Lieutenant Wikeley think it is possible to get cream, when even fresh milk is most difficult to procure?"

Breakfast over, the three of us set forth on regimental camels with their attendant sowars, the latter very keen, especially if allowed to *hallal* our birds and take some of the bag for their own eating. Our shoot to-day is to commence at a place (named Sirki Jangal if I remember right) about eight miles up and rather outside the Bori Valley; here there is a good place for chikor, just too far from cantonments to be much shot over. So we ride straight out there, leaving nearer places to be looked at on our return in the afternoon, only waiting once to try for snipe on a little patch of marsh formed by the overflow of a *karez*; successfully too, for the little patch some fifty yards square holds half a dozen snipe, of which Montresor and Burton (both good shots) account for four. On arrival at Sirki Jangal the camels are tied up, and we take to the hill side forming a line with the camel sowars between the guns. In a long tramp over the stony slopes, intersected by nullahs, we succeed in getting a dozen birds before our expenditure of cartridges makes them too wild. When we decide that the time has arrived, we try for a different kind of game, and proceed to where a line of mud circles about three feet high shows that there is an underground *karez*, which has been tapped by the wily Pathan before it gets far enough from the hill to emerge and flow above ground. These mud erections mark holes like wells going down to the underground stream, and as a rule hold pigeon. We commence operations by going to the highest and throw down a stone or two with no result, the second is equally fruitless, but at the third we are encouraged by the sound of flattering wings, which becomes louder at the fourth, and at the fifth, pigeon begin popping out by twos and threes like birds out of a trap, and make very pretty shooting. By the time we have shot about a dozen of the wells and scared away the remaining birds, we have made quite a decent bag. By this time too we are quite ready for lunch, and still more ready for a drink, so we unstrap a specially constructed *tiffin* box from behind one of the camel saddles, and refresh ourselves before commencing our return down the valley. That return we carry out slowly, riding at times, but often dismounting to beat through any likely bit of ground or *karez*, for in that dry stony country any little stream, a few foot wide with marshy banks, may hold snipe, teal, or even an occasional duck. By the time we reach cantonments we have made quite a decent mixed bag, including all of the above as well as a hare, a few *sisi* (the smallest and best eating partridge), four "Blacks," and even on this occasion an *Honbara*, which, though rare in that country, is found occasionally.

This has given us a longish day, and when we get back we are all ready for a hot tub and dinner; but in spite of being fairly hungry I am afraid that I must confess to being a trifle late for mess. On arrival, after apologising to the President, I seat myself next Colonel "B" of the Baluchis, who happens to have a vacant seat on each side of him. I notice smiles round the table when I cheerfully wish him good evening without eliciting much response, but being quite innocent of the cause, I go on talking unconcernedly until he thaws and becomes more genial. Afterwards I hear that just before my arrival he had been inveighing against officers being late for mess, so that my coming in gaily had of course been like a red rag to a bull, and the others had all been expecting that my advances would draw down a scathing retort on my head.

That same night, while playing whist after dinner, we suddenly heard a rattle and a roar coming down the valley, followed by the house shaking, and then the rattle going on down the valley, an earthquake, and the most terrifying that I have ever heard, probably owing to the shifting of stones in the hills by which we were surrounded. It was so terrifying indeed that one of our four clasped his cards to his bosom and started to leave the mess hurriedly until he saw that the rest of us had not moved. The earthquake did no damage to our mud bungalows, but we heard next day that it had almost demolished the stone staging bungalow at Sinjawi, twenty miles down the road to Harnai, and had considerably damaged the one at Tar Khan, a stage further on.

One more incident and my day is done. At that time I was keeping a spaniel (nicknamed "The Mother" by Gee, because she had had so many families) belonging to Wall, who was on leave. I had beaten her several times for being on my bed when I got back from mess, which had evidently taught her a lesson, for on this occasion as I passed round my hut and looked through the window, I saw her just jumping off the bed on hearing my approaching footsteps. When I got in, however, I found her only *sound* asleep on her own blanket on the floor; *not* blowing the bed to cool the place where she had been sleeping, which as Kipling says "is another story" that I am too truthful to repeat.

GROUP AT FEROZEPORE

Ahmed Khan, Izzat Khan, Holland-Pryor.
Saadut Khan. Azam Khan.
Colonel Burton Hudson
(2nd Lancers.)

IV.—THE MARCH FROM LORALAI TO AMBALLA.

This was a longish march that occupied from the 6th December 1893 to the 24th January 1894, and which took us through many different kinds of country, down to the bottom of the Bori valley, and still on through the stony Baluch Hills until we passed Fort Munro, and came down to a sandy waste with nothing to shoot till we reached the Indus at Dera Ghazi Khan. At that time this place was still undamaged by the river, and the channel was indeed some miles away from the Cantonment. Here we halted a day being hospitably entertained by the "Piffers,"* and reach Multan for Christmas—rather luckily for us, as the turkey we had brought with us for the occasion had found camel riding so unpleasant that he had died prematurely. Our Christmas dinner in the 15th Bengal Lancers' mess was therefore very acceptable.

From there we marched along a "*kacha*" road through sand, *păt*, and smallish jungle (now I believe transformed into fertile country by the Lower Bari Doab Canal), till we had passed the Montgomery district, after which we struck regular forests. There was a good deal of mixed shooting all this part of the march, and most days some of us went out on camels taking *chukkers* on each side of the road along which the regiment was marching, so that we were able to keep an "All Blaze"† going all right.

There had not been many changes among the officers of the regiment since we had left Ferozepore. Wall and Hudson had joined the better part of a year before then, and shortly before the march from Loralai, Colonel Lawrence had said goodbye to the regiment and had gone Home on leave. Colonel Muir had taken over command in his place. Just before the march too we were joined by a doctor named MacLeod, a very good chap but about six foot four in height and heavy in proportion, so that our route was marked by broken chairs at every *dâk* bungalow in which we stopped. The joke made at his expense was that a "Lobengula‡ block" was the only thing fit for him to sit on.

At Raewind we branched off from the main road to Lahore and marched *via* Ferozepore. There we struck cultivation again, and also much to our delight *pukka* roads as well; so that we were able to change from camel to cart transport,—for the first time for over two years.

From Ferozepore Burton and I went for a shoot in Bikanir near Obohur, and had very good fun with the black buck and sand grouse. There is nothing much of interest to say about

---
* A name given to the Punjab Frontier Force on account of their initials "P. F. F."
† Evidently a sort of Hot Pot Stew.
‡ The King of Matabeleland was a very heavy man and sat on a solid block.

our shoot, but I refer to it so as to mention a very good Christmas shoot, which Bower had taken part in, at the same place a few years previously. At the time we were there, Obohur (where by the way there is now a station on the Southern Punjab Railway) though right in the desert, had canals running some miles further on past it. But at Christmas 1888 (I think that was the year) the canal ended there, with a dead end that often flooded with waste water and made a great drinking place for sand grouse, which consequently came there in big flights every day. Bower and his party of three guns made a very big bag, their best day being ninety-six birds, mostly picked out as single birds, so that Bower said it was very like shooting driven grouse in Scotland.

We rejoined the regiment at Ludhiana, where we found that it had shared the camp the previous day with the Gordons who were marching north, and had helped them with their kit over the rather difficult river crossing, which had to be done by ferry. The next day we again shared camp with a Highland regiment, the Argyll and Sutherlands, who gave us a "sing song" at night, with plenty of pipe music much to the enjoyment of our Pathans and to our more or less recently started pipe band. The chief amusement we afforded them was the *hallalling* and cutting up by our Afridis of one of the regimental camels that had slipped up and broken its leg that day on the march. This took place just behind the Adjutant's office tent where I was busy at the time, and I could not think what all the crowd and conversation was about until I came away on finishing my work, when I found the operation just over, and the steaks and joints being removed.

Two days later brought us to Umballa and the end of our long march. We arrived there just at the conclusion of the Proclamation Parade for Lord Elgin on his assumption of the Viceroyalty of India. General Pretyman was then commanding what at that time was the Sirhind District with Kitson of the 60th Rifles as his Assistant Adjutant-General.

The Regiment on Parade at Ferozepore.
Karm Khan.
Medley. Maneh Khan. Hayat Khan.
Mohamed Amin.
Muhamed Akbar.
Hamzullah Khan. Hudson. Holland-Pryor.
Colonel Burton. Mardall Wall. Trotter.
(2nd Lancers.)

APPENDIX III.

THE 17TH CAVALRY STUD FARM.

In 1899 the Indian Government, recognising the increasing difficulty that Silladar Cavalry regiments were experiencing in providing themselves with suitable remounts and at the same time in maintaining their *Chunda* Funds in a satisfactory financial condition, offered the regiments of the Bengal Cavalry grants of land for horse-breeding purposes in the then recently-opened Chenab Canal Colony. This offer was accepted by the 12th Bengal Cavalry, the 13th Bengal Lancers, the 17th Bengal Cavalry and the 18th Bengal Lancers. However the 13th Bengal Lancers eventually did not take up their land, and this was given to the 15th Bengal Lancers instead.

The 17th Cavalry was given Chak No. 231, Rukh Branch. This comprised about eighteen hundred and seventeen acres and was situated about six miles from Lyallpur, and roughly speaking to the south of it. The property was actually made over in 1900, and in that year both the cultivation of the land and the construction of the farm buildings was commenced. At the same time a few old mares were sent down from the regiment in order to start breeding operations.

For the purpose of assisting the regiments to make satisfactory commencements the Government remitted all the water-tax for the first two years and only demanded half the tax for the third year. Cash advances were also made to the regiments to help them to stock their Farms and the 17th Cavalry took advantage of this and obtained the sum of twenty-five thousand rupees.

Nothing more unpromising than the look of the land when it was first taken over can be imagined: it appeared to be merely a sandy waste. It had previously never produced anything except a few rather melancholy looking trees and a little thin scrub jungle. Apart from the barren appearance of the place there were many patches of land that were too high for the canal water to flow over. This apparent desert was however in reality very fertile, and although the work of colonising and cultivating it, and of planning the system of irrigating it, was both difficult and laborious, two years were sufficient to completely change its appearance. General Boudier records that, when he first visited it in May 1902, it already presented a more or less flourishing aspect. However even then there still remained many pieces of high ground which were yet untouched by the water. However the greater part of it was then producing some crops of a sort. As one approached it in the train one could see a number of paddocks situated alongside the railway line, with a rough square of farm buildings at one end. All structures were built of mud and looked rather bare and shadeless; while in the distance, about half a mile away, could be seen an equally bare looking mud-walled village. This was duly registered as "Muirabad" after Colonel Muir, who was commanding the regiment when it was first built.

General Boudier goes on to say that a year later, when he again saw the Farm, the great progress that was really being made was still not very apparent, and although that by then a few trees and attempts at hedges were beginning to peep over the walls, the place still presented a bare and uninviting appearance, especially on a hot weather day. He records however that when he next visited it in 1906, the improvement to be seen was simply marvellous. The bare walls and buildings had practically vanished, being almost completely hidden from the railway by trees and hedges. On entering the Farm he found all the paddocks were abounding in shade for the stock, that the village had grown into a model and shady one, and that careful and painstaking work had so reduced the high ground that nearly all of it had been brought under cultivation. During these three years too, a further grant of land had also been given to the regiment. This consisted of four hundred and seventy-one acres, situated to the East away on the other side of the railway and about a mile away from the original allotment. He had originally seen this piece of land in its uncultivated condition in 1903, but these three years had changed it too into a flourishing looking farm, with the commencement of a second village, which was subsequently named Atkinsonganj.

This name was given to it to keep up the name of General Atkinson, who had managed the Farm from its first commencement until the time when he relinquished the command of the regiment in 1906. It was to his constant thought and excellent management that all the credit, for its subsequently proving so successful (both materially and financially), was undoubtedly due. After 1906 rules and orders, on the lines laid down by him, were regularly codified and embodied as Standing Orders. These rules and orders were in the main so sound and so good that they practically remained unchanged till the day that the farm was broken up and done away with. The only alterations made were introduced as the result of further experience gained, but they merely concerned minor details. The lines on which he had started the Farm were maintained till the end.

SNAPSHOTS AT THE FARM.

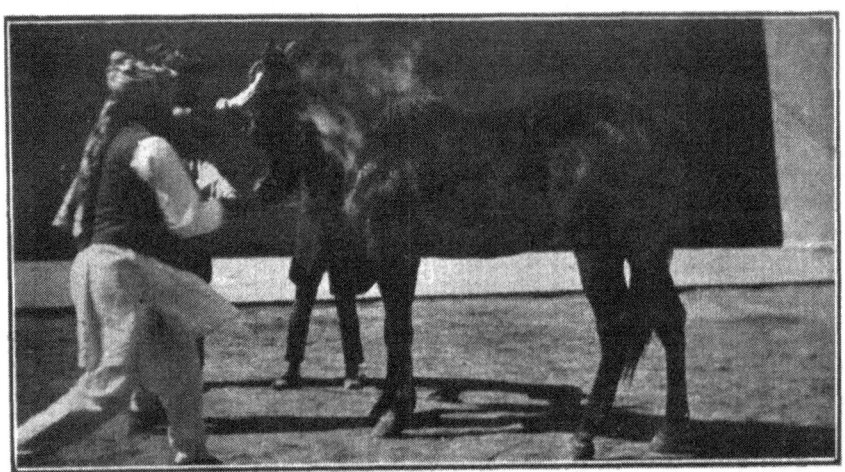

At the Horse Hospital

A paddock scene.

In most of his work at Risalawala (as the place was subsequently called) General Atkinson was ably assisted by a lieutenant to whom almost equal credit is due for the loyal manner in which he carried out all orders and instructions given to him, and for "the sweat of his brow" which he literally and liberally poured out in the arduous work of making the Farm a paying and going concern. This lieutenant was Risaldar subsequently Risaldar-Major Ghulam Muhy-ud-din Khan, Sirdar Bahadur, who, after having taken his turn with other Indian officers for a year during the infancy of the farm, was put permanently in charge of it in the spring of 1903. He remained there for seven years during which time practically the whole of the land, with the exception of some high lying patches, was brought thoroughly under cultivation. Thanks to his careful supervision of even the smallest detail and to his painstaking work, the farm was not only able to pay for the building of the two villages but also for a very large number of other buildings besides, as well as forty-three brood-mares, two stallions and young stock to the value of some fifty-six thousand rupees. At the end of his tenure it had also paid back all but seven thousand rupees of the money advanced by Government when it was started.

Risaldar-Major Ghulam Muhy-ud-din was succeeded by Risaldar (after Risaldar-Major) Rahmat Sher who was there from 1908 to 1911. He was followed by Risaldar Wazir Khan who remained in charge till the breaking out of the war. He was followed by Jemadar Mustafa Khan who was relieved in 1915 by Risaldar (afterwards Risaldar-Major) Bahadur Sher. The latter however proceeded on field service after a tenure of some seven months, and was followed by Jemadar (subsequently Risaldar) Dost Mohamad Khan who remained in charge till 1921 when the property was taken over by Government.

General Boudier took over the affairs of the farm shortly after General Atkinson gave up command of the regiment and from that time until he retired in 1917 he continued to exercise an active control over its management. Associated with him there were at times other officers, one of the principal of whom was Major Wall. The latter however was transferred to Skinner's Horse in 1913 and conditions from then on prevented any continuity of tenure in the assistants. Next to General Atkinson the great credit for the highly successful type of horse produced at the farm is due to General Boudier, and the third village on the estate has been fittingly named Boudierpur to perpetuate his memory. From 1914 onwards the whole of the land was brought under cultivation and those scattered pieces of high land on which water would not flow were finally eliminated.

After General Boudier left the regiment Lieutenant-Colonel Barry-Smith took over charge of the farm and continued personally to manage its affairs till the end.

This completes a short summary of the history of the actual farm, with the exception of the most important part of it and indeed its *raison d'être* the livestock on it. But before leaving this part of the subject, it may be of interest to just briefly mention of what the farm buildings, etc., consisted.

On entering the gate of the enclosure (which by the way the Indian Officer in charge always profusely decorated with an archway of green stuff when expecting a visit from an officer) you passed by the quarters of the Indian Officer, and mounted the steps of a masonary *Baradari*. From this later on, one saw and criticised all the young stock which was produced before you. Here one found one's self in the middle of the rough square of the farm buildings. These consisted of two lines of quarters for the twenty-four sowars of the establishment, bounded at each end by large *godowns* for storing grain, and other produce; there were also *godowns* for dead stock, the office, and the guest-house for Indian visitors. In front of you, through another gateway, was the bungalow for British Officers, this consisted of two bed-rooms, two bath-rooms and another large room which was used for the dual purpose of a sitting-room and dining-room. Beyond the verandah of this living-room a green lawn stretched up to the Horse Hospital, with a garden of fruit trees on its right. Beyond this again was a row of sixteen loose boxes which originally were exclusively kept for mares when foaling. A second similar row of boxes (the two rows being used in alternate years to avoid risk of disease) was also situated behind the bungalow. These foaling boxes were given up as the result of experience. It was proved that even this arrangement was not satisfactory for preventing infection, and in later years all foaling was arranged for in temporary shelters in the paddocks, and these were destroyed by burning each year when their purpose had been fulfilled.

Leaving the *Baradari* and walking round the further *godown* one came in succession to the machine house (with a grain-crusher and chaff-cutter worked by horse-power), a line of houses for followers, stables for mares working on the farm, and the stallion house. This brought one to the end of the buildings, and then one passed into the paddocks, which were nineteen in number. They varied in area from one square (about twenty-eight acres) to about a square and a half. Some of them were divided by a wall in the middle so that the stock could be kept in one-half of the paddock while the other half was being

SNAPSHOTS AT THE FARM.

Animals on 17th Cavalry Stud. Farm.

irrigated. For every two paddocks there was a stable in a small walled enclosure. Here the animals were fed in long feeding troughs built along the wall.

In addition to these nineteen ordinary paddocks there were (about half a mile beyond the furthest), four similar "segregation" paddocks. In these all animals brought to the farm from outside were kept for six months before being allowed to mix with any others.

Besides these segregation paddocks there were, in Atkinsonganj, two paddocks and a horse hospital. These had been built to accommodate infected animals, should it so happen that any infectious or contagious disease had broken out in the stud.

The total acreage occupied by the paddocks was six hundred and fifty-one or a little over a square mile, this with the one hundred and thirty-one acres taken up by the villages, roads, etc., left fifteen hundred and six acres for cultivation. Of this area one hundred and thirty-nine acres formed the Home Farm, on which was grown lucerne and other fodder for the young stock. The remainder was leased out to tenants on what is called the half *batai* system. Under this system the tenant pays as rent half of the actual produce grown on his land. This is handed in as soon as harvested, and is stored in the *godowns* till eaten or sold. This is the ancient system on which all leases used to be given in India. It is in very many ways the most suitable system for the country, and has the advantage of being popular with the tenants and at the same time allowing the landlord great power of supervision both over the class of crops grown, and over the proper cultivation of the land. The system of letting land on a yearly cash rental was tried as an experiment by other regiments, but in all cases it merely resulted either in the accumulation of large uncollectable arrears of rent or in the introduction of middlemen who financed the tenants and bled them accordingly.

The supervision of the cultivation and the collecting of the landlord's share of the crops without loss was a very important part of the work of the Indian Officer in charge of the farm. Several sowars were employed solely to assist him in this work. The remaining sowars were each in charge of a paddock. Each man used to live in this own paddock and spend his time in making friends with all the animals in his charge, feeding them, and looking after their condition generally.

Now turning to the stock on the farm, the modest beginning of a few regimental mares sent for breeding grew until at the time when the stud farm was done away with, there were two hundred and twenty-four horses on the farm, varying in age from fifteen years to about five months. Our aim of getting from it forty really good remounts a year was thus well on the road to realization.

The first foal was born at the farm on the 6th of April 1901. But of course it and those that followed were not fit for the ranks for four years; so in order to start getting remounts, fairly quickly young stock of between one and three years was bought at Horse Fairs and sent to the farm till old enough to be sent up to the regiment.

Being brought up under proper conditions and properly fed, a large majority of these animals turned out excellent remounts, and in many ways this method of stocking the farm had its advantages. But to counterbalance these there were two very serious disadvantages—first that it is difficult to obtain sufficient young stock of the right stamp, and more impossible to tell if a young foal bought in this way, however good looking, would grow into a horse of nearly 16 hands or remain a pony of less than 14-2. Apart from this it was not horse-breeding, the purpose for which the land had been given.

For this reason General Atkinson commenced systematic breeding at once both from mares sent from the regiment and also from all well-bred, well shaped mares and fillies purchased. He began by selecting a certain number of the best as brood mares. The number of brood mares was subsequently fixed at forty but naturally this number varied from time to time. About half the brood mares were normally walers and the remainder country-breds. We also bred from all fillies passed as fit for the ranks and as a rule got from them one foal at four years and another at five years, after which the filly was sent to the regiment as a remount at five and half years of age. In this way we bred from about seventy-five mares and fillies a year. From these we used to obtain about sixty foals a year or a percentage of about eighty per cent., which was very good indeed for India.

For brood mares we originally found that among country-breds the best were those by thorough-bred sires out of Baluch mares These were mostly purchased as young fillies at Dera Ghazi Khan, but we were getting some very good mares of our own breeding by Arab sires, which we hoped would eventually produce for us a regular type of 14-3 remount, which is the best size for Indian Cavalry. As regards breeding from Waler mares, there is a very common idea that they often prove barren or else have not sufficient milk in this country to raise healthy stock. Our experience however was very different, and after having managed the farm for many years, General Boudier has left

TYPES OF 17TH CAVALRY STUD-BREDS.

Major E. G. Atkinson's bay stud-mare Volma, by Keeper Volma (Arab), out of a Mare by Defender (T. B. E.) Grand dam Baluch. Sold to Lord Wimborne in 1923 for the British International Polo Team. Played in all International Trial matches in England during 1924 by Major T. W. Kirkwood.

Played by Major E. G. Atkinson in the two tests England vs. U. S. A., September 1924; afterwards sold in U. S. A. to Mr. Marshalla Field for nearly £800.

it on record that he was strongly of the opinion that carefully selected and carefully mated Waler mares are as good for breeding from as any that can be found.

As regards sires, we originally made use to a large extent of the Government thorough-breds (both Australian and English) standing at Lyallpur; and in 1906 the Army Remount Department sent a thorough-bred waler "Levi" to stand at the farm. Many of the stock of these stallions turned out very well, but others became leggy or "jumped up," and when General Atkinson was in command of the Bangalore Cavalry Brigade, he paid a visit to the old established stud at Mysore. There he heard that the experience gained there was that in this country only Arab sires should be used until by several crosses of that strain, a "stout" mare is produced. After this a thoroughbred can be used to advantage. We latterly therefore proceeded on that principle, only making use of thorough-bred sires in exceptional cases, and the result certainly proved very satisfactory.

The sires latterly standing at the farm were:—

(1) "Artemis" an Ahmednagar bred Arab belonging to the Army Remount Department.

(2) "Crescent," an Arab purchased for the regiment in 1904.

(3) "Haroun-al-Rashid," an Arab purchased in Bombay for the regiment in 1911 because "Crescent," though he had given us some very good remounts, was not quite as high caste a horse as is desirable.

In addition to these we tried the experiment (strongly recommended by General Sir John Watson) of using one of the pure indigenous breeds to produce brood stock. The breed we had selected was the Shahpur District "*Anmohl*" (literally "priceless") breed, and through the assistance of the Honourable Nawab Colonel Sir Umar Hayat Khan Tiwana, we purchased two "*Anmohl*"* fillies, and he kindly allowed us the use of one of his pure bred sires. The experiment on the whole was however a failure.

On the other hand however an experiment of breeding pure Arabs was a great success. Captain Shakespeare obtained two high caste Arab mares from the Sheik of Koweit and four more were purchased from the Government Stud at Ahmednagar. The produce of these were just coming into maturity at the time when the farm was finally broken up.

A tour round the paddocks was of course the most fascinating part of a visit to the farm, as there one could study the future troop horse in every stage of his development, from the ungainly though pretty baby following its mother (and filching as much of her grain as it could) to the more or less fully grown four-year-old only awaiting the order to come up to headquarters. Thanks to their proper bringing up all were equally friendly, and were as ready to nibble your coat or hat as to destroy the young trees in the paddocks, on which they dearly loved to try their teeth.

As you entered each paddock, you found on the gate a board giving the age and sex of the animals it contained. From the time they were weaned (at six months old) the colts and fillies were separated, and they were all divided into lots of twenty to twenty-five of the same age and sex in each paddock. This besides other advantages, enabled the visitor to compare each animal with others of its own age and class and to pick out any either too big or too small.

The height and shank measurement of each of the young stock was carefully noted down in the register maintained for this purpose twice every year, but beyond this not much notice was taken of differences (except in abnormal cases), until the animals were three years old, as experience has shown that some developed very much later than others. At three years however they were all very carefully examined, and any considered unfit for the regiment, or for breeding were marked down to be sold at the horse fairs during the ensuing cold weather.

This was one of the most important duties of the Officer-in-charge of the farm, and his half-yearly visits were times of excitement and hard work for the establishment. Every animal was then brought up to the *Baradari* for his inspection, and all under five years of age were carefully measured. With the older animals this was not a very lengthy operation, but with the yearlings almost any time might have to be spent over it, as the unfamiliar surroundings and the sight of the measuring standard were invariably too much for the feelings of some of them. Eventually many of them had to be half dragged, half carried by four men with hands clasped round quarters and shoulder, and even then the measuring was a difficult business.

Owing to the comparatively poor nutritive quality of Indian grasses it was found necessary to feed the young stock on grain from the time they were weaned. This varied from about a pound for the youngest to four or five pounds for older animals. Formerly the grain given was almost entirely gram, but owing to the heating properties of this, we latterly tried to give only oats that was grown on the farm. In addition to this they were given at different seasons of the year chopped lucern, *chari* and oat hay, and always some bhoosa as well; all mixed up with the grain and

TYPE OF 17TH CAVALRY STUD-BREDS.

Major E. G. Atkinson's b. stud-bred geld. Falcon, by Haroun (Arab), out of the 17th Cavalry stud-bred mare Goshaw, by Peregrine Falcon, (T. B. E.). Grand-dam, a Baluch mare. Played throughout International Trial Matches in England by Major E. G. Atkinson. Sold to Lord Wimborne 1923 after being played in England 1924 by Major I. W. Kirkwood.

given them in the small enclosures mentioned before. The babies too often required milk, to supply which a certain number of cows were kept up.

In conclusion it may be of interest to mention the output of remounts during the time that the farm was maintained. The first batch was sent up to the regiment in March 1902 and in the twenty years which followed, remounts up to a total of seven hundred and three were provided for the regiment. The detail of these annual batches is shown below:—

Year	Number
1902	24
1903	18
1904	39
1905	51
1906	44
1907	48
1908	53
1909	33
1910	41
1911	10
1912	46
1913	18
1914	35
1915	57
1916	16
1917	47
1918	14
1919	29
1920	35
1921	45
Total	703

In addition to these, up to 1906 young mules were also bred or purchased and kept at the farm till fit for work, but it was then found impossible to continue doing this, as the young mule is not only a most troublesome animal to keep in any paddock, but also the increase in the number of horses kept at the Farm used up all the available paddock accommodation and establishment. During those five years however ninety-nine mules were also supplied to the regiment.

Beside the above a certain number of horses found to be growing too big for our standard were sold to the Army Remount Department, for prices from between six hundred and seventy-five rupees for a five-year-old to three hundred rupees for two-year-olds.

While the fillies were kept at the farm till they were five and half years old, colts up till 1911 were sent up as remounts as four-year-olds. But latterly we changed this and arranged to keep them an extra year so that they might become more fully developed and less likely to throw out splints, etc., when first worked. This policy undoubtedly proved to be a success.

In connection with the Horse Farm one used often to be asked as to whether it paid. As far as the actual breeding and rearing of horses was concerned, the answer was that it did not. The regiment could only afford to pay three hundred and fifty rupees for each remount, while in a calculation made about 1909 it was found that each four-year-old cost the farm nearly four hundred and forty rupees without putting on to it any share of the original cost of brood mares, sires, or buildings. This price increased in latter years as food became dearer, and prices again went up latterly when colts were kept an extra year before being sent up to the regiment, because this added greatly to the cost. Towards the end the actual cost of producing a five-year-old remount increased to a sum between twelve or fifteen hundred rupees or perhaps even more. At the same time however the whole farm proved a success financially owing to its being so large that three-quarters of the area could be used for cultivation. The income from the cultivation not only enabled us to feed the stock cheaply, but also provided the funds to cover the actual loss on the breeding of the horses. The rise in prices actually counter-balanced itself largely because we naturally got increased prices for the crops.

The farm is now a thing of the past and the young stock and the brood mares are scattered over India never to be collected together again; and all that remain are the memories and a certain number of horses, many of which have won renown at polo and at horse shows, as well as in the more prosaic role of cavalry troop horses. The brand of the "Star and Crescent" is however fairly well known in India and a horse bearing this brand will never want for a purchaser.

TYPES OF 17TH CAVALRY STUD-BREDS.

Captain J. S. Ballentine's chest. stud-bred geld. Crescent, by Khumra (Anhmohl), out of 17th Cavalry brood mare Bridesmaid (waler), grand-dam (waler.)
A winner in the show-ring as a charger.

Risaldar Alam Sher's (subsequently Risaldar-Major Bahadur Sher's) bay stud-bred gelding, Mohawk by Crescent (Arab), out of Filly No. 605 by Wellbeck (T. B. A.). Grand-dam 17th Cavalry mare Goshawk by Peregrine Falcon (T. B.E.)
A winner in the show-ring.

APPENDIX IV

EAST AFRICAN SQUADRON, 1915-1917.

In describing the two years spent in East Africa by our squadron, the necessity for a brief outline of the campaign, showing very roughly what happened before we arrived and after we had left, is indicated.

With their usual forethought in military matters, the Germans were better prepared for the protection of their colony than we were for ours. They had many more African troops and a plentiful supply of machine guns, ready if necessary to assist their vigorous and efficient administration. Later on they denuded the "Konigsberg" (a cruiser driven into the mouth of the Rufiji River and unable to come out) of all her guns and man-handled these hundreds of miles north to harry our advancing columns.

Our pre-war intelligence regarding the military situation in German East Africa (obtained from the Consular service) was meagre in the extreme. The immediate result of this ignorance was the disastrous fight at Tanga in November 1914, where we landed our troops in a mangrove swamp to be mowed down by machine guns, the existence of which in the country we were unaware. This was to all intents and purposes the opening of the campaign, and the result caused us to retire on Mombassa and think again.

The Indian force, which had been hastily despatched to reinforce the three battalions of King's African Rifles and the few hastily raised local corps forming the local garrison, arrived in two convoys during the months of September and November 1914. The greater part of the force came in the second convoy and took part in the Tanga fight before actually landing in B.E.A. It was soon found that this force, consisting as it did of two mountain batteries, eight regular battalions and four Imperial Service battalions, was insufficient for aggressive warfare. It was only just enough to hold on with difficulty to the Uganda Railway which ran parallel to and rather perilously close to the German boundary.

From then on until the South African contingents arrived in February 1916, the reinforcements were limited to a Rhodesian battalion, a battalion of Territorials from Home and a squadron of 17th Cavalry. Time after time our hopes were raised, by hearing of expected reinforcements but all promised battalions were diverted to Gallipoli or elsewhere and our "side show" had to carry on as best it could.

Meanwhile the Germans were busily employed in raising more and more African levies, and what is more they were, in spite of the vigilance of the " Silent Service " able to arm these. This was thanks to the blockade running of two or three enterprising shipmasters. These latter must have some interesting tales to tell. Needless to say their ships never came direct from Germany to Africa, one was known to have gone *viâ* South America: probably a Swedish vessel.

Throughout 1915 we contented ourselves with endeavouring to keep our own frontier intact, though truth to tell the Germans captured our frontier station of Taveta early in the War and held it until they were turned out in February 1916.

By this time there had arrived two brigades of South African horse and three brigades of South African infantry with three field batteries, also many details from Home such as field hospitals, private batteries of armoured cars, some third rate aeroplanes, motor transport companies and a big gun or two. Later on the conclusion of the Cameroon's campaign a brigade or more of the West African Frontier Force was sent.

General Sir Horace Smith Dorrien who had been sent from England to direct operations having been taken ill at Cape Town, Smuts, a South African politician, well known as a Boer leader in the South African war was appointed to the supreme command. Owing to his energy and resource we, now having superior strength, compelled the Germans to start retiring from Kilimanjaro.

From 1916 onwards, after one stand-up fight just south of Kilimanjaro, the Germans carried out a series of rearguard actions for seven hundred miles right up to over the borders of Portuguese East Africa. By this time our force had been reduced to a few remaining Indian troops and some newly raised King's African Rifle Battalions. It was in these regions that the hardest fighting took place. General Smuts manœuvred the Germans out of German East Africa but never succeeded in inflicting a decisive defeat on them, and when he left East Africa in 1917 the main task still remained to be done.

Eventually, when the Armistice was signed, Von Lettow, the Prussian Colonel, whose dogged nature had held his force together for four years in spite of enormous odds, had doubled back north of Lake Nyassa and was breaking through into Northern Rhodesia. His object, people said, was the idea of trekking right across Africa and trying his luck in the West!

It should here be stated that General Smuts was ordered to England in 1917, and after a short interregunum during which

TYPE OF THE 17TH CAVALRY STUD-BREDS.

Major H. S. Stewart's ch. stud-bred geld. Starlight by the Swale (T. B. E.), out of the 17th Cavalry stud-bred mare Self Love by Young Egotist (stud-bred T. B.) out of a Baluch mare.
A winner on the Indian Turf and twice played by the English Team in the International Polo between England and the U.S.A. Sold to Lieut.-Colonel Richardson, 13th Hussars.

Major-General Hoskins commanded, the command was given to another South-African general, Van Deventer, who held it until the end. This officer laboured under even greater disadvantages than his predecessor for in addition to not being a regular soldier he was handicapped further by not being conversant with the English language. Of course he had a staff of regular officers under him who had to carry on.

There were many and diverse difficulties in the organisation of this heterogeneous army, including as it did white men from the Homeland and many colonies, brown men from all parts of the Indian Continent, *viz,,* from Kashmir to Tuticorin and black men from East, West and South Africa and from the West Indies.

The promulgation of orders was a difficult enough task indeed, but the real difficulty lay in feeding a force spread out in various columns all moving on more or less parallel lines in a southerly direction through virgin forests and unfrequented tracts where roads were almost unheard of. We, of the central column, were fortunate enough to strike an excellent road south of Morogoro for some miles, but for this no thanks were due to the intelligence supplied by the Consular Service.

The two German Railways, *viz.*, the Usambara Valley (from Tanga to Kilimanjaro) and the Central Railway (from Dar-Es-Salam to Lake Tanganiyaka) both ran roughly east and west. Both were thus more or less parallel to our own Uganda Railway. These railways the Germans destroyed successively as they abandoned them, and there was plenty of work for the Indian Railway Sapper companies in order to get them in to running order again.

We first ran a branch line from Voi on the Uganda Railway to Kilimanjaro at the head of the Usambara Valley; this eventually connected the Uganda Railway with the Usambara Valley Line. Afterwards, as we advanced further south, the stores were landed at the port of each railroad in succession. They were run up country as far as necessary, and thence taken to the various columns by motor lorry, Ford-van or porters. Later on when we advanced further south, beyond all railways, the ports of Kilwa and Lindi were utilised as Bases, and supplies were forwarded from these as from the railway.

It must be realised that this campaign was as much a fight against nature as against the Germans. That part of Africa where most of the fighting took place is noted for diseases which attack both man and beast. The commander's thoughts had to be as equally directed towards ways and means of maintaining his fighting strength as they had to the manœuvring of his force in battle.

A description of an East African campaign, however impretentious it may be—would be quite incomplete without some reference to the large amount of big game seen and encountered during the operations. On first arrival, for instance, we noticed that the field telegraph poles were quite unusually tall. On enquiring the reason why, we were told (and truthfully as we discovered afterwards) that communication had at first been seriously delayed owing to the wires constantly being carried away through entanglement with the giraffes' necks. Game had been little disturbed in most of the places where the squadron was sent. At times therefore one could see hundreds of head around one—chiefly of the commoner kind such as *wildebeeste, hartebeeste,* Grant's and Thompson's gazelles, and zebra.

In certain parts it was quite common to have lions roaring near camp every night. The squadron commander was terrified at first of a night panic and was haunted by visions of horses galloping in all directions pursued by ferocious felines. He even went so far as to have large fires kept up nightly to frighten the furious beasts away. But this was soon discontinued and no case actually occurred of a lion penetrating our camp. One night, however, a picquet sentry well wrapped up in two blankets was crouching alone when a lion jumped on his back. The sentry gave vent to an ear-splitting yell, whereupon the lion —evidently realising some mistake—made off with the two blankets which he left in the bush a hundred yards away. Some of the picquet mules were found next morning to have lion claw marks on their backs. Owing to this last fact the sentry got very little sympathy. He was told that the lion had mistaken him for a mule.

On two occasions our patrols had to shoot charging rhinoceros, and it takes a good deal of shooting to kill them with service ammunition. The 'rhino' is a curious relic of former ages. His diminutive eye prevents clear vision, he consequently trusts to his nose. For this reason it is well to keep him, if possible, on the windward side, because he is very apt to charge if disturbed.

As regards our squadron's particular share in the campaign, having "missed the bus" for France, the wire ordering a Pathan squadron to East Africa was received in frigid silence. All realised at once that it was a "side show" and that there was a certainty of being quite out of the picture. But those who were fortunate enough to go will never regret the experience gained.

A composite Pathan squadron chosen equally from 'A' and 'B' squadrons, one hundred and twenty strong, was formed under

TYPE OF THE 17TH CAVALRY STUD-BREDS.

Major H. S. Stewart's b. stud-bred geld. Akbar, by Haroon (Arab), out stud-bred mare 427, by Levi (T.B.A.), grand-dam by Libel Tournament polo pony and winner in the show-ring. Sold to Captain Daly, Royal Horse Guards.

Major R.C. Barry-Smith with Captain V. C. Duberley and Second-Lieutenant B. J. P. Mawdsley as Squadron Officers.

The following Indian Officers accompanied the squadron:—Resaldar Usman Khan, Ressaidar Sajid Gul and Jemadars Wazir Khan and Wazir Mohamad. The strength of the squadron was very shortly afterwards augmented by a maxim gun section sent from the regiment.

We sailed from Bombay on January 25th, 1915 and arrived Mombassa on February 4th. Our ship, a B. I. Persian Gulf Mail steamer of about 2,500 tons had just room and no more for the squadron with their horses and sixty-six mules. There were no facilities for exercising horses on board; the voyage was hot and our time was chiefly taken up in keeping the horses as fit as we could. The only exercise that we could give them was by bringing them out in turn to stand on the hatchways and by moving them from standing to standing. Suffice to say that, by dint of real hard work and assiduous "mucking out," our casualties were nil and the animals arrived in fatter condition than when embarked. Without constant attention, horses on boardship (more especially on low-decked vessels not intended for carrying animals, are apt to suffer dreadfully, chiefly from ships pneumonia caused by the horrible stench from uncleaned standings. This form of pneumonia comes on very suddenly, and unless a sufferer is brought at once into the fresh air he succumbs very quickly. Suffice to say that with plenty of willing men, good food and good weather few casualties should occur.

On arrival at Mombassa we were told that owing to the prevalence of the *tse tse* fly near the coast, it was imperative to get away before dark. What with slinging our horses into deep lighters, unloading them by the same method on to a slippery quay, and packing them into open trucks, we had the greatest difficulty in getting all finished by late afternoon. The loading and unloading was eventually completed with only three or four men laid out from kicks, and a couple of horses injured. A year afterwards we were amused to hear that there a large Remount Depôt containing hundreds of animals had been organized at Mombassa. The *tse tse* fly was later on regarded as a necessary evil.

During the whole of 1915 we spent our time patrolling up and down a line stretching roughly from a point thirty miles south of Nairobi to thirty-five miles north of Kilimanjaro. The most southerly point, a mountain called Longido, changed hands two or three times. For the Germans it was an excellent base from which raids into our territory could be carried out.

The country was fair for cavalry, with rather too much cotton soil, so fast going was inadvisable in most parts; but our patrols did good work. Nearly every full moon saw us out for a week or ten days raiding towards enemy country. But we never could do much with only one squadron, and distances were enormous. The squadron on one occasion covered one hundred and sixty-one miles in five days with no casualties, each horse carrying full marching order.

During the first year we lost a number of horses from African horse sickness, a foul disease the real cause of which is not even yet definitely ascertained but which is believed by many to be the bite of some night-flying insect. Incubation, during which the horse shows no sign of disease, is said to last a week. After this period events happen quickly. The horse refuses his early morning grain and is dead by the evening. We experienced two different kinds of the disease, one in which the animal expelled quantities of "soapsudlike" discharge from the lungs, and in the other the head swelled abnormally and in which there was a smaller amount of discharge from the nostrils. There is no known remedy.

When the spring advance in February 1916 was anticipated we were at Longido waiting for the word to move. Patrols were ordered on three different points at the base of Kilimanjaro thirty-five miles south, to observe whether the Germans still held on to their advanced posts. One of these patrols was commanded by Captain Duberley who was accompanied by Lieutenant Mawdsley and fifty men. Unfortunately it was surprised when the horses were unsaddled and feeding. Both officers behaved with the greatest gallantry, each collecting a few men and dashing out to keep off the enemy until the horses could be saddled and got under cover. Subsequently it was proved that this patrol had been engaged by at least two hundred of the enemy including a mounted infantry detachment of whites. The two *sahibs* (wearing *topees*) were picked off almost at once, and it fell to Jemadar Wazir Khan, an Adamkhel Afridi to bring the patrol out of action as best he could. When almost surrounded, he achieved this with great skill, and was subsequently awarded the I. O. M. The grass where the action occurred was breast high and it was most difficult for those engaged to see what was happening.

Both these officers were a great loss to the regiment. Duberley was a keen, intrepid horseman, a man who knew not the meaning of the word fear who had he lived through the war would most probably have qualified for the V. C.

TYPE OF 17TH CAVALRY STUD-BREDS.

Major H. S. Stewart's b. stud-bred geld. Arch-Priest by Levi (T. B. A.) out the 17th Cavalry stud-bred mare Self Love by Young Egotist (stud-bred T. B.). Grand-dam a Baluch mare. Tournament polo pony and a winner in many show-rings.

Mawdsley, a lad who only joined the regiment some three months before the war, was one of those that had in him all the qualifications that go to make a cavalry officer. His presence with the patrol was unnecessary but he had begged to be allowed to accompany it, and as he was not required elsewhere he was allowed to go.

In addition to the above casualties there were also two killed and three wounded. Of the latter, Lance-Dafadar Khan Sahib was wounded in the leg and hid himself in the bush. After the Germans had left he hobbled out and picking up a lance managed to get back to one of the Longido out-posts thirty miles away after struggling on for six days with no food and practically no water, bringing with him his rifle and one hundred rounds of ammunition. For this he was awarded the I.O.M.

Major Stewart and Lieutenants Knowles and Ibbotson (the latter both members of the I.C.S. who had joined the Reserve of of Officers), reached the squadron in March 1916 as reinforcements. They arrived just after the preliminary fighting in the vicinity of Kilimanjaro had taken place and the enemy had been driven down the Usambara Railway.

These three officers had left India while we were still in standing camp at Longido and had brought with them masses of luggage which they had to shed at various stages on their way up country, as transport became more and more difficult to obtain. They found themselves discharged from a construction train at a point between Mbyuni and Taveta, on an open cotton-soil plain without a house or habitation in sight, with a tin or two of sausages between them and no firewood, and thus laid an excellent foundation to their education in war as it is waged in East Africa.

One of Knowles' chargers pulled up its pegs during the night and disappeared into the darkness and was not recovered for some days, and there were also other alarms and excursions proper to a new country. But the most amusing part of the adventure was the effort to get their various trunks and suit cases in to Taveta the next morning in order to dump them there with anyone that would send them back to the base. Horses, till then nothing but proud and not too perfectly trained chargers, became heavily laden pack horses under protest and before the good work was accomplished the plain was liberally littered with handkerchiefs, ties and collars ; a better fate for them perhaps than being left to rot in an Indian store room.

After a few mild adventures of this kind these three officers joined the squadron at Himo River. They might have just as well waited at Mbyuni had they known the position, for we were then (along with the larger part of the force) on our way back there to form a standing camp for the rainy season, when campaigning is impossible.

At Mbyuni we were joined by some South African units and a small detachment of Flying Corps and had a not unpleasant camp for a couple of months.

The Flying Corps gave trouble by crashing in distant forests and needing patrols to search for them, they were not as clever at finding their way about on the ground as they were in the air, for one of them losing himself in the bush within two miles of Mbyuni was out for about a week without food except what he picked off the trees. Fortunately he survived both his own hunger and that of the lions which abounded in this country.

We had a little polo at Mbyuni, mounted on anything we could get from an S. and T. pack pony to a 16 hand charger. There were many hazards to the game, but it was very good fun.

There was a good deal of game about but not much chance of shooting it as we were not very far from the Germans, however we shot a few quail and spurfowl, and the patrols often got a *kongoni*, or *hartebeeste* when returning to camp. It was amusing to see the swiftness with which an animal was dismembered and stowed away when a patrol had been given permission to take in as much meat as they could get fixed on to their horses in three minutes.

Early in May a certain liveliness in patrolling developed, Knowles and Ibbotson, sometimes in conjunction with the North Lancashire Mounted Infantry, made many journeys to the Pare foothills, and the whole squadron acting as a big patrol went there once.

The North Lancashire M. I. were led by George Atkinson, one of the best bush fighters in the country and a brother of "Joey" Atkinson of the 17th. He got the M.C. and deserved much more. Afterwards he was attached to the squadron for a time when his own force had melted away from fever and horse sickness. At the Mbyuni stage of the campaign the North Lancashire M. I. were mounted on mules with a few ponies to give the mules a lead when it was necessary to change direction or turn about. The mule made several reputations for reckless daring during the campaign, an advance once started, he often continued it whether his rider was willing or not. One gallant peer of the realm was thus carried by his mule right through the German line and out again to safety on the other side during a bush battle near Mbyuni.

The patrol carried out in May by the whole squadron to the Usambara foothills was an uncomfortable affair, we had to spend the night in hollow square each holding his horse to be ready for attack by either rhinos or Germans. It was a dark night and we were in a swampy piece of ground with clouds of mosquitos and a miasma rising from the swamp. Slater to add to his misery was stung by a scorpion about midnight. We almost felt that we were competing with the lads in the Flanders mud for discomfort.

The great advance began on May 20th, and when we started we expected to be out for two or three weeks, but it was as many months before we really stayed long enough in one place for anything but the barest of sustenance to reach us, and we fed for the most part on trek ox and biscuit.

The first object was to push the enemy off the Usambara railway and capture Tanga from the land side having previously failed to take it from the sea.

The squadron was in the first brigade commanded by Brigadier-General Sheppard, and our part was to advance down the Pangani river which runs parallel to the railway and a few miles distant from it.

The advance began from the Moshi outposts with a long night march lasting from 11 P.M. to 9 A.M. when we struck the Pangani river. We watered our horses and were told to get straight out to the front and patrol ten miles returning by evening. We struggled out through the most impossible bush, saw no enemy and were delighted (when we thought there was still a three miles scrimmage through the bush before us), to find a road cut by the Kashmiris which took us back to camp.

We got back about 7 P.M. and then the men had to water, feed and groom—a little—get their own food and sleep, also a little, and be ready to start again at 4 A.M. next morning.

The next day's march was a terror, we started at 4 A.M. and got along splendidly as long as the road prepared overnight lasted. But after that afternoon we got into bush that grew thicker and thicker, till after dark the whole brigade was strung out in single file along a rhino track with some intrepid fellow finding a way at the head of it. Who this intrepid fellow was is lost in obscurity. The squadron had been relieved of patrol work and from 3 P.M. till nearly midnight was leading its horses, as a unit, near the rear of this tremendous 'crocodile.' There could of course be no intervals between units in the dark and the result was as alternation of one minute races and ten minute halts.

We bivouacked at last and all fell off to sleep exhausted; but only to be waked an hour later by ear splitting yells, which made us think that at least the German was among us with the bayonet and his *askaris* were slaking their thirst for blood with their *pangas*. The *panga*, it should be remarked is a heavier straight-bladed edition of the *kukri*.* But the noise died down as mysteriously as it had begun, no orders came and we soon sank off to sleep again. In the morning we found that the cause of all the uproar had been lions that had attacked some mules which in their turn had stampeded over the faces of a company of soldiers sleeping in the grass!

And so the advance continued. Near Old Lassoito we captured part of a German patrol, the honour going to Lance-Dafadar Musalli who spied them in the grass and shot from the saddle with the result that they put their hands up.

The next exciting ride was to the railway at Buiko where the Pangani flows in close to the mountains, we just failed to catch the last German train going out from the Lembani direction after a long ride through 'wait-a-bit' thorn. From this point it was fairly plain sailing to Mkalamo where a trolly line made by the enemy from Mombo on the northern railway to Handeni crossed the Pangani river.

At Mkalamo there was a sharp fight in thick bush, our infantry pushed the German out of their position in an hour or so but suffered heavily in the process. The squadron during this engagement was wedged in on a narrow newly cut road through very thick bush and saw a most striking example of the stopping power of thick bush on rifle fire. The Germans attempted some sort of counter-attack on the left of our force, and from the sound of their rifles they were shooting directly at us at no distant range, so close indeed that when the fire opened a lot of transport coolies just behind us gave a most realistic imitation of snakes by the way they disappeared in the grass without rising off their bellies even on to their knees to crawl. But though several thousand rounds must have been fired hardly half a dozen bullets reached us through the trees.

---

* *Panga* is the Swaheli name for a sword, the weapon referred to above is also known as a *machette*.

A couple of days after this encounter we had the misfortune to lose Knowles; he and Ibbotson were patrolling ahead of the advancing column when they bumped a German picquet and were told to dismount and push on. The bush was so thick that it was impossible to see more than five yards ahead, and for some time we and the enemy each shot at the sound of the other's rifles. But this did not satisfy Knowles and he gallant fellow that he was crept on ahead of his men and must have been seen by the enemy just as he got a sight of them, for he was shot through the neck and the position in which he fell showed without a doubt that he was killed in the very act of firing at the enemy. He had in the short time he was with the squadron gained the confidence and affection of everyone and a reputation for gallantry which made the men willing to follow him anywhere; and when there was danger in front they generally had to gallop to keep up with him.

We followed the trolley line over some waterless country to Handeni where we thought that we must certainly halt to get up supplies, etc., but we had only been there one night and moved next morning into a decent camping place when the order came to push on towards Morogoro forthwith. We accordingly 'pushed' for another week or so and caught one more of the Konigsberg guns which was evidently too heavy for the pace.

A rear guard action was fought at the Lakigura River on June 24th, during which the 25th Battalion (Frontiersmen) of the Royal Fusiliers (popularly known as the "Boozileers") led by their Colonel, O'Driscoll carried the main German position most gallantly with the bayonet.

The squadron remained on the Lakigura River till July 6th and then moved on to Msiha (also known as Makindu), this was only a few miles short of Tuliani. Here the whole column was brought to a halt by lack of provisions and it had to sit down there for a month while transport arrangements were reorganised.

Incidentally we were at this point about eight miles from a very strong fortified position held by Major Kraut, with the one remaining Konigsberg 4·1 inch gun to help him, and excellent observation posts on Kanga mountain which towered above both their position and our camp. The gun paid particular attention to the squadron, probably because the horses gave an excellent mark.

The Afridi was not in the least attracted by the labour of digging himself in until a shell blew up half a dozen poor wretched stretcher bearers in the camp one night. But the next day after this every man might have been a giant to judge by the size of the trees that came in to support the headcover. The poor mules fairly staggered under their loads.

We moved camp once about half a mile to the reverse slope of a steep hill which everyone thought would easily defeat the shells of the 4·1; but this was not so for a shell grazed the top of the hill and burst in the nullah at the bottom of the reverse slope killing or wounding thirteen men cooking their food in what was thought to be the safest place of the whole camp. The slope of the hill and the angle of descent of the shell must have been nearly identical.

The officers' funk-holes were as various in design as the officers themselves. Barry-Smith settled down under a large rock, but evacuated this in favour of a share of the grave that Ibbotson had dug one night when a particularly venomous "hate" was on, and a shell shattered the next rock to his and a bigger one at that.

Atkinson theorised on the smallness of an 'end-on' target and burrowed like a mole; while many and loud objurgations could be heard from the direction of Stewart's tenement where a number of porters under the superintendence of his orderly made him a comparative palace underground. Ibbotson made a double storeyed grave which took a camp bed in the upper storey with a deep dark hole below for special 'hate' nights. None of us got killed so we all won the competition.

During the wait at Makindu occurred the Id which brought the squadron a welcome relief from marching and fighting on empty stomachs, and also in the very nick of time a large consignment of new clothes for off-duty times sent by the ladies of the regiment from India. It would have warmed the cockles of those ladies' hearts as it did ours to see with what joy all the men turned out in their new clean clothes to celebrate the Id, after weeks in rags.

After about six weeks a fresh advance commenced with Morogoro as its objective and the capture of the strong position on the Ruhungu spur as the first move. The entrenchments of this position were on a spur of the Kanga mountain running down to a large swamp at their eastern end.

The position was thus open to attack from the front only, and there the Germans had felled a forest and the trees lay in tremendous confusion just where an attacking force would have been under the heaviest shell fire. Then came a belt of untouched elephant grass and then a cleared zone with a chevaux-de-frise of pointed stakes to take the place of wire. This

EAST AFRICAN SQUADRON.

A troop on parade.

Barry-Smith.   Duberly.   Mawdsley.

chevaux-de-frise was very cleverly made, the stakes strong, sharply pointed and thickly planted in a belt about six yards wide, too wide to jump and to strong to get through without a good deal of delay under machine gun fire.

So it was fortunate for us that movements of other of Smuts' forces southwards from Kondoa Irangi had convinced Von Lettow who had been in support of Major Kraut with his main body, that he must get away south of the Central railway or be brought definitely to battle, which was the last thing that he wished for. When we did advance and try to get round both sides of the Ruhungu position the South Africans on the west of the Kanga mountain, and the first brigade including the squadron through the bush to the east of the swamp, the Germans had just left except a small rearguard and there was no fight at all. It must have been with great regret that the man who had planned that position left it without using it.

The road was now fairly clear to Morogoro which was taken without trouble and the force pushed on southwards into the Uluguru mountains on August 7th.

Stewart remained at Makindu as post commandant, so the officers to go on with the squadron were Barry-Smith, Atkinson and Ibbotson.

When we started into the Uluguru mountains we were in high hopes that the South Africans who had gone round the West of the mountains would close the exit from them towards the Rufigi at Kissaki and that we should bring the Germans to battle and end the fight there. But our hopes were not to be fulfilled, we heard when we were one day into the hills that the South Africans were within twenty miles of Kissaki, then the next day that they had reduced the distance to ten miles, and then we heard no mention of the South Africans again until we had captured Kissaki ourselves and heard that they had bumped the defences of it in two parties and been thoroughly defeated in detail.

During all this time the squadron had been getting weaker and weaker, owing to the ravages of *Tsetse* fly and horse sickness on the horses and fever on the men. During the passage of the Uluguru mountains it was necessary to detail a patrol of fifteen men to go with a flanking column round the East of the mountains to Tulu, and this took up every available man and horse that was fit to go. So Ibbotson took the patrol and Barry-Smith was left in solitary glory commanding a non-existent remainder of the squadron.

The flanking column reached Tulu only a few minutes after the Germans had left, and a couple of days later there was quite a decent little battle at Dutumi, Von Lettow having a large proportion of his force there. But the bush and elephant grass were so thick that neither side could get a satisfactory hold of the other and in the night the Germans withdrew through Behobeho and next day we moved in to Kissaki, the enemy having once more escaped us.

They were now South of the Mgeta river and between it and the Rufigi, and transport difficulties would make it again a long time before we could hope to get round them or pin them down to a fight. One could not help admiring the consumate skill with which they had turned every feature of the country to their advantage and the dogged tenacity with which Von Lettow had held his force together. He went on adding to his reputation however for many months after this.

The material advantage of the attack, apart from the moral affect, was of course more than neutralised by the close country and thick bush which gives a great superiority every time to the man or the force that can sit and wait motionless and see and hear the other side which is forced to be in motion. Time after time our patrols walked on to rearguards and picquets which only fired when we were about twenty yards from them, and we were lucky that they did not cause us much heavier losses than they did.

After the taking of Kissaki the squadron took no further part in the general advance. We had been completely remounted once and nearly completely a second time since May and there were now only about a dozen horses that could go at all and none that were really fit; it had been heartbreaking to take them out ten and a dozen at a time and shoot them in the bush because they were not fit to march any further. Exposure and fever, added to the fighting casualties, had reduced the number of our men to about thirty also, so it was not surprising that orders came for us to return to India.

But two members of the squadron had one more amusing experience before we left. Letters had to be sent in for Von Lettow under a white flag; these incidentally must have contained the demand from Smuts to surrender to which Von Lettow refers in his book on the campaign, and Ibbotson was sent with one sowar and a white flag.

They found the German position, running into a picquet only about a hundred yards beyond the point from which they had turned back a few days earlier. On that occasion they had been out to find the line of communication behind the Germans and had failed after spending the whole day scrambling through almost impassable bush, having to turn back in high elephant grass when evening was approaching. The turn was not a very successful one for two of the patrol were lost in the high grass for some minutes and the others could make no sound to help them as they knew the Germans could not be far off. However they rejoined after a few minutes anxious waiting and, as things turned out, their comrades silence was clearly golden.

But to return to the white flag episode; the picquet was entirely composed of *askari*, and they greeted the emissaries most effusively, it was difficult to get in a word between the ceaseless flow of "*Jambo bwana, jambo sana*" and words to that effect. Eventually however they were persuaded to accompany the emissaries to find a "*mzungu*" (or white man), and took them with their eyes open right in to the rifle pits of the main position.

The "*mzungu*" were not by any means so pleased, and one rushed out to stop any further advance. Then another appeared and cursed the first, third came and cursed the second and so on until it seemed as if all the ranks of the German army up to commander-in-chief must be represented in the obloquy competition. Our representatives however were very politely treated and the letters delivered and then a white man was sent to see them out through the picquet line.

But in the picquet were waiting three scallywag blacks with another white flag. These on enquiry said they were the Englishman's servants. Ibbotson of course at once denied any knowledge of them, and the German began to interrogate them. They persisted in what they had said, and Ibbotson noticed that one of them was drawing himself up gradually under the invective of the German into the position of attention of a soldier being told off; things looked rather blue and when the German could evidently get no further with the matter Ibbotson said that if they said they were his servants they had better come with him, and that anyhow he could not wait.

The German offered no resistance so off they all went, and a very good pace they made until they were out of reach of immediate pursuit. Then they broke off the path into the bush and went into the matter of the identity of the scallywags. These turned out to be German deserters from further back; they had wandered up through the bush intending to give themselves up to our side and seeing a white man with an Indian orderly they followed him and found themselves in the picquet of the Germans as has been said. They had a narrow escape and might well have introduced complications for our party too, but the matter having ended happily they all joined in merriment together and came smiling back to Kissaki.

Shortly after this incident the squadron or such as were left of them started the march back for Morogoro and India. There were only about thirty men all told and a few very sick and tired horses, so they were very thankful to find a returning fleet of Ford supply cars, members of the "*Jigger* Fleet" that had succeeded in keeping them alive for so long, returning to Morogoro themselves. These took our men on board and the one hundred miles journey was done in two days instead of ten.

We waited for a short time at Morogoro, and then went down to Dar-es-Salam, arriving there towards the end of November.

Here we met one of the paradoxes of war organisation, as applied at least by the Army Ordnance Department to the *silladar* system. We were returning without horses, a used-up unit at least for the present, going back to the regiment in India. And they insisted on fitting us out with a whole new supply of saddlery for the complete squadron. It was pointed out to staff officer after staff officer that we would much rather get the stuff in India where it was available, and that they were in great need of all the saddlery they could get at the front, and that this saddlery had just been brought from India after the greatest difficulty and delays in getting shipping. But it was all to no purpose, everyone individually agreed, but orders were orders and there we were. So the stuff was heaved on board again in its unopened boxes and we sailed away with it back to the country of its origin.* The squadron arrived back in Bombay in January 1917.

Barry-Smith was mentioned in despatches and Ibbotson got an M.C.

---

* The idea of course was that the squadron having gone on service with complete equipment should be given complete equipment to return with. Why this transaction was carried out at an overseas base instead of in India can only be understood on the supposition that some financial authority was determined to ensure that the British Government who paid the expenses of the East African Campaign should bear the expense of the supply.

Map showing the route of the 17th Cavalry
IN
GERMAN EAST AFRICA

APPENDIX V.

POLO IN THE 17TH CAVALRY, 1895—1922.

It has been no easy task to record the polo history of the 17th Cavalry, and it is hoped that any inaccuracies will be leniently overlooked.

It is not known as to whether the officers of the old regiment played polo or not, but it is most probable some at least of them did.

We have however the authority of General Boudier for saying that polo was keenly and regularly played by the newly raised regiment at Ferozepore. It was however handicapped by the paucity of officers, as the full strength in those days was only nine, with two probationers! The three full Colonels did not play, so it was practically impossible to raise four good players to form a team.

Station polo then took place only two days a week, but on a third afternoon a regimental game was regularly played. The young Indian Officers and everyone else who could raise a pony (including the Mir Munshi) took part in this. For two years while in camp at Mian Mir the regiment formed the nucleus of a team (completed by one outside from the Devonshire Regiment) raised to give practice to the Twelvth Bengal Cavalry before the Punjab Tournament. That regiment had won this tournament five or six years in succession when the redoubtable Hira Singh formed part of the team.

While the regiment was at Loralai polo was found to be impracticable; the Bori Valley was so thickly covered with stones that a horse could not put his foot down without touching at least three, so a ground was the difficulty.

On arrival at Umballa in January 1894, a start was made immediately under the energetic leadership of Muir (Officiating Commandant). Indeed a batch of ten Arabs was purchased in Bombay in December 1893, to meet the regiment on arrival. No time therefore was lost, but of course it was impossible to get a team together in time for the Tournament of 1894.

1895 was the first year that a team was sent to compete in the Bengal Cavalry Tournament. This team consisted of Mardall (one), Burton (two), Wikeley (three), Muir (back), they defeated the 7th B.C., but were beaten in the semi-finals by the 18th B.L., who eventually won the Tournament.

In 1896 Warre-Cornish (one), Wikeley (two), Boudier (three), Muir (back) were the team; they again reached the semi-finals, beating the 19th B.L., and the 8th B.C., and they again suffered defeat from the 18th B.L., who won the Cup. In November Warre-Cornish, Wikeley, Wall and Boudier reached the finals of the Sirhind Tournament; this being the first occasion that Wall played for the regimental team.

In 1897 twelve teams competed in the Bengal Cavalry Tournament. The regiment was represented by the same team as the previous year except that Burton replaced Boudier. They beat the 2nd P.C. and 4th B.C., but were defeated by the 2nd C.I.H. in the finals after a close game. Later in the same year Muir, Boudier and Wikeley played in the Simla Tournament, but having had no practice on a hill ground were beaten by the 60th Rifles in the first round.

The Bengal Cavalry Tournament of 1898 was not a success as far as our team was concerned; they were beaten on the first round by the 5th P.C. Steel came into the side in place of Wikeley. This was however really a scratch team as owing to the Tirah Campaign then on, the regiment was split up between Mian Mir and Ferozepore and the team had had no practice together. The team was Steel (one), Warre-Cornish (two), Burton (three), and Boudier (back). Next year Smith (one), Henderson (two), Warre-Cornish (three), and Steel (back), played in the Punjab Challenge Cup at Lahore, and after winning the first match were unfortunate in meeting with defeat by Patiala in the second round.

In 1900 the regimental team consisting of Smith, Henderson, Warre-Cornish and Muir were beaten in the finals of the Bengal Cavalry Tournament by the 18th B. L. by two goals. Later on in the same year Warre-Cornish, Henderson, Wikeley and Muir won the Lahore District Tournament very easily.

During the next few years there is little to record as regards polo, the game seemed to have declined in the regiment after the death of Warre-Cornish and during the absence of Muir and Burton. The regiment moved to Rawalpindi and then to Bannu, where serious polo was out of the question. Several new officers joined during these years, namely Wilson, Stewart, Barge, Kirkwood, Dodd, Yeats-Brown and Atkinson, they had ample opportunity to train ponies and learn the game during the time the regiment spent on the frontier.

In 1907 a team risked the arduous journeyings to Lahore for Christmas, and saw how polo should be played. They returned to the frontier with an excellent idea of the standard required with regard to ponies.

In 1908 a team was sent to play at Peshawar during the Christmas tournament, they were Steel, Wilson, Barge and Kirkwood. The ponies were not of a particularly high class while the regiment was stationed at Bannu, but such old stagers as Romeo, Pink 'un, Hafizan, Grey Gordon, Highball, Credition and Ooloo formed a goodish lot to start off with, as soon as the regiment was more pleasantly located in the United Provinces, the home of all sport.

In 1909 the regiment marched to Bareilly and on the way entered a team (Wilson, Kirkwood, Dodd and Atkinson) for the Indian Cavalry Tournament at Umbala, who were beaten unfortunately in the first round by the 32nd Lancers, four to two. Considerable experience was gained, however, with the result that the team from then on did better each year, finally winning the much coveted Cup in 1912. In addition to the Indian Cavalry Tournament in 1909, the regiment entered a Subalterns team for the Civil Service Cup in Naini Tal and reached the finals of that tournament.

In 1910 Henderson returned to play for the regiment and captained the team which played in the Indian Cavalry Tournament (Wilson, Henderson, Kirkwood and Atkinson). They beat the 5th Cavalry, seven to one, and were then defeated by the 36th Jacob's Horse, four to two in the second round. The hot weather of 1910 marked the first victory of the regiment for many years, the Right Wing team winning the Bareilly Monsoon Tournament. Later a team reached the finals of the Naini Tal Civil Service Cup.

In 1911 the regimental team (Kirkwood, Wilson, Henderson and Atkinson) scored their first open success by winning the Connell Cup at the Allahabad Exhibition Tournament. This was a red letter day as the famous all conquering 39th C. I. H. team were beaten by us in the finals, four to three. After this success there seemed every chance of defeating them in the Indian Cavalry Tournament a month later. In the first round the regiment defeated the 32nd Lancers, eight to nothing, then beat the 11th Lancers, seven to four. The semi-finals followed where we met the 39th C. I. H. team. After a splendid game they avenged their Allahabad defeat and beat us four to three; afterwards scoring their third successive victory in the Indian Cavalry by beating the 9th Hodson's Horse in the finals. In the Bareilly Autumn Tournament of 1911 two teams from the regiment entered, the Right Wing team being defeated in the finals. Next followed the Delhi Durbar Tournament. The regimental team, thanks to the sportsmen who so kindly lent their ponies, were able to get three weeks good practice at Delhi, the excellent results of which were seen later. In the Durbar Tournament however the team was stale and suffered defeat by Bhopal, seven to four.

In the year 1912 the efforts of the regiment were at last crowned with success. The same team had now played together for three years and it went to Ambala full of hope and confidence, it was well-mounted, thanks to the whole-hearted way in which it was supported by all officers of the regiment. The ponies played were chosen from the following and were a really good all-round lot :—

> Henderson's Kiel and Mudbas.
> Kirkwood's Qui Vive, Tot, Silver Streak and Sea-mist.
> Atkinson's Moonlighter, Dost and Amber.
> Wilson's Herald, Peter Pan and Richard.
> Boudier's Eedan and Fairy.
> Stewart's Starlight and David.
> Dodd's Grey Gordon and Maharani.
> Brierley's Ivanhoe and Inver.
> Barry-Smith's Begum and Briton.
> Duberly's Hassan.
> Foottit's Milsa.
> Steel's Bluestone.
> Barge's Bletsoe.
> Yeats-Brown's Diam.
> Skipwith's Typhoon.

There were thirteen entries in the Tournament and the regiment defeated—

> 1st Lancers ... ... eleven goals to nil.
> 37th Lancers ... ... four ,, ,, one.
> 9th Hudson's Horse "B" ... eleven ,, ,, ,,

this brought us up against the 3rd Skinner's Horse in the finals with the result we won by four goals to three.

Foottit, Skipwith and Guthrie had joined the regiment shortly previously and turned out really good players, also our doctor, Brierley, who was naturally good at all games and who whole-heartedly supported the regimental polo and lent his first class ponies to the team. Another team composed of Atkinson, Brierley, Skipwith and Yeats-Brown succeeded in winning the Radha Mohan Cup at Delhi, beating the 11th Lancers, eleven goals to one, in the final.

In June the same team except Brierley went up to Naini Tal for the Tournament and again met with complete success beating the Inniskilling Dragoons seven to four, Worcesters twelve to six and in the finals a local team called "The Protestant Boys." This last match was a striking example of the uncertainty of polo, our opponents leading eight goals to love at half time. Suddenly everything went right after this and we equalised in the last chukkar and won after extra time, thus finishing a most successful season.

In September a team, Kirkwood, Brierley and Atkinson, again visited Naini Tal to play in the Civil Service Tournament, beating the Optimists (plus seven) thirteen goals to seven, and the Civil Service (plus eight) ten goals to eight. This brought us to the finals against a good team, the Dolphins, composed of Richardson and Kennedy, 13th Hussars and Baddeley, 15th Lancers. They received one goal start and after a good game and some luck beat us seven goals to six.

In October the Maharaja of Datia presented a handsome cup, to be won outright, for the Bareilly Autumn Tournament. Our team was composed of Kirkwood, Brierley, Dodd and Atkinson, while Guthrie played for a scratch team. In the finals we beat the Inniskilling Dragoons (plus two) by four goals to two.

1913 found us rather short of good ponies as Henderson and Wilson had been Home on leave, and had sold their studs, however thanks to the generous way in which ponies for the team were lent by others, we were able to enter for the Dehra Dun Tournament in January and got good practice for the Indian Cavalry Tournament, which was this year to be played at Delhi for the first time. The same team as the one that won in 1912 was chosen, with Barge as fifth man, the latter was a very keen player, a good trainer of ponies and was always in possession of an excellent string. The ponies were as follows:—

English and Australians.	*Country Breds.*	*Arabs.*
Geraldine.	Dost.	Kiel.
Axelle.	Promised Land.	Inver.
Breeze.	Diamond.	Ivanhoe.

English and Australians.	Country Breds
Betty.	Trigger.
Tot.	Starlight.
Red Mist.	Chustine.
Osprey.	Lally.
Milsa.	Scraffen.
	Eagle Hill.

The country breds are of particular interest to us as nearly all of them were bred in the regimental Stud Farm. Starlight owned by Stewart was a wonderful pony, he was sold to Richardson, 13th Hussars, who took him to England, where he played in 1914 in International polo. Barrett played him in the English team against the Americans in 1921. Arabs had fallen out of favour for two reasons, firstly, the high prices demanded in Bombay for raw ponies of the right type, secondly few can hold their own in first class polo.

At Dehra Dun polo is very keenly played by the Goorkha regiments stationed there, the grounds are absolutely first class. In the first match we beat the 10th Lancers by six goals to three. In the finals our opponents were the 18th Lancers, who won three goals to one.

The team then went to Delhi for the Indian Cavalry Tournament, there were nineteen entries, a record. In the first round our opponents were the redoubtable 26th Cavalry who had come from Bangalore with a big reputation. We were however on the top of our form and won six goals to three. Next round we defeated last year's runners-up, 3rd Skinner's Horse, by eight goals to six. In the semi-finals we defeated 38th C. I. H. by eight to three. This brought us into the finals against the 18th Lancers, who had had a more comfortable journey through the previous rounds. A gale blew the whole time spoiling the game considerably, and the 18th Lancers defeated us by three—one, the same score as at Dehra Dun.

An American Tournament was played at Bareilly later, our team consisted of Foottit, Skipwith, Duberly and Yeats-Brown ; our old friends the Worcesters won this Tournament. Then followed the Radha Mohan Tournament, our team consisted of Foottit, Duberly, Atkinson and Guthrie. We beat the 60th Rifles, C-in-C's Staff, and the 9th Gurkhas and so won the cup for the second year in succession.

In the Bareilly Autumn Tournament we had no success although two teams entered. This was followed by a sporting but unsuccessful venture to Meerut, the team being Cochrane (one), Barge (two), Guthrie (three), Brierley (back). Cochrane gaining his first experience of tournaments.

Next, the regiment entered for the I. P. A. Championship at Calcutta during 'Xmas, ' 1913,' the team being Atkinson (back), Barge (three), Skipwith (two) and Yeats-Brown (one). Brierley was unable to play at the last moment. The first match against the 12th Cavalry ended in an easy win for us by twelve goals to four. We then played the Viceroy's Staff in the semi-finals, and after a good game against a good and well mounted team were beaten by nine goals to four. Brierley's new pony "Kipper" unfortunately had a pastern broken and was destroyed. We then played in the Ezra Cup beating Calcutta (plus four) by five to four, next we defeated a really good side called the Travellers by four to three after getting three goals start. This brought us into the finals against the 12th Cavalry, whom we had beaten easily a few days previously. In this match however everything went wrong, we gave the 12th two goals and were beaten five to three, a sad ending when we should have won easily.

The regiment had now moved to Allahabad, where Yeats-Brown, Skipwith, Foottit and Barge had no difficulty in winning the Connell Cup. The team for the Indian Cavalry Tournament this year was the same as played in Calcutta. Wilson, Kirkwood and Henderson were not available, and Atkinson had to come up from Saugor to play, so we were of course short of practice together and were beaten by the 5th Cavalry by five goals to three in the first round. However fresh players gained experience for future years.

The war now scattered many officers of the regiment, and those left behind in India had to content themselves with station polo. Many new officers joined but usually only stayed a short time before proceeding as reinforcements to the war.

During 1917, the regiment was stationed at Lahore and played a great deal of polo, we now had the assistance of Kirkwood again. Two teams entered for the 'Xmas Tournament and were composed as follows :—" A " team, Brierley, Barry-Smith, Skipwith and Kirkwood. " B " team, Ahmad Yar, Hutchison, Stewart and Guthrie. The "A" team defeated "B" team in the first round, then beat Lahore easily, only to be defeated in the finals by the Patiala team, six goals to three.

It was then arranged to enter a team consisting of Kirkwood, Skipwith, Hutchison and Stewart for the Rawalpindi Tournament held early in 1918, but in one of the final practice matches Stewart had his leg broken by a kick from a vicious pony and the scheme fell through at the last minute.

The regiment again played in the Lahore 'Xmas Tournament, 1918, entering two teams which were as follows:—" A," Persse, Griffiths, Atkinson and Skipwith. " B," Williams, Ballentine, Ahmad Yar and Rukan Din. Kirkwood had left for Russia and Atkinson returned from France. In the first round Mamdot (plus one) beat our " A " team, and the K. D. Gs. defeated our " B " team.

A subsidiary tournament was held and Mamdot (plus one) again just beat our "A" three to two in the finals. Barry-Smith was unfortunately laid up in hospital with a broken leg, and Stewart was still on leave recovering from a similar injury. Many new players had joined and played with great keenness, among them being Hutchison. The Punjab riots and Afghan War rather put a stop to polo for some time.

In 1919 the regiment again played in the Lahore 'Xmas Tournament, the team being Persse, Skipwith, Atkinson and Stewart. They won the first match beating the R. A. F. (plus four) by eight to five, but failing against the 33rd Cavalry (plus four), who won five to four. We really should have won this match as just a few seconds before the " Halt " was sounded the winning goal was hit by Atkinson, but one of the 33rd fell off his pony at this very moment and the umpire in ignorance of the rules (there was no foul or danger to anyone) stopped the game and the goal was not counted. With the widened goals that followed the 33rd scored and won. This incident is mentioned because this was the second Tournament that the regiment lost in this identical manner. The first occasion happened at Naini Tal when the regiment was at Bareilly.

In 1920 Barge returned after many years absence and took a team consisting of himself, Pert, Cochrane and Barry-Smith to Ferozepore. They were not successful however. At the end of April of this year the regiment moved to Rawalpindi, where the polo was distinctly better. We settled down to play seriously again and collected some good ponies. In December two teams played in the Murree Brewery Cup, they were composed of " A " team—Cochrane, Barge, Atkinson and Barry-Smith ; " B " team—Monckton, Greenway, Williams and Dixon. Our "B" team were beaten by the 26th Cavalry first round, and the " A " team beat 22nd Cavalry (plus four) by five to four, 26th Cavalry (plus four) by seven to five, and in the finals defeated the 13th Lancers (plus 3) by seven to four. Unfortunately for the regiment Barge had to go home to the Staff College, shortly afterwards he retired from the Service and was a very great loss to us in every way.

Group at Indian Cavalry Polo Tournament, 1921.

In the meantime however Yeats-Brown had returned after a long absence. A team was sent to play in the Lahore 'Xmas Tournament, Yeats-Brown replacing Barge. In the first round we beat Sialkote (plus three) by seven to four, then the 10th Lancers (plus three) by nine to four, next the Wanderers by six to two. This brought us into the semi-final against Patiala "A". We received three goals start and were just beaten by four to three after a good game.

In the year 1921 the regiment entered for the Indian Cavalry, the Inter-Regimental and the Subalterns Tournament. Kirkwood came out for a few months before resigning, and was therefore able to play for the regiment in its last season. We were quite well mounted and had a good team composed of Cochrane (one), Yeats-Brown (two), Atkinson (three) and Kirkwood (back). The latter arrived in time for a fortnight's practice before going to Delhi for the Indian Cavalry Tournament, there was a large entry. The results were as under :—

17th Cavalry beat 12th Cavalry, nine goals to nil.
,, ,, ,, 10th Lancers, five goals to one.
,, ,, ,, 9th Hodson's Horse, nine goals to three.
,, ,, ,, 28th Cavalry, nine goals to two.

The final, against the 28th, was a very good game. They were led by Henderson who had captained our old team to victory before the war. Thus the regiment won the cup for the second time, and we went off to Meerut for the Inter-Regimental full of confidence. In the first round we defeated the 23rd Cavalry six to two, after a very strenuous game in which the brothers Kirkwood battled on opposite sides. Unfortunately Yeats-Brown had a toss and was knocked out with concussion, this was very bad luck, however Dixon, the most promising of the younger players, came in at half time and played brilliantly. In the second round we defeated the 19th Hussars ten to five, this took us into the semi-finals where we beat the Poona Horse, a strong and highly handicapped side, after a very fast game four to three.

In the meantime the 21st Lancers having only played one game on the other side of the draw had reached the finals. No Indian Cavalry team had ever won the Inter-Regimental before and we were determined to put up a record if possible. Yeats-Brown was still laid up, however Dixon played like a seasoned player. The 21st started off with a couple of goals, however after that we improved and led most of the time, Kirkwood was brilliant in attack and defence and we won a splendid galloping game, which was thrilling till the halt sounded, by five goals to four.

A record was thus made in winning both the Indian Cavalry and Inter-Regimental tournaments in the same season, it will be no easy task for any team in the future to equal this performance.

Our subalterns team Monckton (one), Dixon (two), Greenway (three) and Pert (back), then took over the ponies and played in the Subalterns' Cup. They beat the 18th Hussars Subalterns four to nil and we hoped that they also would create a record by winning this tournament also, which has never been won by an Indian Cavalry Regiment. They played the 21st Lancers Subalterns in the finals and although it was a first class game the 21st won, they being a much older and more experienced lot of players.

Thus the 17th won the blue riband of the Indian Polo in last year of their existence. The spirit however still exists in a team which has become the "Star and Crescents" and is composed of old members of the old regiment. They have since played in and won several tournaments.

The following is a list of the ponies that played in the 1921 team:—

Australian and English.		Indian Country Breds.
Foch.	Lawless.	Volma.
Clinker.	Tulsi Das.	Queen of Sheba.
Retort.	Melisande.	Anne.
Lady Doris.	Nigger.	Chasseur.
Peter.	Anthony.	Vera.
Gardiner.	Chorister.	Waterloo.
Lady Honour.	Ajax.	Harikari.
Lady Jane.	Lady Nora.	John.
Jack.	Night Hawk.	Cliquot.
Snow drop.	Mercia.	Valerio.
Zogg.	Margaret.	Annetta.
		Shahzada.

On return to Rawalpindi a team entered for the Tradesmen's Cup but were beaten. The regiment then left for Waziristan and after the hot weather moved to Lucknow in November, where they were beaten in the finals of the Royals' Cup which was played on handicap.

H. R. H. The Prince of Wales' team won the Commemoration Tournament in November at Lucknow, our team being the runners-up.

It was decided to have a last fling in Calcutta at 'Xmas. A regimental team consisting of Dixon (one), Griffiths (two), Atkinson (three) and Persse (back), played in the I.P.A. Championship, they were very unfortunate in meeting the victorious Jodhpur team in the first round, the latter won a fast galloping game and eventually won the Championship easily.

THE POLO TEAM
THAT WON
THE INTER-REGIMENTAL
AND THE
INDIAN CAVALRY POLO TOURNAMENTS

Regimental Polo Team with the Inter-Regimental and Indian Cavalry Cups.
Kirkwood. Yeats-Brown. Cochrane. Atkinson.

We then played the same team in the Ezra Cup beating Jubbulpur and the Cavalry School "B" (assisted by Pert). In the finals we played the Cavalry School "A" team (plus three) and although down in the last chukkar managed to win by five goals to four.

This was the last tournament in which the 17th Cavalry played as a regiment. At the time the regiment ceased to exist, there were many players of great promise such as Griffiths, Persse, Dixon, Monckton, Pert and Greenway, but many of these have had to leave the service owing to reductions and amalgamations, and they are a great loss to the service in every way.

Of those who were serving with the regiment before the war few remain. Boudier and Wikeley have retired. Steel and Barge have gone into business at Home. Henderson went to command the 28th Cavalry and after playing polo hard with them has now retired also. Barry-Smith, who commanded the regiment at its end and who always helped regimental polo, has retired on a well-earned pension. Wilson, Duberly and Mawdsley gave their lives for their country in the War. Dodd left the regiment to become a Gurkha, Kirkwood resigned and is showing them how polo should be played in England. Without doubt he will play for England against America in the next attempt to win back the Cup.* Skipwith who was a brilliant player has resigned from the service, while Guthrie has transferred to British Cavalry. They were all keen players and helped to make the polo history of the regiment.

It is interesting to notice how the polo of the regiment steadily improved subsequent to 1909, and to consider the causes that led to this result. There is no doubt that the foundation of the success of the regiment lay in the fact that from 1909 onwards there was a determination amongst all the officers that the 17th Cavalry must be made into a first class polo regiment. Other factors were, that the regiment contained no non-polo-players (as everyone not excluding the Medical Officer was a supporter of the game), that all the officers were horse lovers and kept good animals, and last but not least that the 17th Cavalry Polo Club developed practically into a borrowing fund only. The ponies on which the team played were all privately owned animals, being neither club ponies or troop horses.

The fine player without ponies or who merely kept half trained animals to sell at a small profit did not figure in the 17th Cavalry teams. Hence those heart-burning about lending ponies were minimised, bad animals were things to be got rid of quickly

---

* Both Kirkwood and Atkinson were in the English team in 1924.—[Ed. S. and C.]

and horse coping was discouraged. However a well trained high class tournament pony always commands a good price and players could count on eventually recovering their money by training animals, playing them for several years in tournaments and finally selling them before they had grown too old to be any longer considered first class, and when they had another younger animal ready to take the places of those disposed of. We encouraged fellows to keep good ponies and to keep plenty of them. Unless this idea is in force polo will never flourish in a regiment. The polo club as before mentioned being primarily a lending club, the rules limiting the amounts which could be borrowed, were extremely elastic. There was one special rule which was made to encourage the keeping of ponies and this was that no one should play in a regimental team in a first class tournament unless he was in possession of at least three ponies fit to play in the tournament. This rule while not always enforced to the letter showed the spirit of the regiment.

The club, as far as the income of the Tournament Fund would allow, paid the rail fare of ponies to the Tournaments, but all other expenses had to be met by the players themselves. To play in the 17th Cavalry teams men had to economise in other directions. Our players were *bonâ fide* amateurs which is not invariably the case.

The teams were chosen in a peculiar manner, but in a way that proved most successful. Each year in October the General Polo Meeting chose a Provisional Polo Captain. He picked out one other member for the team, these two then selected a third, then the three selected a fourth and the fourth a fifth. The five then met and elected one of themselves as the Polo Captain. He then chose three members of the four remaining to form the team and the man left out became the spare man of the team. Under this system it was just possible that the provisional Captain elected by the meeting might eventually become the fifth man.

This ends the polo record of the 17th Cavalry. It is probably incomplete in many respects but it is hoped that it will be of interest to all members and friends of the old regiment.

APPENDIX VI.

Some Racing Reminiscences of the 17th Cavalry.

This is an attempt to record some memories of the modest racing of the regiment as far as they can now be recalled and to indicate how the officers amused themselves in the days before every subaltern considered the possession of " a motor-bike " as the goal of his ambition and before " *Thé Dansants* " were the " *Chef d'œuvre* " of the day.

Robarts, the first colonel of the regiment, was a very keen racing man and one of the most prominent owners on the Indian Turf. It is unfortunate that the racing records of his time are so fragmentary that even the Royal Calcutta Turf Club have no complete accounts of races prior to 1870. The present writer was fortunate enough to find in the Turf Club library however an old book called " Sonepore Reminiscences, 1840—96," by Harry Abbott. This book contains a certain amount of information regarding Robarts' racing activities and incidentally it explains the absence of records. The following extracts are reproduced in extenso :—

" In 1857 the *Indian Sporting Review,* the only reliable turf guide up to then, died chiefly because its Editor Mr. Hume tried to turn it into a political paper ; naturally the interest its readers took in it fell off and it was not until 1865 that the resuscitation of the old *Oriental Sporting Magazine,* by Mr. W. Gilbert Hickey, gives reliable data to go on."

" Sonepore racing was principally kept up from 1858 to 1864 by Colonel Robarts, Lord Ulick Browne, Kenneth McLeod and H. B. Simpson."

" Colonel Robarts was a funny tempered peppery old fellow and about this time owned a chestunt Australian nag called ' Linton,' who could win almost any race if he chose, but like his owner had a will of his own and he generally bucked his rider off when going to the post and then took an excursion into the country. The Colonel used to go to the starting post armed with a hunting whip, and his son (poor Abdool Ghyas) who rode the brute used to complain bitterly of the old gentleman's behaviour ; he said he did not mind the cuts from the whip which as often reached him as the horse, nor the frequent spills, but it was the fluent native abuse fired at him to which he objected."

* * * * *

(1865.) "Colonel Robarts and his handsome eldest son Abdool Ghyas (whose mother was an Afghan lady) were as usual present."

"Events opened by 'Bricky' Collins* winning the Ledger with 'Dick Hatterick,' his other string Amsterdam being second, 'Marmion' belonging to Colonel Robarts' following them."

"Again the same stable carried of the Chumparun Cup with the mighty 'Vanderdecken' and again Colonel Robarts had to be content with second honours, his colours being carried by 'Challenger.'"

"Colonel Robarts had a look in at last, getting the second class handicap with 'Rockwood,' and that finished the racing for the year."

* * * * *

(1866.) "The entries had been fairly promising, 'Bricky' Collins, Colonel Robarts, Mr. Blocker, Major Windham Mr. Morgan and Captain Cunningham were the principal outside owners."

"A big durbar which was being held up-country, by Sir John Lawrence the then Governor-General of India, kept away a good many army men, but nevertheless the stand was very full; Colonel Robarts and his fine half-Afghan son and   and   being very much in evidence."

* * * * *

"Colonel Robarts' handsome little bay 'Milkmaid' romped home for the Galloway stakes."

"A poor field declared for the Victors Purse, but the lotterly was a good one for ticket takers; 'Blink Bonny' brought Rs. 300, 'Amsterdam' Rs. 500, 'Challenger' Rs. 270 and the tickets Rs. 980."

Dr. Rimmier and 'Bumph' Freeman had now gone into a confederacy and they declared to win with 'Blink Bonny,' so their only opponent was Colonel Robarts' 'Challenger,' but the talent got a nasty shock and the confederates stood agast at seeing the issue when Choochoo on 'Challenger' fairly and squarely outrode Hockney on 'Amsterdam'.

"Only two came to the post for the Losers Handicap, Colonel Robarts' 'Rockwood' conceding Mr. Freeman's 'Blink Bonny' one stone five pounds; the former won from pillar to post."

* * * * *

(1867.) "Colonel Robarts had a fine string of horses, 'Rocket' looking very well considering the hard work that he had done during the last year."

---

* A well known character in Indian Racing, see Horace Hayes "Indian Racing Reminiscences."

"The races commenced on Tuesday, the 5th of November, with the Sonepore St. Leger for maidens. As neither 'Red Lancer' nor the 'Knight of Avenel' were in a fit state to run well, and as 'Orphan' and 'Venture' were facing company rather too good for them at the weights, it looked like Lombard Street to a China Orange on 'Favourite' after her performance at Mysore, especially as she was in excellent condition. And with boozy old George Gooch on her back she romped home: first blood to the Colonel. He followed up his luck by winning the Bettiah Cup with 'Rocket'."

"On the second day the Colonel's stable had another outing for he won the Hutwa Cup with 'Rocket' and the Derby with 'Diamond'. On the third he walked over with 'Rocket' in the Civilian's Cup."

"On the fourth day three of the four events fell to Colonel Robarts, Jimmy steering 'Bellona' for him in the Welter."

"All were glad to see that good sportsman Colonel Robarts do so well."

* * * * *

(1868.) "The next arrival was Colonel Robarts or rather his horses. 'Rocket,' 'Favourite,' 'Bellona,' and 'Growler,' names all well known to fame and the maiden. 'Longden' said to be better than any of them. This stable however was not in its usual force. The Barrackpore race course on which they had been trained* was under water the greater part of the training season and the horses in consequence arrived at Sonepore fat and it was soon seen from the way that they galloped that none of them would humble the pride of the mighty Van; the only one of the lot that was going in good form was 'Favourite'. Colonel Robarts had besides the above horses several maidens but the only ones that eventually appeared in public were 'Warrior' and 'Hector': the former a Waler, and the latter an Arab and a very pretty one too, but too small to be a race horse."

(NOTE —Robarts does not appear to have won any race at Sonepore this year.— Ed. S. & C.)

* * * * *

(1869.) "Debonair, Charley Marten, Colonel Robarts and Monty Turnbull were amongst the visitors."

"The handsome 'Favourite' looked a picture but 'Longden' seemed all off. It was obvious that the quality of the English and Australians had improved greatly since last year, and that the once invincible 'Vanderdecken' and 'Rocket' could no longer hold their own. 'Miss Trelawney' won the Leger, although 'Octoira'

---

* The regiment was then stationed at Barrackpore.

and 'Longden' had been made equally hot favourites; again an outsider in 'Favourite' got home from 'Detrimental' who was villainously ridden by Couchman. Again came an upset in the Derby, Colonel Robarts' 'Cyclone' which only brought thirty dibs in the lottery beat 'Longhope' who fetched Rs. 300 in the lottery and 'Akbar' who brought Rs. 360."

* * * * *

(1870.) Colonel Robarts' 'Bellona' scooped the Planter's Purse on the second day and the Patna Stakes on the last day. 'Silvertail' proved good enough to score again a cup over eight hundred rupees in value, given by Colonel Robarts.

* * * * *

No further mention of Robarts occurs in the book; it appears that he did not again run his horses at Sonepore but in 1871 he is shown as a Steward of the Sonepore races in the prospectus published in the *Oriental Sporting Magazine*.*

Referring further back to the *Oriental Sporting Magazine* we find that in the published reports of the results of the Sonepore meetings that all the horses, referred to as belonging to Robarts in Abbott's book, are shown in the reports as the property of "Mr. W. W." The Calcutta Turf Club List of assumed names goes only back to 1880, so it is impossible to check the matter from that source, but fortunately other evidence is available. The old 17th Bengal Cavalry mess had a racing cup known to be one of Colonel Robarts which fell to the share of Lieut.-Colonel E. G. Newnham when the regiment was disbanded in 1882. This cup is now in the possession of his son Colonel Newnham, late of the Indian Army, and bears the inscriptions:—"*Calcutta Races, 1869-70, Trade's Plate won by Mr. W. W.'s Ch. Aus. G. 'Longden,' 2 miles 3·44, ridden by O. Dignum*" and "*In remembrance of the late Colonel C. J. Robarts who raised the 17th Bengal Cavalry and commanded the regiment for fourteen years, Peshawar, November 1876.*"

It may be taken as a fact that Robarts racing name was "Mr. W. W."

"Mr. W. W.'s" activities on the Indian Turf were by no means confined to Sonepore. His bay Arab horse 'Ruler' won the Calcutta Derby in 1864-65 and his bay Arab horse 'Growler' won it in 1867-68.

Perhaps his greatest achievement was winning that blue ribbon on the Indian Turf, the Viceroy's Cup twice, once in 1869 and once in 1870, with his bay Australian mare 'Favourite'. The 1870 win gave rise to an objection and the Stewards finally

---

* The regiment moved from Barrackpore to Sitapore in 1871.

declared the whole race null and void, and directed that the race be run over again, but the objectors evidently considered that they had no chance of beating 'Favourite' as she was allowed a walkover because no horse appeared against her, when the race was re-run.

Such accounts as are available of those days in the *Oriental Sporting Magazine* make frequent reference to "Mr. W. W.'s" horses. 'Favourite,' 'Longden,' 'Ruler,' 'Growler,' 'Bellona,' 'Rocket,' 'Driver,' 'Antelope,' 'Grey Warrior,' 'Eruption,' 'Bellman,' 'Trump,' 'Euphrates,' 'Doctor,' 'Cyclone,' etc., seem to figure in most up-country and Calcutta meetings. In Cawnpore in 1871 some of the horses begin running as "Mr. Manchester's." Who "Mr. Manchester" was the present writer has no idea except to hazard a guess that perhaps it was the racing name of Abdul Ghyas, Robarts' son (or adopted son) and heir.

Robarts himself died in January 1873 and after his death Abdul Ghyas ruined himself on the Turf and so dissipated Robarts' fortune, which he had inherited.

Horace Hayes in his book "Indian Racing Reminiscences" in writing about Cawnpore Racing says "amongst the pupils (at a Garrison Class at Cawnpore) was poor D'Arcy Thuillier one of the best sportsmen and cheeriest comrades that I have ever met." Thuillier was an officer of the old 17th and died at Dehra Doon as Adjutant of the Viceroy's Body Guard.

Whether any other members of the old regiment were racing men or not can now never be ascertained. Such records are lost in oblivion; but in any case amongst soldiers, keen sportsman like Robarts, who are also sufficiently wealthy to run large racing stables, are few and far between.

After being re-raised in 1885, the regiment was for many years not stationed in places where much racing took place, consequently little general interest was aroused; however both Warre-Cornish with his mare 'Hermia', and also Hewitt with his brown Australian gelding 'Ruapehu,' each managed to win the annual Bengal Cavalry Steeple Chase. 'Hermia' won in the year 1901 and 'Ruapehu' in the year 1905. These successes were however only spasmodic efforts, and they led to no further developments.

In 1907 however, the regiment was in accordance with the general desire of the officers, promised a station in the U. P. and the fact that this move was subsequently delayed by a famine until the winter of 1908-09 served only to make us all the more keen to move into and enjoy to the full, the sports of a "Promised Land." When the regiment came to Bareilly, there we found a course, in bad order it is true, but still a race course in being, even if no real races had taken place on it for some time. It was not long before we all began to take an interest in the sport. The "Gymkhanas" which had long been part of the Bareilly station life were soon recognised not only as affording great amusement but as also offering opportunities of replenishing our purses in a modest way as well. However this was not their sole value, they formed an excellent school for amateur jockeys where any light weight could learn to ride on the flat, and also enabled owners of ponies to see what their animals were worth without going to the expense which entering and running in big meetings involves. Besides this, being full of local interest, they served to keep both the regiment and the station in touch with a traditional English sport

The Bareilly Races during the stay of the 17th Cavalry, owe much of their success to the help they received from the officers of the 17th Cavalry both as owners and officials. General Boudier was a Steward for five years and he on most occasions officiated very successfully in the thankless and difficult task of judging. Besides this he was always ready to help in every way; especially did he recognise as few do, that the Secretary of a meeting had much work to do apart from his military duties. This even if it had stood alone would have been a pillar of strength to the management. Wall was also a Steward for three years. Later, when he left the regiment to join Skinner's Horse, he was replaced by Stewart. "Hender" and Ivan Guthrie, between them carried out for some years the thankless job of starter.

We were lucky also in having with us in the station sporting regiments and batteries who owned and ran horses. Without them we could have done nothing. Gymkhanas depend almost entirely on local entries and it takes more than one regiment to support a meeting. About the time of the arrival of the regiment in Bareilly in 1909 the race course was nearly derelict. There was a grand stand, an enclosure with some stabling, some appliances and a course which appeared to be nearly as hard as a macadamised road. The race course itself, had I believe, been in existence for many years and a broad masonry bridge which carried it over a nullah showed that, at some time during the past, much money had been spent on it. But that time must have been remote. There was an account book which started with the illuminating entry of "cash found in the bank." Presumably the predecessor of the scribe who wrote this, had kept no accounts at all! This famous account book and some odds and ends of paper composed the Club Records.

Everything clerical and practical had to be improvised from the beginning.

However, the occasion had produced a man and before the 17th Cavalry arrived, "Lorry" Godman of the Battery had taken things in hand.

The first task obviously, was to get the course itself into such a condition that racing on it would be possible without laming horses. This took time, and incidentally good "soft going" was not obtained for several years. However, by the winter of 1909-10, Godman had managed to organise some winter gymkhanas and had followed them up by a most successful monsoon gymkhana, which attracted visitors all the way from Jhansi. Everybody supported him—the principal civilians and the regiments all subscribed for cups. This generosity was due to a burst of enthusiasm and it gave the racing a good start. It was never repeated however in our time!

The big Cavalry Camp held during that winter at Gurgaon, kept the regiment away from Bareilly most of the cold season 1909-10, and consequently it was found impossible to carry out any ambitious programme. However, the little we did, was sufficient to bring Dodd to the fore as a popular jockey and his pony Maharani became the foremost local favourite.

A great sensation was caused at one Gymkhana by an animal entered under the name of "Trapper" (who followed the humble avocation of pulling the local bank manager's trap), winning a race; unfortunately for the conspirators it was recognised by a trainer who had come to see the races and the coup that had been planned did not come off, for it was disqualified for running under a false name. Later, under its real name of "Rosemary" and the property of another owner it became one of the most popular of our local race horses. I am glad to record however that these attempts at sharp practice were most unusual at the Bareilly meetings.

A fall whilst schooling a pony at Jhansi, laid Godman up for some time and the Artillery Practice Camp at Delhi closely following this called him away and he resigned the Secretaryship of the Races.

Dodd ran a successful Gymkhana in December 1910, at which Stewart handicapped. We had some ponies up from Agra for this meeting. One of them, Sir John, was supposed to be hot stuff, and afterwards when bought by Curtis of the 60th, turned into a rather famous pony; winning either the Kadir Cup or one of the Cross-Country races that follow it. On this occasion he did nothing. However Dodd, as usual, rode several winners during this meeting, so did Joey and also Foottit who had just joined. Bareilly's " Bonnie," Joey's " Moon-lighter " and Foottit's " Angela," all won closely contested races.

One meeting, however, was enough to show Dodd that the duties of Adjutant could not be combined with those of Race Secretary, so he handed over the management to Stewart, who continued to be Secretary right up till the Spring Meeting of 1914; to manage this last he had to return temporarily from Allahabad.

More gymkhanas were now held, and Bonnie, Tot, Maharani, Hafizan, Lancer, Marguerite, Pink'un, Monarch, David, Huntress, Circuit, Beryl, Gamecock, Highforce, and many other ponies belonging to the regiment figured prominently, much to the pleasure and profit of their owners.

The " Professor " on Highforce, " Joey " on Gamecock and Dodd on a horse belonging to one of the 15th Lancers, all competed in the Indian Cavalry Chase at Amballa, but none of them were fast enough to beat Holden of the 5th Cavalry on Woodlark, which won.

As mentioned before Hewitt's horse Ruapehu had won this cup long ago—so had Warre-Cornish's Hermia, but subsequently to those days we were never able to win anything at this meeting. Of recent years the Indian Cavalry has been turned into more of a " point-to-point " meeting than formerly.

The Bareilly Spring Meeting was revived in 1911, for the first time after many years. The regiment as yet were too modest to enter its horses, and the officers confined themselves to watching the visiting animals run. Officials were hard to get as funds were limited, but Major "Mike " Williamson, perhaps better known under his Turf name of " Mr. Rake," sportingly came as Honorary Handicapper. He was a well-known owner and punter, and his subsequent retirement left a blank on the Indian Turf. Beedham, now one of the biggest trainers in India, formerly a farrier sergeant of the Royal Horse Artillery, was started in the training business by him as his private trainer. This first Spring Meeting did not entirely pass off without friction. In order to sell the lotteries starting declarations, containing the names of the riders, had to go in the night before the race. Some owners failed to comply with this, and there was a lot of unpleasantness in consequence. It was this necessity of putting in starting declarations the night before that had much to do with killing race lotteries in India. Bareilly was one of the last places to keep them going, but eventually we had finally to give them up principally for that reason. There was another reason also; lotteries by custom supplied free drinks; and with this encouragement occasionally foolish young men got more deeply involved than was desirable.

There is little doubt that the modern system of starting declarations, half an hour before the race, is more convenient in every way—but it has robbed racing of much of the former sociability which sprung from acquaintanceships made at the lottery table. Another development of modern years is that bookmakers now are not allowed to open their books till half an hour before the race: in the old days they were willing to start betting as soon as they arrived in a station. As in up country meetings as they always had to see the Secretary first in order to deposit security and get permission to bet, he could get the cream of the odds if he wanted to bet!

'Bareilly,' 'Y. B.', 'Joey,' Duberly, and 'Hender' of the regiment, Jefferies of the Worcesters, Godman of the Gunners, all went off on leave early this year and sold their studs. This put a blight on more racing. And as no new owners seemed to be coming forward, the season closed.

In the winter of 1911 the year of the Durbar, we managed to fit in a couple of gymkhanas before the regiment left for Delhi. 'Y. B.' on Stewart's David, secured an easy victory in a couple of hurdle races. This was the first time we had tried David as a hurdler and he was so successful as to even surprise us, as well as filling our pockets. He continued to be a Bareilly hurdle race favourite for long, quite displacing Fatima belonging to the Royal Scots, which had previously swept the board. Dodd did not have his usual luck at these meetings. Gaussen of the 3rd Skinner's Horse who came over from Meerut with a string, managed to secure a couple of races and was so pleased that he promised to come again and bring his friends, a promise which he later carried out. We always welcomed outsiders. It cheered up the "Books" and made them give better odds.

At the Indian Cavalry Races this year, we ran David in the Pony Chase. He came second but having dropped some lead was disqualified. Yeats-Brown rode only nine stone three and as the pony had to carry twelve stone ten it necessitated two weight cloths to carry the dead weight. Some of the lead slipped out when the pony pecked at a jump. He carried so much dead weight in this race, that I think that here was laid the seed of the mysterious lameness that afterwards affected him. He died finally full of years in 1916, in a paddock at the regimental Farm, where he enjoyed his well earned rest. He was then well over twenty. Starlight managed to pick up a third in the open polo scurry. We little thought in those days, that he would live to be one of the best ponies of the English Team in International Polo. He was by a thorough-bred horse called "The Swale," and his mother "Self Love" was out of a Baluch mare by "Young Egotist." Young Egotist's father, "Egotist," was a horse from General Parrot's famous thoroughbred stud at Saharanpur. which was afterwards taken over by the Government. Starlight was a great credit to the 17th Cavalry Stud Farm, and incidently this mixture of thoroughbred and Baluch has produced the best animals that were bred on the farm. "Self Love," his mother, was one of the best of our brood mares. Dodd's "Maharani," Stewart's "Queen of the Jews," "Archpriest" and "Chasseur," were all also her off-spring.

After the regiment came back from the Durbar, and the excitement of the Indian Cavalry Polo week was over, the Spring Meeting of 1912 came on. This year "Bareilly" ran Banshee and Stewart ran Kim, Starlight, Morning Star and Saglawe, but the only regimental success was a "third" with Starlight. Otherwise the Spring Meeting was a great success in every way. The return of the Infantry Polo Tournament to Bareilly assisted the gate money and the totalisator, and enabled bigger fees to be taken from the "Ring." So well did everything go that at the last minute the Secretary was able to organise a third day which was an innovation entirely, but nevertheless, it proved to be sufficiently successful to turn the meeting for the future into a three day one.

Arthur Fawcett of the R.C.T.C. handicapped for the meeting and lived with us in the Mess, we were all sorry to lose his society when his duties were over. "Pat" Deane, now official starter of the R.C.T.C., (who came over to start from Lucknow, where he was then Race Secretary) was another welcome guest. His cheery manner and amusing stories kept the Mess in laughter for many a day. Old "Doc" Martin, the horse dentist, as well as the polo teams of the 60th Rifles and the Rifle Brigade, was also living with us at the time, so we had a full Mess.

"Doc" Martin was a great character. His speciality was filing horses' teeth. "Horse Dentistry" he called it and he certainly was an artist himself. His bag of instruments was an education to look at, but it was the way that he handled them, that commanded admiration. He used a "crush" of sand bags only and without any tackle would handle the most savage and vicious horses with ease. Before they knew what happened to them, he would have his hand in their mouths and be filing their teeth, and they would be so surprised as to forget to make any fuss at all. He did all the horses of the regiment for us, with great advantage to their subsequent health and condition.

More gymkhanas followed the Spring Meeting, and Kim, Starlight, David and Saglawe, all won races much to the pleasure and profit of the Honorary Secretary. Nor were the successes of the regiment confined to these. Skipwith now began to blossom into a jockey, and soon rode with great success. His pony, Trigger, although it failed in winning the great coup that was planned by Brierley, Y. B., Stewart and Skipwith nevertheless paid well in getting a place. It was an animal purchased from the regiment and quite unknown, and was brought on to the course unclipped, with a long mane looking somewhat uncared for. Naturally it started at very long odds and after all this it was beaten by a head. Its performances later certainly justified the hopes that had been entertained regarding it. Trigger only died a short time ago at a ripe old age as a result of an accident in the 33rd Cavalry. Duberly was another performer and 'Joey' rode many a winner.

Bush of the Worcesters, was a great supporter of the Gymkhanas and rode very well. He would undoubtedly have become a well-known "G.-R." in India, if a Turkish bullet at Gallipoli had not laid him low. His pony Graceful, surprised everybody, except himself by winning three races at one meeting. He was not the only one of the G.-Rs. of those days, whose life was given for his Country. Thursby of the 60th who used to stay with the regiment so often, and Charrington of the Royals and Eustace Crawley of the 12th Lancers whom everybody knew, were all killed in the War. Poor Duberly lies in the African jungle and our "Professor" somewhere in France. Bush's battalion of the Worcesters lost very heavily in Gallipoli, and Gilmour and Townsend, both Bareilly owners and sportsmen, were amongst the fallen, but they were only two of many.

Gilmore picked up an Arab pony from a Pathan dealer which he called Exchange. Its antecedents were quite unknown but everyone thought it was some racing pony which the owner found no longer profitable and had got rid of. Nobody could identify it and whatever it was, it proved to be a gold mine to the owner, in the beginning at Bareilly and later by winning the Army Cup. He finally sold it for a very enhanced price.

Gaussen and Bennett of the 3rd Skinner's Horse, and Rees of the 13th Hussars, came down from Meerut for one of the Gymkhanas to wipe up the field, but their only success was when Rees won the Arab Scurry on Shifter. They did not come again, so it must be presumed that this visit was not a success financially. Richard, Budget, Barehaven, all won races for their owners so the regiment did not do so badly.

During 1912-13, the regiment swept the board at the Gymkhana meetings. Stewart's Starlight won four races, Stewart's Kim three, Skipwith's Serang three, Dodd's Aristocrat one, Skipwith's Trigger three, Duberly's Osprey one, Skipwith's Cristine one, Dodd's Breeze one, Brierley's Barehaven one. There were many other regimental animals, which ran second and third.

In the big Spring Meeting, Steel's St. George won the Bareilly Cup a three mile chase, with Stewart's Kim second. Stewart's Starlight won the Breeder's Plate, and also the Polo Plate.

Skipwith, Atkinson, Dodd, Foottit, again were all successful Jockeys and steered horses to victory in the gymkhanas. Bush of the Worcesters rode Stewart's horses and very well he rode them too.

The regiment left Bareilly early in the winter of 1914 and it proved impossible to hold any gymkhanas before their departure. A big meeting, the first for many years, was held in the autumn and it was intended to make this an annual event. We did not then think of the War. The departure of the 17th Cavalry however marked the end of racing in Bareilly for many years excepting the Spring Meeting of 1914 which Stewart returned to run. Probably the real cause was the breaking out of the War, but it also sustained a blow in the departure of the regiment.

This account of the Bareilly Racing is fragmentary, but if it recalls memories of our old dumb friends, if it recalls the days of happy friendships, and good times, of the days when we lived as cavalry soldiers should live with large stables and little thought of the morrow, then my purpose is served. As I write I can see the revolving wheels of the lotteries and hear the good old cry, "Two hundred rupees in the lottery, and 'David' for sale," and then arises the picture of the Steward's stand on top of the Judge's box, and the horses coming up the straight. How many times have we stood there and watched. Would we could stand there again, and see the old colours flash first past the post.

After leaving Bareilly the regiment moved to Allahabad The race course there is a peculiar one in every way. Stewart was full of plans for improving the course and some of these improvements were actually being carried out when the sudden breaking out of the War stopped all idea of racing in the regiment for many a day.

It was not till the winter of 1917 that any of the regiment attempted to race again, but that year in the Lahore Christmas meeting Pert won a race with his horse " Buffalo."

Some two years later Stewart made an endeavour to win those famous Punjab country-bred races with a horse called Red Lancer which he had bought from the Mona Remount Depôt. However Red Lancer only secured one "third." This was in the Punjab Cup. Skipwith also made various attempts to win races at Lahore with a horse called Muft without success.

By the time that the regiment came to Lucknow on relief from Dera Ismail Khan in 1921 peace conditions had nearly returned. The regiment very soon began to take an active interest in the Gymkhanas which were held about every fortnight in Lucknow. Barry-Smith's Arabian Knight, Stewart's Red Lancer, Cleopatra, Akbar and Druid, Griffith's Fanny, Y. B.'s Antony and Ata Mohamed Shah's Nasrat, all ran with varying success. Joey won the Polo Scurry on Fanny at the special meeting on the occasion of the Prince of Wales' visit. He rode a fine race and beat the Prince who was riding what was supposed to be the best pony in the race.

Shortly after this Barry-Smith and Stewart went down to Gwalior for the special meeting held there on the occasion of the visit of the Prince of Wales and Stewart's horse Red Lancer won the Horse Race. Shortly after this meeting the regiment amalgamated with the 37th Lancers and the 17th Cavalry racing came to an end.

Racing men in India are not always dishonest, as one might gather from the stories that are circulated ; in fact, taken as a body they are good sportsmen. Occasionally it is true individuals to whom this description does not apply are brought into public notice, but many of the "ramps" of the Turf that one hears of, originate in the fertile imaginations of their narrators. The stories told of young men ruined by racing are generally equally fictitious. Occasionally men do come to grief by betting but these are not always owners, and if the word "horse-racing" had never been heard these same men would have found other ways of losing their money. Besides, although it has become the fashion of the time to make a great fuss over the spendthrift, it is well to remember that from the military point of view at least, a man who is prodigal of his purse is frequently equally so with his life. Men who set store by a big balance in the bank may be reasonably expected to wish to live to take advantage of it.

It is sad but true that amateur racing in India is on the decline, although it might be incorrect to make that remark of racing generally. There are, it is true, plenty of fixtures, but the number of professional trainers and jockeys yearly increases. Underneath all the apparent brilliance seeds of decay from the soldiers point of view are sprouting, and in a few years racing in India will become dependent on the interest taken in it by the richer natives of the country. Modern conditions and the strenuous nature of postwar training, prevent soldiers from going in for racing on a big scale, unless they hand their animals over to professionals. Practically speaking they must either do this, or not go in for it at all. The R.C.T.C. has unfortunately made racing more and more professional by making many more rules which cut out the amateur. On their own course at Calcutta horses are now not allowed to run unless trained by professionals.

It will be a bad day for India and for the army when soldiers cease to own horses and run them in races. In the 17th Cavalry racing never did anything but good. Neither will it ever do any harm in any other regiment where sporting ideals are prevalent, and where racing means owning and running horses. It is when soldiers merely watch races from the stand and when their interests are confined to "punting" that disasters occur.

APPENDIX VII.

PIGSTICKING RECOLLECTIONS OF THE 17TH CAVALRY.

Whether the old 17th Cavalry even pigsticked or not is now not known. At any rate they were stationed in places where pigsticking could be done and it is presumed that some at least must have been followers of the sport. That Roberts was a racing and hunting man we know. Whether he was a pigsticker or not is lost in oblivion.

Before the 17th Cavalry came to Bareilly the second time, the re-raised regiment had never been stationed in a place where pigsticking was possible; therefore before 1909 there is little to record. Warre-Cornish however made opportunities for himself, where none apparently existed, and he on his favourite horse Hermia in the year 1901 won the blue ribbon of the pigsticking world, the Kadir Cup.* This has remained a trophy that we have all been most proud of and which we prize greatly. Whenever the writer sees it he thinks how Warre-Cornish would have shone had he been spared to have hunted with the Bareilly Tent Club.

In Wardrop's book "Modern Pigsticking" will be found a note on the "Bareilly Tent Club," contributed by Captain Stewart. It is as follows:—

"The Bareilly Tent Club was founded in 1878. The biggest year's bag on record is one hundred and sixty-nine boar killed in 1897. The average bag is ninety-four. The biggest pig on record is thirty-nine inches. The country consists of *baghs*, *jhow* and grass. The *bagh* country predominates. The short spear is used underhand. The Bareilly pig are very fierce. The country has a lot of blind wells. Small fast handy horses are most useful as the pig have to be caught between covers."

The above gives one a rough idea of the Bareilly pigsticking. In the days when the above mentioned record bag was made, both the Budaon and Moradabad districts were hunted by the Bareilly Tent Club, but when the 17th Cavalry came to Bareilly, the territory of the Tent Club had become much restricted, and these hunting grounds were no longer open to us, as Moradabad and Budaon had organised Tent Clubs of their own. We did go once to Budaon, while the regiment was

---
* See pages 62, 63, 64 and, 65.

at Bareilly, but that was by the special invitation of Cotton, the Collector who, incidentally was the greatest character of the I.C.S. in the United Provinces. Whatever his idiosyncrasies were, he was a great sportsman and a keen pigsticker.

The area of the pigsticking in the actual Bareilly district, was small although well stocked. Its covers were peculiar in their way, and one had to beat thoroughly as they consisted for the most part of almost impenetrable *baghs,* in which the pig used to lie in bamboo clumps and under thorn bushes. Although we did not realise it at first, it was the protection afforded by these dense covers, that induced the pigs to leave their homes in the *Terai* to revel in the sugarcane and other cultivation, which formed such rich feeding. There were also plenty of other covers of grass and *jhow,* but they were never natural sanctuaries, like the great *baghs* of Kaitola and Rat Muggeri.

Below is set forth in tabular form particulars taken from the Tent Club log, of the annual bags, with the names of the Secretaries of the Club from its beginning.

Considering how the territory had been curtailed, it will be seen that the years that the 17th Cavalry were in Bareilly were on the whole particularly good ones. This was in no way the result of chance, but was the reward of hard work and intelligent hunting.

Season.	Secretaries.	Boars Killed.
1878 1879 1880 1881	H. S. Dawkins, Esq., Royal Artillery	No organised Tent Club. Mr. Dawkins ran the Meets privately and there is no record.*
1882	Capt. Basil Spragge, King's Own Light Infantry..	9
1883	Ditto ditto	21
1884	Capt. H. B. Jefferys, Royal Artillery	43
1885	G. McMicking, Esq., Royal Artillery J. H. Balfour, Esq., 13th Bengal Lancers	20
1886	C. F. Knyvett, Esq., Indian Police	14
1887	Ditto ditto	14

* The old 17th Cavalry was stationed at Bareilly during 1881-82 but it is not known whether they then did any pigsticking or not.

Season.	Secretaries.	Boars Killed.
1888	H. L. Webster, Esq., Indian Police	No record of these years in the log.
1889	E. A. Neville, Esq., R. &. K. Railway..	
1890	J. K. Tod, Esq., 7th Bengal Cavalry	10
1891	Capt. F. Pollock, 7th Bengal Cavalry..	17
1892	Ditto ditto	14
1893	C. E. Wild, Esq., Indian Civil Service..	23
1894	Ditto ditto	52
1895	Ditto ditto	71
1896	Ditto ditto / Capt. P. Wheatley, Royal Artillery	122
1897	Capt. R. Fanshawe, Oxford Light Infantry	169
1898	Capt. P. Wheatley, Royal Artillery	102
1899	Capt. G. H. Geddes, Royal Field Artillery	109
1900	Ditto ditto / S. H. Freemantle, Esq., Indian Civil Service	85
1901	Ditto ditto	82
1902	Ditto ditto	125
1903	Major N. Taylor, 14th Lancers	58
1904	Ditto ditto	117
1905	Lt.-Col. G. H. Weller, 14th Lancers	59
1906	Capt. E. A. Hewlett, 14th Lancers	81
1907	Ditto ditto	82
1908	G. R. Maitland, Esq., 14th Lancers	55
1909	K. Barge, Esq., 17th Cavalry / Capt. H. S. Stewart, 17th Cavalry	36
1910	Ditto ditto	99
1911	Ditto ditto	102
1912	Ditto ditto	123
1913	Ditto ditto	78

No account of the Bareilly pigsticking would be in any way complete without a mention of the *shikari* and his assistants. Much depends on a *shikari*—especially if the Secretary is new to the district which his Tent Club hunts. Ahmed Hussain, who was formerly the *shikari* of the Bareilly Tent Club, was a Rohilla Pathan. He was a very clever *shikari*, and as brave as a lion. He was no respecter of persons however, except of those who, in his opinion, were expert pigstickers. It was his failing to adopt this attitude to his employers, but one had to remember that he was old, and had seen much folly.

I can remember quite distinctly my first introduction to him at a meet at Saidupore. We, from a rather indifferent position, have seen a large sow, and a couple of very small boar, break past us. The latter were obviously unrideable and the beat being over, we set about getting for ourselves a drink. At this moment Ahmed Husain rode slowly up on his grey caster. He looked at us with obvious disapproval, and said, "*Jis waqt tum loge diruhkt ke niche sharab pite the ek bara bari sewer chala gya.*"* I presume he made this remark with the laudable object of showing that he considered us greenhorns of no account, but I feel sure he never really knew how near he was on that day to get a beating!

A *shikari* must be mounted to control the coolies, and in this connection it should be remembered that a small pony is as good as a big horse, and that it costs far less to feed. In Kadir country they sometimes mount *shikaris* on camels. These animals however, would have been useless in Bareilly pigsticking.

The *chuprasies* of the Bareilly Tent Club, were Kalan Khan, a decadant Rohilla Pathan who lived near Khaitola, Mehndi, a member of the criminal tribe of *Nuts* and *Pasis* (strangely enough he had blue eyes). There were two others, whose names are forgotten. They were all equipped with old muzzle loading guns from which they used to fire charges of blank or sometimes of small shot at boar unwilling to break.

The *khansama* of the Tent Club, was a hoary old villain who required a daily tonic of fines and abuse to keep him up to the mark. He laboured under difficulties, and although his food was not up to a very high standard, he never actually poisoned us. When I look back, I think perhaps we were lucky. We all remember him at breakfast with his deprecative remark,

---

* "Just when you people were drinking under the tree a very fine boar went away."

"*Aj anda poach hone ke laiy nahin hai. hum 'rumble-tumble' banaenge.*" †

The Tent Club owned a really good medicine box and a first aid set with surgical instruments for the doctoring of men and beasts. These were constantly called into requisition. We were lucky in having the capable 'Bareilly' nearly always out with us. He took on the double part of doctor and "Vet." In his absence the Honorary Secretary officiated for him.

The great feature of the beaters were the *Nuts*. These were members of a criminal tribe and great natural *shikaris*. One *Nut* in a beat, was worth three ordinary coolies, and they drew pay accordingly. The *Jemadar Nut* got a rupee per diem, enormous pay in the days when the ordinary coolie gladly came for two annas per day with a handful *churbaina* (parched gram) for his midday meal. The *Jemadar Nut* was a long thin man of somewhat neat appearance, but very little to look at. It was not till you saw him getting a wounded boar out of a bush, that you realised that he was cheap at a rupee per diem. The long disheveled hair of the ordinary *Nuts*, gave them the appearance of European musicians, and they were named by the members accordingly. These names so took their fancy, that they called themselves by them afterwards, and apparently forgot their original names altogether.

Picture a typical scene : A great shady *bagh*, dimly shown up by the rosy light of the early Indian morning. Dawn is just beginning to break, the air is fairly cool and refreshing after the intense heat of the early part of the preceding night. Round in an irregular circle, are camp beds swathed by white mosquito nets, interspersed with small khaki Kabul tents dotted here and there. Some way off there are lines of picketted horses and rows of bullock carts, while a couple of great elephants gaze with interest on a camel whose sowar is getting ready to go to the railway station, for the daily supply of ice. Everyone is stirring ; the "spears" are washing, pulling on their boots and breeches, or getting out of bed, *syces* and orderlies are saddling horses, mahouts are getting the pads on to the elephants, and the coolies are collecting for the day. As each coolie arrives, the *shikari* gives him a gun wad or a tin disc, so we will know who to pay in the evening, otherwise we should have the whole country side clamouring for pay.

At a long table in the middle, the early birds amongst the "spears," are already sitting down yelling for the *khansama* to bring breakfast. He and the *khidmitgar*, poor devils, are trying

---

† "To-day the eggs are not fit to poach I will make buttered eggs."

to pack up the lunch and the drinks in baskets. Around them, in a circle, sit the patient "*bhimas*" * with their "*bangis*" † and baskets, waiting for their loads. They know later in the day, there will be continual yells for the "*Bangi wallah*," and dire would be the fate of all, if drinks, ice, cigarettes and cheeroots were not forthcoming

At last all is ready. The hunters are fed, cigars and pipes are lighted and the spears mount and are off. Some clamber on to the elephants, the rest get on their horses and the coolies follow behind, shepherded by the *chuprasies*. They are intermingled with *Nuts* and their terriers, and with "*Bangi wallahs*" and their loads. At the head of all rides the *Shikari* on his old white horse. He acts as guide to the procession.

And there we can see Godman on the dun pony he bought from the regiment. "Y. B." on Diavalo—the "Professor" on Highforce—"Bareilly" on Banshee, "Joey" on something hired out of the lines, Allen on one of his little ponies with its kit all tied on with string, Hogan on the famous Bohemian, Jeffries on his old black mare which was cut to pieces in the nullah at Khaitola, "Ginger" Townsend on a caster, old Norbury on his horse with his famous fly-flap stuck in his boot, and many others. The rear will probably be brought up by Stewart on his favourite Molly. He is making sure, that the lunch, the drinks and the medicine chest, have really left camp with "the line." Presently he will canter on and join the *Shikari* to give him the final instructions.

Then the cover is reached and the "heats" are arranged and posted. Then comes the hunting, of which particulars will be told in due course. Then lunch, then more hunting, then home to bathe and dine and sleep. This is a typical day. How many have we had like it? And how many more would we like to have?

Now, having given some little account of the Tent Club, let us briefly record a little of the yearly pigsticking gossip, gathered from such sources as are available.

1909.

The season of 1909, when looked at from the point of view of the number of pig killed, was not perhaps, a great success. Also, a gloom was cast over everything, by the sad death of Patterson of the Horse Gunners, who was staying with Stewart. He died from a fractured skull as the result of an accident caused by a charging boar at Shahi.

---

* The carrier caste also called Kahars.
† Split bamboos on the ends of which balanced loads are carried.

In other ways however, failure was not apparent. To most of us, remain many pleasant memories of those long hot weather days which seemed only too short when spent in shady *baghs* of the jungle, far away from that bright dazzling heat which is reflected from the roads and bungalows of a cantonment. It was, I fancy, a unique season in the annals of the Bareilly Tent Club, for with the exception of our sporting collector Allen, who attended a few meets at the beginning of the season prior to leaving for England, nobody in the garrison had done any pigsticking worth speaking of before, nor did anyone know the surrounding country. The bag of the Tent Club had been dwindling for some years, and the fortunes of the Club seemed at a low ebb. However we were all as yet too inexperienced to do much good, and the season ended with a bag of only thirty-six.

Before the regiment reached Bareilly, it had been settled locally that Kenneth Barge who had gone on ahead, should become Tent Club Secretary. However very shortly after we arrived, he went off to be A.-D.-C. to Sir Jocelyn Woodhouse, so it became necessary to get some one else.

Stewart took over from Barge, but the season was then half gone and this change of management late in the season did not help matters. For some time after Patterson's death no one had much heart to go out, and the rains coming on very quickly, this year made a short season.

1910.

We commenced pigsticking this season much earlier than in the previous one, and as many of the "spears" had now learnt something about the sport and about the country, we had high hopes of a good bag for the year. The opening meet was held at Kaitola, during the Christmas week. For, although according to the Calendar, "Christmas," belongs to the past year, in Bareilly pigsticking, it belongs to the ensuing season. Our bag was six—which established a record for a "Christmas meet" at Bareilly.

Manœuvres and the Cavalry Camp at Delhi, took many members out of Bareilly during January and February, and only an odd meet near Sunker Pul, was held during those months.

Wilson, Yeats-Brown and Stewart went in for the Kadir this year, but without any marked success.

On March 5th, the season was started properly, and meets were held weekly, except during the first week in April when on account of crop cutting, no coolies could be got. One very successful meet was held at Saidupore where we killed nine pig in two days. This surprised even the *Shikari*, for Saidupore previously had always been considered rather a second rate meet. Up to May 7th, when we left for our ten-day meet in Rampur we had slain forty-three boar, and we were full of hope and expectation of a big bag as we had heard glowing accounts of the country in the Rampur State. These hopes for the first few days seemed doomed to disappointment, but subsequently, we were all cheered up by killing five pig in a morning on the way to Paharpur. This temporary run of luck did not last however and finally we left with a bag of thirteen only. Though the bag was small, the runs were long and exciting, and each in itself, was a a liberal education in pigsticking, and we all felt that in another year with the experience that we had gained, we should do much better.

During this meet at the *Mote Jheel*, a famous tiger jungle, "the line" put up a panther. There was of course, much excitement, and as this is the only panther that was actually ever pursued while the regiment was at Bareilly, I record the incident in the words of one of the heat. " I well remember how the sauntering line came to a sudden stop and how the coolies all ran together like animals herding in fear. They thought, as did Ahmed Hussain the *shikari*, that we had come on a tiger. It was a tense moment and one of our elephants, Lukshman Piari, began to trumpet and turntail. Then there was a flash of gold and a panther bounded away through the tall reeds, moving beautifully and noiselessly. We were off after him as hard as we could, the *shikari* on his old white caster armed only with a small whip, leading the way. We never had more than a glimpse of him, the grass was so thick and high. So we returned slightly crest-fallen and started the 'line' again."

The Secretary saw this incident from the pad of one of the elephants in "the line." He had mounted on this on account of a badly injured arm due to an accident some days before. His endeavours to immediately follow the panther with all the elephants, was frustrated by the Rampur "Colonel," who acted as the Nawab's "Liason Officer." The latter was all of a dither at the idea of one of H. H.'s panthers being killed by a pigsticking party, and pointed out with vigour the possibilities of the consequences to himself when that irate potentate should hear of it.

The Rampur State is a very sporting pigsticking country full of ditches barely jumpable and of rivers nearly uncrossable and of ground that it is difficult even to walk over, but the pig are not preserved and are few in number. So it soon became evident that the rest of our ten days' leave could be more profitably

PIGSTICKING SNAPSHOTS.

The Shikari. Hallowes. C. Brierley. Wilson.
Yeats-Brown. Stewart. W. Brierley.
Slingsby. Godman.
GROUP AT A MEET OF THE BAREILLY TENT CLUB.
(Drawing for heats.)

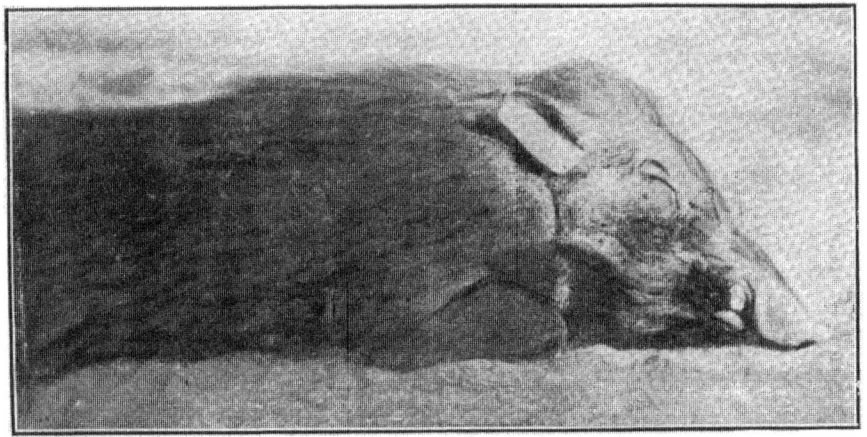

ONE OF THE RAMPUR BOARS.

THE SHAHI COUNTRY.

spent elsewhere if we were still ambitious of getting the hundred pig which had been set-up as the goal to aim at for a season's bag.

A forced march of thirty miles from near Pilaspur in Rampur, to the Canal Bungalow at Kundra, was hurriedly decided upon. We did a morning's pigsticking at Pilaspur, and marched after lunch. The thermometer stood at 105 degrees in the shade and there was nothing to drink from the time of leaving "the line" at Pilaspur till we reached our destination. The road was uncertain, and none of us had ever been over it, but chiefly guided by Godman, who had an instinct for going across country, we finally arrived about midnight. The carts had then just arrived at the camping ground and we finally dined about 1-15 A.M.! To anyone acquainted with the heat of the summer days of Bareilly, these facts will be eloquent. Nowadays, we have all grown older and take our pleasures less energetically. We had a few days' leave still unexpended, and around Rat Muggeri we retrieved our fortunes, killing fourteen pig in two days.

Two four-day meets after this were held, one around Kaitola, Atamara, Shahi and Dunka, and the other at Nawabgunj, Bijamau and Saidupore. Each of these meets accounted for a fair number of boar, so by the 6th of June the bag had reached ninety-two.

Two hard days at Budaon, brought it up to ninety-three, and four days at Rat Muggeri, Kundra and Nawabgunj in the rain, added four more. It seemed hard to be so near and yet so far from the "hundred," but an attempt to get the necessary three pig out of Kaitola, was utterly defeated by a rain storm.

Subsequently, after repeated efforts in the "breaks" of the rains, another boar was killed, so we ended the season with ninety-eight pig and a parah.

We were all very bucked up with our success however and the monsoon preventing more jaunts into the country, we decided on a final meet at the Bareilly Club in the form of a pigsticking dinner. This function was subsequently made an annual fixture. If any faith is to be placed in numbers, these were the most popular meets of the Tent Club, for they certainly were the best attended. The excellence of the songs and speeches may be judged from the remark of Allen, that this was the first time he ever remembered having sat over the wine till half-past one on Sunday morning! "Pigsticking" in the ladies' room of the club, over jumps made of the furniture, followed. Billiard cues made handy spears. Yells of "Colonel Sykes and Colonel Rooke have each broken a spear," warned the more responsible members that the unlimited breaking of pet cues of prominent old gentlemen, might raise a storm, so a "chariot race" home, in bazaar "phittans" without the drivers, was suggested to break up the party. Several *garrywallahs* were still looking for their carriages and pairs about Church time Sunday morning, but in the end these were all found undamaged, in various officers' compounds. Godman was one "Jehu" and Street of the Worcesters was another. "Jock" Anderson the "Vet" fell out on the way home and woke up under a tree on the road side next morning, wondering how he had got there!

Brierley's two brothers, one from Peshawar and the other from Hong Kong, paid the Tent Club a visit during this season. Their father and mother should have been proud to have bred three such fine sportsmen. Hallowes, of the 15th Lancers, who was on long leave in India, was another visitor.

1911.

This season opened well, and the Christmas meet held at Kaitola, was a great success. We had gone out with modest hopes for many of the spears were new to the game, and the previous year's record of six had been pronounced by all who set up to know, as a great stroke of luck that would not be repeated.

It seemed strange to be out in the Tent Club camp, and not to see the old familiar faces of Norbury, Wallace, "Y.-B.," Godman and "Joey." We missed "Kirk's" cheery countenance too, but then he had been a consistant deserter, ever since he went home to marry a wife. However, if some of the old guard were absent promising recruits were not wanting to take their places, and a cheery party of ten "spears" sat down to dinner the first night. Four pleasant days were spent in hunting in the mornings and afternoons, and in playing auction bridge in the evenings. The sport shown was excellent, beating the record of the year before, and establishing a new one of nine boar.

Pigsticking in the "cane," although a splendid sport, does such a lot of damage that it was decided to follow the custom of previous years, and to confine ourselves to the one meet at Christmas, and to wait until such time as the "cane" might be cut before going out again. However, even after the cane was down, Races and Polo, Marriages and Manœuvres, "Weeks" and other gaieties interfered with further meets (except for an abortive one near Thakur Sheo Bakhsh Singh's village in the Faridpore direction) for the next month or so. And even after all these festivities were over, it took some of the gallant hunters several more weeks to thoroughly solve the problem of obtaining suitable mounts at suitable prices; so pigsticking proper, did not begin till the meet held at Panwaria on April 4th.

A new departure had been made this year, by publishing in advance, a printed programme of the fixtures of the season, so that members might know beforehand where and when pigsticking was likely to be, and so make their arrangements accordingly. The meets were consequently arranged, so as to follow the run of the pig as nearly as possible, and also to thoroughly complete one " circle " before holding a meet in the other.

This arrangement proved to be a great success in every way, especially as regards hunting the pig. The Khaitola "circle" provided many more pig than it had ever done formerly, but part of this success, may have been attributable to some thinning out of the jungle which had been done there. There can be no doubt that it was thoroughly necessary to keep stirring up the big *baghs* of Rat Muggeri and Kaitola, if one wanted the other covers to hold. These were the places where the pig used to breed, and where they would, if left to themselves, all congregate.

The first meet at Panwaria on the Ganges was a failure as far as getting any pig went. The *jhow* jungle there had always required cutting, but with other places to go to, any money available could always be used to better advantage elsewhere. The next meet at Saidupore produced six pig, and at Kaitola and Shahi which followed, we killed sixteen more.

From here the Tent Club went to Rampur, but met with nothing but failure. Two days were enough to show us the uselessness of remaining there, and we decided to clear out. We concluded that it was useless continuing to go to Rampur until such time as the Nawab could be induced to preserve. When anyone who pleases can shoot or net a pig, there are naturally few left to "stick."

A long dusty march brought the Tent Club to Dunka, and the morning after arrival, we started pigsticking. The river, however had just changed its course, leaving quick-sands everywhere. There were several good pig about but one kept losing them in thick patches of *jhow* and we finished that day without getting anything. Next day we beat down the river to Shahi, rather disheartened, having now been out five days without having killed a pig. A blank day at Shahi reduced the party to two (Stewart and Godman) and then the luck changed. We got a good boar out of a small *bagh* on the road to Atamara. This kind of marching and pigsticking on the way, is a very pleasant way of spending a day. We used pad elephants as "cover hacks" and the coolies were reduced to a minimum. They consisted mainly of the *Jemadar Nut* and his followers with their little mongrel terriers. Each cover as it came in sight, was reconnoitred, the spears got on their horses and the cover was then beaten out. Perhaps a run and a kill would result, perhaps it would not. Anyhow, there were always other covers further on and a camp to work towards in the evening.

Next morning we put up another boar in an *arrah* crop near the Atamara Bagh, and killed it before it could find shelter in the *bagh*. The same afternoon, some recruits having turned up, we drove out and killed three more boar from the Iktiarpur Bagh, although that place had been well beaten only ten days previously.

Great hopes were now centred on the Atamara Bagh of which we had heard such good reports. We had been reluctantly obliged to leave this cover alone after doing Kaitola a short time before on account of the other covers nearer at hand taking more time than was anticipated. However, now it was reported to be full of pig. Twelve spears turned up to take part in the slaughter, but sad to relate, they went away disappointed. It is true a score of big sows and almost a hundred squeakers came out but only one boar. His death must have made many widows. This ten-day meet, on the whole, was not a success and the goal of " one hundred " seemed very far off on Sunday April 27th, when we returned to Bareilly.

Thursday, however, saw a well attended meet at Gurgayia (Rat Muggeri), and by the time that Sunday had again come round, sixteen good boar had been added to the bag. The feature of this meet was the good sport obtained in the grass at Baroor, which we had under-rated previously.

The next week-end we spent around Nawabgunj, getting four days excellent sport and sixteen boar for the bag. Eight days pigsticking had now accounted for thirty-two pig, so we determined to give this part of the country a rest and to return to the Kaitola " circle."

A good muster of spears collected at Kaitola on Thursday and five pig were killed. On Friday the spears were reduced to three, but we managed to get a couple of pig from outlying patches, and that afternoon the Tent Club now reduced to two spears, moved on to Shahi.

Shahi and Dunka never produce many pig, but to the true sportsman, they give the best enjoyment that can be found in any part of the Bareilly country. There, it is not enough to have a fast horse and to ride for the "first spear;" the country demands that instinctive co-operation between all the members of a heat, that only comes through long practice. In short here we must "hunt" rather than "chase" the boar. On Sunday, June 11th, sixteen boar were killed. This brought the bag up one hundred and two.

It was finally decided to make this the concluding meet of the season. It would have been folly to have beaten either Rat Muggeri or Kaitola again, because they were just beginning to be full of squeakers about a week old. It was possible to get pig in outlying patches, but it was difficult to get "spears." It was here we missed some of the absent ones, who, at the mere rumour of the likelihood of a pig, would venture anywhere in any weather.

The season was closed with the usual Tent Club dinner. The bag had been one hundred and two boar.

1912.

Circumstances prevented the Christmas meet being held at the usual time and it had to be put off for a little. The following account of it by one of the spears who was out for the first time is set forth below in extenso :—

On the 23rd of January we sallied forth in the brake for a few days' pigsticking ; this was the long deferred Christmas meet. There was a west wind blowing, rather cold too, inasmuch as our Honorary Secretary, although a native of a cold climate, having forgotten to bring out his thick coat, was obliged to give over the ribbons and take protection behind Y. B. who had had the forethought to bring one with him. Skipwith steered the brake quite successfully until he came to the level crossing, when by some misfortune he dropped a rein. The team however managed to get through without any damage to anything, except to the nerves of the highly strung Brierley.

Horses met us at Sunka Pul whence we rode out to our camp near Khaitola. Here we were met by Jacob (one of the Mess Goanese), who attended to the wants of "our inner men," and then we started out to beat the *bagh*. The Honorary Secretary and the cunning Brierley had the good sense to bag the best side of the nullah and got the only two runs of the day. They only brought one of the pig down though, which measured thirty and a quarter inches and weighed one hundred and ninety-five pounds.

Having had tea, we proceeded to a most interesting and picturesque entertainment—the paying of the coolies. Imagine to yourself a dark wood, the only light, that of a flickering hurricane lantern; a circle of men squatting on the ground, each holding in his hand a metal disc. In the centre of the ring stands the Honorary Secretary and the *shikari*. The former holds a stick, the latter a lantern. The Honorary Secretary raps each man in turn on the head and starts counting up to sixteen, while the *shikari* collects the metal discs. Then the Honorary Secretary raps a man rather harder on the head, this is to make him understand that he is the sixteenth man and has to stand up. When every man present has received a tap on the head, money is produced and is doled out to each sixteenth man, who then has to pay off the fifteen men on his left.

The next item is to measure and weigh the pig, while the "first spears" examine the tushes that they have won, and give their opinion as to the age and quality of the pig they have killed. The *syces* press round and mark the pig that their *sahib* has killed, it being their perquisite to take away the hair and skin. The *Nuts* then cut up the pig and start cooking it. These *Nuts* are the mainstay of the beaters in the Bareilly Tent Club. They come of a gypsy tribe and wear their hair long, like all nomads. "Paderewski" and "Kubelik" are among the best known *Nuts* in the Tent Club; they will go fearlessly into cover to beat out a wounded pig; also they keep a most useful lot of dogs that give tongue whenever a pig is on foot in some tangled bamboo *bagh* where no man can force his way.

Friday morning was a bad day for the *khansamah*, as he was detected in a heinous offence; he had brought out no golden syrup. If there is one thing the Honorary Secretary likes with his porridge, it is golden syrup.

The first *bagh* produced a pig which was fiercely chased by "Y.-B.," backed up by Skipwith. On killing it, it turned out to be a sow! Woe to Y. B. who caused Skipwith to blood his first spear in that of a sow; the extenuating circumstances were that the sow was armed with a good pair of tushes, and wore a beard like a boar.

The sugarcane was beaten unsuccessfully till about midday, when the hawk-eyed Ata Mohamed* spotted a pig slipping away in the distance. We all gave chase and "Y.-B." managed to secure 'first spear' just in time to save the pig from disappearing into a large patch of sugarcane. (Height, thirty inches; weight, two hundred pounds.)

---

* Stewart's orderly, a bold pigsticker.

Half an hour later we got on to another pig, which also fell to "Y.-B.'s" able spear, Stewart having turned aside from the pursuit with a broken curb chain. (Height, twenty-seven inches; weight, one hundred and fifty pounds.) Lunch followed but was prevented from being an absolute success by the Honorary Secretary cutting his finger, which necessitated the elephant being brought up and the medicine box opened.

A beat and a long wait produced another pig which dodged from patch to patch and gave a succession of short runs before it got into the open. Stewart should have got the pig, but his horse shied off and gave Skipwith an opportunity to get the first spear. It was a small pig, whose tushes were only worth keeping as a remembrance of one's first. (Height, twenty-seven inches; weight, one hundred and forty pounds.) Thence home to dinner followed by piquet between Stewart and Brierley, whilst "Y. B." aided by some excellent "Justerini" compiled the Tent Club log.

The field on Saturday was augmented by two more "spears". Balfour of the 16th Rajputs and Slingsly of the 22nd Cavalry. We trekked some way and finally got *khabbar* of a pig in some sugarcane near a village. A pig came out, ran through the village and disappeared into some sugarcane. We spent some time in trying to beat it out only to find it was too small. We got back to our places, to find that in the meantime the big pig had gone away, but had been marked down. We proceeded to beat this patch and "Y.-B." got away after one pig and killed him after a good run across the open. (Height, thirty inches.) Five minutes afterwards Skipwith got away by himself and brought another pig to book. This was a big pig, measuring thirty and a half inches and weighing two hundred pounds. After lunch we had no sport till four P.M., when Slingsly and Stewart got away on to a pig which the former succeeded in killing. Whilst the spears were standing over the pig the keen sighted Ata Mohamed again spied a horseman who, we presumed, was galloping after a boar. We all gave chase and presently came up with Stewart. Our queries of "which way!" elicited no reply but "Get to blazes out of it." It didn't require much intellect to guess that something was wrong, so we pulled up and watched our hard riding Honorary Secretary trying to control his steeplechaser Kim whom he was endeavouring to make into an efficient pigsticker. Soon he headed for a sugarcane patch and we thought that going through that would be enough for the horse. But no, it took three broad patches of sugarcane before Kim stopped, and Stewart has made a note that a breast plate is useful to prevent the saddle being brushed of backwards when galloping through sugarcane. Bolting horses are tiresome and heating, so no one was surprised when the elephant was called up.

"*Revenons a nos sangliers.*" About half an hour later we all got away after a smallish pig which jinked and dodged from patch to patch, giving all of us a chance. It eventually made for a heap of dry sugarcane leaves and tried to hide under this but was unsuccessful, Brierley gave it a good spear, but it was most tenacious of life however, and more than three other spears were necessary to finish it off. Directly after this we got on to a good pig which was speared first by Brierley, and although it was speared twice more, the thrusts were too far back and the pig, being a good plucked one, kept on running. We chased him in and out of a temple garden, a pond and a thick bamboo grove until darkness overtook us. However the pig was not brought to book. On Sunday we went back to try and beat him out but could find no trace of him.

Atkinson and Henderson motored out from Bareilly and joined us this day. They did not bring good luck, however, as we wandered from place to place without getting anything, and only seeing three small squeakers. We finally decided to have lunch and during this meal, the headman of a village near brought in good news, namely, that he knew where some pig were. For a wonder he was telling the truth, and after a time a good pig got away followed by Skipwith, Stewart and Ata Mohamed on David. Stewart got on him on the jink, but Ata Mohamed was "seeing red" and made straight for Stewart bumping him and riding him off the pig altogether. The road now being clear Skipwith got on to the heels of the pig when Ata Mohamed came tearing after him also and speared the pig a second or two before Skipwith. He actually speared the pig across the forelegs of Skipwith's horse and the second after he had done so, the spear was sent flying out of his hand by the horse's leg, luckily falling with the point away. Ata Mohamed disappeared into the blue for a short while and then came back to face Stewart's wrath. However, by this time the Honorary Secretary's anger had abated. It was very bad luck on Stewart to have lost this "first spear" when he was sure to have got it, by being thus rudely hustled out of the way by his own orderly on one of his own ponies. However, when one sells all one's trained horses, and starts again with new ones, one can't expect many "first spears."

Atkinson's horse Gamecock overreached rather badly while after this pig and after a short halt while the Honorary Surgeon of the Tent Club had dressed the wound, we went on to look for more sport. We were not long in coming across it and after quite a good run a boar was speared by " Y.-B." (Height, twenty-eight inches.) This was the last pig we got, making a total bag of ten for the three and a half days. This was one better than the Christmas meet of the previous year.

*　　*　　*　　*　　*　　*

After this there was no pigsticking for some time but on Sunday morning, February 4th, we killed two big pig out of Kurma *Bagh*. The first was set afoot by a very clever bit of work on the part of Lakshman Piari, the she-elephant who has so often helped the Tent Club. The pig broke through a village scattering all the inhabitants and a herd of wallowing buffaloes, and gave a very nice little run receiving a fatal spear at the edge of some sugarcane, in which he was subsequently found dead. The sportsmen had hardly time to look at him, however, for they were hollowed away after a black form disappearing over the horizon towards Ikhtiapur. The pig stopped and thought for a minute on finding that he was chased, but Brierley on Banshi hustled him so that he lost his head. He ran into some *arrah* first, then jinked left handed to make back for Kurma *Bagh* again. The horses were pretty done up by this time, for it was a mile before they had got on terms with him at all, but he was caught eventually after a pretty hunt and died feebly. Pig are very gross and soft at this time of the year, and die largely from lack of breath. After this, our luck deserted us. A long morning and forenoon in the sugarcane was followed by a run after a "dream" pig, imagined by one of the spears. Then a real pig was found, and was *honked* backwards and forwards in the cane by the nimble Miss Piari (who got cut in the off-fore in the process) until at last the boar lost patience and charged out at a line of beaters that had been placed so as to prevent him breaking in that particular direction. He rushed first at Brierley, but turned off before he ran on his spear, and charged a cooly instead ripping up his shin. Yeats-Brown meanwhile, had come dashing up, just as Kalan Khan (a Tent Club *chaprassi*) was doubling after the pig (for some unknown reason) with a loaded gun. The pig was the cynosure of every eye, and " K. K." and " Y.-B." (who were neither of them looking where they were going), met with a loud crash, the *chaprassi* discharging a charge of shot as the horse passed swiftly over him! Luckily no serious damage was done, but of course the pig escaped while the injuries of the elephant, cooly and *chaprassi* were being inspected. Kalan Khan was badly shaken, but after a little stimulant he pluckily insisted on seeing the day out on the elephant. Half an hour laetr, he reported seeing two immense pig of equal size and identical shape (query whisky?) in some young wheat. One there was, sure enough, who went off like smoke, and was killed after a good fight. He proved to be an exceptional pig and must have kicked the beam at two hundred and fifty pounds but the balance was not working properly, so we could not weigh him. And so home.

"Bohemian," who had now become the property of Hogan, contributed a comic finale to the day (for everyone except his rider) by lying down in the nullah outside Bhojeepura. As the train was late, there was time to practise some of the surgery for which the Tent Club is famous, and amongst other operations, Lakshman Piari's wound was bound with a first field dressing that was just long enough to go once round her shapely ankle.

On the 16th of March we had another day in the crops at Sankarpul, and got two good pig.

Brierley on Highforce and Barehaven had a try for the Kadir this year, but although he had a pleasant time, he did not get on very far.

We have told of the "Christmas" and other meets held up to March 16th. We had secured by that date fifteen boar which made an excellent beginning for the year. There was no more pigsticking after that until April 6th, when the club met at Saidupore. Two good days here produced nine boar more. This meet nearly afforded a catastrophe; for "Joey" and a certain "Thakur" both going at full speed, collided at right angles. Luckily no harm was done; it remains in our memory as an amusing incident only. That it was not a dreadful accident, however, is due to the favour of the gods; the Thakur only missed impaling Joey on his spear by an inch.

The following week-end saw us in the Kundra Bungalow, the grass, however, was far too long and thick, so the sport was not what it should have been; still by doing the Baroor grass and some small *baghs* on the way there, the week-end accounted for twelve.

A meet at Nawabganj followed. The final day of this meet established a record for Bijamau. We killed nine, so on April 21st, the bag stood at fifty-two. This seemed to augur well for the success of the season, but in the following meet at Khaitola, Shahi and Dunka, four hard days only accounted for three.

However, a couple of days in the week after that at Atamara and Iktiarpur, cheered us up again, for here we got nine. "Joey" and "Y.-B." each had a mishap at Iktiarpur. They were in a heat composed of Brierley and themselves and what happened, is best told in one of the victims' own words.

"One hot weather morning early in May, I started off by train to join the Tent Club at a place called Ikhtiarpur about three miles from Bhoojeepura station. As usual the train was late, so I did not arrive in camp until after the other sportsmen had left for a neighbouring *bagh*. After a hurried breakfast I set out in the direction they had taken, and suddenly saw Brierley and "Y.-B." riding, what proved to be a fine boar, which they accounted for after some little trouble. As this was the "heat" to which I was supposed to belong, I at once joined it. We dismounted and were discussing the prospects of sport, while 'the line' was beating in our direction and after a little while a boar went away in the direction of a very big *bagh* called Kaitola. Luckily it was our pig, so we mounted and set off on what was to prove a most adventurous ride, which involved the death of five pig and a few casualties. The going being good and our horses fresh, it did not take long to account for the first. While returning to our place another pig was seen taking the same line, we waited for him behind a tree until he had made his point, and then galloped after him and laid him low. By this time our horses were rather blown. On leaving the dead pig, a wonderful sight met our gaze. In the distance, about a mile away, was the *bagh* which was being beaten: the intervening space was an open plain, and across this plain was streaming a line of pig, of all sizes and sexes, about a quarter of a mile in length. They rushed through a herd of cattle scattering them in all directions; away we tore straight at them, wishing we had our fresh horses; then each of us selected a boar and with much difficulty separated him from his relatives. "Y.-B." was after a very fast lean pig which ran so hard that his horse "Ur," which was already blown, could gain little on him for a long time. At last he managed to get up with the pig and stuck him. The latter started jinking which completely wore out the tired "Ur." Probably disappointed that his speed was not taking him out of danger, the boar tried by a circular course to get back into Iktiarpur. However, with a last great effort "Y.-B." managed to get in a dangerous crossing spear, which brought down horse and rider and pig in an entangled heap on the ground. Here they remained for half a minute struggling hard; luckily perhaps for Y. B his horse was too blown to rise, and as the point of his spear was in the pig and rest of it under the horse, the pig was quite unable to move. "Y.-B." after a desperate struggle to get clear (in which he put his hand into the pig's mouth by mistake!) at last got free and made a bee-line for a friendly tree. The pig in the meantime got up and cruelly punished "Ur," cutting him behind the elbow so that the assistance of Brierley and the medicine chest became necessary.

While the horse's wounds were being attended to, the pig trotted off to a bush nearby, and sat there, until Stewart, who was called by the coolies arrived and killed it.

In the meantime I had separated my boar and had ridden him towards a neighbouring *bagh*. "Newminster," my horse, was very blown by the two previous runs, and it was with the greatest difficulty I got on terms with the pig just before he dashed into the *bagh*. I managed to spear severely but rather far back. On he went, through the *bagh* and out the other side. I had another chance and ought to have settled his account, but this time, although I got a good spear into him, the head of the spear broke off and remained buried in the pig.

Now what was to be done? Unfortunately the pig decided before I did, and immediately charged. It being quite impossible to keep him off my horse with a broken spear, I turned tail, and just managed to prevent "Newminster" being cut. The boar was by this time surrounded by several village dogs, and made his way to a nullah. As there was no one in sight and my *syce* with another spear was a mile and a half away, I foolishly decided to follow the pig on foot and to try to kill him by hitting him on the head with the butt of the spear. This, I might explain, was covered with a very heavy piece of lead, in order to balance the spear. As the banks of the nullah were steep and about six feet deep. I thought I would be able to get close above him and so administer a fatal blow. I managed to persuade some "coons" or Aryan brothers that my horse was much too tired to really do them any damage and that if they would hold him while I advanced on the pig I would reward them. The pig, in the meantime, had completely recovered from his run, and sat surrounded by village dogs, one of which he managed to cut. Taking the broken spear in my hand, I advanced with the heavy butt end in the air ready to deal the fatal blow. The dogs of course bolted, and in doing so no doubt roused the boar's suspicions of impending danger. Anyway the long and short of it was, I had only just looked over the edge of the nullah at him when he immediately dashed up the bank straight at me and charged. No doubt everyone who has the misfortune to have read so far, will wonder, as indeed I did, why I did not hit the boar on the head as he came over the bank. But it is not a particularly easy thing to hit with a loaded stick, an animal which travels faster than a race-horse for a short distance. The pig certainly got the best of it this time, and over I went on my back. Luckily my legs were in the air and so I was able to deliver a few harmless kicks. My next impression was seeing the pig standing across me, looking a winner all over! He did nothing however, until I struggled, when he proceeded to get in a few cuts with his remarkably sharp tushes; but as I felt nothing, I concluded that I was still unhurt and that up to then only my clothes and boots had suffered damage.

Something, however, had to be done, so I thought the best way to escape would be to roll down the steep bank of the nullah. Down we went, the pig a short head behind; and on reaching the bottom he got in a good cut and slashed a hole in my right thigh. Luckily at this juncture, when there was no doubt at all who was getting the best of it, an unfortunate village dog came in view. The pig catching sight of it, charged and laid it low, and I escaped up the other bank and sat down to investigate the damage. Luckily there was only one wound, but altogether there were five or six cuts through my boots and breeches; some of the former looked as if they had been done with a razor. A pig's tush being very dirty and poisonous, I got on my horse and made straight for camp, promising numerous rewards to the spectators (who never thought of assisting), if they would keep an eye on the pig until some one came up to kill him. In Brierley's skilful hands I was soon put right and sewn up. The boar by the greatest luck was not a big one and his tushes were small, otherwise the damage would have been serious. We returned to the scene of action later but the spectators and the pig had vanished. The latter had evidently made good his escape into Kaitola *Bagh*.

It was distinctly annoying, as his tushes, though, small, would have been an interesting memento of the occasion. Another time I shall take very good care not to tackle a wounded boar with a broken spear single-handed, and suggest that others in the same predicament take this advice also.

Brierley rode the rearmost pig and killed him skilfully, after a jinking run without special adventure, but his professional duties kept him busy for some time.

* * * * * *

The above contains a tactical lesson: Both "Joey" and the pig bearing in mind Napoleon's maxim, assumed the vigorous offensive, the result was a draw!

Following this came another good week at Kundra, accounting for fifteen and a second week at Nawabgunj, where eleven more were killed; so on May the 19th, the bag stood at ninety.

A hard though comparatively unsuccessful two days at Khaitola, brought it up to ninety-three, which seemed to promise that records would be broken. This however, was the result of hard work. In our enthusiasm we had almost forgotten that pig-killing is an amusement, not a business. Consequently, a reaction set in. " Y.-B.," " Joey " and Skipwith went to Naini Tal to play polo. Many horses were laid up and everybody seemed to think of stopping pigsticking for the season. However, Brierley, Warren and Stewart tried some odd afternoons round Khaikhera and Sental, a part of the country previously little hunted. They had excellent fun and fair sport getting eight boar in four outings. Brierley's motor bike and sidecar, proved a blessing here; one left the mess after lunch and was back by dinner, having accounted in the interval for many miles and several boar.

About June 15th, things began to look up again, the expected rain had not come, and people began to find week-ends in Cantonments long and dull. So it was decided to try a few days again at Kundra. The party for these three days was in many respects a unique one, for amongst others contained two ladies. Miss Bellingham, " Y.-B's " cousin, and her friend Miss Hewett, the daughter of the L.-G., sportingly determined to brave the heat and minor discomforts of camp life, in order to see the sport, and this determination they continued to show in their riding. Although Miss Hewett took a nasty toss in the *kunker* pits, the ladies were not at all discouraged, and saw most of every run and were always in at " the death." Lockett of the 17th Lancers, since famous as the Polo Captain of England, also put in a day with us. It was a pity that his leave did not permit him to stay longer, as the first day at the Kundra and Gurgayia meet, seldom shows good sport.

After this, we had a Sunday at Khaitola, a Sunday at Nawabgunj, and a Sunday at Atmara. During the Nawabgunj meet, a boar with nine and a half inch tushes was killed. This was a record in the Bareilly Tent Club. Stewart had the luck to get " first spear " and these tushes now serve him for wine labels.

Atamara was the final meet, as here the rains broke in earnest. However, this season we bagged one hundred and twenty-three boar. The third biggest bag on record and the best for many years. It also, as mentioned above, included the boar with best tushes ever recorded as killed in the Bareilly Tent Club.

There was still the Tent Club dinner. This as usual was held at the Bareilly Club. " Y.-B." had much to say in selecting the " Menu " and he also arranged to provide the members with a wonderful selection of wines and drinks, each course having its own wine. It was felt that due honour must be done to " the bag " in more ways than one. The cost of the dinner eventually came to eight rupees a head, with twenty rupees additional for a share of the drinks, and that was in the days when drink and food was still cheap. There is no doubt that it was a great banquet. After dinner an extensive toast list was executed, without mishap. Stewart who was in "the chair" in proposing "Pigsticking," pointed out the past season had been the best since 1904. " Y.-B. " proposed our absent members, and Brierley in replying, announced the fact of Godman's early departure for South Africa. Godman whose health was drunk, responded for " the shikari and his staff " in a witty speech and told us how sorry he was to go. His departure was an irreparable loss to the Bareilly pigsticking, for his attendance had been constant at all the meets for the past three years. By his sporting spirit and unselfish riding, he had endeared himself to all the members of the Tent Club. Alas now he lies " somewhere in France." The Honorary Secretary then proposed " Preservers of Pig," coupled with the name of Allen, our Collector. In responding Allen who was a veteran at the game, gave some interesting reminiscences of his early days after boar. After several other speeches from Wilson, Townsend and Secondé, the banquet ended in a vote of thanks to the Honorary Secretary for the fine sport he had shown during the season. Somewhat later, the banqueters dispersed to their homes, having in spite of the drink bill, inflicted little damage on the Club property or on themselves.

1913

The year as usual opened with the Christmas meet. This meet is really one of the most pleasant of all the fixtures of the year, because this is the one time that one gets cool weather out pigsticking. Winter pigsticking is perhaps not so exciting as the hunting of later in the season, but there is always the certainty of a pleasant day in the country. Some sugarcane patch or wheat field is certain to contain a boar. One may be getting bored and thinking that the day will be blank after all. When suddenly there is a chorus of shouts from the line followed by the yaps of Chabli, Majira, Jim or Bachu, and a scurry and excitement amongst the beaters. The *shikari*, the *chaprasies* and the Jemadar Nut are pointing—the boar is away and you are after it.

Early this season Yeats-Brown, Stewart and Skipwith went down to Muttra to compete as a team in the " Muttra Cup " which this year had been inaugurated by the Inniskilling Dragoons, and which is the most sporting pigsticking event in India. The other teams were two from the Inniskilling Dragoons, one from Skinner's Horse, two from the Gunners at Meerut, and one from the 13th Hussars.

The 17th did not have much luck, both Yeats-Brown and Stewart's horses came down in the first run and Skipwith was not able to kill the pig by himself. In the second run they had the pig practically killed when he dodged into some extraordinary thick *jhow* where he was lost. They got all the others. Undoubtedly the best team won however. The party sent down by Wardrop's Battery got every pig, they rode after, Much of their success was due to their thorough training; they rode the pig in a peculiar formation: one man rode the pig, another covered him, the third rode level with the coverer on the left flank. If the pig jinked, the nearest man followed him and the other two fell in their places in the formation without any words.

The records of 1913 are not so full of anecdotes and accounts of adventure as those of former years. Four years intensive pigsticking makes one attach less importance to incidents that have become commonplace; consequently they have not been written down.

It is sad to relate that during this year the advance of modern ideas had also its effect on the sanctuaries, and the civil authorities allowed much of the cover at Kaitola to be cut down. Worse still was the fate of Nawabgunj, where the Agricultural Department started an experimental sugar plantation, and where they installed a *babu* who was actually encouraged by the authorities to shoot the pig. The *bagh* covers thus got fewer and fewer, but there yet remained the grass and jungle.

Kundra was our stand-by, we took over thirty pig out of it, and this and the grass near by was where we had the day of all days; the day the workers were rewarded, and the cunning ones done down. The morning produced only one pig, so having eaten our lunch and drunk our beer, we hacked quietly back to the line; but before we reached it away went Wallace on a young horse, without a spear. We galloped for our spears but it was too late, he was gone. Then we had a glorious time, a hot time, a thirsty time, scarcely time to change a horse, not time to drink and only now and then a second in which to wipe our heated brow. Six pig between two thirty and five thirty was our bag, and then we only stopped because of the dark and the horses. The kunker pits availed nothing, we negotiated them more than once without losing a pig. Of course we saw, rode and lost the "big pig", but he was a devil, he was the cause of four tosses and two lame horses. Then dark fell and there was much anxious thought for the morrow, which brought however four pig to one heat inside the hour, two horses cut and one toe bitten by a charging pig. A change of camp and more spears brought the total for the meet up to nineteen pig, a grand meet for some of us who had ridden after fully sixteen of those killed—what luck for any man to have.

The final bag for the season totalled seventy-six. This was certainly not so good as that of 1912, which had amounted to one hundred and twenty-three. And certainly it was not so full of thrills and excitement, yet there were some glorious days that were good enough to be treasured in memory against the days when we are far away from the great spaces of the Ganges Basin. May those days yet be distant, may it be long before we are compelled to think of pigsticking in recollection only, and yet when we look back on the memory of those days of slain boars, dead horses and friends of the past, how vividly they come to life again. How well we remember the magic of those golden hours, when sunlight lay on all things under the vault of turquoise, when we fought the boar on the plains of Bareilly and saw and enjoyed India as no man can see and enjoy it from cantonments.

A mention of the Christmas Meet of the Tent Club about December 1913 is quoted below. With it ends the associations of the 17th Cavalry with the Bareilly Tent Club :—

"Fee, fi, fo, fum, I smell the blood of an old grey boar." That was what Skipwith wanted to be able to say, but it did not come off. We had hoped to see red, ride red and talk red once more before leaving Bareilly, but fate was unkind, the wind cold, our colour blue. The shikari had said, " *Soor to hain* " and then paused. This pause was meant to signify I doubt if you will be men enough to catch him. This was the last Christmas Meet we were to have with the Bareilly Tent Club, and the bag was nil !

If racing is the Sport of Kings, then pigsticking is the King of Sports. It teaches you not only how to ride and how to fall, but to rise to fall again. Cochrane was out for his first time and it was disappointing not to be able to show him the real thing. The next best was to listen open-mouthed to the stories, and " Shirt " can always make his yarns picturesque when he is in the mood. Part of this effect lies no doubt in the extravagance of his language, but I cannot quote here (the Editor is the devil of a fellow for Purity). What a meal would breakfast be at a Tent Club Meet without Beer and without " Do you remember ? " Who can forget the Honorary Secretary's happily told tales of " Swift toss up the……," his " patent-unfailing-get-well-quick " remedy. How he and Paterson tried to jump the nullah at Shahi and, landing in the middle, swam quickly and safely over. How Bohemian lay down in the river coming home ! How Fizzer having fallen, lay, too tired to rise, how the great hog of Saidupur jumped up and bit Hogan's horse in the back, and all about that misty and furious morning at Atmira, which accounted for eight pig and two horses How a dead pig was carried off, a horse speared, a man laid low, a fight, a prison and then long and close closeting with officials, furious wires from Simla, and then peace. These and other tales, how often are they told, how eagerly listened to, a fund on which to draw for all and any time. "Sorry be the man who never has the luck to listen to the annals, or worse far worse, never the opportunity of himself scoring his name deep in the log of some Tent Club."

* * * * * *

The last year of the Bareilly Pigsticking of the regiment was disappointing, as far as the bag went. The causes were varied. One undoubtedly was that we had killed a great many of the best boar of the district in the three preceding years, another has been mentioned; that is, the sanctuaries had been interfered with. No pigsticking country can survive that treatment. Tent clubs are ever at the mercy of the civil officials, and it is sad to state the more modern kind of officials are not in sympathy with the pastimes of the "brutal and licentious soldiery," still less do they pursue the sport themselves like their predecessors did A further cause was perhaps that the members of the Tent Club were less well mounted during 1913 than they had been in previous years, also in some cases their keenness had become blunted. Meets with indifferent promises of sport no longer attracted them. The expenses of four years of pigsticking had also lightened the pockets of the 17th Cavalry. Pigsticking was and is an expensive sport. First and foremost come the actual Tent Club charges; these of course vary but a rough estimate of the daily Bareilly charges was as follows:—

		Rs.	a.	p.
Messing	...	3	0	0
Share of cartage	...	1	0	0
Drinks	...	1	8	0
Share of coolies	...	4	8	0
Total	...	10	0	0

Besides Rs. 1-8-0 was charged for each "first spear." This went to the *shikari* and the *chaprasies*. Cartage of private kit was of course additional to the above.

The Secretary set a high standard for the Club in 1910, which continued to be more or less carried out till the end. This idea was to have four days pigsticking each week-end of the season. Thursday and Sunday being holidays, this really only entailed getting two days' leave a week; Commanding Officers gladly gave this in most cases.

To carry out this scheme however, it was necessary for all the Tent Club carts and for many of the private baggage carts of the regular members as well, to remain more or less permanently out in the district only coming in occasionally for the purpose of refitting. The horses and *syces* and generally a bearer or *khidmitgar* for each 'spear,' had to be left with the private carts. This was an excellent arrangement, but it involved expense. Pigsticking horses were not always easy to come by, however in the 17th Cavalry we had certain advantages. Some of us bought, others of us hired animals out of the regiment. The *Chanda* Fund let out a horse for pigsticking purposes for three months for fifty-two rupees; thirty-six rupees of this went to the *Chanda* Fund and sixteen rupees to the sowar who was nominally mounted on the horse. The horse was fed by the regiment and the hirer took the risk of having to pay something for depreciation should the horse be injured whilst pigsticking. It was a good arrangement for all concerned. The difficulty lay in being able to pick out of the ranks a suitable, fast, handy and staunch horse. Here I might remark, that my experience with regard to staunchness is as follows: Nearly all Arabs are natural pigstickers, Walers can to some extent be trained to be staunch, but country-breds ever remain as they appear when they first see the pig.

We picked up much valuable experience at Bareilly and it is a pity that this experience should be lost. I will therefore give a few words of advice to novices based on what we learnt.

Go out pigsticking on a good horse. You can get a new horse, but not a new neck. Well trained handy horses are seldom cut; it is the ill-trained brute who brings you and himself to grief, therefore school your horse carefully. Try for an animal with a good shoulder. You want "something in front of you" out pigsticking. When you do decide on a horse, try and train him like a tournament polo pony. It will repay you a thousand times.

HAVE A SHARP SPEAR, and don't fancy any old bamboo with a head on it will do. A pigsticking shaft should be specially selected. It should be short, thick at the butt, and should rapidly taper to the head. *Don't cut the shaft to fit into the head.* The head must be big enough to fit on *over* the shaft. Put a big lump of lead on the butt so that you can hold the spear near the end. With a well sharpened spear made on these lines, you should seldom get a horse cut by a boar. It is the men with the blunt spears that are always in trouble. Syces understand spear sharpening very well if they are given a suitable file.

Don't use cheap saddles out pigsticking If you do, one day your arch will spread and you will find your best horse with a sore back just when you want him most. Sowter knows what is required, patronise him.

Wear a double thickness Cawnpore Tent Club *topee*. If you fall this will probably save your head. A thin coat of hard faced material that will not catch in thorns (with a spine pad), should be worn, unless you prefer to hunt in a shirt. In any case, you require a spine pad. Do not turn up yourself or allow your *syce* to come out in white or other conspicuous coloured clothing, disregard of this will ensure you seeing no sport. You will also certainly be very soundly cursed by the Secretary if he knows his job. Wear cord breeches, thin ones will rub you. Wear boots to protect you from thorns, they are more convenient than gaiters.

Remember to cut down your kit as much as possible, but do not forget that pigsticking is a pastime, and do not go in for making yourself uncomfortable. Wardrop in " Modern Pigsticking " says quite correctly, that there is no reason because you hunt the pig to live like one.

The above notes for beginners are rather outside the scope of these recollections. I have included them in case that any one should be interested in our experiences at Bareilly. Those who really wish to read all about pigsticking, should study Baden Powell's " Pigsticking or Hog Hunting" and Wardrop's " Modern Pigsticking."

In 1909 we were full of eagerness and enterprises, arrangements and ideas. A meet of the Club involved a *bunderbust* similar to that of a campaign. In those days, in spite of all this something generally went wrong, the " spears " lost their way, the drivers went astray, or worse still, there were no pig. Still keenness increased instead of diminishing. As time went on experience made things easy. Keenness made big bags. Just as the keenness began to diminish, so did the bags, but I know that this was only transitory, if we had remained another year.........but it is no use speculating.

The 17th Cavalry pigsticking, at Bareilly, is finished, and so is the account of it.

* * * * * *

Some Pigsticking Aphorisms recorded by the Honorary Surgeon.

(*i*) Start the day with Beer—preferably a big bottle. Continue the day with Beer. This causes the Boar to look smaller than it really is during the chase, but has a wonderful reverse magnifying effect in the evening, when the incidents of the day are under discussion. Conclude the day with Beer. This engenders sleep.

(*ii*) In difficult country ride behind the Honorary Secretary. He will see you through all right.

(*iii*) In country characterised by long grass and *kunker* pits never ride in a heat with " Y.-B.," unless prepared to lose your life. He will subject your somewhat timid pace to a merciless criticism.

(*iv*) When the going is so bad, that pig repeatedly escape, ask the Honorary Secretary to dismount from his elephant and give you a lead. He will probably do this, and then go back on the elephant, and advise you to go to a more practical cover.

(*v*) Always let sleeping dogs lie, that is to say never unnecessarily address at breakfast, members of the Tent Club with a known liver habit.

(*vi*) Before selecting places, take care to ask the *shikari* which way the pig are likely to break. Then announce that to be the worst station and volunteer to stand there.

(*vii*) If your vocabulary is a poor one, attend an interview between the Honorary Secretary and the *khansamah*. You will thereby acquire many gems of rhetoric.

APPENDIX VIII.

THE WEEKLY DURBAR.

The *Silladar* system of raising troops is of great antiquity, dating back at least to the time of Timour and Atilla. It is described in another place, but the *Durbar*, with which it is intimately associated, deserves a note to itself.

From a loosely organised body of feudal soldiers, the *Silladar* regiments became eventually a sort of contractors to Government, supplying fighting men at so much a head. The Commandant was in a sense the Managing Director of a limited liability company in which each man held, or was entitled to subscribe for, from three to a forty-five pounds of debenture stock, the debentures being secured on horseflesh and equipment. This company contracted with Government to supply six hundred and twenty-five cavalrymen, fully mounted, provisioned and equipped, for the sum of about thirty pounds per annum per capita, and it was by far the cheapest cavalry in the world and was extraordinary good value for the money expended.

The finance of the system made the *Durbar* a necessity. No important decision affecting the interests of the regiment could be taken without consulting the stockholders, represented by the British and Indian Officers of the regiment assembled at the weekly board meeting or *Durbar*. There was no voting on any proposal but any officer British or Indian could give his opinion. Other ranks of the regiment were at liberty to attend and listen to the proceedings but were obliged to stand there in silence. No history of the Seventeenth Cavalry would therefore be complete without a description of this typically Oriental function which formed so integral a part of regimental life.

Durbar was usually held under some convenient tree near the lines. There was usually a considerable crowd assembled to hear the affairs of the regiment discussed and to see justice dealt out to offenders. Under a shady banian tree the Commandant's table and chair are set. Near him are chairs for the Adjutant, the senior Major and the other officers. On two parallel benches, placed at right angles to the British officers, sit the Indian officers, and at the fourth side of the square thus formed, facing the Commandant, are marshalled the various persons to be brought before the *Durbar*.

The officers being assembled, the *Mir Munshi*, or chief accountant, opens the proceedings by reading aloud the minutes of the last meeting, which are then signed by the Commandant. Next, the eight Kote-Daffadars report on the property and personnel of the regiment stating that so many men, so many horses, so many followers, so many rifles, etc., etc., are present; ending with "*baqui khairiyat*"—"All's well." Finally the *Mir Munshi*, who has come to the front and taken his place by the Kote-Daffadars, reports the amount of cash in the regimental treasure chest.

That ends the routine. Now each half squadron commander stands up in turn and brings forward the business of his half squadron, sowars for leave, syces to cut their names, horses to be seen, articles of equipment to be inspected, prisoners, recruits. One by one, sheepish or stolid or suspicious, according to their tribes and dispositions, the recruits are led up, future officers some of them, to be seen by their comrades assembled, like Mowgli at the Council Rock. Hawk-faced Afridis, like wild animals led into captivity, ringleted Khuttucks, milk faced Peshawaries, Yokels from the Punjab Grecian profiled and stolid as the "*bhiles*" they drive, one by one, they are led, like victims of some ancient rite, before the Commandant's table. Enquiries are made as to their relations, the capital (called the *assami*) they are prepared to invest in the regiment and their sponsors. In pre-war days no soldier could gain admittance to an Indian cavalry regiment without an introduction from a member of that regiment.

When the recruits have been seen and offenders dealt with, the men in their stable dress of grey or white crowd in close behind their Indian officers. First, perhaps, the Commandant has some announcement to make, concerning manoeuvres or discipline. Then the price of grain is sure to be discussed by the senior Indian officers. Some grass farm question will also be discussed in all probability, and the forge, engine, "line" building, grain *godown*, horse hospital, Quarter-Masters' stores and all the multiplicity of detail (often rendered more complex than it need be by the Oriental fondness for having two men do the work of one), will come up for orders. No authority was, or could be delegated by the Commandant. Naturally, he trusted certain people more than others, but by immemorial custom, all decisions had to emanate from him

While this is going on, the junior officers whisper together in a state of acute boredom. At last some interruption occurs to remind the C. O. that it is long past lunch time, and that in another hour he is expected on the polo ground. Sometimes it is a dog fight, more often the Adjutant plans a diversion in the shape of a messenger from the office with an urgent telegram to be attended to...

Which of us, whose memories extend to pre-war days, does not remember the " grey blanket question," or the " lance bucket *juggra*"? Do the shades of *sikligars* of bygone days come out with *tulwars* and spurs in their skeleton fingers, to exhibit them to Burton's wraith? Does the spirit of Hamzullah, with a *dumchi* or a *phraki* or a *boyhkband* before him, still hold forth in its high pitched voice to the assembled shades? Or does the opiate voice of a fat Quarter-Master Daffadar speak to us of the new masks and breastplates for " *Gutka-butate*," that anomatopeic term for skill at arms? Perhaps all this goes on in the limbo of forgotten things. But our time is passed. The *Silldar* system has gone. We are become a company of ghosts...

No one sits under the banyan tree now. The regimental officers are too busy for *Durbar* nowadays. They are all in that bleak building over there, sweating over pay sheets and returns...

APPENDIX IX.

THE RISE AND FALL OF THE SILLADAR CAVALRY OF INDIA WITH AN EXPLANATION OF THE SYSTEM.

As the 17th Cavalry was a *silladar* regiment, it is therefore felt that no history of the regiment would be complete without a short sketch of the *silladar* system. The Government of India abolished that system soon after the great war; and, just before amalgamation with the 37th Lancers, the 17th Cavalry was converted into a regular or non-*silladar* regiment.

The old system is already partly forgotten, and before long its memories will become vague and traditional, and soon when the last officers of the old regime have passed on to the pension list, most of the interesting particulars will be completely forgotten.

The *Silladar* Cavalry regiments of India as a military organisation were unique amongst modern armies. In some respects they were similar to the Cossacks of Russia, and like them they were a survival and development of the old methods of raising armies which had passed away elsewhere some hundreds of years before.

As they were organised before the Great War, they were the cheapest force of cavalry in the world to maintain, for not only did they provide regimentally their horses, transport, and equipment, but also, within limits, they defrayed the cost of feeding themselves, their horses and transport animals. They also built and maintained the "lines" in which they were accommodated.

Long before the arrival of the British in India the term *silladar* was current to describe a soldier, who owned his own horse and arms. It is derived from the Persian words "*Sillah*" (a weapon) and "*Dar*" (the bearer). The irregular cavalry who fought in the wars of the various States of which India was at that time composed, were free lances, who sold their swords to the highest purchaser. These were distinct from the regular, or "*Pagah*" Cavalry of the State Armies, and they were generally the personal following of a leader, who sold their services to the best advantage and looked after their interests as his own. They did not necessarily remain long in one service but moved about according to the financial inducement offered. In fact they were not dissimilar to the " Free Companions " of mediæval Europe, and were sometimes called " *Khudaspas* " (horse owners).

When the East India Company began to exercise political power. it began to find it necessary to command on occasions the services of considerable forces of cavalry, and it took advantage of the custom obtaining in the country and contracted with guerilla leaders to supply such bodies of irregular cavalry as might be required from time to time. In the course of time this system was found to have certain marked disadvantages. These irregular mercenaries were unreliable and undisciplined and often deserted at the critical moment. The Company then gave up the idea of employing these freebooters and raised several regiments, both in Bengal and Madras, on the " *Pagah* " or regular system.

However, in 1809, light horsemen were urgently required and Skinner and Gardner were ordered to raise for the Company two corps of irregular cavalry on the *silladar* or *khudaspa* system. These corps eventually became the 1st, 2nd and 3rd Bengal Cavalry. These irregular cavalry regiments laid the foundation of what afterwards became the *silladar* cavalry of the Indian Army.

The difference between the *silladar* units organised by Skinner and Gardner and the corps of *Khudaspas*, who had been employed previously, lay in the establishment of what were called " *Assamis* " and " *Chanda* " Funds.

The " *Assami* " was the value of the property, which each trooper was bound to maintain in order to be an efficient soldier and the following was the way it was made up :—

Value of a horse on which to mount the soldier.

Value of a half share of a transport pony, on which to carry two soldiers' kit and equipment.

Value of the uniform, arms and equipment of the soldier.

Value of a half share of a tent to accommodate the two soldiers forming a *jori* or pair.

Value of one and a half month's pay which every *silladar* had to deposit with the regiment to help to provide the working capital.

In the beginning the men provided the actual animals and articles, which were valued by the regiment and credited to the men's accounts. In the later development of the system cash equivalents were arranged. These cash equivalents were technically termed " prices."

The *Chanda* Fund was a fund for the insurance and provision of a horse for each *silladar* for the whole period of his service. It had two sources of income, firstly, the monthly subscription from each *silladar*, and secondly, the compensation paid by the East India Company for each horse dying, or being killed in their service, thirdly, by the sale price of casters; latterly the actual capital of the fund was increased by the initial deposit of the horse prices of the *silladar* enlisted, who brought cash instead of horses. The necessity for the establishment of such a fund had been proved by the reluctance, exhibited by the *Khuaaspas*, to risk their horses' lives in battle, because the loss of their horses was their own personal loss and involved their becoming dismounted men.

After the establishment of the *Chanda* system, the horse brought with him by the *silladar* was valued, for the purpose of insurance with the *Chanda* Fund. When the *silladar* was discharged he took away with him, either his original horse, if he wished for it or cash to the amount at which it was valued when he enlisted. As the system got farther standardised each man was obliged to bring a horse of a certain value or if the value of the horse that he actually brought was short of that value he was obliged to pay down in cash the amount by which the horse was short valued. As time went on the custom of each man bringing his own horse with him when he enlisted died out, and the men instead either brought with them (or were lent it by the regiment) a fixed sum of money based on the estimated amount required to purchase a horse. This money they received back on discharge. This money as previously mentioned was technically known as "the Horse Price." The eventual result of this modification was that the *Chanda* Funds in the end became the *ipso-facto* owners of all the horses in the regiments.

About 1898 the Government gave large grants of land to regiments for horse breeding in the new Punjab Canal Colonies which were then being opened to settlement. These Horse Runs when properly run gave great assistance to regiments in mounting themselves. An account of the 17th Cavalry Horse Run will be found elsewhere.

Since the beginning in the *silladar* cavalry it had been the practice for each pair (*or jori*) of troopers and each Indian Officer to own a baggage animal, usually a country pony, for the purposes of transport. About the year 1890 in view of the success of the *Chanda* system, as applied to horses, regiments began to organise Pony *Chandas* to supply and maintain these baggage animals.* These proved to be great successes and with the

---

* See page 24 for an account of the introduction of this system into the 17th Cavalry.

accumulation of funds which thus resulted, regiments were soon able to replace the country pony by the more expensive mule, which experience had proved to be more suitable. To help the regiments to organise mule transport Government lent each regiment eighty-nine Government mules who thus remained as a Government transport reserve maintained at no cost to the State.

Each mule had an attendant who was the private servant of the owner or owners, of the mule. This servant cut the grass required daily by the horses of his master or masters, did any other work which might be required of him by his master or masters, and besides this worked on the *rukh* or grass farm allotted to the regiment for the provision of grass of the horses and mules. On the march these mules carried the baggage of the regiment, and in cantonments they carried fodder from the "*rukh*" to the lines.

This transport system gave great mobility to *silladar* regiments, for they were able to move anywhere in India, at a few hours notice without assistance, because they were self-contained as regards transport. The rationing of men, horses, and mules was also independant of the Supply and Transport Corps and was done very efficiently by the regimental *buniahs*.

This transport system came to an end in 1914, in the early days of the Great War, because the Government of India commandeered all the *Chanda* mules maintained by *silladar* regiments as well as those above mentioned which were on loan from Government.

In later years individual regiments further developed the *Chanda* system and applied it to the provision and maintenance of tents, saddles, arms and equipment of all descriptions, until, in some regiments, the *silladar* remained the actual bonâ fide owner only of the uniform that he wore, the rest of his *Assami* being represented by the deposits called "Prices" which on enlistment he had paid into the various *Chanda* funds. These funds supplied him with and maintained for him the various military equipment and arms required to equip a cavalry soldier, with the exception of rifles, pistols, ammunition, and certain technical equipment which were supplied and maintained free by the Ordnance Department. In the 17th Cavalry there were three *Chanda* funds, the Horse *Chanda* which supplied the horses, the Mule *Chanda* which provided the mules and the Equipment *Chanda* which arranged for all equipment. The only personal property of the rank and file was their uniform.

Chanda Funds of all descriptions were classed by the committee which sat at Simla in 1920, as Public Funds, and were therefore taken over by Government on the conversion of a regiment; the equity of this procedure as regards *Chandas* other than the Horse *Chanda* is rather open to question, as the administration of these funds, the donations and subscriptions, which they received, and the rules under which they were conducted were nowhere laid down in official publications but only in regimental standing orders of the regiments which maintained them. They had all been voluntarily organised by regiments themselves in the interests of efficiency.

In addition to the ordinary *silladars* many regiments contained men called *baghirs*. This meant that their *assamis* were owned by others. Indian officers often owned one or more *baghirs*. The actual difference between the mounted and dismounted rate of pay was given to the actual owners of the *assami* of the *baghir*.

In 1861, when the whole of the Army in India was reorganised after the Mutiny, it was decided, in view of the superior loyalty that had been shown by the regiments that had been raised on the *silladar* or irregular system both before and during the Mutiny, to raise no more regular regiments, and to continue in the service those *silladar* regiments, which had not mutinied and to raise others to take the place of the regular and irregular cavalry which had mutinied and had been disbanded. The regular regiments of the Madras Army which had not mutinied were continued on the old footing, and until quite recently these three regiments were the only three regular cavalry regiments of the Indian Army.

The *silladar* of the days of the Mutiny was little different to his predecessor of the days of Skinner and Gardner, but he was very different from the *silladar* of the days before the Great War, because the former even up to time of the Mutiny, generally brought his own horse, arms and equipment, or at least brought cash to the value of these; whereas the latter brought only a portion of his *assami* in cash and effected a loan for the balance of it. Generally also he was invariably supplied with articles of a regimental pattern after joining. This procedure had been adopted for the sake of uniformity, which was previously lacking.

For a considerable number of years before the Great War it had been the custom for regiments to enlist as *silladars* men who were unable to bring with them in cash the full amount of money required to purchase an *assami*. The amount of cash in each case accepted varied with the wealth of the races from which the regiments were recruited, and this deposit in the case of Transfrontier tribesmen sometimes was reduced as low as fifty rupees.*

---

* All recruits brought some money.

After the outbreak of the Great War it began to be necessary to accept recruits who were unable to bring even modified cash deposits which had previously been standardised for their class. And eventually towards the middle of the War it was found necessary to give up the idea of asking for any cash deposits at all.

But this made no interference with either theory or practice in the administration of the system because the regiments in which such men were enlisted lent them out of regimental funds the money required to complete their *assamis*, or in the case of men without *assamis*, the full amount of an *assami*. Interest on such loans was charged at six per cent and repayment was arranged by small monthly instalments. In cases where regimental funds ran short of cash the Government would advance money on interest to enable regiments to finance themselves.

The regiments live in " lines " or barracks made of mud brick. Each *jori* (or pair of men) had a separate room. The horse " lines " or stables were situated in between the barracks. Most of the " lines " (or barracks and stables) were originally built under regimental arrangements and paid for either out of the regimental funds or by the *silladars* themselves. It seems probable that the *Chanda* and " price " system was applied to maintenance of lines because in the Central India Horse the remains of a system of this nature were still carrying on in the year 1922, when they were converted to a regular basis. However in the 17th Cavalry it appears the cost of construction of the Ferozepore lines came directly out of the pockets of the *silladars*.* It is probable that in most cases the expense was not great, and that the mule attendants originally did most of the work of building and maintaining the " lines." A regiment on transfer, handed over the " lines " to the relieving regiment, who satisfied themselves that the lines were in a habitable state of repair.

In 1890 a Combine was formed, called the " Bengal-Punjab Cavalry Lines Combine," and in 1901 another followed called the " Bombay Cavalry Lines Combine." To these Combines passed the ownership of all the lines built by the *silladar* cavalry with the exception of the lines of the Central India Horse. The " Bengal-Punjab Combine " eventually owned eighteen sets of old lines and five sets of new lines. The " Bombay Combine " owned five sets of old lines and two new sets. The Military Works Funds also owned three sets of old lines and one new set at stations where the *silladar* cavalry had never built any. Perhaps these stations were garrisoned originally by the Madras

---

* See page 20.

regular cavalry. In 1912 the Government of India assumed the responsibility of erecting and maintaining such new lines as might be required, and finally in 1919 the Combines were abolished and the provision and maintenance of all lines became a Government liability.

Until 1912, when Government took over the lines, each regiment of *silladar* cavalry recovered monthly the sum of one hundred and seventy-five rupees from the men, and paid this amount into their local repair fund, which was used to keep the lines of that particular station in repair. On relief by another regiment the balance in this fund and the accounts of it were handed over to the relieving regiment. In addition to this each regiment belonging to the Bengal-Punjab Cavalry Combine paid a further sum of two hundred and forty rupees per mensem to the President of that Combine. This was in liquidation of the joint loan of ten lacs eighty-three thousand four hundred and fifty rupees granted by Government to the Combine for building. The subscriptions of all ranks to the Line Fund were laid down in Army Regulations, India, and if these were not sufficient, regimental funds had to make up the balance.

After 1912 four hundred and fifteen rupees were recovered from each regiment of *silladar* cavalry monthly, the only exceptions being the regiments on service, from whom Government took the actual subscriptions recovered from the men, instead of four hundred and fifteen rupees.

The *silladar* system has gone, but India is a country of cycles. The system was indigenous to and popular in the country and in time it may be revived in a modified manner.

It had many advantages—the following may be mentioned:—

1. It was an extraordinary cheap system of raising cavalry not only were the direct costs less owing to the careful administration and economy in regiments (designed to keep the expenses of the *silladars* as low as possible), but also the indirect costs were nil, as those expensive services and departments, *i.e.* the supply, transport, ordnance, clothing, remounts, military works, veterinary, etc., had no responsibilities with regard to *silladar* units.

2. Any articles of equipment required were obtained without either trouble or delay, and the necessity of clerical labour to maintain all the equipment ledgers and other hugebooks now required for audit

purposes was avoided, also there were practically no " objection " statements to answer.

3. Horses unsuitable for cavalry purposes could be quickly cast and disposed of, and fresh remounts purchased without any of those troublesome references, which are necessary when dealing with animals the property of Government.

4. Owing to the superior status of a *silladar* in the popular Indian estimation a superior social class of men were recruited by the *silladar* cavalry.

5. Owing to the system of every man having money invested in the regiment his material interests were bound up in remaining loyal in times of crisis. This was proved during the Mutiny in 1857.

6. Every man on discharge went back to civil life with a small capital sum in cash.

The disadvantages were more apparent than real. The opponents of the system always go back to the point that the system would not work in modern war. This is of course beyond dispute, but no *silladar* officer had ever contemplated that it would; the pre-war regulations clearly provided for the procedure in passing from private to government supply. It is true that this perhaps threw a strain on the services and departments; but, in India, administrative departments are more easily improvised than cavalry soldiers. When one has to chose between the two alternatives of effective peace establishments of administrative non-combatants and effective peace establishments of combatants, it is safer in India to go for the combatants. In Europe where every man is a potential soldier the case is somewhat different.

The second point that is generally emphasised is the assertion that the system required a clever business man to run it and that many a capable cavalry soldier was obliged to spend the time he should have been training his men, in puzzling over his accounts and in managing the business affairs of the regiment. This is a matter of opinion, but answering the present objection statements of Government Departments probably takes more time than the *silladar* accounts and regimental administration ever did. A man who was incapable of administering a *silladar* regiment would probably be incapable of administering a regular regiment also. As far as junior officers were concerned the variety of the problems which they were called on to settle gave a training to their minds which can never be duplicated in a regular unit.

The third point frequently mentioned was diversity in the pattern of uniform and equipment. This diversity as regards equipment was much exaggerated. As Messrs. Cooper Allen & Co. of Cawnpore supplied the whole *silladar* cavalry, standardisation could easily have been arranged. In most cases the diversities were inherited and not deliberately designed, regiments had no objections to a system of standardisation which did not involve loss to the *silladars*. Any unit could have been standardised by gradual replacement. The differences in uniform were confined to full dress. They harmed no one and merely encouraged *esprit de corps*.

It is true that at the end of the war the *silladar* system had to be ended or mended. The increased cost of everything would have necessitated a large increase of pay to the *silladars* if it had been intended to mantain the system. This however would have in no way equalled the direct and indirect costs consequent on the introduction of the regular system.

The old *silladars* before the war cost Government about fifty-four rupees per capita per month, including the pay of the British Officers and the upkeep of the mule transport. The modern regular costs nearer one hundred and twenty-five rupees per month and he has no mule transport. Of course it must be remembered that during this time prices have risen and soldiers have been given free rations. The horse's ration has also been increased but this is balanced by the fact that each *silladar* paid for part of a mule's ration which Government does not do.

Good or bad, the *silladar* system has gone, but, whatever our opinions, let us remember the system was one that produced many fine regiments and that possessed particular attractions to those soldiers who were born with an aversion to "red tape" and who found themselves at home in the irregular cavalry of India.

APPENDIX X.

STATEMENT OF THE REGIMENTAL ACCOUNTS OF THE 17TH CAVALRY SHOWING THE FINANCIAL POSITION OF THE REGIMENT AT THE TIME OF ITS CONVERSION TO A NON-SILLADAR BASIS.

The accounts of the regiment as they stood at the time of conversion are set forth in the following statements :—

The first account shown is the final regimental balance-sheet as prepared for the standing Silladar Cavalry Conversion Committee. This is in the form of the usual monthly balance-sheet prepared by all silladar regiments.

The Committee for the purpose of the conversion accounts divided this regiment balance-sheet into four separate statements.

(1) *Balance Sheet A.*

This statement shows the balances of the Funds taken over by Government, and the liabilities to be assumed and settled by Government.

(2) *Balance Sheet B.*

This statement shows the accounts that would liquidate themselves on the closing up the silladar system.

(3) *Balance Sheet C.*

This statement shows Private Funds remaining with the regiment.

(4) *Balance Sheet D.*

This statement shows the regimental assets in cash and securities and how these were distributed.

There will also be found a statement (prepared by order of Finance Branch at Army Head Quarters) showing the number of *assamis* purchased by Government and the average cost of an *assami*.

267

SILLADAR CAVALRY CONVERSION COMMITTEE.
ACCOUNTS OF THE 17TH CAVALRY.
Regimental Balance Sheet on the date of conversion.

	Rs.	a.	p.		Rs.	a.	p.
* Horse Price Account	1,25,400	0	0	* Horse *Chanda* Fund	92,257	15	7
* Mule Price Account	26,000	0	0	* Mule *Chanda* Fund	3,411	9	3
* Equipment Price Account	48,600	0	0	* Equipment *Chanda* Fund	1,909	7	2
Forge Fund (Horse Hospital Account)	3,577	0	9	Horse Shoes Account (Forge Fund)	683	9	3
Treasure Chest Account (in Bank)	69,268	15	11	Horse Stud Farm Account	3,622	12	1
Assami Kit Account (value of kits purchased in *Assamis*)	56,566	7	9	Government Advance for Conversion Account	2,00,000	0	0
Stores purchased by the Local Committee Account	15,675	13	1	Unpaid *Assami* Account (*Assamis* of Seconded (Men).	534	13	5
Advance Account	2,078	6	7	Miscellaneous Fund	1,01,564	14	6
Horse Hospital Clipping Account	89	11	8	School Fund	865	11	7
Line Account	2,416	15	9	Lead and Cartridge Fund	40	3	4
Assami Loss Account	3,127	2	9	Training Grant Account	14	0	0
Major K. Barge's Account	20	6	0	Tailor Alam Din's Account	6	6	6
Major T. Kirkwood's Account	300	2	0	Arms Repair Fund	1,325	6	9
Major H. S. Stewart's Account	175	13	4	Bayonet Fighting Account	319	11	0
Messrs. Cox and Co.'s Account	22	4	0	Circle Paymaster's Account (D. D. O.)	6,663	11	1
Fixed Deposit Account	52,540	0	0	Discharged Men's Account	1,563	15	4
Mochi Shop Account	113	14	6	Vehoa Detachment Grain Account	5,950	4	0
Office Fund	1,788	13	4	Engine Fund	16,929	7	11
Officer in charge Engine Fund's Account	358	2	8	Family Allotment Account	306	0	0
Payment Ration Account	33	11	6	Workshop Account	1,585	14	8
Quarter Master's Account	41	10	11	Captain Majoribank's Account	60	0	9
Rejected Stores Account (Stores in hand not taken by the Local Committee).	747	13	1	Mansehrah Grain Account	4,611	6	9
Stores due from Officers' and Squadrons' Account	65	10	9	Multan Ration Account	166	4	0
Savings Bank Account	2,870	11	0	Lieutenant Pratt's Account	450	0	0
Suspense Account	46,949	11	1	O. C. Store Account	8,891	1	0
Spinner and Company's Account	170	0	7	Syces' Pay Account	8,202	15	10
Tank Squadron Field Account	500	0	0	Committee Disallowances Account	451	11	7
Risaldar Wazir Mohamed's account	21	5	11				
Wanu Squadron Field Account	285	0	0				
Lieutenant Zikarya Khan's Account	2,563	12	11				
Gram purchased by the Local Committee Account							
Total	4,62,379	4	10	Total	4,62,379	4	10

* These six accounts were adjusted by the Silladar Cavalry Conversion Committee for an establishment of 506 the strength of the regiment on the date of conversion, instead of for an establishment of 625 on which they had previously been based.

SILLADAR CAVALRY CONVERSION COMMITTEE.

ACCOUNTS OF THE 17TH CAVALRY.

Balance Sheet "A."

Balance Sheet of the Public Funds handed over to Government.

Due by Government.	Rs.	a.	p.	Due to Government.	Rs.	a.	p.
Horse Price Account	1,25,400	0	0	Horse *Chanda* Fund	92,257	15	7
Mule Price Account	26,000	0	0	Mule *Chanda* Fund	3,411	9	3
Equipment Price Account	48,600	0	0	Equipment *Chanda* Fund	1,909	7	2
Value of kits purchased in *Assamis*	56,566	7	9	Forge Fund (Horse Shoes Account)	683	9	3
Value of stores purchased by Local Committee	15,675	13	1	Horse Stud Farm Account	3,622	12	1
Value of Grain purchased by Local Committee	2,563	12	11	Government Advance for Conversion	2,00,000	0	0
Forge Fund (Debtor Balance)	3,577	0	9	Committee Disallowances	451	11	7
Horse Hospital Clipping Account (Debtor Balance)	89	11	8				
Balance of cash refundable to Government from the Statement of Assets	23,864	2	9				
Total	3,02,337	0	11	Total	3,02,337	0	11

SILLADAR CAVALRY CONVERSION COMMITTEE.

ACCOUNTS OF THE 17TH CAVALRY.

Balance Sheet "B."

Balance Sheet of the Funds in course of Liquidation.

Due to the Regiment.	Rs.	a.	p.	Due by the Regiment.	Rs.	a.	p.
Advance Account	2,078	6	7	Unpaid *Assami* Account of Seconded Men	534	13	5
Assami Loss Account	3,127	2	9	Tailor Alam Din's Account	6	6	0
Major K. Barge's Account	20	6	0	Circle Paymaster's (D. D. O.) Account	6,653	11	1
Major T. Kirkwood's Account	300	2	0	Discharged Men's Account	1,563	15	4
Major H. S. Stewart's Account	175	13	4	Vehoa Detachment Grain Account	5,950	4	0
Payment Ration Account	33	11	6	Family Allotment Account	306	0	0
Quarter Master's Account	41	10	11	Captain Marjoribank's Account	60	0	9
Cost of Stores due from Officers' and Men's Accounts	65	10	9	Lieut. Pratt's Account	450	0	0
Suspense Account	46,949	11	1	O. C. Store Account	8,891	1	0
Spinner & Co.'s Account	170	11	0	Syces' Pay Account	8,202	15	10
Tank Squadron Field Account	10	0	7	Multan Ration Account	166	4	0
Risaldar Wazir Mohamed's Account	500	0	0				
Wana Squadron Field Account	21	5	11				
Lieutenant Zikarya Khan's Account	285	0	0	Balance credit carried to the Statement of Assets	20,994	5	0
Total	53,779	12	5	Total	53,779	12	5

SILLADAR CAVALRY CONVERSION COMMITTEE.

ACCOUNTS OF THE 17TH CAVALRY.

Balance Sheet "C."

Balance Sheet of the Private Funds retained by the unit and of those Public Funds not handed over to Government.

	Rs. a. p.		Rs. a. p.
Value of Stores not taken over by Local Committee	747 13 1	Miscellaneous Fund	1,01,564 14 6
Line Account (Debtor Balance)	2,415 15 9	School Fund	865 11 7
Mochi's Shop Account (Debtor Balance)	113 14 6	Lead and Cartridge Fund	40 3 4
Office Fund (Debtor Balance)	1,788 13 4	Arms Repair Fund	1,325 6 9
O. C. Engine Fund (Debtor Balance)	358 2 8	Bayonet Fighting Account	319 11 6
		Engine Fund	16,929 7 11
		Workshop Account	1,585 14 8
		Mansehrah Grain Account	4,611 6 9
		Training Grant Account	14 0 0
Balance or cash required to meet liabilities from the Statement of Assets.	1,21,832 1 2		
Total	1,27,256 12 6	Total	1,27,256 12 6

270

SILLADAR CAVALRY CONVERSION COMMITTEE.

ACCOUNTS OF THE 17TH CAVALRY.

Balance Sheet "D."

Statement of the Assets to be retained by the Unit and how distributed.

	Rs. a. p.		Rs. a. p.
Treasure Chest	Nil.	Cash required to meet liabilities as per—	
Treasure Chest Account (in Bank) ..	69,268 15 11	Balance Sheet "A"	23,864 2 9
Messrs. Cox & Co.'s Account	22 4 0	Balance Sheet "B"	Nil.
Fixed Deposit Account	52,540 0 0	Balance Sheet "C"	1,21,832 1 2
Savings Bank Account	2,870 11 0		
Credit Balance from Balance Sheet "B" ..	20,994 5 0		
Total ..	1,45,696 3 11	Total ..	1,45,696 3 11

SILLADAR CAVALRY CONVERSION COMMITTEE.
ACCOUNTS OF THE 17TH CAVALRY.

Government Account of the Assamis purchased from the Silladars of the 17th Cavalry.

Government Assets.		Rs.	a.	p.	Government Liabilities.		Rs.	a.	p.
Total of the Funds surrendered to Government					506 *Assamis* @ Rs. 511-10-8		2,56,566	7	9
Horse *Chanda* Fund		92,257	15	7	Value of the Stores purchased by the Local Committee.		15,675	13	1
Mule *Chanda* Fund		3,411	9	3					
Equipment *Chanda* Fund		1,909	7	2	Value of the Grain purchased by the Local Committee.		2,563	12	11
Horse Stud Farm Account		3,622	12	1					
Forge Fund (Horse Shoes) Account		683	9	3	Forge Fund (Debtor Balance)		3,577	0	9
Total		1,01,885	5	4	Horse Hospital Clipping Account (Debtor Balance)		89	11	8
Amounts due to Government									
Committee Disallowances		451	11	7	Amount due to Government, being balance refundable on Conversion.		23,864	2	9
Amount of the Government Advance for Conversion.		2,00,000	0	0					
Total		2,00,451	11	7					
GRAND TOTAL		3,02,337	0	11	GRAND TOTAL		3,02,337	0	11

Detail of an Assami.*

		Rs.	a.	p.
Horse Price		250	0	0
Mule Price		50	0	0
Equipment Price		100	0	0
Value of Uniform and Equipment		111	10	8
Total		511	10	8

* This does not include the item of "Regimental Fund," because this item was merely refunded to the men on the abolition of the system. Nevertheless a month and half's pay should be added to the above to arrive at the amount which a sowar had to arrange for on enlistment as a Silladar.

† This was the strength of the regiment on the date of conversion, the other *assamis* up to a total of 625 (which was the pre-war establishment) had been purchased previously by debiting the Horse prices, Mule prices and Equipment prices to their respective *Chanda* and by taking the remaining Uniform and Equipment into stores where it was eventually paid for by Government in the "value of stores purchased by the local committee".

APPENDIX XI.

REGIMENTAL LIST AS IT STOOD AT THE TIME OF AMALGAMATION.

17TH CAVALRY.
[Amalgamating with 37th Lancers (Baluch Horse).]

Raised at Muttra in 1857, as the Muttra Horse. Became the Muttra Police Corps the same year; the Rohilkhand and Auxiliary Police Levy, 1858; 'Robarts' Horse,' 1858; the 17th Regiment of Bengal Cavalry, 1861; was disbanded, 1882. Re-raised at Mian Mir 1885, by Colonel E. H. E. Kauntze, under its former designation. Became the 17th Regiment of Bengal Lancers, 1900; the 17th Bengal Lancers, 1901; present designation 1903.

"Afghanistan, 1879—80."

LUCKNOW.

Composition—2 Squadrons of Punjabi Musalmans, 2 of Pathans.
Uniforms—Blue. *Facings*—White.
COLONEL—Major-General William A. Lawrence ... 13 May 1904.

First Commission.	Names and Ranks.	Army rank.	REMARKS.
	COMMANDANT.		
20 May 93	Barry-Smith, Lt.-Col. R. C.	19 June 17	
	SQUADRON COMMANDERS. (4).		
28 May 00	Stewart, Maj. H. S.	1 Sep. 15	2nd-in-Command *(temp.)*, member of the Silladar Cavalry Conversion Committee.
	* * * *		
	* * * *		
	* * * *		
	SQUADRON OFFICERS. (9).		
19 Sep. 09	Barge, Maj. K., D.S.O., M.C.	18 Jan. 18	*Staff Coll., Camberley, Jan. 21 (Sr. Divn.), leave pending retirement.*
21 Jan. 03	Kirkwood, Maj. T. W., O.B.E	21 Jan. 18	*Lv., ex India, pending retirement.*
5 Aug. 05	Yeats-Brown, Maj. F. C. C., D F.C.	5 Aug. 20	*l.*
19 Jan. 07	Atkinson, Maj. E. G.	1 Sep. 15	
11 Dec. 07	Foottit, Capt. J. A. W.	21 Sep. 15	
24 Aug. 12	Cochrane, Capt. R. P. I.	4 Aug. 16	
	* * * *		
	* * * *		
	ATTACHED.		
20 May 15	McCay, Capt. R. C., D.S.O.	20 May 19	*Wazir Force.*
1 June 15	Campbell-Harris, Capt. C.	16 June 19	*Wazir Force*
23 June 15	Persse, Capt. S. H.	23 June 19	
16 Dec. 14	Williams, Capt. C. C.	16 Sep. 19	*Wazir Force*
20 Dec. 15	Sydenham, Capt. A. F.	20 Dec. 19	*Mechanical Transport, India.*

274

First Commission.	Names and Rank	Army rank.	Remarks.
	Attached—(concluded).		
12 May 15	Turner, Capt. E.	12 Feb. 20	
16 Aug. 16	Ballentine, Capt. J. S.	16 Aug. 20	Adjutant (officiating).
23 Sep. 16	Griffiths, Capt. W. S.	23 Sep. 20	
25 Feb. 17	Clews, Capt. L. C.	26 Feb. 21	*Wazir Force.*
18 June 17	Pert, Lieut. C. E.	18 June 18	*Cavalry School, Saugor.*
21 Dec. 17	Freston, Lieut. T. A.	21 Dec. 18	*Attending University in U. K.*
24 Apl. 18	Wilson, Lieut. J. H. A.	24 Apl. 19	*With 31st Lancers.*
3. Aug. 18	Dixon, Lieut. V. H.	31 Aug. 19	Quarter Master (officiating).
16 Dec. 18	Pratt, Lieut. H. S.	16 Dec. 19	*Lv., ex India, medical certificate.*
20 Dec. 18	Monckton, Lieut. E. P. S.	20 Dec. 19	
15 Apl. 19	Greenway, Lient. J. A.	15 Apl. 20	*Lv., ex India, medical certificate.*
29 Jan. 20	Child, Lieut. C. H.	29 Jan. 21	*Wazir Force.*

Honorary Officer.

17 Apl. 21	Malik Khizar Mohamed Khan Hayat Tiwana.	17 Oct. 20	Hony. Lieut. I.L.F.

INDIAN OFFICERS.

Risaldar-Major.

		Jemadar.	Rissaidar.	Risaldar.	Risaldar-Major.
18 Mar. 94	Rahmat Sher, I.D.S.M.	1 Aug. 05	1 Jan. 12	11 Apl. 16	16 June 20. Order of British India 2n. class.

Risaldars.

19 Mar. 00	Bahadur Sher	12 Mar. 02	16 Oct. 09	11 Apl. 16
8 July 94	Wazir Khan, I.O.M.	1 Oct. 09	20 Sep. 16	1 Mar. 20
1 Mar. 06	Malik Alam Sher Khan, I.D.S.M.	1 Jan. 12	1 Sep. 17	7 May 20
16 Sep. 07	Ata Muhammad Shah	15 Mar. 08	14 Aug. 16	1 Apl. 21
1 Oct. 09	Dost Muhammad Khan	10 Oct. 09	22 Sep. 17	1 Apl. 21
1 Jan. 04	Wazir Muhammad, M.B.E.	8 Sep. 14	1 Mar. 20	1 Apl. 21
1 Mar. 13	Sultan Sikandar Khan	24 Dec. 15	7 May 20	1 Apl. 21
1 Aug. 95	Inayatullah Khan	22 Mar. 16	16 June 20	1 Apl. 21

Jemadars.

19 Dec. 08	Malik Ghulam Husain Khan.	24 Dec. 15	
2 June 11	Arbab Muhammad Husain	26 Mar. 16	
12 July 16	Malik Ahmad Yar Khan	12 July. 16	
1 Oct. 09	Ahmad Ali Khan	22 Sep. 17	Woordie Major.
1 Mar. 98	Pir Dad Khan	5 Oct. 17	
15 Feb. 06	Said Raza	1 Jan. 18	Quarter-Master Jemadar.
24 Mar. 01	Alam Khan	24 Jan. 18	
24 July 11	Mohammad Aslam Khan	9 Apl. 18	

APPENDIX XII.

LISTS OF BRITISH OFFICERS WHO HAVE EITHER BELONGED OR WHO HAVE BEEN ATTACHED TO THE REGIMENT.

THE FULL LIST OF THE BRITISH OFFICERS OF THE 17TH CAVALRY.

Appointed prior to August 4th, 1914.

Name.	Date of joining the Regiment.	Regimental appointments.	Particulars of Services, etc.
1. Robarts, Charles James.	25-11-58	1st Commandant 1858—73.	Died as a Colonel 6-1-73. For details of his services, see Appendix I.
2. de-Kantzow, Charles Adolphus.	25-11-58	Commandant of de-Kantzow's Horse.	Transferred to the Political Department, 1860. Retired as a Colonel. Died at Brighton. For details of his services, see Appendix I.
3. Adley, William Henry.	1-4-59	1st Medical Officer.	First Commissioned 2-9-50. Transferred to the 15th Bengal Lancers in 1869. Deputy Surgeon-General, Allahabad, 22-6-77. Retired, 31-3-82.
4. Watson, Thomas James.	1-4-59	1st Adjutant 1858—60. Squadron Commander 3rd Commandant, 1878—82.	First Commissioned 20-2-51. Transferred from 46th N. I. and appointed Adjutant of Robarts' Horse 21-4-59. Commandant 24-4-78 to 1-7-82. Commandant of the 9th Bengal Lancers 18-10-82 to 2-12-87 Died in New Zealand in 1907. Indian Mutiny 1857—59, mentioned in despatches. Bhutan, 1865-66, Jowaki 1877, Afghan War 1879-80. Mutiny medal with clasp, Bhutan medal, Afghan medal.
5. Glasscock, Talbot Bradford Middleton.	30-5-59	Squadron Officer. 3rd Adjutant, 1865—76. Squadron Commander.	First Commissioned 11-8-57. Transferred from the 50th N. I on appointment to the regiment. Transferred to the 1st Bengal Cavalry 8-8-76. Retired as Colonel and Second-in-Command of that unit

Name.	Date of joining the Regiment.	Regimental appointments.	Particulars of Services, etc.
			1887 Died at Brighton 1900 Served in the Indian Mutiny, Bhutan Campaign and Afghan War. Mutiny medal with clasp, Bhutan medal with clasp, Afghan medal.
6. Clifford, Richard Melville.	10-5-60	Squadron Officer.	First Commissioned 25-6-58. Transferred from the 60th N. I. on appointment to the regiment. Transferred to the 16th Bengal Cavalry 9-3-77. Commandant of the 2nd Bengal Cavalry. Retired as a Major-General. Served the Hazara Campaign 1868, Sudan Expedition 1885. Indian General Service medal. Egyptian medal. Bronze Star.
7. Hoggan, George Welland Henry.	28-8-60	Squadron Officer. 2nd Adjutant, 1860—65.	First Commissioned 4-4-54. Transferred from the 4th N. I. on appointment to the regiment. Appointed Commandant, Fort Abajai, 9-3-77. Retired as a Lieutenant-Colonel 23-5-1882. Died in England. Served in the Indian Mutiny.
8. Lindsay, Arthur Fergusson.	12-8-61	Squadron Officer.	First Commissioned 12-8-61. Transferred to the Oudh Police 15-4-62. Subsequently joined 8th B. C. Died at Sea as a Major 29-9-81
9. Hodson, Vernon James.	20-12-62	Squadron Officer.	First Commissioned 20-11-58. Appointed from 4th European Light Cavalry. Died at Dinapore 27-11-63.
10. Webster, Hamilton Bell.	5-3-63	Squadron Officer.	First Commissioned 4-12-57. Appointed from 4th European Light Cavalry. Reverted to the 4th European Light Cavalry 11-8-63. Retired as a Captain 24-4-68.
11. Best, Henry White	20-1-64	Squadron Officer.	First Commissioned 20-12-45. Appointed from 5th European Light Cavalry. Reverted to the 5th European Light Cavalry 1865. Died at Agra in 1870. Served in the Mutiny and seige of Delhi. Mutiny medal.

Name.	Date of joining the Regiment.	Regimental appointments.	Particulars of Services, etc.
12. Newnham, Edward George.	20-1-64	Squadron Officer.	First Commissioned 4-8-59. Transferred from General List Infantry on appointment to the regiment. Transferred to the 6th Bengal Cavalry 1-7-82 on the disbandment of the old regiment. Died at Naini Tal 14-6-87 in the rank of Lieutenant-Colonel. Served in the Bhutan Expedition 1865-66 (medal). Afghan war 1879-80 (medal).
13. Boileau, Frederick Durie.	27-4-65	Squadron Officer.	First Commissioned 8-6-61. Transferred to the regiment from the General List Infantry. Died at Sonepore, 9-11-65.
14. Bentall, Clement Edward.	1-9-65	Squadron Officer.	First Commissioned 20-5-69. Transferred to the regiment from the General List Cavalry. Transferred to the 1st Bengal Cavalry 23-3-70. Died at Allahabad 3-9-78 as a Captain.
15. Patten, James Alexander Mountford.	8-7-65	Squadron Officer.	First Commissioned 20-4-34. Transferred to the regiment from the 1st European Light Cavalry. Reverted to the 1st European Light Cavalry 13-11-65. Retired as a Captain 13-5-68.
16. Dickson, John Ballantyne.	1-7-65	Squadron Officer.	First Commissioned 20-1-60. Transferred to the regiment from the General List Cavalry. Transferred to the 18th B. C. 20-10-65 and subsequently exchanged into the 16th Lancers (British Service.) Retired as a Major-General 2-2-01. Served in South African War 1879: Zulu Campaign (mentioned in Despatches), Soudan Expedition 1884-85 action of Abuklea, severely wounded. South African War 1899-01 Despatches London Gazette 16-4-01. Major-General 9-2-00. South African medal 1879. Egyptian medal (two clasps). Kedive's Star, South African Queen's medal

Name.	Date of joining the Regiment.	Regimental appointments.	Particulars of Services, etc
			with five clasps. Companion of the Order of the Bath. Companion of the Order of St. Michael and St. George. Retired 2-2-01. Died in England 1925.
17 Swiney, Hugh Bladen.	12-2-66	Squadron Officer. 4th Adjutan, 1876-77.	First Commissioned 20-12-60. Transferred to the regiment from the General List Infantry. Adjutant of the regiment at Peshawar 1875. Commandant of the Calcutta Volunteer Lancers 15-1-75. Killed in an affray with the Jowaki Afridis 21-11-77.
18. Compton, Digby..	3-1-66	Squadron Officer.	First Commissioned 26-8-54. Transferred to the regiment from the 2nd European Light Cavalry. Died at Landour 22-9-66.
19 Drummond, William Lyttleton Powys.	4-3-67	Squadron Officer.	First Commissioned 9-12-53. in the Indian Staff Corps. Joined the regiment as a Captain Transferred to the 12th B. C. 22-12-68. Died in England on sick leave 10-8-71. Served at the Siege of Delhi and organized and commanded a regiment of Police Cavalry during the Oudh Campaign of 1858 Four times mentioned in Despatches. Served in the China War 1860-61 with 1st Sikh Cavalry and subsequently on the staff of Sir R. Napier. Mutiny medal with clasp and China medal.
20. Lindsay-Carnegie, Donald Christian Strachan.	17-1-67	Squadron Officers.	First Commissioned 30-3-58. Joined the regiment on transfer from 4th European Light Cavalry as a Captain. Transferred to the 6th B. C 19-2-69, reappointed, 4-8-70. Reverted to the 4th European Light Cavalry. 22-2-78. Retired in the rank of Major 5-10-81. Died in Scotland 1923.
21. Craigie, William Burkett.	5-11-67	Squadron Officer.	First Commissioned 4-12-59. Joined the regiment from

Name.	Date of joining the Regiment.	Regimental appointments.	Particulars of Services, etc.
			the General List Cavalry. Transferred to the 6th Bengal Cavalry 23-1-68 and subsequently to the 2nd Bengal Light Cavalry. Retired as Major 4-12-79.
22. Gower, Basil Henry Stevens.	2-1-68	Squadron Officer.	First Commissioned 7-11-62 in the 59th Foot and transferred to regiment. Died at Bareilly 14-2-81.
23. Jones, Hugh Davies	10-3-68	Officiating Medical Officer.	First Commissioned 20-5-54. Transferred 16-9-68. Was Surgeon of the Viceroy's Bodyguard 1865. Died at Barrackpore 16-9-68.
24. Graham, Thomas Chadwick.	21-3-68	Squadron Officer.	First Commissioned 25-11-54. Joined the regiment from the 4th European Light Cavalry as a Captain. Transferred to 4th B. C. 8-1-70. Reverted to the 4th European Light Cavalry. Retired 12-2-80 as a Brevet Lieutenant-Colonel. Served in the Mutiny against Ghowts in Gugaria and in the Siege and capture of Lucknow at the taking of Bareilly 1858 and in the Sordon Field Force 1858. Wounded at the capture of Fort Deghan. Mutiny medal and clasp.
25. Morris, Frank Bird	27-5-68	Squadron Officer.	First Commissioned 4-10-61. Joined the regiment from the General List Infantry. Transferred to Central Province Police 19-10-68. Died at Nagpore as District Superintendent, Police, 29-12-1878.
26. Potter, Henry ..	17-10-68	Officiating Medical Officer.	First Commissioned 23-7-61. Transferred to the 18th Native Infantry 18-12-76. Subsequently became Medical Store Keeper at Mian Mir. Served in the Indian Mutiny 1858-59. Mutiny medal. Retired as Brigade-Surgeon 2-11-91.
27. Grant, Alexander Gibb.	28-10-68	Officiating Medical Officer.	First Commissioned 1-4-64. Transferred to the 1st Bengal

Name.	Date of joining the Regiment.	Regimental appointments.	Particulars of Services, etc.
28. Chalmers, Edward Willock.	12-5-71	Squadron Officer.	Cavalry 4-3-69. Retired as Surgeon- Major 1-8-86. Served in the Afghan War 1879-80. Afghan medal. First Commissioned in the 11th Foot (North Devons) 21-8-67 Appointed to the regiment. from the 11th Foot. Transferred to the 7th Bengal Cavalry 1-7-82, on disbandment of the regiment, and subsequently appointed to the Remount Department. and retired as Lieutenant-Colonel and First Superintendent of Remount Depôts 14-8-99. Served on N.-W, Frontier. Jowaki, 1877-78, Afghanistan, 1878-80, Burma 1886—88. Indian General Service medal with two clasps and Afghan medal.
29. Ryall, Browne William.	31-1-72	Officiating Commandant.	First Commissioned 14-1-46. Joined as officiating Commandant from 3rd B.C. Transferred to the 14th Bengal Lancers as Commandant 2-1-78. Retired as Colonel 12-9-81, promoted Major-General. Served in Sonthal Insurrection: received the thanks of the Government of India, Served with 2nd Hyderabad Cavalry as Adjutant in Central Indian Army, Battle of Banda (wounded and horse wounded), capture of Kirwee and all other affairs up to 1-6-5 8. Commanded 1st Sikh Cavalry in Shahabad Campaign 1858. Frequently mentioned in despatches. Strongly recommended for Victoria Cross or gallant conduct at Battle of Banda.
30. Graham, Frederick William.	2-1-73	Officiating Commandant. 2nd Commandant.	First Commissioned 26-7-47. Joined the regiment as Officiating Commandant from the 6th B.C. Appointed Commandant 17-2-73. Retired 10-4-78 and died shortly afterwards. Served in Bur-

Name.	Date of joining the Regiment.	Regimental appointments.	Particulars of Services, etc.
			mese War 1852-53, in the Indian Munity in Oudh, Chinhut 30-6-57 slightly wounded and horse wounded Defence of Lucknow Residency, slightly wounded. Took part in the Sorties, 29th September and 2nd October, and in all subsequent operations at Lucknow. Completed the Oudh Campaign with Brigadier Hall's column. Mentioned in Despatches. Brevet of Major Burma medal, Mutiny medal with two clasps.
31. Shoubridge Herbert William.	6-3-73	Squadron Officer.	First Commissioned 21-7-59. Joined the regiment as a Captain. Appointed Fort Adjutant, Attock, 4-6-74. Died at Poona as Lieutenant-Colonel, 8-9-85, Served in the Afghan War 1878-79. Bazaar Valley Expedition medal.
32. Thuillier D'Arcy Wentworth.	13-6-76	Squadron Officer.	First Commissioned in 26th Foot. Appointed from 1st Battalion, 8th Foot. Appointed Adjutant of H.E. the Viceroy's Body Guard, 22-10-78. Died at Dehra Dun 13-6-81, from abcess on the liver.
33. Macdonald, Denis Peter.	8-12-76	2nd Medical Officer.	First Commissioned 1-4-73. Transferred to the 5th Bengal Cavalry 8-7-82, on the disbandment of the regiment afterwards appointed to Civil Medical Department, Punjab, and retired with rank of Lieutenant-Colonel 1-4-93. Died in England. Served in the Jowaki Expedition, 1877-78; Afghan War, 1878-80, Chin-Lushai Expedition 1889-90. Afghan medal, General Service medal with two clasps.
34. Trotter, Robert Francis.	9-4-77	Squadron Officer. 5th Adjutant, 1877—81. Squadron Commander.	First Commissioned 8-12-69 in the 4th Hussars. Transferred to the 7th B.C. 1-7-82 on disbandment of the regiment. Re-appointed 15-10-85. Transferred to the

Name.	Date of joining the Regiment.	Regimental appointments.	Particulars of Services etc.
		Second-in-Command.	13th B. L 1-10-98, and retired 8-12-01. Commanded the regiment for three months in autumn of 1900. Served in the Jowaki Expedition, 1877-78; Afghan War, 1879-80; Capture of Ali Masjid. During the beginning of the Great War, 1914, served as Commandant of the Cavalry Base Depôt, Marseilles. Indian General Service medal; Afghan medal with clasp, 1914-15 Star; British War medal; Victory medal.
35. Wood, Edward James Fandon.	29-11-77	Squadron Officer.	First Commissioned 1-1-73. Transferred to the 10th B. C., 16-5-78; commanded that regiment and retired 1-1-05. Served in the Jowaki Expedition, 1877-78; Afghan War, 1878-80; Occupation of Kandahar and Khelat-i-Ghilzai, Affair of Jugdulluk. Mentioned in despatches. General Service medal with clasp, Afghan medal. Was Private Secretary to Governor of Punjab.
36. Heathcote, Mark Henry.	10-4-7	Second-in-Command.	First Commissioned 20-12-54. Joined as Second-in-Command. Transferred to the 14th B. L. as Commandant 18-1-82. Died at Lahore as Brevet-Colonel and C. B. 22-10-83. Served in Sikhim Expedition, 1861 (mentioned in despatch;) Duffla Expedition 1874-75 (mentioned in despatches). Operations against the Nagas 1875 (mentioned in despatches); Perak Expedition 1876 (mentioned in despatches)., medal with clasp and Brevet of Lieutenant-Colonel, Afghan War 1878-80, both Bazaar Valley Expeditions, advance to Kabul, action of Charasiah operations at Kabul. Mentioned in despatches three times. Medal with clasp. Created Companion of the Bath.

Name.	Date of joining the Regiment.	Regimental appointments.	Particulars of Services etc.
37. Probyn, Francis Hoel.	6-5-79	Squadron Officer.	First Commissioned 20-12-54 in the 40th Foot. Transferred to 9th B. C. 2-3-82. Killed in Soudan Expedition 19-2-84 while attached to the 10th Hussars. Passed the Staff College Camberley in 1881. Served in the Afghan War, 1879-80 (medal).
38. Montresor, Welby Francis.	5-11-79	Squadron Officer. Squadron Commander.	First Commissioned 19-10-77 in the 10th Hussars and subsequently to the regiment. Transferred to the 16th B. C., 29-12-80. Re-appointed 1-10-85. Retired as Major, 1896. Died January, 1909.
39. Robarts, Charles James.	13-2-80	Squadron Officer.	First Commissioned 2-12-73. Appointed from the 3rd Hussars. Transferred to the 2nd B. C., 17-12-80 and became Adjutant of that regiment. Appointed Cantonment Magistrate 1892. Retired as Lieutenant-Colonel 5-5-05. He was a nephew of Colonel C. J. Robarts, first Commandant of the regiment. Served in the Afghan War, 1879 and in Egypt 1882, actions of Kassasin and Te-el-Kabir. Afghan medal, Egyptian medal with clasp, Khedive Bronze Star.
40. Campbell, Alexander William Dennistoun.	7-10-79	Squadron Officer.	First Commissioned 30-12-71 in 16th Lancers. Appointed to the regiment from the 15th Hussars and 7th B. C. Had originally passed into Indian Civil Service and resigned. Appointed Cantonment Magistrate 6-4-82. Retired as Lieutenant-Colonel 1-2-00. Served in the Afghan War, 1879-80. Occupaton of Kandahar and Khelat-i-Ghilzai and operations in Yaghistan. Afghan medal. First Commissioned 10-3-28.
41. Cones, George Augustus.	6-2-80	Officiating Medical Officer.	Only attached for a few months as Surgeon Left the regiment when it marched to Kabul.

Name.	Date of joining the Regiment.	Regimental appointments.	Particulars of Services etc.
42. Willes, George Frederick.	13-4-8	Squadron Officer.	Transferred to the 9th B. L. 1-7-82 on the disbandment of the regiment, afterwards transferred to the 15th B.L and retired as Major 25-6-01. Served in the Afghan War 1878-80 (medal).
43. Lawrence, William Alexander.	16-6-81	Squadron Commander. 5th Commandant, 15-10-88 to 5-7-95. Colonel of the 17th Cavalry, 13-5-04 to 8-7-24.	First Commissioned as Cornet 7th Dragoon Guards, 4-2-81, subsequently transferred to the 21st Hussars and admitted to the Bengal Staffs Corps. Served with the Guides, the Viceroy's Body Guard, in Civil Employ in Assam and the 1st Bengal Lancers. In 1881 was appointed to the 17th Bengal Cavalry and when the regiment was mustered out he was posted to the 14th Bengal Lancers. In 1885 when the 17th were re-raised he was reposted to the regiment. He was appointed Commandant, 17th Cavalry, and subsequently Colonel of the regiment. Major-General 8-11-97. Transferred to Unemployed Supernumary List in 1900. Died 8-7-24. Served in Afghanistan, 1878-80. Battle of Ahmed Khel. Mentioned in despatches Brevet of Lieut.-Colonel. Medal with clasp.
44. Kauntze, Ernest Henry Edward.	26 1-82	Squadron Commander. 4th Commandant, 1885 to 10-10-88.	First Commissioned 11-5-55. Appointed from the 7th Dragoon Guards to the 6th B. C. and afterwards to the 11th B. L. and thence to the regiment. Transferred to the 7th B. C., 1-7-82 on disbandment of the regiment. Re-appointed 1885 as First Commandant of the re-raised regiment. Died 1910. Promoted a Brevet-Colonel 11-5-85. Served in the Crimean Campaign 1883 after the fall of Sebastopol.

This closes the list of officers appointed to the old regiment.

Name.	Date of joining the Regiment.	Regimental appointments.	Particulars of Services etc.
45. Sartorius, Reginald William.	18-9-85	Second-in-Command.	First Commissioned 2-1-58. Joined the regiment as Second-in-Command on its being re-raised, from General Duty. Served in the Indan Mutiny, 1858-59. Relief of Azimgarh and operations in Gorakhpur District, Khasia and Jyntia Hills Expeditioin (Assam), 1862-63. Bhootan Campaign, 1864-65. Ashanti War, 1873-74 (Brevet of Major) Afghan War, 1878-79. Indian Mutiny medal, Bhootan medal with clasp, Afghan medal, Ashanti medal, Victoria Cross, Companion of the Order of St. Michael and St. George. Retired 12-9-90. Died 8-8-07.
46. Muir, Charles Wemyss.	18-9-85	Squadron Commander. 6th Commandant. 5-7-1895 to 12-4-1902.	First Commissioned in the 6th Foot 7-7-69, subsequently transferred to the 6th B.C. and thence to the regiment. Was Adjutant and subsequently Commandant of the Viceroy's Body Guard. Appointed Commandant of the regiment 5-7-95. Promoted to Colonel 7-7-99. Appointed "Colonel-on the Staff" at Delhi from 12-4-02 to 12-4-05. Retired 12-4-07. Subsequntly served in France during the Great War as a D.A.Q.M.G. Died in England. 27-12-20 Served in the Afghan War, 1880. March from Quetta to relief of Kandahar; Soudan Expedition, 1885 (A.-D.C. to O.C. Indian Contingent). Mentioned in despatches. Burmese Expedition, 1885-87; Frontier of India, 1897-98; Operations in Samana and in Kurram Valley; Tirah 1897-98; capture of Sampagha and Orhanga Passes (on the staff). Mentioned in despatches (London Gazette 5-4-98). Afghan medal, Egyptian medal with two clasps, Kedive's Star, Burmese medal with clasps,

Name.	Date of joining the Regiment.	Regimental appointments.	Particulars of Services etc.
47. Medley, Ernest James.	15-9-85	6th Adjutant 1885—88. Squadron Commander.	Indian General Service medal with three clasps British War medal and Victory medal. Companion of the Order of the Bath, and Companion of the Order of the Indian Empire. First Commissioned in 12th Foot 11-5-78 and transferred to 7th B.C. Joined the regiment as Adjutant on its being re-raised in 1885. Retired on pension 11-5-06. Served in the Afghan War, 1878-80. Afghan medal.
48. Burton, Edmund Boteler.	15-9-85	Sqadron Officer. 7th Adjutant 1888-90. Squadron Commander. 8th Commandant. 15-10-06 to 14-4-11.	First Commissioned in the 33rd Foot 13-8-79. Transferred to the 15th Bengal Lancers 15-9-84 and subsequently to the 17th Bengal Cavalry, 17-10-85. Adjutant 20-10-88 to 13-10-90. Squadron Commander 15-10-91 to 14-10-06. Commandant 15-10-06 to 14-4-11. General Officer Commanding the Secunderabad and Meerut Cavalry Brigades 15-4-11 to 1-6-13 with the rank of Brigadier-General. Retired with rank of Colonel 1-6-13. Served as Commandant of the Andaman Military Police Battalion, 1902-03; Consul for Arabistan, 1903. Employed on Reconnaissances in Persia 1890-91 and 1897. Served in the Mahsud Wazir Expedition, 1881; the Egyptian Campaign, 1882; (Battle of Tel-el-Kabir), the Burmese Expedition 1886-87 (mentioned in despatches); the Chitral Expedition (Field Intelligence Officer mentioned in despatches) France and Italy 1917-18. Companion of the Bath. Egyptian medal with clasp and Kedive's Star, Burma medal with two clasps, the old Indian General Service medal with two clasps, the British War medal and Victory medal. Fellow of the Royal Geographical Society. MacGregor Memorial medal.

Name.	Date of joining the Regiment.	Regimental appointments.	Particulars of Services etc.
49. Darrah, Maurice Zouch.	15-9-85	Squadron officer.	First Commissioned 11-8-80. Appointed to the Burma Commission 1887. Killed in Upper Burma 1887 while leading the attack on the stockade at Pyin-ul-win (Maymyo).
50. Bower, Hamilton	15-9-85	Squadron Officer. Squadron Commander. Second-in-Command.	First Commissioned in 11th Foot, 23-10-80. Promoted Brevet-Major 18-11-96. Brevet-Lieutenant-Colonel, 29-11-00 and Brevet-Colonel, 1-6-04. Substantive Colonel, 1-12-08 and Major-General 15-2-09. Raised and and Commanded the Chinese Regiment at Wei-hei-Wei 1889. Served as D.A.Q.M.G. (Intelligence) 18-4-93 to 4-5-98. Commanded Legation Guard, Pekin, 1-12-01 to 24-11-06. Rejoined the regiment at Bannu in 1908. Appointed officiating Brigade Commander of the Dehra Ismail Khan Brigade and subsequently as G.O.C. of the Assam Brigade, 1-12-08. Commanded the Abor Expedition, 1912. He was well known for his journeys in Central Asia 1889 and 1891. Served in the Dongola Expedition 1896 as D.A.Q.M.G. (Intelligence). Brevet of Major, China, 1900. Relief of Tientsin and relief of Pekin in Command of the Chinese regiment, mentioned in Despatches. Brevet of Lieutenant-Colonel. Abor Expedition, 1912 (G.O.C. of Force), created Knight Commander of the Bath 23-8-12. Egyptian and British medals; 1896; China medal, 1900; Indian General Service medal; Macgregor Memorial Gold medal; Gold medal of the Royal Geographical Society and Humane Society medal for saving life.
51. Griffiths, William Edwin.	15-9-85	3rd Medical Officer.	First Commissioned 1-10-72. Indian Medical Service.

Name.	Date of joining the Regiment.	Regimental appointments.	Particulars of Services etc.
			Trasnferred to the 20th Punjab Infantry 31-8-92. Served in the Afghan War 1878-79, (Engagement at Mattoon and forcing the Shutar gardan Pass) and in Mahsud Waziri Expedition 1881. Afghan medal.
52. Mardall, William Sleigh.	23-3-86	Squadron Officer. 8th Adjutant. 1890-92 Squadron Commander.	First Commissioned in the Royal Marines 1-2-81. Subsequently appointed to the 2nd B. I., and thence to the regiment. Transferred to the 31st D.C.O. Lancers as Second-in-Command 6-6-06. Subsequently appointed Commandant of that regiment. Died October 1912.
3. Browne, George	18-4-86	Squadron Officer.	First Commissioned in the Border Regiment, 5-12-83. Transferred to 4th Bengal Cavalry, and thence reverted to the Border Regiment.
54. Stewart, James Fearnley.	11-5-86	Squadron Officer.	First Commissioned in the Scottish Rifles 10-3-83 and from there transferred to the regiment. Subsequently transferred to Commissariat Department 9-5-88, and thence to the 14th B.L. Served in the Judge Advocal General's Department from 7-5-00 to 31-5-04. Subsequently appointed Second-in-Command of an Indian Infantry Battalion and died in India about 1905.
55. Boudier, Edward William.	14-4-87	Squadron Officer. 9th Adjutant 1892-95. Squadron Commander. Second-in Command. 9th Commandant. 15-4-11 to 28-2-17.	First Commissioned in the Royal Artilley 8-7-84 and appointed to Bengal Staff Corps as a probationer, attached to the regiment. Admitted to the Staff Corps, 14-10-88 and appointed permanently to the Regiment 15-5-90. Appointed Adjutant 8-5-92. Promoted Captain, 5-7-95. Raised the 57th Silladar Camel Corps 15-3-01. Rejoined the regiment and officiated as Commandant June to October

Name.	Date of joining the Regiment.	Regimental appointments.	Particulars of Services etc.
			1903. Proceeded to Somaliland 1-9-03 as Commandant, 2nd *Ekka* Train Somaliland Field Force. Appointed Second Squadron Commander 1-10-06. Officiating Commandant 15-5-06 to 15-10-06 and 8-11-09 to 14-4-11. Commandant 15-4-11 to 28-2-17 and Lieutenant-Colonel 8-7-10 Colonel, 3-6-15. Appointed Recruiting Officer, Bengal, 9-4-17 and Inspector of Depots, Lucknow District, 14-4-18. Appointed Brigadier General (temporary) 14-4-18. Served with the Afghan Field Force 1919 as Red Cross Comissioner, Subsequently Brigade Commander, Amballa Brigade till 15-9-19. Retired with the Honorary rank of Brigadier-General 31-1-21. East African medal with clasp, Indian General Service medal with clasp, Delhi Durbar medal.
56. Griffin, Cecil Pender Griffiths.	4-12-87	Squadron Officer	First Commissioned 5-2-85 Transferred to the 1st B.L. 1-5-90. Subsequently commanded the Aden Troop. Served in Tirah 1897-98, China 1900. Relief of Pekin and actions of Piet Sang and Yaungtsun. Mentioned in despatches. Companion of the Distinguished Service Order. Indian General Service medal with two clasps, China medal with clasp.
57. Clark, William Ronaldson.	5-4-88	Officiating Medical Officer.	First Commissioned 31-3-87 Indian Medical Service. Transferred 19-12-89.
58. Peacock, Henry Barnes.	9-5-88	Squadron Officer	First Commissioned 13-10-86 in the 7th Hussars and transferred to the regiment. Subsequently transferred to the Political Department.
59. Holland-Pryor, Pomeroy.	14-1-91	Squadron Officer	First Commissioned in the 3rd Dragoon Guards 16-11 87. Appointed to the regiment on transfer to the Indian Army,

Name.	Date of joinign the Regiment.	Regimental appointments.	Particulars of Services etc.
60. Wall, Edward Watkin.	16-1-91	Squadron Officer.	14-1-91. Appointed Transport Officer in Sind in 1892 and in 1893 appointed to the 13th B.L. Held the appointments of D.A.A.G. (1899), A.A.G. and Assistant Military Governor, Orange Free State, 1900, and Commandant of the Kimberly Column 1901 during the South African War. Recruiting Staff Officer, Army Headquarters, India, 1903, D.A.A G. and A M.S., Northern Army, 1906. Charge of H. M's Indian Orderly Officers 1909. A.A.G. (offg.) Army Headquarters 1911. Transferred to the 1st D.Y.O. Lancers as Second-in-Command 1912 and became Commandant of that unit 1914. G O.C. of 6th Cavalry Brigade and Cavalry Division (Mesopotamia), 1917. G.O C., 14th Infantry Division (Mesopotamia), 1918. G.O.C, Cavalry Brigade, Bolarum 1919. G.O.C., 10th Cavalry Brigade, Afghanistan, 1919. G O.C., 1st Cavalry Brigade, Risalpur, 1919. D A. & Q.M.G. Southern Command, India, 1922. G.O.C, Poona District, 1925. Served in Waziristan (1894). North West Frontier 1897. Tirah Expedition, 1897-98. South Africa, 1899-02. Great War, 1914—18. Afghanistan, 1919. Medals—Indian General Service medal 1886, Indian General Service medal, 1897, Queen's South African medal King's South African medal; Indian General Service medal 1919; Queen's Jubilee medal; Delhi Durbar medal. Companion of the Bath. Companion of St. Michael and St. George. Companion of the Distinguished Service Order. Member of the Victorian Order. Major-General 28-1-21. K.C. B. (1926) on retirement. First Commissioned in the Devonshire Regiment 30-1-86

291

Name.	Date of joining the Regiment.	Regimental appointments.	Particulars of Services, etc.
		Squadron Commander. Second-in-Command.	Transferred to the 11th (P.W.O) Lancers 22-9-89 and to the 17th Bengal Cavalry 9-3-91. Promoted Captain 30-1-97. Major, 30-1-04, Lieutenant-Colonel 30-1-12. Colonel, 4-6-17. Transferred to Skinner's Horse and appointed Commandant, 12-8-13. Served in France November 1914 to August 1916 (three times mentioned in despatches). Indian Frontier, 1917. Bushire Field Force September 1918 to June 1919 (Base Commandant, Bushire, mentioned in despatches). Companion of the Order of Saint Michael and Saint George (4-6-17). 1914-15 Star, British War medal, Victory medal and Delhi Durbar medal. Retired July 1920.
61. Hudson, Arthur Keith.	15-4-91	Squadron Officer. Squadron Commander (substantive pro tem).	First Commissioned in the Connaught Rangers, 9-11-89 and transferred to Indian Staff Corps. Captain, 9-11-00. Placed on Half Pay 21-9-06. Died in 1922.
62. Cassidy, Christopher Clements.	15-9-91	Officiating Medical Officer.	First Commissioned, 31-1-91. Indian Medical Service. Died of wounds received in the Maizar Outrage in Waziristan 1897.
63. Wikeley, James Masson.	1-6-92	Squadron Officer. 10th Adjutant 1895-98. Squadron Commander. Second-in-Command.	First Commissioned in the Royal Warwickshire Regiment 5-2-87. Transferred to the 10th B.L. and from there to the regiment. Appointed Recruiting Officer for Punjab Mohamedans in 1910. Subsequently rejoined the regiment in 1914 as Second-in Command Transferred to the 28th Light Cavalry as Commandant and retired in 1920. Served on the N.-E. F. Chin Lushai Hills, 1889-90 ; Tirah, 1897-98. (Orderly Officer to G. O. C.) Actions of Sanpagha and Arhanga Passes, Reconnaisance of Karwa Defile, Action of 7-11-97.

Name.	Date of joining the Regiment.	Regimental appointment.	Particulars of Services etc.
			Reconnaisance of Saran Sar and action of 9-11-97. Operations against Khani Khel Chaw Kanins. Operations in Bazar Valley. Great War, 1914-21. Operations in Baluchistan and Persia. Two Indian General Service medals—one with one clasp, the other with two. British War medal, Victory medal.
64. Marshall, Daniel Grove.	31-8-92	24th Medical Officer	First Commissioned, 31-.3-88 Indian Medical Service Appointed to succeed Surgeon-Major Griffiths. Retired 23-3-05. Died in Scotland. Served on the N.-W. Frontier 1897-98. Operation in Tochi Valley and in China 1900. Indian General Service medal with clasp, China Medal with clasp.
65. Macleod, John Norman.	4-12-93	Officiating Medical Officer.	Indian Medical Service attached. Transferred 4-12-94.
66. Warre-Cornish, Francis Thackery.	16-11-95	Squadron Officer 11th Adjutant 5-2-98 to 20-10-01.	First Commissioned in the Somerset Light Infantry and transferred to the Indian Staff Corps. Winner of the Kadir Cup 1901 and the Bengal Cavalry Steeple Chase. Died at at Rawalpindi 20-10-01.
67. Henderson, Robert Wynne.	12-1-96	Squadron Officer 12th Adjutant 10-2-02 to 7-4-02. Squadron Commander.	First Commissioned, 10-10-94 in Indian Unattached List and appointed to the regiment, appointed to the 28th Light as Commandant in February 5th 1920. Promoted Colonel on 3-6-23. Retired on 4-8-24. Served in Chitral 1899 Relief of Chitral N. W. Frontier of India, 1897-98, Samana Kurram Valley and Buner. Tirah 1897-98. South African War 1902—Transvaal. Tibet 1903-4. The War of 1914-21, Egyptian Expeditionary Force 3-12-16 to 31-10-13 Brevet of Lieutenant-Colonel. Twice mentioned in despatches. Indian Frontier medal 1890-4 clasps

Name.	Date of joining the Regiment.	Regimental appointment.	Particulars of Services etc.
			Queen's South African War medal—2 clasps. Tibet medal—clasp British War medal. Victory medal. Companion of the Distinguished Service Order.
68. Cowper, Maitland	23-5-98	Officiating Second-in-Command. Officiating Commandant.	Attached temporarily to the regiment from the 10th Bengal Lancers. Officiated as Commandant. Second in Command and Squadron Commander from 29th May 1896 to 11th May 1897. Then held the rank Captain. Subsequently Commanded the 10th Lancers (Hodson's Horse) 1901 and is now Colonel of Hodson's Horse. Retired as a Major-General. War Services.—Chitral Relief Force 1895. War of 1914-21. D. A. and Q. M. G. to Force (Mesopotamia) Oct. 1915 to Sept. 1916. Companion Order of the Bath. Companion Order of the Indian Empire. India Frontier medal 1895 with clasp, Relief of Chitral. 1914-15. Star Victory medal with Palms. British War medal 1914-15. Medal, Delhi Durbar, 1903. Medal, Dehli Durbar 1911. Second class order of the White Eagle of Servia.
69. Granger, Thomas Arthur.	30-5-96	Officiating Medical Officer.	Attached, Indian Medical Service, and later transferred. Retired 1-8-22.
70. Whitchurch, Harry Frederick.	12-1-97	Officiating Medical Officer.	Attached Indian Medical Service, transferred to 1st Gurkhas, July 1897. Victoria Cross. Died 16-8-07.
71. Steel, Richard Alexander.	18-7-97	Squadron Officer. Squadron Commander.	First Commissioned, 5-10-92 in the 7th Dragoon Guards, subsequently transferred to the 87th Royal Irish Fusiliers and then to the Indian Staff Corps. Was first sent to a Bombay Infantry Battalion and subsequently in 1897 to the 13th Bengal Lancers and finally posted to the

Name.	Date of joining the Regiment.	Regimental appointment.	Particulars of Services etc.
			regiment. Was A.-D.-C. to Lord Curzon when Viceroy in 1899. Went to China as A.-D.-C. to the G. O. C. of the British Force. Passed the Staff College Camberly in 1904 and afterwards went to Japan to study the language. Passed as an Interpreter in Japanese and was attached to the Japanese Cavalry. Subsequently served as an unpaid instructor at the Cavalry School. From there was appointed to the Staff of H. I. H. the German Crown Prince during his tour in India. Appointed Military Attaché in Persia in 1913. Served as G S.O.I with Indian Corps in France 1914-15 and subsequently at the War Office London during 1916-1920 Served on N. W. Frontier of India 1897-98 (Mohmand); China, 1900; (Peitsong Youngstun) mentioned in despatches. War of 1914-21, mentioned in despatches, 17-2-15. Brevets of Lieut.-Colonel and Colonel. Belgian Order of the Crown 4th class. French Legion of Honour, 5th class. Japanese Order of the Rising Sun, 3rd class. Italian Order of St. Maurice and St. Lazarus, 4th Class. Russian Order of St. Stanislans, 2nd class. Servian Order of the White Eagle (with swords) 3rd class, Companion of the Order of St. Michael and St. George. Companion of the Order of the Indian Empire. German Red Eagle 2nd class for service with German Crown Prince. Indian Frontier medal 1895. 1 clasp. China medal, clasp Delhi Durbar medal (1911). Retired in 1921 as a Colonel.
72. Woodright, William Henry Edward.	28-8-97	Officiating Medical Officer.	Attached Indian Medical Service, subsequently transferred.

Name.	Date of joining the Regiment.	Regimental appointments.	Particulars of Services etc.
73. Ferris, John Tate	1-15-98	Squadron Officer	First Commissioned on 1-10-87 in the 5th Dragoon Guards. Transferred to the Central India Horse, March 1898 Died, 22nd August 1898.
74. Barry-Smith, Raymond Cope.	1-15-98	Squadron Officer. 13th Adjutant 7-4-02 to 7-4-06. Squadron Commander. 2nd in Command. 10th Commandant 17-6-17 till amalgamation with the 37th Lancers.	Commissioned in the Gloucestershire Regiment and transferred to the Indian Staff Corps, 8-7-98 Commanded the Service Squadron of the regiment in East Africa. Temporary Commandant 1-2-17 to 16-6-17. Commandant 17-6-17 to 16-6-22. Transferred the 15th Lancers on amalgamation as the First Commandant of that Unit. War of 1914—21. 1914—15 Star, British War medal. Victory medal. Mentioned in despatches 8-2-17. Waziristan, 1921. Indian General Service medal with clasp. Retired, 3-12-22.
75. Atkinson, Francis. Garnett.	1-10-98	Second in Command. 7th Commandant. 13-4-1902 to 15-8-1906.	First Commissioned on 1-9-76 in the Royal Marines. Transferred to the Indian Staff corps and appointed to the 13th Bengal Lancers. Transferred to the regiment as Second-in-Command on 12-4-02. Appointed to Command the Banglore Cavalry Brigade 16-8-06. Retired as a Brigadier General. Served in Egypt, 1882; Kassassin and Tel-el-Kabir. North-West Frontier of India, 1897—98; (Shabkadar)—mentioned in despatches; (Mohmand)—Brevet of Lieut.-Colonel. War 1914-21. Specially Employed. Egyptian medal and Bronze Star; Indian Frontier medal 1895 Companion of the Order of the Bath.
76. Stephenson, John	15-2-98	Officiating Medical Officer.	Indian Medical Service. Attached.
77. Hayward. William Davey.	23-1-99	Officiating Medical Officer.	Indian Medical Service Attached.

Name.	Date of joining the Regiment.	Regimental appointments.	Particulars of Services etc.
78. Shakespear, William Henry Irvine.	21-3-99	Squadron Officer. Quarter Master.	Indian Unattached List, Quarter Master, 23-10-02. Transferred to the Indian Political Department, 2-1-04. Promoted Captain 22-1-07. Traversed Arabia from Roweit to Suez in 1914. Awarded the Companion-ship of the order of the Indian Empire on 1-1-15. Killed in a tribal battle on 24-1-15, near Majama, Central Arabia.
79 Harvey, William Frederiak.	17-11-99	Officiating Medical Officer.	Indian Medical Service, Attached. Trnsferred to Civil Employ Afterwards Head of the Pasteur Institute Kasauli and subsequently Head of the Bacteriological (Research) Institute Kasauli. Companion of the order of the Indian Empire, M.B.
80. Bailey, Frederik Marhmau.	26-10-01	Squadron Officer.	Indian Unattached List, transfered to the 32nd Pioneer, January 1903 and subsequently to the Political Department. Served in Tibet, 1904; Abor Expedition 1911; Flanders, Gallipoli N.-W. Frontier, Mesopotamia and Russian Turkestan, 1914-18; Afghan War 1919. Tibet medal, Indian General Service medal two-clasps. 1914—15 Star, British War Medal, Victory medal Companion of the Order of the Indian Empire.
81. Hewitt, Dudley Raisford.	1-5-02	Squadron Officer.	First Commissioned in the East Lancashire Regiment from the ranks of the Tasmanian Bushmen on 19-5-00. Transferred to the Indian Army and appointed to the regiment; subsequently transferred to the Remount department. Queen's South African medal with three clasps 1914—15 Star. British War medal, Victory medal.

Name.	Date of joining the Regiment.	Regimental appointments.	Particulars of Services etc.
82. Wilson, Denis Daly	29-7-02	Squadron Officer. 14th Adjutant 8-4-06 to 7-4-09. Squadron Commander.	First Commissioned in York and Lancashire Regiment and served with it the operations round Ladysmith and Spion Kop, also in the operations in Natal and Transval 1899—1901. Transferred to Indian Army in 1902, Adjutant April 1906 to April 1909. Squadron Commander, 10-10-1913. Proceeded to Staff College Camberly December 1913. Appointed to the General Staff 46th Division on outbreak of War and served with it in France. Subsequently appointed in March 1916 to command the 5th Battalion Sherwood Foresters and was killed in action at Gommecourt at the Somme on July 1st 1916. Twice mentioned in despatches. Queen's South African medal with seven clasps. 1914 Star. British War Medal. Victory Medal and the Military Cross.
83. Vincent-Watson, Arthur Henry.	13-11-02	Squadron Officer	First Commissioned 20-1-00. Transferred to the 2nd Punjab Cavalry, June 1903. Resigned 21-8-06.
84. Barnes, J. A.	5-12-02	Officiating Medical Officer.	Indian Medical Service Attached. Left 10th October 1903.
85. Young, Thomas Charles Mac-Combie.	10-4-03	Officiating Medical Officer.	Indian Medical Service, Attached, October 1905. Transferred to Civil Medical Department Director of Public Health, Assam 1924, since reverted to Military Employ.
86 Dodd, Arthur Harvey Russell.	19-1-04	Squadron Officer Quarter-Master 15th Adjutant 8-4-1909—1913. Squadron Commander.	First Commissioned in the Indian Unattached List, and posted to the regiment. After vacating the appointment of Adjutant was appointed Station Staff Officer, Meerut. Subsequently became Brigade Major, Meerut Cavalry Brigade. Proceeded to Mesopotamia in 1917

Name.	Date of joining of Regiment.	Regimental appointments.	Particulars of Services etc.
			with the "Dunster Force." Subsequently served on the Head quarters Staff of the Mesopotamian Expeditionry Force as General Staff Officer Second grade, as D. A. A. and Q. M. G Cavalry Division, D. A. A. and Q. M. G., and A. A. and Q. M. G. Persian Force. Was mentioned four times in despatches and given Brevet of Lieutenant-Colonel. Subsequently nominated to Staff College Quetta, and on completion of course transferred to the 3rd Q.A. O., Gurkha Rifles Subsequently General Staff Officer Second Grade at Karachi and at Army Head Quarters. British War medal, Victory medal, Delhi Durbar medal.
87. Sumner Fred. William.	23-3-05	5th Medical Officer.	Indian Medical Service. Appointed as fifth Medical Officer of the regiment on the retirement of Major Marshall. Posted in April 1909 to United Provinces as Civil Surgeon. In September 1914 proceeded with East African Expeditionary Force and served with it in various appointments till invalided in 1918. While in England held the appointment of Consulting Surgeon First Southern General Hospital (Birmingham). Proceeded on Field Service to the Third Afghan War in 1919. Reverted to Civil employ in December 1919. Proceeded on leave pending retirement in March 1925. 1914-15 Star, British War medal. Victory medal. Indian General Service medal with Clasp F.R C.S.(E).
88 Kirkwood, Thomas William.	1-3-04	Squadron Officer Quartermaster. Squadron Commander (Temporary.)	First Commissioned in the Unattached List and posted to the regiment. Proceeded to Russia in 1914 to study the language. Served with the Cavalry Corps in France and

Name.	Date of joining the Regiment.	Regimental appointments.	Particulars of Services etc.
			subsequently returned to India in 1915 and was appointed Commandant, Marine Lines Drafts, Camp, Bombay. Subsequently rejoined the regiment and proceeded to Siberia in 1918 with the Knox Mission with Admiral Kolchak. Retired in 1921. Mentioned in despatches 1914 Star, British War medal, Victory medal, Officer of the Order of the British Empire. Delhi Durbar medal. Order of the Rising Sun of Japan.
89. Barge, Kenneth	1-1-05	Squadron Officer. Squadron Commander-(temporary). Second-in Command (temporary).	Commissioned 9-9-03 in the Cameronians. Had previously served in 3rd Argyll and Sutherland Highlanders (Militia) from 14-12-01 to 8-9-03. Served with them in the South African War 31-1-02 to 23-9-02. Transferred to the Indian Army 6-1-05. A.-D.-C. to G. O. C. Northren Army (India) 5-3-10 to 6-10-13 A.-D.-C. to H. E. the Commander-in-Chief (India) 4-12-10 to 27-5-12. Adjutant and officiating Adjutant, Imperial Cadet Corps 1-3-13 to 15-9-14. Served in France, 29-1-15 to 7-12-17. Commanded a Signal Troop. Was G. S. O. (III), Brigade. Major and G. S. O. (II) Attached to the War Office 1-1-18 to 22-5-18. G. S. O. (I.) Liaison Officer between War Office and the Balkans 23-5-18 to 17-1-20. Mentioned in despatches. Proceeded to Staff College, Camberly 15-12-20. Retired 5-1-22 with the rank of Lieutenant-Colonel on account of sudden and unexpected death of his elder brother. Queen's South African medal with two clasps. 19-14-15 Star, British War medal, Victory medal. Military Cross. Distinguished Service Order. White Eagle of Servia with Swords. The Delhi Durbar medal.

Name.	Date of joining the Regimental	Regimental appointments.	Particulars of Services etc.
90. Stewart, Harold Souther.	2-8-06	Squadron Officer. Squadron Commander. Second-in-Command (temporary.) Commandant (temporary).	Commissioned in the Royal Field Artillery, May 23rd, 1900. Lieutenant Royal Field Artillery. Served in the 71st and 11th Batteries R. F. A. Transferred to the Indian Army, September 1906. Squadron Commander, December 15th, 1913. Served in France 1914-15 and in East Africa 1915-17. Brigade Major, Jhansi Brigade March to August 1917. Appointed Second-in-Command (temporary) September 1917. Commandant (temporary) July 1st to December 24th, 1919. Served in the Punjab Disturbances 1919 and in Afghan War, 1919. Served in Waziristan Field Force, 1920 and again in 1921. Member of the Silladar Cavalry Conversion Committee, 1st April 1921 till disolved finally at Aden in March 1924. Transferred to the 16th Lancers on amalgamation in 1922 but never joined, being appointed at first, General Staff Officer, and subsequently Deputy Assistant Director, Auxiliary and Territorial Forces of the Presidency and Assam District. Transferred to 15th Punjab Regiment. Promoted Lieut.-Colonel 1914-15 Star, British War medal, Victory medal, Indian General Service medal with clasps for the Afghan War and Waziristan. Appointed Commandant 2nd/15th Punjab Regiment.
91 Yeats-Brown, Francis Charles Claypon.	31-12-00	Squadron Officer. 16th Adjutant, 1913-1917. Squadron Commander (temporary).	First Commissioned in Indian Unattached List, 5-8-05. War of 1914-21. Served in France with the Indian Cavalry Corps, subsequently proceeded to Mesopotamia with Royal Flying Corps. Twice mentioned in despatches. Waziristan, 1921. Transferred to the 15th Lancers on amalgamation.

Name.	Date of joining the Regiment.	Regimental appointments.	Particulars of Services etc.
92. Wilcox, Lionel Harold.	27-2-08	Squadron Officer	Distinguish Flying Cross. Retired 1924. 1914 Star, British War medal, Victory medal, Indian General Service medal. Retired in the rank of Major 1924. First Commissioned in the A. S. C. subsequently transferred to the 17th Infantry, 8-10-09.
93. Atkinson, Eric Garnet.	26-8-08	Squadron Officer Squadron Commander (temporary). Second-in-Command (temporary). Commandant (temporary).	Son of Brigadier-General F. G. Atkinson. First Commissioned in Indian Unattached List. Served with the West Yorkshire Regiment. A. D. C. to the Governor of Madras 1912-13. Served in France from 23-8-14 to 14-3-18. Attached 15th Hussars, 5th Lancers, 36th Jacobs Horse and Cavalry Signals. On return to India acted as Squadron Commander, Second-in-Command, and Commandant of the regiment and was given acting rank of Lieutenant-Colonel in 1918. Commanded the Service Squadron of the 17th Cavalry in the Third Afghan War. Transferred to the 15th Lancers on amalgamation and appointed Commandant of the Viceroy's Body Guard. Mentioned in despatches for Services in France, Afghanistan and Waziristan. 1914 Star, British War medal, Victory medal, Indian General Service medal with two clasps and King George's Coronation medal. A member of the British Polo team sent to America in 1924.
94. Phipson, Edward Selby.	..	Officiating Medical Officer.	Indian Medical Service Attached. Subsequently transferred. Port Officer, Aden, 1923. Distinguished Service Order.
95. Brierly, Wilfred Edward.	14-5-09	6th Medical Officer.	Indian Medical Srvice. Appointed Medical Officer of the regiment on the posting of Captain F. W. Sumner to

Name.	Date of joining the Regiment.	Regimental appointments.	Particulars of Services etc.
			Civil employ. Served in France with the Indian Cavalry Division (3rd Skinner's Horse) 1914-16, in East Africa 1916 and in Waziristan 1919-21. Held the temporary rank of Liutenant-Colonel 1-4-20 to 2-2-22. Left the regiment in December 1918 when Regimental Medical Officers were abolished. 1914-15 Star, British War medal, Victory medal Indian General Service medal and Delhi Durbar Medal. Bachelor of Medicine. Fellow of the Royal College of Surgeons.
96. Foottit, James Augustus Warwick.	9-10-09	Squadron Officer. Adjutant, (Officiating.) Squadron Commander (temporary).	First Commissioned 1-12-07 in the Prince of Wales' West Yorkshire Regiment. Transferred to the Indian and posted to the regiment. Appointed officiating Adjutant of the regiment, vice Yeats-Brown (on service) and served as such from 1914-1917. Served with Mesopotamian Expeditionary Force 1917. Was subsequently appointed Staff Officer to the Inspector of Infantry in India, subsequently officiated in other appointments and transferred to the 15th Lancers on amalgamtion. In 1922 was made a Military Advisor to the Indian State Forces in Hyderabad and Mysore and subsequently in the Central India States Force. Finally made Chief Commandant Mysore State Forces, 1924.
97. Duberley, Vernon Conrad	0-6-10	Squadron Officer.	First Commissioned in the Royal Field Artillery. Transferred to the 17th Cavalry. Accompanied the special Service Squadron to East Africa. Killed in action in East Africa 1916 with the 17th Cavalry Service Squadron.

Name	Date of joining the Regiment	Regimental appointment.	Particulars of Services etc.
98. Skipwith, Charles Grey Yule.	3-1-11	Squadron Officer 17th Adjutant 14-3-19 to 16-9-20 Second-sn-Command (temporary.)	First Commissioned in the Indian Army Unattached List. 8-9-09. Served with the West Yorkshire regiment Posted to the 17th Cavalry Served in France with the 3rd Signal Squadron R. E. 7-9-14 to 29-5-15. Twice mentioned in despatches, Returned to India and subsequently became Adjutant. 1914 Star. British War medal, Victory medal Delhi Darbar medal. Retired in 1920 as a Captain.
99. Lee, Alfred John.	8-5-11	Officiating Medical Officer.	Indian Medical Service Attached for a short time only.
100. Guthrie, Ivan Douglas.	8-10-11	Squadron Officer. Squadron Commander (temporary).	Transferred to the regiment from the Royal Scots to which he was gazetted, 27-5-08. Proceeded to France in charge of the Lucknow Cavalry Brigade Amunition Column. Held appointments as General Staff Officer, 3rd grade, 46th Division and as Brigade-Major, 36th Brigade in the 12th Division. Returned to India in July 1917 and subsequently was attached as Second-in-Command to the 2-25th Punjabis. Awarded Military Cross. 1914-15 Star, British War medal, and Victory medal. Transferred to the Inniskilling Dragoons and subsequently to the 10th Royal Hussars.
101. Barnet, James William.	2-11-12	Officiating Medical Officer.	Indian Medal Service, Attached. Commissioned Feb. 1908. Captain Feb. 1911. Major Feb. 1920. Served in Somaliland 1908-10. France, Mesopotamia and Aden Field Force, 1914-18. East African General Service medal, 1914 Star, British War medal and Victory medal. M.B. Ch.B.
102. Kamat, Dwarkanath Dhamaji.	25-1-13	Officiating Medical Officer.	Indian Medical Service, Attached.

Name.	Date of joining the Regiment.	Regimental appoinments.	Particulars of Services, etc.
103. Cochrane, Richmond Pelham Inglis.	28-10-13	Squadron Officer. 18th Adjutant. 1920-21.	Indian Unattached List. Served with Highland Light Infantry and 8th Hussars. Proceeded to Mesopotamia with 12th Cavalry subsequently served with the Royal Flying Corps. Rejoined the regiment at the end of the War and made Adjutant. 1914-15 Star, British War medal, Victory medal. Transferred to the 15th Lancers on amalgamation. Retired in 1923 as a Captain.
104. Mawdsey, Barton James Platt.	16-3-14	Squadron Officer.	First Commissioned in the Indian Unattached List 22-1-13. Promoted Lieutenant 22-4-15. 1914-15 Star, British War medal, Victory medal. Accompanied the service squadron to East Africa. Killed in action in East Africa in 1916 with the the 17th Cavalry on 6-2-16.
105. Gow, Peter Fleming.	..	Officiating Medical Officer.	Indian Medical Service, Attached for a short time, Companion of the Distinguished Service Order.

ATTACHED OFFICERS.

Appointed subsequently to August 4th 1914.

No.	Name.	Date of joining the Regiment.	Particulars of Services etc.
106	Robertson, Frederick Ewart.	4-12-14	First Commissioned in the Indian Army Reserve of Officers. Appointed from the East Indian Railway Volunteer Rifle Corps. Demobilized with the rank of Captain at the end of the War. Now Chief operating Superintendent of the E. I R. Volunteer Officers' Decoration, 1914-15 Star, British War medal, Victory medal. Served with Indian Cavalry Corps in France.
107*	Henderson, Walter Lewis.	24-12-14	First Commissioned on 4-12-14 in the Indian Army Reserve of Officers. Was a Captain in the Indian Volunteers, and was commissioned as a Lieutenant. Proceeded to France to join the 15th Lancers, 23-5-15. Served in France 1915, Mesopotamia 1916; Persia and Persian Gulf 1916-19; Military Cross 3-6-19 1914-15 Star; British War medal and Victory medal Resigned 1-9-20.
108	Ashe, Wellesley St. George.	29-12-14	First Commissioned in the Indian Army Reserve of Officers, 4-12-14. Transferred to the Indian Cavalry Corps France in 1915. Resigned 22-11-17. Queen's South African War Medal; 1914-15 Star; British War Medal; Victory Medal. Formerly a planter in Assam.
109	Whitaker, Basil	30-12-14	First Commissioned in the Indian Army Reserve of Officers 4-12-14. Formerly a planter in Assam and in the Dutch East Indies. Proceeded to Mesopotamia as a reinforcement but subsequently rejoined the regiment in India. Later Commanded a Silladar Camel corps and served in Waziristan. Demobilized as a Captain at the end of the War. British War medal, Victory medal. Indian General Service medal.
110	Floyer, Earnest Ayscoghe.	2-3-15	First Commissioned in the Indian Army Reserve of Officers. Formerly a planter in Assam. A nephew of Colonel Watson (3rd Commandant) and cousin of Capt. F. T. Warre-Cornish. Served in the Abor Expedition as a member of a Machine Gun detachment supplied by the Assam Valley Light Horse. Transferred to the Egyptian Expeditionary

No.	Name.	Date of joining the Regiment.	Particulars of Services, etc.
			Force as a reinforcement. Served with the Patiala Lancers and with Royal Flying Corps. Was shot down and taken prisoner by the Turks 5-3-07, mentioned in despatches. Relinquished commission as a Captain on 1-5-22. Indian General Service medal. 1914—15 Star. British War medal, Victory medal, Military Cross.
111	Watson, Harold Reginald West.	19-1-15	First Commissioned in the Indian Army Reserve of Officers. Had previously been in the Bombay Light Horse. Transferred to the 18th King George's own Lancers, 18-5-1915. Served in France and Palestine. Mentioned in despatches September 1918. 1914-15 Star, British War medal, Victory medal, Volunteers Officers' Decoration, Territorial Long Service medal. Demobilized at the end of the war with the rank of Captain.
112	Abercrombie, John Robertson.	27-2-15	First Commissioned in the Indian Army Reserve of Officers on 17-2-15. Transferred to the 18th King George's Own Lancers, April 1916. Served in France till March 1918 and in Palestine from March 1918 to February 1919. Awarded the Military Cross as an immediate award for operations in Palestine, September 1918. Mentioned in F. M. Sir Douglas Haig's despatches for the Cambray Operations, November and December 1917. British War medal, Victory medal. Demobilized at the end of the War with the rank of Captain.
113	Anstey, Alec, C.	15-3-15	A settler in East Africa, and a Lieutenant in the East Africa Formerly in the Westminister Dragoons Mounted Rifles, attended to the Service Squadron of the 17th Cavalry in East Africa, subsequently rejoined his own unit.
114	Puckle, George Hole.	28-4-15	First Commissioned in the Indian Army Reserve of Officers. A member of the Indian Police. Transferred to the 36th Jacob's Horse.
115	Knox, James Hay Graham	8-8-15	Joined up on the outbreak of War and proceeded to East Africa. First Commissioned in the Indian Army Reserve of Officers, 7-8-15. Joined the Service Squadron of the 17th Cavalry in East

No.	Name.	Date of joining the Regiment.	Particulars of Services, etc.
			Africa on being Commissioned. Returned with the squadron to India and joined the regiment. Subsequently transferred to 35th Scinde Horse and given a regular Commission in the Indian Army. Appointed to 35th Scinde Horse and served in the Arab Rebellion in Mesopotamia. Awarded the Military Cross, 1914-15 Star, British War medal, Victory medal and General Service medal. Retired on the reduction of Indian Army, 29-6-22.
116	Baradawaja, Davendra.	19-5-15	Temporarily attached in Medical charge. Subsequently transferred. A Temporary Officer in the I. M. S.
117	Ibbotson, Archie William.	17-5-15	First Commissioned in the Indian Army Reserve of Officers. A member of the Indian Civil Service. Served with the Service Squadron of the 17th Cavalry in East Africa and returned to India with the Service Squadron. Acted as Adjutant 17th Cavalry for a short period. Transferred to the 18th Lancers in April 1917. Subsequently held several third grade staff appointments and was Staff Captain to the Force in Turkistan 1918-19. Demobilised as Captain 24-6-1919. British War medal, Victory medal, General Service medal, Military Cross. Military Member of Order of the British Empire.
118	Vickers, Hugh Gordon Muschamp.	5-7-15	First Commissioned in the Indian Army Reserve Officers, 18-6-15. A member of the Indian Civil Service Transferred to 16th Cavalry 27-9-15. Killed in action in Mesopotamia, 30-10-18.
119	Sarkar, Sureswar.	30-8-15	Indian Medical Service. Temporarily attaches in medical charge. Subsequently transferred.
120	Brock, George Selby.	12-11-15	Indian Medical Service. Temporarily attached in medical charge. Susequently transferred. Died 7-10-18.
121	Blakiston, John Francis.	11-12-15	First Commissioned in the Indian Army Reserve of Officers. Transferred to the C.I.H. 2-10-16 and shortly afterwards proceeded to France as a re-inforcement. Returned to India on 21-3-18 and acted as Adjutant C.I.H. Depot about eight months. Demobilized as a Captain about the beginning of 1919. A member of the Indian Archæological Service.

No.	Name.	Date of joining the Regiment.	Particulars of Services, etc.
122	Slater, Duncan McLauchlan	0-2-15	11th Rajputs, attached to the Service Squadron of the 17th Cavalry in East Africa as Machine Gun Officer. Subsequently rejoined his own unit. 1914-15 Star. British War medal and Victory medal; Officer's Cross of the Legion of Honour. Transferred to 13th Frontier Force Rifles.
123	Kirkwood, John, Henry Morrison.	15-2-16	Formerly in the 4th Dragoon Guards, served with the Russian Cavalry in 1915 Special Service Officer, East African Force. Attached to the Service Squadron of the regiment for a short time and then went to France to join the Household Cavalry. Was a member of the House of Commons for some years.
124	Onraet, Pierre Trevor.	8-3-16	First Commissioned in the Indian Army Reserve of Officers, 19-2-16. Transferred to Mesopotamia in September 1916 and posted to 23rd Cavalry. Mentioned in Despatches in 1918. Returned with that unit to India and served with that unit through the Punjab Riots and Afghan War 1919. A Reserve Officer of the 11th P.A.V.O. Cavalry.
125	Knowles, Andrew Brooks.	10-3-16	First Commissioned in the Indian Army Reserve of Officers. A member of the Indian Civil Service. Was first posted to the Guides Cavalry. Was sent direct from that unit as a reinforcement to the Service Squadron of 17th Cavalry in East Africa. Killed in action at Mkalmo on 11-6-1916 after shewing great gallantry. British War medal and Victory medal.
126	Cazalet, Robert George.	10-3-16	First Commissioned in the Indian Army Reserve of Officers. Commanded the 17th Cavalry Remount Squadron in Mesopotamia from November 1916 to September 1919. Twice mentioned in Despatches. Promoted Captain 2-10-17 and Demobilized in that rank 9-9-19. Returned to his former post on the Jodhpur State Railway. British War medal and Victory medal.
127	Pont, Leon Victor.	4-4-16	First Commissioned in the Indian Army Reserve of Officers, 20-2-16 from the ranks of the Indian Volunteers. An officer of the Eastern Bengal Railway (Signal Department) who had served nine years in the Yeomanry and Volun-

No.	Name.	Date of joining the Regiment.	Particulars of Services, etc.
			teers. Transferred to 36th Jacob's Hors in May 1916. Subsequently served in Mesopotamia with the Railway Service. Promoted Captain 20-2-20. Relinquished Commission 1-5-22. British War medal and Victory medal.
128	Small, Gerald Agnew.	8-3-16	First Commissioned in the Indian Army Reserve of Officers. A member of the Indian Educational Service. Transferred as Assistant Recruiting Officer, Lucknow, September 1917. Subsequently made O. C. of the 4th Meerut Cavalry Brigade Signal Troop, January 1918. Demobilized on 26-6-20 as a Captain.
129	Hallowes, John Hope.	10-5-16	Major 15th Lancers (Cureton's Multanis) attached for temporary duty. Rejoined his own Unit, September 1917. Served in France and Mesopotamia. Subsequently served with the 41st Cavalry. Retired as a Lieutenant-Colonel 1914-15 Star, British War medal, Victory medal.
130	Atkinson, George Prestage.	5-7-16	First Commissioned, 20-4 1910 in the Loyal Regiment (North Lancashire). Had previously served in the ranks of 1st Bnl. Gordon Highlanders 2 years 186 days.. Eldest son of Brigadier-General F. A. Atkinson and elder brother of Major-E. G. Atkinson. Attached to the Service Squadron of the 17th Cavalry in East Africa. Had previously commanded a Mounted Infantry company who gradually disappeared in the course of the operations—Served in East Africa 18-12-14 to 24-2-17 Palestine 13-5-17 to 18-5-18 ; France 27-5-18 to the end of the War. Took part in a great number of actions on all fronts and was four times mentioned in despatches and was given Brevet of Major. Companion of the Distingnished Service Order, Military Cross, French War Cross with Palm, 1914-15 Star, British War medal, Victory medal. Serving with 2nd Battation of the Loyal Regiment 1926).
131	Wallace, Alexander Ross.	16-8-16	First Commissioned in the Indian Army Reserve of Officers. A member of the Indian Civil Service. Served as Quartermaster and Adjutant of the regiment. Transferred as Special Service Officer to the Patila Lancers, August 1918. Demobilized at the end of the War.

No.	Name.	Date of joining the Regiment.	Particulars of Service etc.
			British War medal and Victory medal. Took a proportionate pension from the I C.S. and is now Head-master of Cargilfield School, Midlothian, Scotland.
132	Clark, Robert Napier.	Did not join.	First Commissioned in the Indian Army Reserve of Officers 18-8-16 and brought on the list of the regiment on being commissioned. Was immediately appointed Railway Transport Officer, Karachi. Promoted 18-8-17. His name was subsequently removed from the list of the regiment. Relinquished his commission 1-5-22.
133	Cones, Herbert Alfred Michael.	21-8-16	First Commissioned in the Indian Army Reserve of Officers. A member of the Indian Police to which he was appointed 7-12-08. Posted to the C.I.D., Allahabad, 1-7-14. Commissioned in I.A.R.O, 1-8-16. Captain (tempy.) 1-8-16. Major (tempy.), 1-4-20. Demobilized, 1-4-21 with rank of Major. Served in Mesopotamia 1-8-16 to 1-4-21. Held appointments of Commandant Police Bagdad, Deputy Inspector General of Police, Irak, and officiating Inspector General of Police, Irak. Served in the Arab Rebellion. (Mentioned in despatches). British War medal, Victory medal and General Service medal.
134	Pyne, Herbert Percy.	1-9-16	First Commissioned in the Indian Army Reserve of Officers, 21-8-16. Transferred as Assistant Cable Censor, Rangoon, in December 1916. Relinquished Commission 1-5-22.
135	Lloyd, Stanley..	23-9-16	First Commissioned in the Indian Army Reserve of Officers. Transferred to the 18th K. G. O. Lancers in 1918. Served in Palestine. Invalided to England in March 1919. Demobilized in November 1919. British War Medal and Victory Medal. A Tea-planter in Assam.
136	Ballentine, John Steventon.	19-1-17	First Commissioned in the Unattached List, Indian Army. Appointed 19th Adjutant, 17th Cavalry. Promoted Captain, 16-8-20. Transferred to the 15th Lancers on amalgamation and became the 1st Adjutant of the new regiment—Served with Aden Field Force 1916—17, Trans-Indus 1919, Waziristan 1921, British War medal, Victory medal and Indian General Service medal with clasps.

No.	Name.	Date of joining the Regiment.	Particulars of Services, etc.
137	Pert, Claude Ernest.	23-1-17	First Commissioned in the Indian Unattached List as Second Lieutenant, June 18th 1917, promoted Captain, June 18th, 1921. Served in Palestine with a Baluch Regiment and subsequently with the Imperial Service Cavalry. Rejoined the 17th Cavalry and was transferred to the 15th Lancers on amalgamation. Subsequently appointed Adjutant of the Governor of Bombay's Body Guard. British War medal and Victory medal.
138	Peck, Arthur Wharton.	Did not join	Appointed on 1-3-17 from the 25th Cavalry F. F as Commandant, to succeed Colonel Boudier, vacated the appointment 19-6-17, never having joined the regiment, remaining Seconded on Service Brevet Colonel and Brigadier General employed under the War Office, promoted Major-General. Retired 20-3-21. Companion of the Order of the Bath. Companion of the Order of St. Michael and St. George.
139	Thomson, John Lambert.	21-3-17	First Commissioned in Indian Army Reserve of Officers, 21-3-17. Transferred first to the Convalescent Section, Deesa and subsequently to Remounts. Relinquished Commission, 1-5-22.
140	Bowden, Cecil Charles Hooper.	..	Came to India with Territorial Artillery in August 1914. Given a Commission in the Indian Army Reserve of Officers, 21-3-17. Resigned his Commission to go to Cadet School, Quetta. Recommissioned in Indian Army Unattached List, 13-11-17. Appointed to the 38th Central India Horse. Attached to the Supply and Transport Corps. Promoted Captain, 31-8-21. Retired with gratuity, 4-1-23.
141	Elles, Frederick William Cesari.	..	Given a temporary Commission in the Indian Army from the ranks of the Royal Engineers Transferred to the Royal Flying Corps shortly afterward; released from Army Service, 12-2-19. Relinquished Commission, 1-9-21.
142	Tozer, Donald Charles Essery.	4-5-17	Arrived in India, 9-11-14 with the 1st & 3rd (Devon) Battery R. F. A. Was given a commission in the Indian Army Reserve of Officers, 23-4-17. Attached to the regiment and subsequently transferred to the 32nd Lancers, 25-8-17. Given a regular commission in Indian Army, 23-1-18. Promoted Captain, 4-1-23. Serv-

No.	Name.	Date of joining the Regiment.	Particulars of Services, etc
			ed in the operations in Mesopotamia 22-6-18, to 31-10-18; the operations Kurdistan and the Arab Rebellion, 1-11-18 to 3-3-21. Awarded the Military Cross. British War medal, Victory medal and General Service medal with two clasps.
143	Platts, John Carrick.	9-5-17	First Commissioned in the Suffolk Regiment, probationer for the Indian Army. Transferred to the 10th (D. C. O.) Lancers (Hodson's Horse), 8-11-17. Served in Mesopotamia with that regiment. Previously served in France with his own Unit. Promoted acting Captain, 17-9-18, Captain 25-6-19. Killed in action, 7-3-20. British War medal, Victory medal, General Service medal.
144	Carter, Arthur Charles.	10-6-16	First Commissioned in the Indian Army Reserve of Officers, 4th May 1917. Subsequently transfered to the 29th Horse. Relinquished Commission as a Captain, 1st May 1922.
145	Preston, Thomas	11-6-17	First Commissioned in the Indian Army Reserve of Officers 19-5-17. Transferred as Assistant Cable Censor, Rangoon, in September 1917. Relinquished Commission 1-5-19.
146	Campbell-Harris, Clifford	15-6-17	First Commissioned in the Royal Sussex Regiment, a probationer for the Indian Army. Proceeded on Service in Mesopotamia with the Guides Cavalry and the 11th K. E. O. Lancers, June 1918 to January 1921. Rejoined the regiment, April 1921. Transferred to the 7th Light Cavalry, October 1921. Promoted Captain, 16th June 1919. Served in France, February 1916 to March 1917; Mesopotamia, June 1918 to January 1921; Waziristan April 1921 to November 1924. British War medal, Victory medal, Indian General Service medal.
147	Ferguson, Stanley McEwan.	27-6-17	First Commissioned in the 10th Battalion Seaforth Highlanders, 1915. Served in France with the 8th Battalion Seaforth Highlanders, 1916-17. Appointed a probationer for Indian Army and posted to the regiment. Squadron Officer of 'D' Squadron. Died at Lahore on 15th September 1918. British War medal and Victory medal.

No.	Name.	Date of joining the Regiment.	Particulars of Services, etc.
148	Hutchison, James Riley Holt.	30-6-17	Captain Lanarkshire Yeomanry. Served with 19th Lancers Indian Army in France. Sent to India as a probationer for Indian Army and Attached to the 17th Cavalry, 30-6-17 Appointed to 17th Cavalry, June 1918 acted as 'B' Squadron Commander (temporary). Resigned the Service, March 1919. Served in France, Gallipoli, Egypt and Palestine. 1914–15 Star. British War medal and Victory medal. In business in Glasgow.
149	Williams, Charles Claire.	3-8-17	Appointed as a probationer in the Indian Army Reserve of Officers from the 51st Battalion Training Reserve and subsequently given a regular commission in the Indian Army Transferred to the 7th Light Cavalry, October 1921 and subsequently to the 7th Rajput Regiment. Served in France and Waziristan, the Punjab Disturbance and in the third Afghan War. Received the special thanks of the Government of India for services during the Punjab Riots. Awarded 1914-15 Star, British War medal Victory medal and Indian General Services medal.
150	Rayner, George Hugh.	3-8-17	First commissioned in the Royal Warickshire Regiment 10-7-13. Appointed as a probationer in the Indian Army Reserve of Officers, transferred to the 29th Punjabis 8-12-17. Relinquished appointment and reverted to the British Services 16-4-19.
151	Lushington, Harry Ernest Cordue	3-9-17	First Commissioned in the Indian Army Reserve of Officers. A member of the Indian Police. Transferred to the Sarhad Levy Corps East Persia as Adjutant 25-5-18. Special duty with Political Department in Quetta, 28-9-19. Demobilized 20-1-20. Now in the Ceylon Forest Service.
152	Cameron, William Wyllie Leslie.	16-9-17	Appointed to the Indian Army Reserve of Officers on probation August 1917. Highland Light Infantry. Transferred to Indian Farms Department, January 1918, rejoined the regiment May 1918 and subsequently transferred to the Military Accounts Department. Invalided to England, March 1919. Promoted Captain 2-10-19. Demobilized 2-3-20. British War medal.

No.	Name.	Date of joining the Regiment.	Particulars of Services, etc.
153	Taylor, Walter..	30-9-17	First Commissioned in the Indian Army (temporary) commission 1-9-17. Transferred to 2-27th Punjabis. Relinquished Commission 1-9-21.
154	Cotton, Trevor Charles.	26-9-17	Enlisted in December 1915 as a gunner in the 77th Howitzer Battery, R. F. A., subsequently posted to No. 2 Amunition Column, R F.A. Gazetted to a temporary commission in the Indian Army 13-9-17, transferred to Egyptian Expeditionary Force and attached to the 2-7th Gurkha Rifles and served with them in Palestine. Returned to India with the unit and took part in surpressing the Punjab Disturbances 1919. Subsequently posted to the 8th/9th Gurkhas and was present in Thal during the investment of that post by the Afghan Army in 1919. Demobilized in September 1919, but recalled to Army Service and sent to the 32nd Lancers in Mesopotamia at the time of the Arab Rising. Finally relinquished commission in August 1921. Now serving as Assistant Secretary to the Y.M.C.A., Simla. British War medal, Victory medal, Indian General Service medal, and General Service medal.
155	Bles, David Goodfrey.	4-11-17	First Commissioned in the Indian Army Reserve of Officers. A member of the Indian Civil Service. Served in Political Deparment, Mesopotamia 1918. Demobilized June 1919. Took a proportionate pension from the I. C. S. and is now a publisher in London. British War medal, Victory medal.
156	Bion, Roy Harold.	16-12-17	First Commissioned in the Indian Unattached List 29th June 1915. Posted to the 13th Lancer's Depôt and subsequently attached to the regiment. Transferred to the 57th Wilde's Rifles, F. F. on 21st April 1918. Resigned from the service in January 1919. Now a planter in Bihar and a member of the Bihar Light Horse.
157	Garle, John Aubrey Barton.	29-1-18	First Commissioned in the West Kent (Queen's Own Yeomanry September 1912. Transferred to the Indian Army Reserve of Officers (on probation) as a Captain in January 1918. Served in Gallipoli, Egypt, Suez Canal and Senussie Fronts and in Palestine. Demobilized at the

No.	Name.	Date of joining the Regiment.	Particulars of Service, etc.
			end of the War in the rank of Captain. Formerly a member of Lloyds. Now farming in South Africa. 1914-15 Star, British War medal, Victory medal.
158	Macintyre, Alexander.	12-2-10	First Commissioned in the Scottish Horse 1-10-16. Appointed to the Indian Army Reserve of Officers as a probationer. Transferred in July 1918 to Egypt. Relinquished Commission 1-5-22.
159	Rusell, Coral Sherwood Cowper.	12-2-18	First Commissioned in the 18th Northumberland Fusiliers 3-4-15 and appointed to the Indian Army Reserve of Officers on probation. Transferred 21-5-18 to 2-12 Punjab Regiment. Relinquished Commission 1-5-22.
160	Chamberlain, Wilfred Gerard.	2-3-18	First Commissioned in the 8th King's Regiment 5-8-16, and appointed to the Indian Army. Transferred to 2-73rd. Relinquished Commission, 1-5-22. Served in France October 1914 to October 1917 (Gassed) 1914 Star, British War medal, Victory medal.
161	Griffiths, William Stanley.	2-3-18	Appointed as a probationer to the Indian Army from the Yeomanry. Served in Palestine, 1916-18. Afghanistan-1919, Waziristan, 1920. Transferred to the 15th Lancers on amalgamation. Subsequently retired. British War medal, Victory medal, Indian General Service medal and Territorial medal.
162	Gordon, Gilbert	14-3-18	First Commissioned in the Indian Army Reserve of Officers. An Assam Planter. Released from Army Service in 1919. Relinquished Commission, 1-5-22 and returned to Assam. A member of the Assam Valley Light Horse. Since deceased, (1925).
163	Freston, Thomas Antony.	21-3-18	First Commissioned in the Indian Unattached List. Served with the Trans-Indus Squadron of the 17th Cavalry from June to October 1919. Seconded for Study at Oxford University Corpus Christi College, November 1919 to September 1922. Resigned on appointment to the Indian Civil Service. Now serving in Bihar and Orissa. British War medal, and Indian General Service medal.

No.	Name.	Date of joining the Regiment.	Particulars of Services, etc.
164	MacCay, Ross Cairns.	30-3-18	Appointed as a probationer for the Indian Army from the Field Artillery Australian Imperial Force with the rank of Lieutenant. Had held the rank of Major in Australian Artillery. Promoted temporary Captain 26-10-18, Captain 13-5-19. Transferred to 7th Light Cavalry, 20-10-21 and subsequently to the 6th Rajputana Rifles. Served as Staff Captain and Brigade Major Sialkot Cavalry Brigade while with 17th Cavalry. Served in Gallipoli, France, Suez Canal and Waziristan. Companion of the Distinguished Service Order, 1914-15 Star, British War medal, Victory medal and Indian General Service medal.
165	Sydenham, Alwyn Francis.	30-3-18	Appointed as a Probationer for the Indian Army from the 13th Light Horse, Imperial Australian Force. Subsequently transferred to the Mechanical Transport section of the Supply and Transport Corps. Retired with gratuity, 28-9-22.
166	Persse, Sydney Henry.	17-4-18	First Commissioned in the 23rd B. N. London Regiment, appointed to Indian Army Reserve of Officers as a probationer. Subsequently granted a regular commission. Transferred to the 15th Lancers on amalgamation. Served in France, Third Afghan War and Waziristan. 1914-15 Star, British War medal, Victory medal, Indian General Service medal.
167	Barry, Charles Bissell.	19-6-18	First Commissioned in the Indian Army Reserve of Officers. A member of the Indian Civil Service. Demobilized as a Second Lieutenant 31-12-18. British War medal.
168	Tait, John	29-6-18	First Commissioned in the Indian Army Reserve of Officers, 7-6-18. Transferred to 31st Lancers 22-5-19. Relinquished Commission, 1-5-22.
169	Ritchie, Adam Alexander.	26 7-18	First Commissioned in the Indian Army Reserve of Officers. A member of the Indian Educational Service Released from Army Service in 1919. Relinquished Commission, 1-5-22.
170	Seigh, Gervase Paget.	1-8-18	First Commissioned in the West Riding Regiment 23-1-14, appointed to the Indian Army on probation. Transferred back to West Riding Regiment, 12-4-19. Retired with gratuity, 8-6-22.

No.	Name.	Date of joining the Regiment.	Particulars of Services, etc
171	Withinshaw, Leslie.	17-8-18	First Commissioned in the Indian Army Reserve of Officers. An officer of the Indian Police, released from Army service 1919, relinquished commission, 1-5-22. Now employed as Head of the Watch and Ward Department, East Indian Railway.
172	Harper, Leonard Graeme.		First Commissioned in the Unattached List for Indian Army, 21-8-18; transferred to the 5th Light Infantry and subsequently to 128th Pioneers. Retired with gratuity, 17th October 1922.
173	Dixon, Vivian Hastler.	3-9-18	First Commissioned in Indian Unattached List. Served in the Waziristan Field Force April to November 1921. Transferred to the 15th Lancers on amalgamation, subsequently retired on the special terms in 1922. British War medal, Indian General Service Medal.
174	Wilson, John Hector Alexander.	21-10-18	First Commissioned in the Indian Unattached List. 24-4-18. Transferred to the 31st (D. C. O.), Lancers, 22-5-19 Retired with gratuity 4-11-22.
175	Collins, Lionel	3-11-18	First Commissioned in the Indian Army Reserve of Officers 20-11-14. Remained only a few days and was on the 3-11-18 transferred to the Karpurtala Infantry. Promoted Captain 20-11-18. Relinquished Commission 1-5-22.
176	O'Dwyer, John Chevalier.	18-12-18	First Commissioned in the Indian Army Reserve of Officers. Son of Sir Michael O'Dwyer, Lieutenant-Governor of the Punjab. Transferred to the 31st Lancers in May 1919. Appointed Cipher Officer, Waziristan Field Force Head Quarters, June 1919. Demobilized November 10th 1919 but remained on Cadre of the I. A. R. O. Indian General Service medal with two clasps.
177	Pratt, Herbert Sydney.	23-12-18	First Commissioned in the Indian Unattached List Promoted Lieutenant 16-12-19. Retired on Invalid and Disability Pensions, October 7th, 1922.
178	Corkhill Edwin Cristian.	10-1-19	First Commissioned in the Indian Army Reserve of Officers 11-9-18. Only remained with the regiment for about ten days. Promoted Lieutenant 11-9-19. Relinquished Commission 1-5-22.

No.	Name.	Date of joining the Regiment.	Particulars of Services etc.
179	Whyte, Alastir Douglas.	12-1-19	Seconded from the South African Mounted Riflemen for services Overseas, May, 1918. Appointed to Indian Army Reserve of Officers, September 1918 and attached to the 17th Cavalry. Promoted Captain 10-7-19. Released from the Indian Army and returned to his permanent appointment in the South African Permanent Forces in October 1919. Acted as Adjutant of the regiment in 1919. Served in the Natal Native Rebellion 1906 and South-West Africa, Egypt, and India 1914-18. Natal Native Rebellion medal 1906, 1914-15 Star, British War medal, Victory medal.
180	Lucas, Francis Edmond.	17-1-19	First Commissioned in the 3rd Hussars, 15-9-18 and appointed to the Indian Army, on probation. Transferred to the 31st Lancers 22-5-19 Retired with gratuity, 4-11-22 Served in France in 1918 British War medal and Victory medal.
181	Clews, Lionel Charles.	21-1-19	First Commissioned in the Yorkshire Light Infantry, 26-2-17. Indian Army Probationer. Transferred to the 28th Light Cavalry, April 1922. Resigned his commission and retired with gratuity, 5-10-22. Served in France 1916-17. British War medal Victory medal. Served in the third Afghan War. Indian General Service medal and clasp.
182	Moffat, Leslie Palmer.	8-2-19	First Commissioned in King Edward's Horse, 10-12-15. Appointed as a probationer for the Indian Army, attached 44th Cavalry, 14-0-18. Transferred to 17th Cavalry, 8-2-19. Subsequently transferred to 22nd Cavalry and demobilized, November 1919. Awarded the Military Cross, 19-5-18. Served in Irish Rebellion and in France and Italy, the Punjab Riots and various frontier actions. British War medal and Victory medal.
183	Worgan, Rivers Berney.	7-3-19	Major and Brevet-Lieutenant-Colonel, 20th Royal Deccan Horse, attached as temporary Commandant. Commanded an infantry battalion and subsequently a Brigade in France and later on a Brigade in the Wazir Force. Served as Military Secretary to H R. H. the Duke of Connaught 1920, as Military Secretary to H. R. H. the Prince of Wales 1921, and as Military Secretary to H. E. the Viceroy

No.	Name	Date of joining the Regiment.	Particulars of Services, etc.
			1924. Brigade-Commander Bangalore Brigade 1926. Served in the South African War, 1900-02. France and Aden, 1914-18, Punjab Disturbances, 1919, Waziristan, 1919-20. Despatches London Gazette 1-1-16, 15-6-16, 4-1-17, 28-12-17, 10-6-21. Brevet of Major and of Lieutenant-Colonel with Distinguished Service Order for France. Commander of the Victorian Order, Companion of the Order of the Star of India, Queen's and Kings medals with two clasps each for S.A. War, 1914 Star. British War medal, Victory medal, Indian General Service medal.
184	Monckton Edward Philip Simon.	30-3-19	First Commissioned in the Indian Unattached List as Second Lieutenant 20-12-18. Lieutenant. 30-12-19. Quartermaster (tempy.) 3-4-20 to 31-5-21. Served in Waziristan Field Force, April 1921 to December 1921. Transferred to the 15th Lancers on amalgamation. Retired on the Special Terms in 1922. Indian General Service medal.
185	Greenway, John Alexander.	21-4-19	First Commissioned as a Second Lieutenant in the Indian Unattached List, 15-4-19. Transferred to the 15th Lancers on amalgamation.
186	Child, Claude Herbert.	5-2-20	First Commissioned in the Indian Unattached List. Transferred to the 7th Light Cavalry in 1922. Doing duty with the Indian Army Service Corps. Served in Waziristan, April 1921 to September 1923. Indian General Service Medal.
187	Dinwiddie, Ronald Maitland.	15-1-20.	First Commissioned in the Lanarkshire Yeomanry 20-6-15. Promoted Captain 20-6-19. Given a temporary Commission in the Indian Army Reserve of Officers. Remained with the regiment until May 1920 Demobilized 18-12-21.
188	Turner, Eric	..	First Commissioned in the 6th Dragoon Guards, 12-2-14 and appointed to the Indian Army as a probationer. Transferred to the regiment from the Guides Cavalry. Retired with gratuity 12-12-22.
189	Marjoribanks, Stewart Dudley.	..	First Commissioned in the Indian Unattached List. Came to the regiment from the 38th Central India Horse. Subsequently transferred to the 7th

No.	Name.	Date of joining the Regiment.	Particulars of Services, etc.
			Light Cavalry. Now serving with the Indian Army Service Corps. Served in Waziristan 1921. Indian General Service medal with clasp.
190	Spottiswoode, George Andrew Gordon.	27-5-21	First Commissioned in the Indian Army Unattached List. Came to the regiment from the 33rd Light Cavalry. Transferred to 7th Light Cavalry, 31-10-21. Served in Waziristan 1921. Indian General Service medal with clasp. Waziristan 1920-21.
191	Western, Charles Edward Murray.	15-7-21.	Major 37th Lancers attached for Temporary duty. Rejoined his own unit in November 1921.
192	Malik Khizar Mohamed Hayat Khan, Tiwana.	17-10-20	First Commissioned in Indian Land Forces as Honorary 2nd Lieutenant and appointed to the regiment as an Honorary Officer. On amalgamation tranferred to the 15th Lancers. Promoted Honorary Captain.

INDIAN OFFICERS OF THE REGIMENT.

There is no record of any Indian Officers prior to October 1876, except three, that were shown among the British Officers in the Army List when they became "Bahadoors." There is also no record of the War services of most of these Indian Officers, but all who were enlisted by 1859 must have fought in the Mutiny under de Kantzow. Similarly, we may take it for granted that those in the regiment from 1877 to 1880 took part in the Jowaki Campaign and Afghan War.

Name.	Date of joining service.	Commissioned.	Left Regiment.	REMARKS.
1. Ahmad Yar Khan	..	..	1869	Appears in the Army List for October 1864 as Ressaldar and "Bahadoor" from 8-8-64.
2. Ali Yar Khan	..	..	1874	Appears in the Army List for July 1872 as Naib-Ressaldar and "Bahadoor" from 5-6-68; disappears from the cadre in October 1874 still as Naib-Ressaldar.
3. Raja Ram	26-10-57	26-10-67	1-7-82	Received his commission as Ressaldar, 26-10-57; Ressaldar-Major, 24-4-66. Retired on disbandment of regiment with a gratuity of one year's dismounted pay of rank.
4. Kumrooden Khan	30-10-31	..	1-5-81	Was received as a transfer on the regiment being formed in 1858, probably as Naib-Ressaldar. He first appears in the Army List for January 1875 as Naib-Ressaldar and "Bahadoor" from 12-10-73; Ressaldar, 1-5-76; 3rd class Order of Merit gained at the Seige of Lucknow.
5. Muhammad Oomur Khan.	7-5-59	15-1-59	1-7-82	Ressaidar, 1-6-59. Ressaldar, 1-7-69. Retired on disbandment of the regiment with one year's dismounted pay of rank.
6. Masjidi Khan	4-3-46	24-5-59	1-5-78	Ressaidar, 1-4-67. Was married to a Hazara wife, and left many descendants of marked Tartar physiognomy. His descendants were in the 17th Cavalry up to 1910, mainly employed in administrative duties.

Name.	Date of joining service.	Commissioned.	Left Regiment.	Remarks.
7. Mahbub Khan	18-6-57	23-6-58	1-5-81	Received as a transfer in 1858 as a Jemadar. Ressaldar, 1-5-70. Came to Ferozepur in 1886, and again in 1891 to see the regiment. He was employed in the Bhawalpur State Army, and died there. He held many certificates and letters of recommendation describing him as a man of extraordinary courage. He had been several times wounded in action. 2nd Class Order of Mérit for great gallantry in action with 3rd Sikh Cavalry.
8. Boodh Singh	15-10-57	1-1-58	25-1-81	Ressaidar, 6-5-76. Transferred to Robarts' Horse with 108 sabres of the Meerut Military Police on 24th November 1858. Specially mentioned for gallantry, and given a reward of Rs. 200 for killing the rebel Chieftain Sah Mull.
9. Kapur Singh	8-2-58	8-4-67	1-7-82	Promoted Ressaidar and appointed Woordi-Major, 1-5-76. Ressaldar, 1-5-81. Retired on disbandment of the regiment with a gratuity of one year's dismounted pay of rank.
10. Salvant Singh	23-5-58	9-12-58	1-5-32	Ressaidar, 1-5-78.
11. Mytab Singh	21-12-58	20-1-59	9-1-79	Retired on pension as a Jamadar.
12. Harbhajan Singh	24-10-57	28-9-59	1-5-78	Retired on pension as a Jamadar.
13. Durga Singh	2-2-58	1-5-76	1-7-82	Ressaidar, 25-1-81. Retired on the disbandment of the regiment with a gratuity of one year's dismounted pay of rank.
14. Mahmud Khan (Kohistani Afghan).	15-4-59	1-5-76	15-4-91	Ressaidar, 1-5-81. Transferred to the 7th B. C. on disbandment of the regiment and re-transferred to it when it was re-raised in 1885. Ressaldar 8-9-85. Ressaldar-Major, 1-2-88. He came of a very good Afghan family and his uncle was Wali of Cabul about 1840. He was married to a sister of Mahomed Amin, afterwards Ressaldar-Major of the regiment. He was given land at Sargodha, and died at Ludhiana in 1898. His son

Name.	Date of joining service.	Commissioned.	Left Regiment.	REMARKS.
				Muhomed Akbar was Kote-Daffadar of L. C. Half Squadron and became Ressaidar in the 57th Camel Corps. The second Risaldar-Major of the new regiment.
15. Kudrat-ullah Khan	14-5-59	1-5-76	4-1-78	Pensioned as a Jamadar.
16. Abdul Rahman ..	6-4-59	4-1-78	1-7-82	Retired on disbandment of the regiment with a gratuity of one year's dismounted pay of rank.
17. Baldeo Singh ..	5-5-58	1-5-78	1-7-82	Ressaidar, 1-5-82. Transferred to 5th B. C. on disbandment of the regiment. Ressaldar, 25-4-88. Pensioned with 32 years' service, 10-5-91. Still living in Moradabad, (1911).
18. Hazara Singh ..	10-5-59	1-5-78	1-7-82	Ressaidar and Woordi-Major, 1-5-81. Appears in Army List for July 1882 on list of unemployed Native Officers on disbandment of regiment. Appointed to the 2nd Bengal Lancers, January 1883. Ressaldar 18-9-85. Ressaldar-Major, 18-7-90. Order of British India 2nd class, 24-8-92. War services:—Bhootan Campaign 1865, Medal and Clasp. Jowaki Expedition, 1877; Clasp Afghan War, 1879-80, Medal, Egyptian Campaign, 1882 Medal and Clasp and Khedive's Bronze star.
19. Niaz-oola Khan ..	1-7-59	9-1-79	1-7-82	Retired with a gratuty of one year's dismounted pay of rank on disbandment of the regiment.
20. Moti Singh ..	15-1-59	5-1-81	1-7-82	Retired with a gratuity of one year's dismounted pay of rank on disbandment of the regiment.
21. Muhamad Azim Khan.	23-2-72	1-5-81	1-7-82	Appears in the Army List for July 1882 on the list of unemployed Native Officers on disbandment of the regiment. Appointed to 8th Bengal Cavalry and promoted Ressaidar, 18-9-85. Ressaldar, 2-7-86. Ressaldar-Major, 1-5-92. Retired on pension, 16-10-02.

Name.	Date of joining service.	Commissioned.	Left Regiment.	Remarks.
				War services :—N. W. Frontier of India, Jowaki, 1877, Medal with Clasp. Afghanistan, 1879-80, Medal.
22. Taj Mahomed Khan (Yusufzai).	1-5-76	1-5-81	9-4-92	Transferred to the 7th Bengal Cavalry on disbandment of the regiment. Retransferred to it when re-raised in 1885, and formed the Yusufzai Half-squadron at Mian Mir and Ferozepore. Ressaidar, 8-8-85. Ressaldar, 15-4-91. Retired on pension. North-West Frontier of India, Jowaki, 1877-78, Medal with Clasp. Afghanistan, 1879-80, capture of Ali Majid, Medal with Clasp.
23. Wazir Ali Khan..	6-4-72	1-5-82	1-7-82	Appears in the Army List for July 1882 on list of unemployed Native Officers on disbandment of the regiment. Afterwards appointed to 1st Bengal Lancers: Ressaidar, 1-5-85. Ressaldar, 1-3-90. Ressaldar-Major, 17-7-01. Order of British India, First Class, 11-8-04. Retired on pension, 1-3-06. N.-W. Frontier of India, Jowaki, 1877, Medal with Clasp. Afghanistan, 1879-80. China Medal, 1900. Relief of Pekin, Action of Peitsang, Action of Jangtsun, Medal with clasp.
24. Rustam Ali Khan (Hindustani Musalman).	25-8-52	7-8-77	1-2-88	Indian Mutiny Medal. N.-W. F. of India, Jowaki, 1877-78, Medal. Afghanistan, 1879-80. Capture of Ali Masjid, Medal with Clasp. Ressaldar, 1-5-82. Appointed to the regiment as Ressaldar-Major from 4th Bengal Cavalry, 8-9-85. Retired on pension. The first Rissaldar Major of the new regiment.
25. Bhai Khan (Punjabi).	23-10-64	1-11-80	1-5-89	Sudan 1884, Medal and Khedive's Bronze Star. Appointed to the regiment as a Ressaidar from the 9th B. C., 8-9-85. Ressaldar, 1-3-86. Retired on pension.
26. Muhammad Akbar Khan (Kazilbash).	15-8-66	1-5-82	16-11-01	Afghanistan, 78—80. 1st Bazar Valley Expedition. Affair at Jagdallak. March to action.

Name.	Date of joining service.	Commissioned.	Left Regiment.	Remarks.
				at Kandhar. Medal with Clasp, Bronze Star. Egyptian Campaign, 1882. Medal with Clasp, Bronze Star. Appointed to the Regiment as a Ressaidar, from 13th B. L., 8-9-85. Ressaldar, 1-2-88. Ressaldar-Major, 1-12-00. Retired on pension. The fourth Risaldar-Major of the new regiment.
27. Khan Karam Khan (Utmanzai, Pathan).	1-6-74	21-1-81	1-6-02	Afghanistan, 1879-80. Action of Takhtipul, 4-1-79. Actions of Ahmedkhel (Horse wounded) and Urzoo. Patrol-Thana (Horse wounded). Medal with Clasp. Appointed to the regiment as a Ressaidar from the 1st Punjab Cavalry, 8-9-85. Ressaldar, 1-5-89. Retired on pension. Cousin of the Khan of Khalabat. Raised a large portion of H. Troop or (left D. Half Squadron) in 1885.
28. Sarbuland Khan (Khalil, Pathan).	2-8-64	8-9-85	1-10-92	Egyptian Campaign, 1882. Action of Tel-El-Kabir, Medal with Clasp, Bronze Star. Appointed to the regiment as a Jemadar from 6th B.C., 8-9-85. Ressaldar, 1-3-86. Retired on pension.
29. Muhammad Amin Khan (Kazikhel, Afghan).	1-9-76	8-9-85	16-10-09	N.-W. F. of India, Jowaki 1877-78, Medal. Afghanistan, 1879-80. Capture of Ali Masjid, Medal with Clasp. Appointed to the regiment as a Jemadar from the 7th B. C., 8-9-85. Ressaidar, 1-2-88. Ressaldar 1-12-00. Ressaldar-Major, 1-8-05. Order of British India, 2nd Class. Orderly Officer to H.M. The King-Emperor, 1908. Retired on pension. Subsequently Municipal Councilor and Subregistrar Ludhiana. Died in 1916. He was the son of a Sirdar who accompanied Shah Shuja to India. The sixth Rissaldar-Major of the new regiment.
30. Izzat Khan (Adamkhel Afridi).	1-4-64	1-5-82	1-12-00	Egyptian Campaign, 1882. Action of Tel-El-Kabir, Medal with Clasp, Bronze Star. Appointed to the regiment as

Name.	Date of joining service.	Commissioned.	Left Regiment.	REMARKS.
				a Ressaldar from 6th B. C. 5-12-85. Present at Diamond Jubilee Celebration, 1897. Jubilee Medal. Ressaldar-Major, 15-4-1891. Order of British India, 2nd Class, 17-11-1892. Order of British India, 1st Class, June 1897. Retired on pension. The third Risaldar-Major of the new regiment.
31. Saadat Khan (Sulemankhel Afghan).	27-6-73	8-9-85	1-8-05	Egyptian Campaign, 1882. Action of Tel-El-Kabir, Medal with Clasp, Bronze Star. Appointed to the regiment as a Jemadar and Wordie-Major, from the 6th B. C. Ressaidar, 1-3-86. Ressaldar, 9-4-92. Ressaldar-Major, 16-11-01. Retired on pension. The fifth Risaldar-Major of the new regiment.
32. Ghulam Hussen Khan (Kasur Pathan).	9-1-86	9-1-86	10-8-86	Direct Commission. Son of the Ressaldar-Major of the 10th B. L. of the Kasur Family. Resigned.
33. Mohommed Usman Khan (Papalzai Afghan).	9-1-86	9-1-86	29-11-94	Direct Commission. Transferred to the 7th Bombay Lancers.
34. Mahomed Hossain Khan (Utmanzai Pathan).	13-2-86	13-2-86	31-10-01	Direct Commission. Raised a large part of the H. Troop (or left D. Half Squadron F.) in 1885. Wordie-Major and Ressaidar, 9-4-92. Retired on pension. Son of the Khan of Khalabat, Khan Zaman Khan.
35. Hayat Khan (Tiwana).	15-2-86	15-2-86	4-3-95	Direct Commission. Died at his home. One of the Tiwana Maliks.
36. Kazi Latif (Kazikhel Pathan).	7-3-69	1-3-86	16-11-90	Afghan War, 1879-80. Action of Maxina Medal. Appointed to the regiment from the 5th Bengal Cavalry. Retired on pension.
37. Kadir Khan (Khalil Pathan).	1-6-86	1-6-86	27-1-89	Direct Commission. Raised a large portion of the B. and D. Troops (*i.e.*, left A and left B. Half Squadrons) in 1885. Died in Peshawar of Abscess of Liver. Son of Afridi Khan, Commandant, Khyber Rifles. Father of Lieutenant Bahadur Sher Khan Resaldar-Major of the 15th Lancers, and formerly of the 17th Cavalry.

Name.	Date of joining service.	Commissioned.	Left Regiment.	REMARKS.
38. Rahbuddin Khan (Adamkhel, Afridi).	30-3-78	10-8-86	9-5-01	Egyptian Expedition, 1882. Action of Tel-El-Kabir, Medal with Clasp, Bronze Star. Appointed to the regiment from the 6th Bengal Cavalry. Retired on pension. Cousin of Rissaldar-Major Izzat Khan
39. Hamzulla Khan (Babar, Pathan).	1-5-76	1-8-87	1-1-12	Afghan War, 78-9-80. Actions of Ahmed Khel, and Padkao., Medal with Clasp. Appointed to the regiment from the 19th Bengal Lancers. Ressaidar 1st October 1892. Ressaldar, 16-11-01. Ressaldar-Major, 16-10-09. Order of British India, 2nd Class, 4-5-09. Order of British India, 1st Class, 2-5-12. Honorary Captain. Retired on pension. The seventh Rissaldar-Major of the new regiment.
40. Manneh Khan	7-6-66	1-2-88	8-7-98	Afghan War, 1878-9-80. Action of Ahmed Khel, Medal with Clasp. Appointed to the regiment from the 1st Bengal Cavalry. Ressaidar, 1-5-89. Retired on pension.
41. Ahmad Khan (Adamkhel, Pathan, Afridi).	12-9-74	28-1-89	22-12-06	Egyptian Expedition, 1882. Action of Tel-El-Kabir, Medal with Clasp, Bronze Star, Chitral Relief Expedition, 1895. Medal with Clasp. Ressaidar, 8-7-98, Ressaldar, 1-6-02. Retired on pension.
42. Ghulam Kadir Khan (Punjabi).	20-12-85	1-5-89	1-1-95	Transferred to the 7th Bombay Lancers.
43. Sayyid Zamin Ali Shah (Afghan of the Nawabs of Sardhana).	28-3-91	28-3-91	12-7-92	Appointed to a Direct Commission. Resigned.
44. Azam Khan (Kambarkhel, Afridi).	12-3-89	15-4-91	16-8-00	Resigned. Was subsequently murdered. It is reported that the deed was done by his own brother Jan Mohammad, Malik of the Kambarkhel Afridis, but there is some doubt in the matter.
45. Ghulam Mohiyudin Khan (Rajput).	1-2-82	9-4-92	6-7-14	Appointed from the 8th Bengal Cavalry as Mir Munshi. Ressaidar, 1-12-0. Ressaldar, 1-8-05 Ressaldar-Major, 1-1-12.

Name.	Date of joining service.	Commissioned.	Left Regiment.	REMARKS.
				Did excellent work at the Regimental Farm, which he managed for 8 years. Order of British India, 2nd Class. Died at home, April 1924. Retired 6-7-14. The eighth Risaldar-Major of the new regiment.
46. Abdullah Khan (Khalil, Pathan).	4-12-85	12-7-92	1-10-95	Resigned.
47. Nikab Gul Khan (Khattak).	25-12-85	1-10-92	15-2-04	Ressaidar, 21-3-02. Retired.
48. Ismail Khan (Afridi).	1-6-80	29-11-94	5-9-05	Came to the regiment from the 6th B. C. Served in the Egyptian Expedition, 1882. Action of Tel-El-Kabir. Medal with Clasp, Bronze Star. South African War, 1900. Served with the Remount Department, Medal. Retired.
49. Raja Gauhar Rahman Khan (Gakhar.)	1-1-95	1-1-95	13-5-02	Resigned. Nephew of Raja Jahandad Khan. Direct Commission.
50. Malik Dost Mahomed Khan (Tiwana).	26-1-86	5-3-95	1-2-18	Ressaidar, 15-11-01. Ressaldar, 22-12-06. Accompanied the Indian Contingent sent to London for the Coronation, 1911. Medal. Order of British India 2nd Class, 1916. Ressaldar Major, 6-7-14 until retirement in January 1918. The ninth Rissaldar Major of the new regiment.
51. Kaim Khan (Adamkhel, Afridi).	1-11-88	1-10-95	15-11-01	Wordie-Major and Ressaidar, 1-11-01. Died of Pneumonia at Rawalpindi in 1901. Son of Ressaidar-Major Izzat Khan, and father of Jemadar Diam Khan.
52. Aslam Khan (Mohmand Pathan, from Luhianad).	3-7-82	8-7-98	30-11-10	Egyptian Campaign, 1882. Medal and Bronze Star. Ressaidar and Wordie-Major, 16-11-01. Retired. Now employed as Risaldar Major with the Nawab Bahadur of Murshidabad.
53. Muhamad Amir Khan, (Mohmand of Peshawar Pathan,) Arbab.	13-10-96	16-8-00	15-3-08	Resigned on appointment to Police. Ressaidar, 1-6-02.

Name.	Date of joining service.	Commissioned.	Left Regiment.	REMARKS.
54. Mir Alam Khan (Hazara, Pathan).	1-3-78	?-12-00	1-8-05	Appointed from the 1st Punjab Cavalry. Retired.
55. Usman Khan (Kambarkhel Afridi).	12-3-89	11-5-01	14-4-18	East Africa January 1915 until January 1917. Ressaldar, 22-12-06. Ressaldar, 6-10-09. Went to Australia with Indian Contingent in 1902. Retired on pension, April 1918.
56. Barkat Shah (Adamkhel, Afridi).	20-12-85	13-10-01	13-11-04	Retired. Related to Ressaldar-Major Izzat Khan.
57. Malik Sher Ali Khan (Tiwana).	16-6-86	16-11-01	16-10-08	Ressaldar, 5-9-05. Retired.
58. Rukan Din Khan (Awan, Shahpur District).	20-5-86	16-11-01	1-3-19	Served with the 17th Cavalry Remount Squadron in Mesopotamia. Wordie-Major, 1-8-05. Ressaidar, 15-10-08. Ressaldar, 6-7-14. Retired 1-3-19. British War Medal and Victory Medal.
59. Bahadur Sher Khan (Khalil, Pathan).	19-3-00	21-3-02	15-2-22	Received a direct Commission after two years' service as a N.-C. O. Son of Jemadar Kadir Khan, grandson of Afridi Khan, Commandant, Khyber Rifles. Wordi Major, 15-10-08. Ressaidar 16-10-09. Ressaldar, 11-4-16. Served in East Africa with the 17th Cavalry Squadron March 1916 until January 1917. Mentioned in Despatches for good work on Field Service in East Africa. Served with the Service Squadron of the 17th Cavalry in the third Afghan War. Served in Waziristan 1921. Transferred to the 15th Lances on amalgamation as the First Ressaldar-Major of the new unit. Granted the Honorary rank of Lieutenant, 6-11-25. British War Medal, Victory Medal, Indian General Service Medal with two Clasps.
60. Sultan Khan (Gakhar).	6-5-02	14-5-02	6-5-20	Served with 13th Lancers in Mesopotamia. A Direct Commission. Son of Raja Karamdad Khan of Kahuta. Ressaidar, 1-12-10. Ressaldar, 1916, with 13th Lancers on F. S. Retired. Has since died at his home. British War Medal and Victory Medal.

Name.	Date of joining service.	Commissioned.	Left Regiment.	REMARKS.
61. Sikandar Khan (Hazara Pathan).	10-12-85	1-7-02	9-12-02	Served in Afghan War, 78-79-80 Medal. Appointed from 13th Bengal Cavalry. Retired.
62. Said Akbar Khan (Malikdin Khel, Afridi).	15-1-02	23-12-02	26-3-06	Direct Commission. Son of Subedar-Major and Honorary Captain Yasin Khan of the 24th Punjab Infantry. Resigned.
63. Muhamad Akbar Khan (Utmanzai)	23-11-99	13-10-04	26-11-07	Chitral Relief Force, 1895, Medal with Clasp. Soudan, 1897. Medal and Khedive's Medal. Formerly served in the 1st Bombay Lancers. Retired.
64. Sajid Gul Khan (Khatak).	18-1-94	1-8-05	1-3-20	Chitral Relief Force, 1895. Served East African January 915 until January 1917. Ressaidar, 6-7-14. Retired. Indian contingent to England, Peace Celebration, 1919. Indian General Service Medal (1895) with Clasp. 1914-15 Star British War Medal, Victory Medal. Ressaldar, 1-1-12. Retired 1920.
65. Rahmat Sher Khan (Adamkhel, Afridi).	18-8-94	1-8-05	15-2-22	Tirah Expedition, 1897-98, taking of Sanpaga and Arhanga Passes. Medal with 2 Clasps. With 19th Lancers in France and served with the Service Squadron of the 17th Cavalry in the Third Afghan War and in Waziristan. Mentioned in despatches, 1921. Acompanied R. M. Izzat Khan to the Diamond Jubilee in 1897. Order of British India 2nd class. Indian Distinguished Service Medal, 1914-15 Star, British War Medal, Victory Medal, Indian General Service Medal with two Clasps. Diamond Jubilee Medal. Was the eleventh and last Risaldar Major, the 17th Cavalry.
66. Mustafa Khan (Gakhar).	1-12-85	5-9-05	15-2-17	Chitral Relief Expedition, 1895. Medal with Clasp. Retired.
67. Zikariya Khan (Afghan from Peshawar District).	1-12-86	20-3-06	19-6-20	Had previously served in the Afghan Army. Ressaldar, 15-3-08. Ressaldar, 1-1-12, Ressaidar-Major, 1918. Ap-

Name.	Date of joining service.	Commissioned.	Left Regiment.	REMARKS.
				pointed Honorary Lieutenant on retirement. The tenth Ressaidar-Major of the new regiment.
68. Gauhar Ali Khan (Rajput, Janjuah).	10-5-85	22-12-06	15-2-19	Ressaidar, 4-9-14. Retired
69. Ata Mahomed Shah Khohistani Sayed (Afghan).	16-9-07	15-3-08	15-2-22	Given a direct Commission after serving nine months as a N.-C. O. Ressaidar, 4-8-16, Ressaldar, 1-4-21. A member of a noble Afghan family of which many members are still high in the Amir's service. Served with the 17th Cavalry-Remount Squadron in Mesopotamia, and in Waziristan, 1921, Transferred to the 15th Lancers on amalgamation. British War Medal, Victory Medal and Indian General Service Medal.
70. Tikko Khan (Gakhar).	25-2-89	15-10-08	16-4-20	N.-W.F. of India, 1897-98. Action of Shabkadar. Mohmand Expedition. Medal with Clasp. Wordie-Major, 1-12-09. Transferred from 13th B. L. Ressaidar, 22-3-16. Retired.
71. Wazir Khan (Adamkhel, Afridi).	18-7-94	1-10-09	11-2-22	Served with the 17th Cavalry Squadron East Africa, January, 1915—January 1917, and in Waziristan, 1921 Ressaidar, 9-11-16. Indian Order of Merit, 6-2-16. Retired, 1922. Mentioned in dispatches for service in East Africa, 1914-15. Star, British War Medal, Victory Medal, Indian General Service Medal with Clasp.
72. Dost Muhamad Khan (Utmanzai, Hazara District).	1-10-09	16-10-09	1-1-22	Direct Commission. Son of Ressaldar Khan Karam Khan. Served at the Regimental Farm, 1915—21. Given a Sanad and a Sword of Honour for service in the Punjab Disturbances, 1919. Ressaidar, 22-9-1917. Rissaidar 1-4-21 Retired.
73. Daim Khan (Adamkhel, Afridi).	8-1-04	1-12-10	26-3-16	Son of Ressaidar and Wordie-Major Kaim Khan and grandson of Ressaidar-Major Izzat Khan. Resigned his Commission in March 1916.

Name.	Date of joining service.	Commissioned.	Left Regiment.	Remarks.
74. Malik Alam Sher Khan (Tiwana).	2-3-06	1-1-12	15-2-22	Served with the 18th K. G. O. Lancers in France. Awarded the I. D. S. M. and mentioned in despatches for his services there. Ressaidar, 1-9-17. Rissaldar, 7-5-20. Recalled from service to the regiment in India owing to the shortness of Indian Officers Served in Waziristan, 1921. 1914-15 Star, British War Medal, Victory Medal. Indian General Service Medal, and Clasp. Transferred to 15th Lancers on amalgamtion. Subsequently transferred to the Remount Department, 1922.
75. Mohamad Sarwar (Sulemankhel, Afghan).	24-3-04	7-7-14	1-2-20	Son of the late Ressaldar-Major Saadat Khan. Served in France, 1916. Retired 1918. British War Medal and Victory Medal.
76. Mohamad Raza (Awan, Shahpur District).	17-2-98	8-7-14	31-10-20	Served with the 18th Lancers in France. Ressaidar, December 1917. Retired, 1920. British War Medal and Victory Medal.
77. Wazir Muhamad (Khalil, Pathan).	1-1-04	8-7-14	15-3-22	Served in East Africa, January 1915—January 1917, with the 17th Cavalry Service Squadron, and in Waziristan, 1921. Ressaidar, 1-3-20. Ressaldar, 1-5-21. Retired, 1922. 1914-15 Star, British War Medal, Victory Medal and Indian General Service Medal. Appointed a member of the Order of British India for good work with the Remount Department.
78. Malik Ghulam Husain Khan (Tiwana).	19-12-08	24-12-15	31-1-22	Nephew of Ressaldar-Major Malik Dost Mohammad Khan Bahadur. A relation of the Hon. Nawab Colonel Malik Sir Umar Hayat Khan, Tiwana. Served in Waziristan, 1921. Indian General Service Medal and Clasp. Retired in 1922
79. Sultan Sikander Khan (Rajput, Kassar).	11-3-13	24-12-15	1-2-22	A direct Commission. Served in Waziristan, 1920. Indian General Service Medal, Ressaidar, 7-5-20. Ressaldar, 1-5-21. Retired in 1922.

Name.	Date of joining service	Commissioned.	Left Regiment.	REMARKS.
80. Inayatullah Khan (Baber, Pathan).	1-8-95	22-3-16	15-2-22	Served with the Remount Department in the South African War. Served in East Africa, January 1915—March 1916, in the third Afghan War and in Waziristan, 1921. Acting Woordie Major, 14-8-16. Ressaidar, 16-6-20. Ressaldar, 1-5-21, brother of Ressaldar-Major (Honorary Captain) Hamzulla, Khan. Transferred to the 15th Lancers on amalgamation. Queen's South African Medal, King's South African Medal, 1914-15 Star, British War Medal, Victory Medal, Indian General Service Medal with two Clasps. Retired.
81. Arbab Muhamad Husain (Khalil, Pathan).	2-6-11	26-3-16	15-2-22	Transferred to the 15th Lancers on amalgamation. Served in Waziristan, 1921. Indian General Service Medal.
82. Ata Muhamad Khan (Rajput).	4-5-96	12-7-16	1-10-20	Brother of the late Ressaldar-Major Ghulam Mohiuddin Bahadar Retired 1920.
83. Malik Ahmad Yar (Tiwana).	12-7-16	12-7-16	1-1-22	A nephew of the Hon. Nawab Colonel Malik Sir Umar Hayat Khan Tiwana, K.C.I.E.., C.B.E., M.V.O., Member of the Council of State. Served in Waziristan, 1921. Indian General Service Medal. Direct Commission. Retired 1922.
84. Muhamad Hasan Khan (Rajput, Bhatti).	1-12-93	13-7-16	1-6-20	Retired. Served with the Remount Squadron of the 17th Cavalry in Mesopotamia, 1916-1913. British War Medal, Victory Medal.
85. Nizam-uddin (Afghan).	14-8-16	14-8-16	2-12-20	A grandson of the late Colonel Aslam Khan and a cousin of Ressaldar Ata Mahomad Shah. A direct Commission. Resigned. Served in Third Afghan War. Indian General Service Medal with clasp.
86. Bahadur Ali Khan	15-12-98	27-8-16	'19	Served in Mesopotamia with the 17th Cavalry Remount Squadron. British War Medal and Victory Medal. Retired..

Name.	Date of joining service.	Commissioned.	Left Regiment.	Remarks.
87. Sharif Khan (Mishwani).	2-1-96	9-12-16	'19	Served with the 17th Cavalry Remount Squadron, Mesopotamia. British War Medal, Victory Medal. Mentioned in despatches. Retired, 1919.
88. Muzaffar Khan (Tiwana).	16-2-03	11-4-16	11-4-16	Promoted to serve in the 71st Government Camel Corps Became a Ressaldar and has since retired.
89. Fateh Khan (Tiwana).	18-11-98	12-4-16	1920	Promoted to serve in a Camel Corps where be became a Risaldar, subsequently rejoined the regiment and retired, 1920, with the rank of Jamadar.
90. Mohamad Akbar (Afridi)	8-1-04	20-9-16	1920	Served in East Africa, 1916-17 Retired. British War Medal and Victory Medal, son of Ressaidar Ruabadin Khan.
91. Ahmad Ali Khan (Awan).	1-10-09	22-9-17	15-2-22	Woordie Major 1917. Transferred to the 15th Lancers on amalgamation. Subsequently transferred to the Remount Department.
92. Gustasab Khan (Rajput).	1-10-13	22-9-17	..	A direct commission after four years service in the ranks. Was a relation to the Raja of the Junjuars. Resigned.
93. Pirdad Khan (Awan).	1-3-98	5-10-17	31-1-22	Served with the 13th Lancers in Mesopotamia. Served in Waziristan, 1920. British War Medal, Victory Medal, and Indian General Service Medal. Retired.
94. Sher Muhamad Khan (Tiwana).	16-5-05	14-10-17	8-11-18	Served with the 18th K.G.O. Lancers in France Transferred to 41st Cavalry. Since retired. 1914-15 Star, British War Medal, Victory Medal.
95. Sher Bahadur (Tiwana).	6-3-94	3-12-17	1-3-20	Quarter-Master Jamadar. Retired, 1920.
96. Said Raza (Bangash, Khattak).	15-2-06	1-1-18	1-4-22	Served in Waziristan 1921. Indian General Service Medal with Clasp. Quarter-Master Jemadar. Retired.
97. Alam Khan (Awan).	24-3-01	24 - 8	4-2-22	Served with the 17th Cavalry Remount Squadron, Mesopotamia, and in Waziristan, 1922

Name.	Date of joining service.	Commissioned.	Left Regiment.	Remarks.
98. Mahboob Khan (Mohmand of Peshawar.)	12-4-18	12-4-18	10-4-19	British War Medal, Victory Medal and Indian General Service Medal with Clasp. Retired. A Direct Commission. Resigned his Commission, 10-4-19.
99. Shah Gul Khan (Khattak).	1-10-02	16-4-18	16-4-19	Retired.
100. Abdullah Khan (Babar, Pathan).	1-6-06	24-9-18	..	Sent as a re-inforcement to the 22nd Cavalry as a Dafadar, 8-7-17 in Mesopotamia, was there promoted to Jemadar. He was awarded the I.D.S.M. for gallantry and initiative in the action of Tuzkurmatli on 25-4-18 Having been detached with eight sowars on a flank to check some enemy cavalry who were threatening our force, he pursued and although entired unsupported and fired on by several parties of the enemy, cowed them by his boldness. His party captured 128 prisonerss 16 laden carts, 15 camels and 33 other pack animals. Son of Ressaldar-Major and Honorary Captain Hamzullah Khan. Transferred to the 22nd Cavalry. Since retired. British War Medal and Victory Medal.
101. Muhamad Aslam Khan (Khattak, Akora).	24-7-11	9-4-18	15-2-22	Served with the 19th Lancers in France, and in Waziristan 1921. Transferred to the 15th Lancers on amalgamation. 1914-15 Star, British War Medal, Victory Medal, and Indian General Service Medal.
102. Abdullah Khan (Awan).	15-8-05	7-11-18	12 4-15	Commissioned while serving with a Government Camel Corps. Never rejoined the regiment. Promoted Ressaldar (Camel Corps) 1-6-19. Served in Third Afgan War and in Waziristan. Serving with the 44th Camel Corps 1926, 1914-15 Star, British War Medal, Victory Medal Indian General Service Medal with two Clasps.
103. Muhamad Azam (Farsiwan).	17-12-06	7-11-18	..	Nephew of late Ressaldar-Major Muhammad Amin Khan Bahadur.l, Retired. British War Medal, Victory Medal.

APPENDIX XIII.

THE ROLL OF HONOUR.

OFFICERS WHO APPEAR IN THE REGIMENTAL LIST AND WHO WERE KILLED IN ACTION OR WHO DIED AS THE RESULT OF WOUNDS RECEIVED IN ACTION.

Serial No.	Name and rank.	Particulars.
1	Captain H. B. Swiney	Killed in an affray with Jowaki Afridis, 21st November 1877.
2	Lieutenant M. Z. Darrah	Killed while leading the attack on the Stockade of Pym-ul-Win (Maymyo), 1877.
3	Captain C. C. Cassidy (I.M.S.)	Died of wounds received in action at the Maizar Outrage in Waziristan, 1897.
4	Captain V. C. Duberly	Killed in action while commanding a detachment of the 17th Cavalry in East Africa.
5	Lieutenant B. J. P. Mawdsley	Killed in action with a detachment of the 17th Cavalry in East Africa.
6	Captain (and temporary Lieutenant-Colonel) D. D. Wilson, M.C.	Killed in action while commanding the 5th Battalion of the Sherwood Foresters in France.
7	Lieutenant A. B. Knowles	Killed in action with a detachment of the 17th Cavalry in East Africa.
8	Lieutenant H. G. M. Vickers	Killed in action in Mesopotamia on 30th October 1918.
9	Captain J. C. Platts	Killed in action in Mesopotamia, 7th March 1920.

No particulars of N.-C. Os. and men killed on service or dying at the result of wounds or illness contracted on service prior to 1914 are available in the records.

LIST OF N.-C. OS. AND MEN BELONGING TO THE LATE 17TH CAVALRY WHO FELL IN THE GREAT WAR, 1914-18, OR DIED OF WOUNDS OF DISEASE AS THE RESULT OF FIELD SERVICE IN THE GREAT WAR.

Serial No.	Regtl. No.	Rank and Name.	Particulars.
1	1974	Sowar Nazar Gul	Died from Gun Shot wound on 14th March 1915 in B. E. Africa.
2	2255	Sowar Mian Gul	Died on 11th June 1915 in B. E. Africa.
3	2281	Sowar Pir Dost	Died of wounds in East Africa, 5th August 1915.
4	1385	Dafadar Said Gul	Severely wounded and died in B. E. Africa, 8th February 1916.
5	1982	Sowar Hasham Ali	Killed in action, I. E. Force " A ". (France.)
6	2418	Sowar Khalid Gul	Killed in action on 9th March 1916, B. E. Africa.
7	1396	Dafadar Zaid Gul	Killed in action in B. E. Africa, 11th March 1916.

Serial No.	Regtl. No.	Rank and Name.	Particulars.
8	2123	Sowar Zeri Gul	Died of disease on 21st April 1916, I. E. Force "A". (France.)
9	2209	Sowar Hasham Ali	Died of wounds, 30th May 1916 in East Africa.
10	2241	Sowar Saadat Khan	Killed in action on 23rd June 1916 in France.
11	1883	Sowar Alam Khan	Killed in action on 24th June 1916 in B. E. Africa.
12	2712	Sowar Mir Gul	Killed in action on 24th June 1916 in East Africa.
13	2225	Sowar Hikmat Khan	Died of wounds in East Africa, 27th June 1916.
14	2108	Sowar Mohd. Ibrahim	Died of disease on 11th July 1916 in East Africa.
15	2464	Sowar Said Amir	Killed in action, 25th July 1916.
16	2478	Sowar Akbar Khan	Killed in action, 25th July 1916, East Africa.
17	2398	Sowar Jahan Dad Khan	Died of disease on 24th October 1916 in East Africa.
18	2404	Sowar Jiwan Khan	Believed killed in action, 17th December 1916.
19	2776	Sowar Fateh Khan	Died on 2nd January 1917 in Mesopotamia.
20	2742	Sowar Chan Pir	Died on 13th April 1917 at the War Hospital, Bombay, after return from Mesopotamia.
21	1517	Dafadar Atta Mohammad	Died of disease at Bundar Abas (Persia), 1st July 1917.
22	2000	Sowar Said Hassan	Died of disease in France on 9th April 1918.
23	2656	Sowar Zaman	Died in Mesopotamia on 7th July 1918.
24	2641	Sowar Mian Din	Died of disease on 20th October 1918 in Mesopotamia.
25	2312	Sowar Sher Dil	Died of disease in Egypt on 21st October 1918.
26	2262	Sowar Pir Mohammad	Killed in action on 1st November 1918.

LIST OF N.-C. OS. AND MEN BELONGING TO THE LATE 17TH CAVALRY WHO WERE KILLED OR DIED OF WOUNDS OR DISEASE AS THE DIRECT RESULT OF WARS OTHER THAN THE GREAT WAR.

1	1560	Dafadar Wazir Khan	Died of disease on 20th June 1919 at Peshawar (N.-W.F.P.).
2	3087	Sowar Ghulam Jalani	Died of cholera at Peshawar on 21st June 1919.
3	3139	Sowar Sardar	Died of Cholera on 21st June 1919, N.-W. F.P.
4	3737	Sowar Mohammad Shah	Died at Wana on 16th October 1921.

Add to the list of men who died in the Great War.

No. 61/1837 Reservist Abdul Rahim died on shipboard of pneumonia, 24-12-1914.

No. 72/1886 Reservist Saidan Shah died in France, 1915.

APPENDIX XIV.

COPIES OF THE DEEDS EXECUTED REGARDING THE DISPOSAL OF THE FUNDS AND PROPERTY OF THE OFFICERS' MESS AND THE POLO CLUB OF THE 17TH CAVALRY.

Copy of the Agreement between the Officers, 17th Cavalry and the Trustees of the 17th Cavalry Polo Club regarding the property of the Officers' Mess, 17th Cavalry and the funds of the 17th Cavalry Polo Club.

This Inventure made the first day of May 1922 *between* the Officers of the 17th Cavalry at present at Lucknow British India (hereinafter referred to as The Vendors) of the one part and the Trustees of the 17th Cavalry Polo Club (hereinafter referred to as the Trustees) of the other part *witnesseth as follows*:—

Whereas the Officers of the 17th Cavalry have for some years past formed among themselves a club to the funds of which the said Officers have subscribed regularly and which has been known as the Polo Club and the management of this Club has been vested in the hands of a Committee who have administered the funds of the Polo Club in accordance with the rules governing the constitution of the said Club, *and whereas* the funds of the said Club are the private property of the Officers of the 17th Cavalry.

And whereas at a Special Meeting of the said Officers of the 17th Cavalry held at Lucknow on the eight day of December, one thousand nine hundred and twenty-one, a proposal was made that the funds of the said Club should henceforth cease to be administered by the said Committee and that the same should hereafter be transferred to and become vested in the hands of Trustees to be appointed for the said purpose and that the said funds so transferred be held by the said Trustees in trust for the Club and that the fund should in future be known and designated the 17th Cavalry Polo Club and this proposal was duly agreed to and passed by the meeting and entered in the minutes of the meeting.

And whereas at a subsequent Special Meeting of the said Polo Club held at Lucknow on the 30th day of April 1922 at which the following Officers were present Lt.-Col. Barry-Smith, Major H. S. Stewart, Captain J. A. W. Foottit, Captain W. S. Griffiths,

Lieutenant E. P. S. Monckton, Major E. G. Atkinson (by proxy), Captain S. H. Persse (by proxy) and Captain J. S. Ballentine (by proxy) the above resolution was duly confirmed and duly entered in the minutes of the meetings.

And whereas a sum of ten thousand one hundred and twenty-four rupees nine annas and one pie (Rs. 10,124-9-1) which represents the aggregate of the credit balances transferred from the Entertainment Fund, the Plate Fund, the Library Fund, the Store Fund and the Billiard Fund, all of which monies are the private property of the Officers' Private Fund of the 17th Cavalry Officers, was on the second day of January one thousand nine hundred and twenty-two paid over by the Mess President, 17th Cavalry, to Lt.-Col. Barry-Smith, one of the Trustees of the 17th Cavalry Polo Club and received by him and on behalf of his Co-Trustees and the receipt of which said sum he hereby acknowledges.

And whereas it was subsequently resolved that out of the Rs. 10,124-9-1 before mentioned a sum of Rs. 1,124-9-1 should be applied for other purposes a repayment of the said sum of Rs. 1,124-9-1 was made by the Trustees to the Mess President leaving a sum of Rs. 9,000 (nine thousand rupees) only in the hands of the Trustees.

And whereas by a resolution of the said meeting duly passed and entered in the Minute Book on the eighth day of December, one thousand nine hundred and twenty-one and purporting to be signed by the President of the said meeting it was resolved that the Mess Dead Stock, the property of the Officers' Mess, 17th Cavalry, should be taken at a valuation of sixteen thousand five hundred and ninety-six rupees eleven annas six pies (Rs. 16,596-11-6) such valuation being the depreciated value of the said Mess Dead Stock as shown in the Mess Books and that the said Dead Stock be sold to the Trustees for the said sum in order and for the purpose that the said Trustees may with the said monies liquidate the debts existing at the present time of the Officers' Mess, 17th Cavalry, and that such sale was duly made to the said Trustees and confirmed by the meeting.

And whereas it was further resolved at the said meeting that the Trustees be and are hereby empowered to deal with the whole or any part of this fund either by loan or sale of the Dead Stock to the Mess of the new amalgamated regiment at their discretion.

And whereas it was further resolved at the said meeting that the First Trustees of the Club shall be the following six Officers who were officers of the 17th Cavalry at the outbreak of the late Great War (4th August 1914) and are borne on the rolls, of Officers of the 17th Cavalry at the date of these presents, namely :—Lt.-Col. Barry-Smith, Major H. S. Stewart, Major F. C. Yeats-Brown, Major E. G. Atkinson, Captain J. A. W. Foottit and Captain R. P. I. Cochrane, be and are appointed Trustees and Administrators of the Funds of the 17th Cavalry Polo Club aforesaid and that power be given to these original Trustees to appoint fresh Trustees when their number falls below three in India during the absence on leave or retirement in Europe of these Trustees or of such Officer Trustees leaving the regiment or the country permanently with the exception of Lt.-Col. R. C. Barry-Smith who has consented to remain a permanent Trustee *now this indenture witnesseth* that in pursuance of the premises and in consideration of rupees nine thousand (Rs. 9,000) paid by the Vendors to the Trustees (the receipt whereof the Trustees hereby acknowledge) the Vendors as beneficial Owners hereby convey unto the Trustees the said sum of Rs. 9,000 and the Mess Dead Stock representing in value the sum of rupees sixteen thousand five hundred and ninety-six eleven annas and six pies (Rs. 16,596-11-6), upon trust for the members of the Club to be loaned, sold or otherwise dealt with by the Trustees as they shall from time to time in their discretion determine.

In witness whereof of the parties hereunto have set their hands and seals on the day and year first above written.

* * * * * *

Copy of the Deed nominating Trustees to control of the 17th Cavalry Polo Club Funds and property purchased from the Officers' Mess, 17th Cavalry.

Know all men by these presents that at a special meeting of the Officers of the 17th Cavalry Mess held at the Officers' Mess, Lucknow, on the 5th December 1921 and at which the following Officers were present, Lieutenant-Colonel R. C. Barry-Smith, Major H. S. Stewart, Captain E. G. Atkinson, Captain S. H. Persse, Captain W. S. Griffiths, Captain J. S. Ballentine and Lieutenant V. H. Dixon at a General Meeting the following resolutions were agreed to and passed and at a subsequent meeting held at Lucknow on the 30th April 1922 at which the following Officers were present, namely, Lieutenant-Colonel R. C. Barry-Smith, Major H. S. Stewart, Captain W. S. Griffiths, Captain J. A. W. Foottit, Lieutenant E. P. S. Monckton, these resolutions were modified as under—

1. The Meeting resolved that the credit balances in the following funds, *viz.* the Entertainment Fund, the Plate Fund, the Library Fund, the Store Fund and the Billiard Fund, amounting to a total of Rs. 10,124-9-1 which is the private property of the Officers of the 17th Cavalry should be transferred into one

fund as the Private Fund of the Officers of the 17th Cavalry and as they were entitled to have these funds divided amongst themselves they have instead resolved to appoint Trustees from among their pre-war officers of the regiment, the Trustees so appointed to receive Rs. 9,000 of this and to leave the remaining Rs. 1,124-9-1 as a Private Fund to the Mess to be subsequently disposed of to discharge other liabilities.

2. It was also resolved that the Public Funds of the Mess, namely, the Mess Fund which is in debt to the extent of Rs. 1,749-12-0 and the Dead Stock Fund which is in debt to the extent of Rs. 14,548-14-7 should both be liquidated by sale of the Mess Dead Stock which is valued at Rs. 16,858-1-9 and that the sale be made to the Trustees of the 17th Cavalry Polo Club for the sum of Rs. 16,593-11-5 who shall be empowered to loan, sell or otherwise deal with Mess Dead Stock as they should think advisable and that they might sell, give or lend the whole or any part thereof to the Mess of the amalgamated regiment.

3. It was further resolved that the Trustees of the 17th Cavalry Polo Club should comprise the following six officers of the 17th Cavalry, Lieutenant-Colonel R. C. Barry-Smith, Major H. S. Stewart, Major F. C. C. Yeats-Brown, Major E. G. Atkinson, Captain J. A. W. Foottit and Captain R. P. I. Cochrane who were with the regiment at the outbreak of the Great War on the 4th August 1914 and who are with the regiment at the present time and that these original Trustees shall be given the power to appoint new Trustees whenever the number of Trustees falls below three in India during the absence on leave, or retirement in Europe of these Trustees or of such Officer Trustees leaving the regiment or the country permanently with the exception of Lieutenant-Colonel Barry-Smith who has consented to be a permanent Trustee.

Now these presents witness that in pursuance of the resolutions aforesaid of the general meetings aforesaid it is agreed that a proper Trust Deed be drawn up to the intent and for the purpose of giving effect to the resolutions.

In witness whereof the members of the general meetings have hereunder set their hands and seals, this first day of May, one-thousand nine hundred and twenty-two.

*   *   *   *   *   *

Copy of the Agreement for the formation of an Officers' Mess for the newly amalgamated Regiment in substitution of the separate Officers' Messes of the late 17th Cavalry and the 37th Lancers.

An agreement made the first day of May 1922 *between* the Trustees of the 17th Cavalry Polo Club (hereinafter referred to as the Trustees) Lucknow of the one part and of the Officers of the 37th Lancers (who are the Officers of the 37th Lancers and who are borne on the Roll of Officers of the 37th Lancers on the date of this agreement) and hereinafter referred to as the Officers, 37th Lancers also of Lucknow of the other part.

Whereas at a Mess Meeting of the Officers of the 17th Cavalry and the Officers of the 37th Lancers was held at Lucknow, on Wednesday, the twenty-fifth day of January, nineteen hundred and twenty-two for the purposes of forming the Mess of the newly amalgamated Regiment to take the place of the separate Messes of the two defunct regiments and at which the following Officers were present:—

Of the 17th Cavalry.
1. Lt.-Col. R. C. Barry-Smith.
2. Major H. S. Stewart.
3. Captain E. G. Atkinson.
4. Captain J. A. W. Foottit.
5. Captain R. P. I. Cochrane.
6. Captain W. S. Griffiths.
7. Captain J. S. Ballentine.
8. Lieut. V. H. Dixon.
9. Lieut. E. P. S. Monckton.

Of the 37th Lancers.
1. Major J. St. C. D. Stewart.
2. Major E. Lorimer.
3. Major C. E. M. Western.
4. Captain A. L. P. Anderson.
5. Captain R. L. Watkis.
6. Captain G. S. R. Webb.
7. Captain G. G. Collyns.
8. Lieut. W. E. Merrill.
9. Lieut. T. G. Llewellin Evans.
10. Lieut. W. B. S. Webb.
11. Lieut E. M. Holt.
12. Lieut E D Tilden.
13. Lieut. C. S. Sankey.
14. Lieut. A. B. Ellis.

The draft of an Agreement between the Trustees of the 17th Cavalry Polo Club, the Purchasers of the Dead Stock of the 17th Cavalry and the Officers of the 37th Lancers and their Trustees was read and adopted by the meeting.

Whereby it was mutually agreed as follows:—

1. In the interpretation of this agreement the expression "The Trustees" shall mean the Trustees of the 17th Cavalry Polo Club of Lucknow and the expression "the Officers, 37th Lancers," shall mean the Officers who are now at the date of this agreement Officers of the 37th Lancers Regiment.

2. The new Mess of the amalgamated regiment being unwilling to take over the existing liabilities of the Mess Fund and the debts of the Mess of the 17th Cavalry, the Mess of the 17th Cavalry have sold their Dead Stock to the Trustees of the 17th Cavalry Polo Club who as beneficial owners of the said Dead Stock have undertaken to discharge the liabilities and debts aforesaid.

3. That the Presentation Plate and other articles of a sentimental value which belong to the Officers of the 17th Cavalry are and remain the absolute property of the Trustees of of the 17th Cavalry Polo Club and in the same way, the Presentation Plate and other articles of a sentimental value which are

possessed by the Officers of the 37th Lancers are and shall remain the absolute property of the said Officers or of any Trustees that may be appointed on their behalf hereafter.

4. That the parties hereto agree to lend the plate and other articles mentioned in para. 3 above to the Mess of the amalgamated regiment who shall insure the same against loss, destruction or damage by fire, theft or any other calamity and the sum for which the things shall be insured shall be determined by a joint committee of the 17th Cavalry Officers and Officers of the 37th Lancers and the said committee, shall also select the office with whom the said policy or policies of insurance shall be effected and this Committee shall also determine the amount of premia to be paid, dates of payment, method of payment and duration of policies and any other matters incidental thereto.

5. Each of the contracting parties undertakes to furnish a complete list setting forth in detail each article and the value assigned by them against it in such lists or the Inventories of their respective properties and if considered necessary each of the contracting parties shall countersign the Lists or Inventories of the other party, and these lists and receipts shall be attached to this agreement and form part of it.

6. The Mess Committee of the Amalgamated Mess undertakes to provide suitable storage room and be responsible for the safe custody and securing of the articles aforesaid and to deliver them up to each of the parties whenever called upon to do so.

7. Each of the contracting parties reserve unto themselves the right to terminate the conditions under which the loan of the articles aforementioned have been made to the amalgamated Mess whenever in their opinion it is considered that the circumstances have changed and warrant their so doing.

8. That in the case of the destruction, loss, or damage by fire, theft or other calamities whatsoever the monies that shall be recovered under the policies of Insurance shall be and become payable immediately to the party or each of the parties in proportion to the loss that may have been sustained by them.

9. Each party shall have the Dead Stock that they are contributing to the amalgamated Mess valued by an outside Valuer where this may be possible and in case an outside Valuer cannot be had or if it is found that his services are too expensive then and in that case the valuing shall be done by the members of a joint Committee of Officers appointed for the purpose.

10. That the 37th Lancers shall contribute their Mess Fund and their Dead Stock to the Amalgamated Mess but as the 17th

Cavalry Mess Fund is in debt such debt will be settled by the regiment and the 17th Cavalry have therefore no Mess Fund to hand over to the Amalgamated Mess.

11. That the total value of the Dead Stock that is made over by the 37th Lancers to the Amalgamated Mess and accepted by the said Mess together with the amount of the Mess Fund of the 37th Lancers shall be credited to the Officers of the 37th Lancers in the books of the amalgamated regiment.

12. That the Trustees of the 17th Cavalry Polo Club shall hand over to the Amalgamated Mess on the same terms and be credited with the value such Dead Stock value as shall equal in amount the combined value of the Mess Fund and the Dead Stock handed over by the 37th Lancers.

13. That a General Meeting of the Amalgamated Mess or a Committee appointed by such Meeting shall after considering the provisions of paras. 9, 10, 11 and 12 herein written decide what Dead Stock is necessary to the requirements of the Amalgamated Mess and thereafter should there remain any surplus Dead Stock the same shall be disposed of as follows :—

- (a) If such surplus consists of property handed over by each of the parties to the Amalgamated Mess under paras. 11 and 12 above written, the proceeds thereof shall be credited to the Funds of the Amalgamated Mess.
- (b) Where such surplus Dead Stock is not of the description mentioned in para. 11 above such surplus Dead Stock or the proceeds thereof shall be disposed of by the two parties to this agreement as they each think fit.

14. That upon a dissolution of the present amalgamated regiment or in the case of the aforesaid regiment having to be disbanded on account of a further reduction of the Indian Army Establishment or for any other reason then upon the said dissolution or disbandment taking place, each of the contracting parties has agreed to take each a half of the existing assets at the date of such disbandment or dissolution and that the same shall thereafter be considered and treated as their respective properties which each party shall be at full liberty to deal with as they may think fit.

15. Each party to this agreement hereby undertakes to discharge the debts and liabilities of their respective Messes and to collect all monies due and owing to them and to close and settle their accounts and it is further expressly agreed and understood that the Amalgamated Mess shall under no circumstances be held

liable for or incur any responsibility for any liabilities or debt of the 17th Cavalry or the 37th Lancers' Mess except to the extent and purpose hereinbefore contained and the Amalgamated Mess shall only be liable for such debts as it has contracted on and from the date of the Amalgamation.

16. The Mess of the Amalgamated Regiment shall purchase from the Messes of the 17th Cavalry and the 37th Lancers such Oilman's Stores and Groceries as it may require for its own consumption and the values of the articles so taken by the Amalgamated Mess shall be fixed by a Joint Committee of Officers of the said two regiments which shall be specially convened for the purpose and the prices determined by the said Joint Committee shall be accepted as final by the aforesaid messes.

17. And finally it is agreed that each of the contracting parties shall at all times loyally and faithfully render to each other all the assistance necessary for the purpose and to the intent hereinbefore contained and that each party shall disclose to the other any errors, omissions or irregularities that may come to their knowledge.

18. Such party undertakes that in the event of any dispute arising between them touching these presents they shall refer the matter to arbitration each party appointing one arbitrator and notifying to the other party in writing the name of the arbitrator so appointed by them or where they agree upon a sole arbitrator each party shall express in writing their willingness of the choice of the person so appointed and they undertake to be bound by the decision of the arbitrator or arbitrators whose decision shall be accepted as final and conclusive.

In witness whereof the parties have set their hands and seals on the day and date first above written.

* * * * * *

Copy of the Agreement between the Trustees of the 17th Cavalry Polo Club and the President and Members of the 37th Lancers Polo Club for the formation of the 17th/37th Cavalry Polo Club.

Memorandum of agreement made this first day of May 1922 between the Trustees of the 17th Cavalry Polo Club at present of Lucknow in the United Provinces of Agra and Oudh in British India (hereafter referred to as the Trustees) of the one part and the President for the time being and from time to time the elected Representative of the Officers and Members of the Polo Club of the 37th Lancers also of Lucknow aforesaid (hereinafter referred to as President) of the other part witnesseth as follows:—

1. The Trustees and the President on behalf of their respective Polo Clubs agree to form an amalgamated Polo Club

shall hereafter and from the date of these presents be known and referred to as the Polo Club 17th/37th Cavalry.

2. The Presidents will lend to the 17th/37th Cavalry Polo Club the sum or sums of money derived from the Contingent Fund, the Interest Fund and other similar funds the monies of which are the private property of the 37th Lancers Polo Club (as distinguished from the money which forms the deposits of Officers of the 37th Lancers and which they have the right to demand to be repaid) for a period of five (5) years.

3. The Trustees will lend to the 17th/37th Cavalry Polo Club such sum of money as shall be equal in amount to that contributed by the President to the funds of the 17th/37th Cavalry Polo Club on the date of amalgamation also for a period of five (5) years from the date thereof.

4. The President agrees to transfer and does hereby transfer to the amalgamated Polo Club such sums of money deposited by the Officers of the 37th Lancers in the 37th Lancers Polo Club such deposits being at present represented by monies owing and due from Officers of the 37th Lancers for the 37th Lancers Polo Club and the said debts shall until the money has actually been realised be and remain and the security to those officers of the 37th Lancers Polo Club who have already made payments to the late 37th Lancers Polo Club fund as well as all monies that will be collected by the amalgamated club, but any money which the Trustees may at any time lend to the 17th Cavalry Polo Club in accordance with the provisions of para. 5 hereof shall not be applied in repayment of the said deposits nor shall such monies be considered as securities therefor.

5. The Trustees agree to lend to the 17th/37th Cavalry Polo Club for a period of five (5) years such sum of money as shall be equal in amount to the total of the deposits of the Officers of the late 37th Lancers Polo Club which has been transferred to the 17th/37th Cavalry Polo Club as provided in para. 4 above and it is hereby agreed that if any officer of the late 37th Lancers Polo Club is repaid his deposit then a like sum shall be transferred to the Trustees out of the funds of the 17th/37th Cavalry Polo Club.

6. All monies paid by and received from the officers of the amalgamated regiment by the 17th/37th Cavalry Polo Club shall not be subject to the provisions of paras. 3 and 4 first above mentioned.

7. Any monies which the Trustees may lend as aforesaid to the 17th/37th Polo Club shall be free of interest.

8. On the completion of the five years on the day of May 1st, 1927, the Trustees and the President reserve to themselves full liberty of action in respect of disposal of their respective funds, but if it should be mutually agreed between the parties hereto that this agreement should continue for a further term of years then and in that case the provisions of this agreement shall continue in force for the extended period, but not otherwise.

9. If at any time within the five years the Trustees should see fit to advance money to the 17th/37th Cavalry Polo Club in excess of the amount provided for herein they shall be at liberty to charge interest thereon.

10. Upon the dissolution of the present amalgamation or in the event of the disbandment of the present amalgamated regiment the 17th/37th Cavalry Polo Club shall repay to the Trustees and the President all monies that may have been leased to them and that are still outstanding on the date of such dissolution or disbandment immediately and at latest within six months therefrom.

11. The 17th Cavalry Polo Club and the 37th Lancers Polo Club each agree to make a free donation of two hundred and fifty rupees (Rs. 250) to the Tournament Fund of the amalgamated regiment.

In witness whereof the parties have hereunto set their hands and seals on the date and year first above mentioned.

APPENDIX XV.
A LIST OF THE REWARDS GIVEN TO THE INDIAN MEMBERS OF THE LATE 17TH CAVALRY FOR GOOD SERVICE.

Name and Rank.	Year.	Land Grants.	Other rewards.
Jamadar Boodh Singh	1857	..	Reward of Rs. 200 for killing in action Shah Mull, a noted rebel leader, and capturing a Standard.
Naib Rissaldar Kumroodin Khan.	1857	..	Third Class, Order of Merit.
Jamadar Mahbub Khan	1857	..	Second Class, Order of Merit.
Sowar Nur Gul	1857	..	Third Class, Order of Merit.
Sowar Sher Muhammad	1857	..	Third Class, Order of Merit.
Risaldar Ahmad Yar Khan Bahadur.	1864	..	Second Class, Order of British India.
Naib Risaldar Ali Yar Khan Bahadur.	1868	..	Second Class, Order of British India.
Risaldar Major Mahmud Khan.	1887	3 squares.	
Risaldar Hazara Singh. (Subsequently Risaldar Major of 2nd Bengal Lancers.)	1892	..	Transferred to the 2nd Bengal Lancers in 1882, when the old 17th Bengal Cavalry was disbanded, and received the Second Class, Order of British India in that Regiment.
Dafadar Fazal Dad Khan	1893	..	MacGregor Memorial Medal.
Risaldar Major Izat Khan Sirdar Bahadur.	1897	..	Order of British India, First Class. Proceeded to England as a representative of the Indian Army at Queen Victoria's Diamond Jubilee. Awarded Queen Victoria's Diamond Jubilee Medal.
Risaldar Manneh Khan	1900	3 squares.	
Dafadar (Salutri) Rajab Khan.	1900	1½ squares.	
Kote Dafadar Pir Muhammad.	1900	1½ squares.	

Name and Rank.	Year.	Land Grants.	Other Rewards.
Sowar Umar Ali Khan	1903	..	Long Service and Good Conduct Medal with Gratuity.
Lance Dafadar Faizullah Khan.	1904	..	Long Service and Good Conduct Medal with Gratuity.
Risaldar Wazir Ali Khan. (Subsequently Risaldar Major of the 1st Bengal Lancers.)	1904	..	Transferred to the 2nd Bengal Lancers in 1882, when old 17th Bengal Cavalry disbanded. First Class, Order of British India in that Regiment.
Dafadar Munir Khan. (Subsequently Risaldar Major of a Camel Corps.)	1905	2 squares from the Camel Corps.	Order of British India Second Class in that Camel Corps.
Risaldar Major Saadat Khan	1905	5 squares.	
Risaldar Major Muhammad Amin Khan Bahadur.	1905	3 squares	Second Class, Order of British India. Honorary Magistrate, Municipal Commissioner and Sub-Registrar of Ludhiana. Orderly Officer to His Majesty King Edward VII Medal of the Victoran Order.
Risaldar Ahmed Khan	1905	3 squares.	
Risaldar Muhammad Husain.	1905	3 squares.	
Dafadar Sangar Khan	1905	2 squares.	
Dafadar Muhammad Mir	1905	2 squares.	
Dafadar Sikandar Khan	1905	2 squares.	
Dafadar Ditta Khan	1905	2 squares.	
Dafadar Habibullah	1905	2 squares.	
Trumpeter Fateh Din	1905	2 squares.	
Sowar Fateh Khan	1905	2 squares.	Long Service and Good Conduct Medal with Gratuity (1908).
Sowar Allah Yar Khan	1905	2 squares.	
Dafadar Alam Khan	1905	..	Meritorious Service Medal with Annuity.
Sowar Gheba Khan	1905	..	Long Service and Good Conduct Medal with Gratuity.
Sowar Nur Mohammad	1905	..	Long Service and Good Conduct Medal with Gratuity.

Rank and Name.	Year.	Land Grants.	Other Rewards.
Dafadar Chaudhri Khan	1906	..	Long Service and Good Conduct Medal with Gratuity.
Sowar Adalat Khan	1606	..	Long Service and Good Conduct Medal with Gratuity.
Lance-Dafadar Khan Beg	1906	..	Long Service and Good Conduct Medal without Gratuity.
Sowar Gulab Singh	1907	..	Long Service and Good Conduct Medal with Gratuity.
Lance Dafadar Azim Khan	1907	..	Long Service and Good Conduct Medal without Gratuity.
Dafadar Arif Ullah	1907	..	Meritorious Service Medal with Annuity.
Sowar Nur Muhammad	1907	..	Long Service and Good Conduct Medal with Gratuity.
Lance-Dafadar Makarrab Khan.	1908	..	Long Service and Good Conduct Medal with Gratuity.
Sowar Warriam Khan	1908	..	Long Service and Good Conduct Medal without Gratuity.
Sowar Agha Gul	1909	..	Long Service and Good Conduct Medal without Gratuity.
Sowar Lall Mir..	1909	..	Long Service and Good Conduct Medal with Gratuity.
Dafadar Gul Hassan Khan	1910	..	Meritorious Service Medal with Annuity.
Sowar Nawab	1910	..	Long Service and Good Conduct Medal with Gratuity.
Farrier Khuda Baksh	1910	..	Long Service and Good Conduct Medal without Gratuity.
Sowar Mir Afzal Khan	1910	..	Long Service and Good Conduct Medal without Gratuity.
Sowar Muhammad Hassan	1911	..	Long Service and Good Conduct Medal with Gratuity. Coronation Durbar Medal, 1911.
Dafadar Ghaniullah	1911	..	Meritorious Service Medal with Annuity. Coronation Durbar Medal, 1911.
Jemadar Mustafa Khan	1911	..	Coronation Durbar Medal 1911.
Dafadar Akram Khan	1911	..	Coronation Durbar Medal 1911.

Name and Rank.	Year.	Land Grants.	Other rewards.
Dafadar Sargul	1911	..	Coronation Durbar Medal 1911.
Kote-Dafadar Mohammed Sarwar.	1911	..	Coronation Durbar Medal, 1911.
Kote Daffadar (subsequently Jemadar) Khadi Gul.	1911	..	Coronation Delhi Durbar Medal 1911.
Dafadar (Head Salutri) Rahman Beg.	1911	..	Coronation Delhi Durbar Medal 1911.
Acting Lance-Daffadar Abdul Majid.	1911	..	Coronation Delhi Durbar Medal 1911.
Acting Lance-Daffadar Gulmin.	1911	..	Coronation Delhi Durbar Medal 1911.
Camel Sowar Nawab Khan	1911	..	Coronation Delhi Durber Medal 1911.
Sowar Nekawaz Khan	1911	..	Coronation Delhi Durbar Medal 1911.
Sowar (subsequently Acting Lance-Daffadar) Nur Khan.	1911	..	Coronation Delhi Durbar Medal 1911.
Acting Lance-Daffadar (subsequently Daffadar) Yar Gul.	1911	..	Coronation Delhi Durbar Medal 1911.
Acting Lance-Daffadar (subsequently Daffadar) Said Ali Shah.	1911	..	Coronation Delhi Durbar Medal 1911.
Acting Lance-Daffadar (subsequently Daffadar) Amir Shah	1911	..	Coronation Delhi Durbar Medal 1911.
Sowar Agha Gul	1911	..	Coronation Delhi Durbar Medal 1911. Subsequently in 1919 granted a political pension in consideration of the services of his father (an Afghan Sirdar) at the time of the murder of the Cavagnari Mission in Kabul.
Sowar (subsequently Acting Lance-Daffadar) Khan Baz.	1911	..	Coronation Delhi Durbar Medal 1911.
Acting Lance-Daffadar (now Daffadar) Said Gul.	1911	..	Coronation Delhi Durbar Medal 1911.

Name and Rank.	Year.	Land Grants.	Other rewards.
Acting Lance-Daffadar Ajaib Khan.	1911	..	Coronation Delhi Durbar Medal 1911.
Sowar (subsequently Daffadar) Dalel Khan.	1911	..	Coronation Delhi Durbar Medal 1911.
Sowar (subsequently Daffadar) Nazim Gul.	1911	..	Coronation Delhi Durbar Medal 1911.
Sowar (subsequently Acting Lance-Daffadar) Said Ali.	1911	..	Coronation Delhi Durbar Medal 1911.
Acting Lance-Daffadar (subsequently Lance-Daffadar) Saadat Khan.	1911	..	Coronation Delhi Durbar Medal 1911.
Acting Lance-Daffadar Hassan Ali.	1911	..	Coronation Delhi Durbar Medal 1911.
Acting Lance-Daffadar Lall Khan (1)	1911	..	Coronation Delhi Durbar Medal 1911.
Sowar Mohammad Khan ..	1911	..	Coronation Delhi Durbar Medal 1911.
Camel Sowar (subsequently Lance-Daffadar) Sangar Khan.	1911	..	Coronation Delhi Durbar Medal 1911.
Sowar (subsequently Daffadar) Sajawal Khan.	1911	..	Coronation Delhi Durbar Medal 1911.
Acting Lance-Daffadar (subsequently Daffadar) Ali Mardan.	1911	..	Coronation Delhi Durbar Medal 1911.
Acting Lance-Daffadar (subsequently Daffadar) Hayat Mohammad.	1911	..	Coronation Delhi Durbar Medal 1911.
Sowar Hayat Mohammad..	1911	..	Coronation Delhi Durbar Medal 1911.
Sowar (subsequently Jemadar) Bahadur Ali.	1911	..	Coronation Delhi Durbar Medal 1911.
Sowar (subsequently Lance-Daffadar) Mohammad Ali.	1911	..	Coronation Delhi Durbar Medal 1911.
Sowar (subsequently Lance-Daffadar) Dawar Khan.	1911	..	Coronation Delhi Durbar Medal 1911.
Acting Lance-Daffadar Abdul Sittar.	1911	..	Coronation Delhi Durbar Medal 1911.

Name and Rank.	Year.	Land Grants.	Other rewards.
Acting Lance-Daffadar (subsequently Daffadar) Wazir Khan.	1911	..	Coronation Delhi Durbar Medal 1911.
Trumpeter (subsequently Trumpeter Major) Sher Dil.	1911	..	Coronation Delhi Durbar Medal 1911.
Sowar (subsequently Daffadar) Atta Mohammad.	1911	..	Coronation Delhi Durbar Medal 1911.
Farrier Ali Bakhsh	1911	..	Coronation Delhi Durbar Medal 1911.
Sowar (Quarter-Master Clerk) Ali Mohammad.	1911	..	Coronation Delhi Durbar Medal 1911.
Acting Lance-Daffadar Jahan Khan.	1911	..	Coronation Delhi Durbar Medal 1911.
Acting Lance-Daffadar (subsequently Jemadar) Fateh Khan.	1911	..	Coronation Delhi Durbar Medal 1911.
Acting Lance-Daffadar (subsequently Lance-Daffadar) Atta Mohammad.	1911	..	Coronation Delhi Durbar Medal 1911.
Acting Lance-Daffadar (Subsequently Squadron Daffadar Major) Sher Mohammad.	1911	..	Coronation Delhi Durbar Medal 1911.
Sowar Khan Mohammad	1911	..	Coronation Delhi Durbar Medal 1911.
Acting Lance-Daffadar Hakim Khan.	1911	..	Coronation Delhi Durbar Medal 1911.
Acting Lance-Daffadar (subsequently Daffadar) Sikandar Khan.	1911	..	Coronation Delhi Durbar Medal 1911.
Acting Lance-Daffadar (subsequently Jemadar) Ahmed Ali.	1911	..	Coronation Delhi Durbar Medal 1911.
Sowar (subsequently Acting Lance-Daffadar) Kale Khan.	1911	..	Coronation Delhi Durbar Medal 1911.
Sowar Wilayat Shah	1911	..	Coronation Delhi Durbar Medal 1911.
Sowar (subsequently Lance-Daffadar) Bahram Khan.	1911	..	Coronation Delhi Durbar Medal 1911.
Sowar Ghulam Ali	1911	..	Coronation Delhi Durbar Medal 1911.

Rank and Name.	Year.	Land Grants.	Other Rewards.
Sowar (subsequently Daffadar) Mohammad Sher.	1911	..	Coronation Delhi Durbar Medal 1911.
Sowar Shab Madar	1911	..	Coronation Delhi Durbar Medal 1911.
Sowar Umar Khan	1911	..	Coronation Delhi Durbar Medal 1911.
Government Syce Samanda	1911	..	Coronation Delhi Durbar Medal 1911
Dafadar Jinde Khan	1911	..	Coronation Durbar Medal 1911.
Kote-Dafadar Norzali	1911	..	Coronation Durbar Medal 1911.
Lance-Dafadar Zaid Gul	1911	..	Coronation Durbar Medal 1911.
Kote-Dafadar Fazal Shah..	1911	..	Coronation Durbar Medal 1911.
Lance-Dafadar Khan Beg.	1911	..	Long Service and Good Conduct Medal without Gratuity.
Lance-Dafadar Rahman-ud-din.	1911	..	Long Service and Good Conduct Medal with Gratuity.
Sowar Ghulam Haider Khan	1912	..	Long Service and Good Conduct Medal without Gratuity.
Lance-Dafadar Muna Lal ..	1912	..	Long Service and Good Conduct Medal with Gratuity
Sowar Rehmullah	..	..	Long Service and Good Conduct Medal with Gratuity.
Sowar Muhammad Khan ..	1912	..	Long Service and Good Conduct Medal with Gratuity.
Risaldar Major and Honorary Captain Hamzullah Khan, Sirdar Bahadur.	1912	..	Order of British India First Class. Honorary rank of Captain on retirement. Coronation Durbar Medal, 1911.
Risaldar Major Ghulam Mohy-ud-din, Bahadur.	1913	..	Order of British India Second Class. Coronation Durbar Medal, 1911.
Lance-Dafadar Sher Dil ..	1913	..	Long Service and Good Conduct Medal with Gratuity.
Sowar Jalal Khan	1913	..	Long Service and Good Conduct Medal with Gratuity.

Rank and Name.	Year.	Land Grants.	Other Rewards.
Sowar Shadman Khan	1913	..	Long Service and Good Conduct Medal without Gratuity.
Sowar Khan Baz	1914	..	Long Service and Good Conduct Medal with Gratuity.
Dafadar Faiz Muhammad	1914	..	Long Service and Good Conduct Medal with Gratuity.
Sowar Jahan Khan	1914	..	Long Service and Good Conduct Medal without Gratuity.
Sowar Sher Khan	1915	..	Long Service and Good Conduct Medal without Gratuity.
Lance-Dafadar Ahmed Yar	1915	..	Long Service and Good Conduct Medal with Gratuity.
Dafadar Alam Khan	1915	..	Meritorious Service Medal with Annuity.
Sowar (Farrier) Jafar Khan	1915	..	Long Service and Good Conduct Medal with Gratuity.
Dafadar Khan Sahib	1915	..	Indian Order of Merit.
Sowar Muhammad Hussain	1915	..	Indian Order of Merit.
Sowar Karim Dad	1916	..	Long Service and Good Conduct Medal with Gratuity.
Lance Dafadar Hayat Muhammad.	1916	..	Long Service and Good Conduct Medal without Gratuity.
Dafadar Yar Gul	1916	..	Long Service and Good Conduct Medal with Gratuity.
Sowar Sangar Khan	1917	..	Long Service and Good Conduct Medal with Gratuity.
Sowar Nek Aawaz	1917	..	Long Service and Good Conduct Medal with Gratuity.
Sowar Sultan Ali Khan,	1917	..	Long Service and Good Conduct Medal without Gratuity.
Dafadar (Now Jemadar) Ghulam Sarwar.	1917	..	Indian Meritorious Service Medal.
Dafadar Abdullah Khan, I.D.S.M. (Subsequently Jemadar in 22nd Cavalry.)	1917	..	Indian Distinguished Service Medal. Coronation Delhi Durbar Medal, 1911.
Dafadar Major (Now Jemadar) Madat Mhan.	1918	..	Indian Meritorious Service Medal.

Rank and Name.	Year.	Land Grants.	Other Rewards.
Dafadar Allah Khan	1918	..	Long Service and Good Conduct Medal with Gratuity.
Lance-Dafadar Raj Wali.	1918	..	Long Service and Good Conduct Medal without Gratuity.
Sowar Banaras Khan	1918	..	Long Service and Good Conduct Medal with Gratuity. Coronation Delhi Durbar Medal, 1911.
Risaldar Khan Dost Muhammad Khan.	1919	..	Sword of Honour and Sanad from the Punjab Government for services in the Punjab Riots 1919.
Risaldar Major Malik Dost Muhammad Khan, Bahadur.	1919	2 squares	Sent to England as representative of the Regiment at Coronation of His Majesty King George V. Second class, Order of British India. Coronation Delhi Durbar Medal 1911 with Clasp for Coronation England.
Risaldar Major and Honorary Lieutenant Zikryia Khan.	1919	2 squares	Honorary Lieutenant on retirement. Honorary Magistrate, Nowshera.
Risaldar Major Rahmat Sher Khan, I.D.S.M, Bahadur.	1919	2 squares	Indian Distinguished Service Medal. Second Class, Order of British India. Queen Victoria's Diamond Jubilee Medal.
Risaldar Muhammad Usman Khan.	1919	2 squares	Honorary rank of Risaldar Major on retirement.
Risaldar Wazir Khan	1919	..	Indian Order of Merit Jangi Inam of Rs. 10 monthly.
Dafadar Qudrat Ullah	1919	1 square.	
Sowar Zarif Khan	1919	1 square.	
The son of late Farrier Hikmat Shah.	1919	1 square.	
Risaldar Sultan Sikandar Khan.	..	6 squares from Civil Authorities.	
Risaldar Tika Khan	1919	..	Jangi Inam of Rs. 10 monthly. Coronation Delhi Durbar Medal 1911
The son of late Dafadar Amir Ali Khan.	1919	..	Jangi Inam of Rs. 5 monthly.

Rank and Name.	Year.	Land Grants.	Other Rewards.
Risaldar Inayat Ullah Khan	1919	..	Jangi Inam of Rs. 10 monthly. Honorary rank of Risaldar Major on retirement and Sword of Honour from the 15th Lancers. Welfare Officer, District Soldiers' Board, Peshawar.
Risaldar Wazir Muhammad	1919	..	Member of the Order of the British Empire. Coronation Delhi Durbar Medal 1911.
Risaldar Muhammad Raza Khan.	1919	..	Jangi Inam of Rs. 10 monthly.
Risaldar Sajjid Gul	1919	..	Sent to England as the representative of the Regiment at the Peace Celebrations 1919. Honorary Assistant Recruiting Officer for Pathans, Kohat District. Coronation Delhi Durbar Medal, 1911.
Dafadar Major Shad Mohammad Khan.	1919	..	Indian Meritorious Service Medal.
Dafadar Hayat Mohammad	1919	..	Long Service and Good Conduct Medal without Gratuity.
Dafadar Nadir Khan	1919	..	Long Service and Good Conduct Medal with Gratuity.
Sowar Maraj Gul	1919	..	Long Service and Good Conduct Medal with Gratuity.
Lance-Dafadar Pahlwan Shah.	1920	1 square	Caronation Durbar Medal, 1911.
Lance-Dafadar Azimullah	1920	..	Long Service and Good Conduct Medal with Gratuity.
Lance-Dafadar Muzaffar Khan.	1920	..	Long Service and Good Conduct Medal with Gratuity.
Dafadar Sher Muhammad..	..	..	Meritorious Service Medal with Annuity.
Squadron Dafadar Major Mathra Dass.	1920	..	Meritorious Service Medal with Annuity, Coronation Darbar Medal, 1911.
Sowar Saifullah Khan	1922	..	Long Service and Good Conduct Medal with Gratuity
Dafadar (Armourer) Muhammed Din.	1922	..	Honorary rank of Jemadar on retirement. Indian Meritorious Service Medal with Annuity in 1921.

Rank and Name.	Year.	Land Grants.	Other Rewards.
Khan Bahadur Moulvie Qazi Abdul Hakim.	1925	1½ squares	The Titles of 'Khan Sahib' and 'Khan Bahadur.' Delhi Coronation Durbar Medal 1911
Risaldar Malik Alam Sher Khan.	1925	1½ squares	Indian Distinguished Service Medal and Jangi Inam of Rs. 10 monthly.
Risaldar Gauhar Ali Khan	1925	1½ squares.	
Jemadar Pir Dad Khan ..	1925	1¾ squares	Jangi Inam of Rs. 10 monthly.
Dafadar Malik Ghulam Hassan.	1925	1 square	Delhi Coronation Durbar Medal 1911.
Trumpeter Major Shah Wali.	1925	1 square	Meritorious Service Medal with Annuity, 1918.
Farrier Dafadar ur Alam	1925	1 square.	
Risaldar Bahadur Sher Khan. (Subsequently Risaldar Major of the 15th Lancers.)	1925	..	Honorary rank of Lieutenant, while still serving with the 15th Lancers.

APPENDIX XVI.
DEED RELATING TO THE PRIVATE SILLADAR FUNDS OF THE 17TH CAVALRY.

NOTE.

It having been found that undue delay in publication would result from the inclusion of the deed relating to the above funds in the regimental history, it has been decided to issue the book without it.

Any subscriber who specially desires a copy of the above deed may at some time in the future obtain a printed copy suitable for inserting at the back of the book, provided that sufficient subscribers apply to make printing worth while.

The capital of the Private Silladar Funds has been invested in Government Securities and kept separate and intact, so as to make the re-raising of the regiment at any time practicable. The Funds at the face value of the securities amount to nearly one lakh and sixty thousand rupees.

www.ingramcontent.com/pod-product-compliance
Lightning Source LLC
Chambersburg PA
CBHW070313240426
43663CB00038BA/1702